George Lawson

Practical Expositions of the whole Books of Ruth and Esther

George Lawson

Practical Expositions of the whole Books of Ruth and Esther

ISBN/EAN: 9783337159788

Printed in Europe, USA, Canada, Australia, Japan

Cover: Foto ©ninafisch / pixelio.de

More available books at **www.hansebooks.com**

PRACTICAL EXPOSITIONS

OF

THE WHOLE BOOKS OF

RUTH AND ESTHER;

WITH THREE SERMONS ON THE DUTIES OF PARENTS
TO THEIR CHILDREN.

BY GEORGE LAWSON, D. D.

MINISTER OF THE ASSOCIATE CONGREGATION, SELKIRK; AND PRO-
FESSOR OF THEOLOGY OF THE ASSOCIATE SYNOD OF SCOTLAND.

WITH A MEMOIR OF HIS LIFE AND WRITINGS.

PHILADELPHIA: WM. S. RENTOUL.
1870.

RENTOUL'S LIBRARY
OF
STANDARD BIBLE EXPOSITIONS.

Of this valuable series there are now published, in uniform 8vo. size, 1 vol. each:—

I. WARDLAW'S (RALPH, D.D.) EXPOSITORY LECTURES ON the whole Book of ECCLESIASTES: 432 pages.—"It is like the sword of Goliath, 'there is none like it.'"

II. STUART'S (REV. A. MOODY) EXPOSITION OF the whole of THE SONG OF SOLOMON: 544 pages.—Rev. Dr. Paxton of New York writes to the Publisher:—'I am glad to hear that you are about to republish Rev. A. Moody Stuart's Commentary upon THE SONG OF SOLOMON. I have been familiar with this work for a number of years and esteem it very highly. I have five or six other commentaries upon "The Song" in my library, but for all the practical purposes of the ministry I find this to be the best.'

III. LAWSON'S (GEORGE, D.D.) EXPOSITORY LECTURES AND DISCOURSES ON the whole Books of RUTH AND ESTHER; with Three Sermons on the Duties of Parents, and a Memoir of the Author: 450 pages.—"There is a peculiar charm in the writings of that sage-like, apostolic man, Prof. LAWSON; in them most important, original, pregnant thoughts are continually occurring." Prof. John Brown, of Edinburgh.

PREFACE
OF THE PUBLISHER OF THIS EDITION.

The Writings of Dr. George Lawson have been suffered so long to fall out of print both in Great Britain and America, that their excellence is but little known to the new generation which has sprung up since he passed away. It is with difficulty that the diligent and indefatigable book hunter can now find a single copy of his charming Expositions of the Books of Ruth and Esther, or of his other most instructive works.

The Publisher has considered, that no books could be selected by him as more suitable to form a part of his LIBRARY OF SPECIAL EXPOSITIONS OF BOOKS OF THE BIBLE, than Dr. Lawson's Lectures and Discourses on Ruth and Esther. To these he has appended Dr. L's. three admirable Sermons on the Duties of Parents—to which a number of fresh Notes have been added applicable to the circumstances of our own time; and he has prefixed to the whole an interesting Memoir of the author and his Writings, by Dr. Henry Belfrage. The Memoir will be found sufficiently full and minute to gratify the reader's natural desire of an intimate acquaintance with our author's blameless and amiable Christian life and character.

'The memory of the just is blessed'; and the Publisher feels happy to contribute, even in his humble sphere, to perpetuate the memory and blessed example of so eminently godly a man as Dr. Lawson; and to re-produce, for the benefit of the present generation, some of the most instructive and useful of his writings.

This is peculiarly a volume of precious reading for Christian families. It is instinct with practical instruction both for parents and youth. The weight and importance of the matter is only equalled by the elegant simplicity of the style.

PHILADELPHIA, 1869.

CONTENTS.

	PAGE
Memoir of Dr. Lawson and his Writings,	ix

LECTURES ON THE WHOLE BOOK OF RUTH.

INTRODUCTION, ... 1

LECTURE I.

Chap i. 1-5.—Elimeleck and his family go to sojourn in the land of Moab, ... 7

LECTURE II.

Chap. i. 6-10.—Naomi's return to her own country, . . 19

LECTURE III.

Chap. i. 11-15.—The same subject continued, . . . 29

LECTURE IV.

Chap. i. 16-18.—Ruth's steadfastness to her religious profession, . 40

LECTURE V.

Chap. i. 19-22.—Ruth's arrival with Naomi at Bethlehem, . 48

LECTURE VI.

Chap. ii. 1-4.—Ruth goes to glean, and meets with Boaz, . 59

LECTURE VII.

Chap. ii. 5-14.—Boaz speaks kindly to Ruth in the harvest field, 70

LECTURE VIII.

Chap. ii. 15-23.—Boaz' directions to his reapers to treat Ruth kindly—her success in gleaning, &c., ... 84

LECTURE IX. PAGE

Chap. iii. 1-9.—Ruth, at the instigation of Naomi, lays herself down at the feet of Boaz, and requests him to cast his skirt over her, 95

LECTURE X.

Chap. iii. 10-18.—Boaz promises to Ruth to marry her, if her husband's nearest kinsman did not insist upon his prior right. He dismisses her with a present to her mother-in-law, who expresses great satisfaction with her kind reception by Boaz, 107

LECTURE XI.

Chap. iv. 1-10.—Boaz, in the presence of ten elders of Bethlehem, procures the consent of Ruth's nearest kinsman to his marriage with her, ... 119

LECTURE XII.

Chap. iv. 10-22.—Ruth's marriage, and the birth of Obed, . 131

DISCOURSES ON THE WHOLE BOOK OF ESTHER.

INTRODUCTION, ... 149

DISCOURSE I.

Chap. i. 1-9.—Ahasuerus's feast, ... 152

DISCOURSE II.

Chap. i. 10-22.—The disobedience and divorce of Vashti, . . 161

DISCOURE III.

Chap. ii. 1-11.—Extraordinary method used to supply the place of Vashti, ... 176

DISCOURSE IV.

Chap. ii. 12-23.—Esther made Queen of Persia—By her means Mordecai discovers to the king a conspiracy formed against his life, ... 185

Discourse V.

Chap. iii. 1-6.—The elevation of Haman—His pride, and resolution to revenge fancied indignities received from Mordecai upon the whole nation of the Jews, ... 196

Discourse VI.

Chap. iii. 7-15.—Haman obtains from the king a decree for the destruction of the Jews, ... 205

Discourse VII.

Chap. iv. 1-11.—The grief of Mordecai and the other Jews at hearing of the bloody edict—Mordecai solicits Esther to intercede with the king in their behalf, ... 218

Discourse VIII.

Chap. iv. 12-17.—Mordecai insists on the charge to Esther to go in unto the king—She complies with his desire; but requires him to procure for her the help of the solemn prayers of all the Jews in Shushan, ... 228

Discourse IX.

Chap. v. 1-14.—Esther goes in unto the king, and finds favour in his eyes—Haman, inflamed by revenge, prepares a gallows for Mordecai of fifty cubits high, ... 244

Discourse X.

Chap. vi. 1-13.—Haman is compelled to confer a singular honour upon Mordecai, which he hoped to procure for himself, . 257

Discourse XI.

Chap. vi. 14-vii. 10.—Haman's fall and death, . . 268

Discourse XII.

Chap. viii. 1-14.—Mordecai is advanced to great honours—Liberty is procured for the Jews to defend themselves against the intended Massacre, ... 279

Discourse XIII.

Chap. viii. 15-ix. 5.—Mordecai's greatness, with the happy change in the condition of the Jews, ... 291

Discourse XIV.

Chap. ix. 6-19.—Numbers of the slain—A second battle at Shushan, 302

DISCOURSE XV.

Chap. ix. 20–32.—Ordinance of Mordecai and Esther for observing the days of Purim, ... 312

DISCOURSE XVI.

Chap. x.—Greatness of Ahasuerus—Character and grandeur of Mordecai, ... 324

SERMONS ON THE DUTY OF PARENTS TO THEIR CHILDREN.

Sermon I. Ephesians vi. 4, ... 335
Sermon II. Same Text, ... 350
Sermon III. Same Text, ... 381

A MEMOIR

OF

DR. LAWSON AND HIS WRITINGS.

BY

HENRY BELFRAGE, D. D.

Dr. Lawson was born in the parish of West Linton in the shire of Peebles, Scotland, in 1749, and by the care of very pious parents was trained up in the fear of God. It has often been remarked how many of our men of genius have sprung from the peasantry of Scotland, and that on the mountain's side they felt the first movements of that inspiration by which the world has been charmed; and men of God have delighted to look back to the still waters, where, in their early days, they mused on the Shepherd of Israel, and to the wood and the glen where they poured out their hearts to the Lord. From his earliest years his attention was engaged by religion, or subjects connected with it; and by the tuition of the venerable men at whose feet he sat in his course of study he improved rapidly in holy wisdom. He was uniformly characterized by that modesty which is at once the ornament and the guardian of youth, and by a rare union of quickness of apprehension, laborious and unremitted application, and a retentiveness of memory altogether uncommon.

After completing his course of study he was licensed to preach the Gospel; and after a unanimous call by the people, was ordained minister of the Associate Congregation of Selkirk in 1771, and continued in that charge for the long period of forty-nine years. The comparative retirement of this situation furnished him with ample opportunities of study, and these he improved with the greatest eagerness. Few have enriched their minds so amply with the best knowledge as he did. While some ministers have wasted their time in visiting and gossiping and have tried this expedient to gain popularity; while others from eagerness to be rich have engaged in secular business; and while others have devoted their best energies to literary pursuits; he felt that his people had a claim to all his efforts; and that his time should be spent in doing them good, or in fitting himself for it. Accordingly, devoted as he was to study, he never felt reluctant to leave his library, at the call of duty; but at the earliest or the latest hour went forth to admonish, or to console, as the providence of God called him. When reluctance to such duties rises in the minds of the studious, it would be well for them to reflect, how hearts may be bleeding in sorrow which they might be the means of comforting; and how those may be sinking in destruction whom they might pluck as brands from the burning. The sacrifices thus made to duty God will compensate, by a light and vigour which will more than make amends for the efforts which are remitted.

The Scriptures were his daily study. For many years he made a point of committing to memory a portion of the Bible in the original. A friend once remarked to him, that he supposed if the Bible was lost he (Dr. L.) could furnish it exactly from memory. In reply he remarked that he believed he could, excepting perhaps some of the passages containing names merely. He could state the contents of the different chapters, the respective parts of which they consisted, and how many verses were occupied with each. It was his nightly custom to read a passage of Scripture before he retired to rest, as a subject of meditation while he was awake. Meditation, he used to say, was an important, but much neglected duty; and that it would be well for some, if they read less and reflected more. It is on the food digested that nourishment and health depend. This acquaintance with the Scriptures was not only most conducive to the furtherance of his own piety and comfort, but fitted him for giving the best counsel to others in every perplexity, and for improving with facility and in a manner truly happy, every topic and event to which he was called to advert.

His acquaintance with the best theological works, ancient and modern, was extensive and accurate. He greatly relished, and often read in the original Greek, the works of Chrysostom. The writings of Owen, and especially his practical works, he highly valued. There are few who have not heard with surprise and regret the harsh and contemptuous terms in which the works of Owen were spoken of by Hall. We must consider the opinion he expressed, so opposite to that of the wise and good for ages, as originating in the eccentricity of his genius; and are confident that, however high his authority, it will not in the least degree lessen the veneration felt for the memory of that truly great man. The sermons of Massillon and Saurin he read with pleasure, and in the original French. No translation which the world has yet seen has done them justice · and in reading those of Massillon especially, we search in vain, in sentences cold and tame, for the vivacity, and fire, and pathos of that eloquence by which kings were humbled, and courtiers devoted to dissipation were awed into seriousness, or melted into tears.

The writings of Jonathan Edwards he carefully studied, and Campbell on the Gospels, and other approved works of sacred criticism; and it was pleasing to mark with what simplicity and perspicuity he could state the result of their most elaborate inquiries; make passages abstruse and difficult intelligible to persons of ordinary capacity; and point out the lessons of wisdom which were thus set in a more striking light, or freed from difficulties which were felt to be perplexing.

He devoted a portion of his time through the week to the perusal of works of practical piety; such as the writings of Trail, Boston, and Brown. For the works of Trail he had a peculiar relish. There is a holy unction and sweetness in them by which the devout mind is charmed. It was by such reading that he learned to apply with fidelity and wisdom the truths of the Gospel for the advancement of piety in his own soul, and to qualify himself for speaking to the hearts of others. He used to speak of prayer as the best guide in the search after truth; besought the Father of lights to make him to know wisdom in the hidden part; and felt this as the great object of his solicitude, that he might receive with meekness the engrafted word which was able to save his soul.

But he did not neglect classical literature, philosophy, and history. Plutarch's lives was a favourite book of his, and from the incidents he details, and the maxims of wisdom with which they abound, he introduced into his discourses many very appropriate and useful quotations; and from his lips they fell with a simplicity and gravity widely different from the levity and exaggeration of many such details. He was familiar with Homer and the lesser Greek poets, and occasionally quoted them with great readiness. The sages and the heroes of Greece and Rome he valued as monitors, to teach us the diligence with which we should seek for a higher wisdom, and strive for a brighter glory.

The whole range of history, ancient and modern, was quite familiar to him. Works of taste and genius he delighted to peruse, and by them he felt his mind relieved after severe study; but never did he devote to them aught of the time which was claimed by more serious engagements, or contract by them a disrelish for mental occupation of a graver cast. So admirable was the intellectual discipline which he maintained, that lighter scenes and feelings were not suffered to distract his attention in serious enquiry, but were employed as stimulants in the ways of wisdom.

It was a circumstance which beautifully characterized his spirit and manner as a scholar, that amidst his own acquirements he maintained uniform modesty, and delighted to do justice to the talents and attainments of others. No jealousy or envy wrought in his breast, and so far from courting opportunities for displaying his research, his aim was mildly to instruct or encourage others to be diligent. It is easy to see with what effect from the lips of such a man that counsel would come, which is so needful in associations of youth,—'Let us not be desirous of vain glory, provoking one another, envying one another.' To excite emulation, and yet to maintain humility and brotherly kindness, requires the utmost skill of a religious instructor.

As a minister of the Gospel, it was his great object to make his people stand complete in all the will of God, and for this purpose he expounded the Scriptures in a manner clear, lively, and attractive. He could avail himself of the stores of his mind with the greatest readiness, to illustrate and enforce their various lessons; and places of the Bible which are sometimes passed by as too abstruse for the comprehension of the people, or too barren for utility, he delighted to open up, and to bring forth the gold treasured in them. Regarding 'all Scripture as given by inspiration of God, and as profitable for doctrine, for reproof, for correction and for instruction in righteousness,' he laboured so to expound it 'that the man of God might be perfect, thoroughly furnished for all good works.'

In his ministry he showed admirable skill in improving remarkable dispensations of Providence, whether of a public or a private character; he always selected some text appropriate to such occasions, and illustrations suited to console or to impress. In a congregation in the neighbourhood, some confusion and alarm had been excited by the sliding of one of the beams of the gallery of the chapel, which was much crowded, it being the day of the dispensation of the Lord's Supper. Most happily, no lives were lost. Next day he preached on that text, 'And David was displeased because the Lord had made a breach upon Uzzah,' in which discourse he showed in a solemn and striking manner how much we owed to the Divine patience in these slighter tokens of his hand; how deserving we were of much severer blows; and that, instead of murmurs, the voice of gratitude and praise became us, to Him who in wrath remembers mercy.

On one occasion an alarm was excited during public worship, that his own chapel was falling; and in the agitation and tumult produced by it there was great danger of serious injury, and even of the loss of life. Next Lord's day he preached on that text, 'Unless the Lord had been my help, my soul had almost dwelt in silence.' Incidents of this kind are sometimes permitted to occur, to teach us to serve God with fear, and to worship under the impressions of eternity.

After the fall of a wall in Selkirk, by which several persons were severely hurt, he preached on the Sabbath following on 1 Kings xx. 30,— 'But the rest fled to Aphek, into the city; and there a wall fell upon twenty and seven thousand of the men that were left.' This passage of Scripture was admirably adapted to teach his hearers to feel what they owed to the patience of God in sending visitations of calamity so lenient in comparison of what he had sent, or could send; and to impress upon them this truth—that in scenes where they may think they have found a refuge from His anger, he may make them monuments of his power to destroy.

At the opening of a new church in Lauder, the subject of his discourse was Hosea viii. 14, first clause,—'Israel hath forgotten his Maker and builded temples.' It is a most necessary caution which these words suggest to men in all ages, not to consider the zeal which they manifest for the forms of religion, or the peculiarities of a party, as a sure test of the love and the fear of God. It has been in the lowest decline of piety that the most magnificent edifices have been reared for its worship; and it was the hypocritical and rapacious Scribes and Pharisees who built the tombs of the prophets, and garnished the sepulchres of the righteous.

I shall only mention as another instance of the singular felicity with which he selected appropriate texts to particular occasions, and derived suitable and striking lessons from passages which to many would have seemed to suggest nothing suited to their purpose, that at an election of elders his text was Prov. xxvi. 6,—'He that sendeth a message by the hand of a fool cutteth off the feet, and drinketh damage.' This is a passage which teaches very strikingly the mischiefs which may arise from entrusting duties of importance to the management of those whose indiscretion may divulge what ought to be kept secret; whose rashness may render useless the best plans for utility; and whose simplicity may be imposed on by every fair pretense.

It should be mentioned as a peculiar character of his ministry, the amplitude, particularity, and earnestness with which he discoursed on relative duties. Some hearers of the Gospel are unwilling to have topics discussed which expose their negligence, or their severity; and would wish sermons occupied with subjects more general and soothing; but every wise and good man must feel that a just idea of the extent and value of relative duties is of the utmost necessity to the happiness of families, and to the maintenance of religion from age to age. Deficiencies in such duties he exposed and rebuked with no sparing hand; and fidelity he encouraged by the examples of the holy men of old, and by the beautiful pictures which he drew of the filial piety by which a father was cheered in the decline of his days, and of the consolations and hopes which were mingled with the tears shed by it at a mother's grave.

In the more private duties of the pastoral office he was diligent and faithful. In such duties he whose delight is in popular applause and public display feels no interest, and either neglects them, or hurries over them in a cold and formal manner; but a man of God feels that they call him to the most solemn intercourse he can have with his people, and that in the lowliest dwelling there is an eye which marks his feelings, and an ear which listens to his counsels, infinitely more important than the notice of the multitude. A good man's heart is poured out in him, when he thinks on his leading the orphan to the feet of Jesus, and making the widow's heart to sing for joy.

It was his custom when visiting his congregation, to ask the head of each family, what was the chapter last read at family worship. Whatever was the chapter, he proceeded immediately, without asking for a Bible, to comment on it, and apply it to the circumstances of the family. A general descant on religion will excite little interest, but when the members of a family are addressed in a mode suited to their age, habits, employments, and prospects, it is felt that a word spoken in season is like apples of gold in pictures of silver.

In his examinations, he paid particular attention to the instruction of the young; and in his manner there was a happy union of gravity and sweetness, fitted to excite love and awe. Gravity alone may terrify, but it will not win; and petulance may be encouraged by an unwise familiarity. 'The young kept silence at his counsel, and the light of his countenance they cast not down.'

He did what he could to establish meetings for social prayer throughout his congregation; and in this pious labour he would encourage them by such assurances of holy advantage as these,—'As ointment and perfume rejoice the heart, so doth the sweetness of a man's friend by hearty counsel:' and 'If any two of you shall agree as to any thing that they shall ask, it shall be done for them of my Father who is in heaven.'

In visiting the sick he was regular and faithful; and, whatever was the disease, he never shrunk from his duty. In a letter to a young friend who had asked his advice on the subject, he says, 'I always felt it my duty to visit the sick although their diseases were infectious. There is little danger of infection in so short a visit as is proper in such cases, and precautions against danger may be used. We are always safest in the path of duty, and God is a powerful preserver.' While the kindness of his disposition made the task of consoling and encouraging delightful, he was fearful of saying peace when there was none, and judged it safest to urge immediate and penitential application to the grace of the Saviour; and to point out the strong consolation and the certain safety of those who 'flee for refuge to lay hold on the hope set before them.' It is more gratifying to witness in such scenes the tears of penitence than flights of rapture; and the soul longing for God's salvation, rather than exultation in its attainment. The dullness of hearing under which he laboured for a number of years kept him from receiving many communications from the sick and dying as to their religious experience; but there were some cases in which Providence made known to him what Christ had wrought by him, as an instrument of his grace, to make sinners obedient by heart and word and deed. He had the satisfaction of receiving from some of the sick and dying, testimonies to the power of his ministry in their conversion to God, their light in perplexity, their encouragement in duty, and their hope in affliction. These are precious testimonies which do not flatter, but encourage; which do not puff up, but solemnize; and the scene in which they are given, associates them with the day of judgment, when the seals of our ministry shall rise up and call us blessed; and when Christ shall rejoice with us in the travail of his soul, and the efficacy of his grace.

In other places where he occasionally ministered, God sometimes gave testimony to the word of his grace. I may mention an instance of this. A man in G—— who lived without even a profession of religion, happened to hear him preach. A sentence to this effect, that 'persons in a Christian land who neglect the Gospel must be more guilty and wretched than heathens,' struck him to the heart: he regularly attended public worship ever after, connected himself with the church, and maintained to his death the character of a consistent and pious man.

After the death of the eminently learned and pious Professor John Brown of Haddington, he was appointed his successor as Professor of Theology, by the Associate Synod in 1787. Institutions of this kind may seem to some to have their most proper seat in large cities, where students may have it in their power to attend to other branches of education, which may be necessary accomplishments in a public Teacher; but in such a sequestered situation as Selkirk their attention is concentrated on Theology, and there they are more intimately associated than they could be in a wider sphere. An intercourse is maintained highly friendly to improvement, and friendships are formed which become a blessing for life. Many of the young men once under his care, have looked back on the associations of their early days with delight, when 'as iron sharpeneth iron, so doth a man sharpen the countenance of his friend.' And though virtue should be guarded by the impression of the inspection of a brighter eye, and the account to be given to a higher tribunal than any which men occupy, yet the idea of the strict attention paid in such a scene by all around to their movements, is friendly to the formation of those habits of caution, self-denial, and strict propriety of conduct, which are so necessary to the respectability and the influence of the clerical character.

During the five sessions which were the appointed course of study, Dr. Lawson gave an exposition of the System of Theology, in lectures rich in sentiment, concise yet clear in language, and in arrangement most judicious. Deeply skilled though he was in divinity, he avoided all technicalities of expression, and elucidated the most abstruse points in a perspicuous manner. In his prelections, theology came not forth in the armour of the schools—dark, rusty, and cumbrous; but in the armour of light—simple, easy, and pointed. His critical lectures presented illustrations of the dark passages of Scripture, of the customs and manners of the East, of the peculiarities of the Sacred style, of the ancient versions of the Scriptures, of the figurative modes of speech occurring in the Bible, of the mode of illustrating types and explaining prophecies, of the Holy Land in its history and productions, and of the writers, the design, and the periods of writing of the different parts of the sacred canon. It is easy to see what diligent and extensive research were necessary in the execution of such a plan, and how great its usefulness must have been. His examinations were so happily managed as to enable him to judge of the proficiency of his pupils; and his remarks on their discourses so candid and judicious, as to commend themselves to the approbation of all who heard them. His manner was marked by mild solemnity, and his prayers and counsels by the unction of a heart full of the Holy Ghost. His demeanour to them exhibited the happy medium betwixt the indulgence which youth is so apt to abuse, and the reserve it feels so galling. In him there was nothing of that inquisitorial jealousy which has led some to pry into every indiscretion; or of that sluggishness which never follows the young beyond the precincts of their Seminary. He approved himself at once as their guardian and their father. He invited them to his house on suitable occasions, and made them welcome to the use of such books in his library as they wished to consult; when any of them required his counsel, it was given in a manner the most friendly; and when any of them were sick, he watched over them with the solicitude of a parent. When we think on the many young men who have been trained by him, and who are labouring in various places in Britain, in Ireland, and in America, we feel it impossible to estimate the results of his instructions, admonitions, and prayers.

As a proof of his great prudence in the discharge of this office, it may be mentioned, that on one occasion a present was sent to the library of the students of some books, among which were six copies of Paine's Rights of Man. This was done at a period when the nation was agitated by political speculation; and such a gift, to such a seminary, was fitted to poison the ardent minds of youth, and excite them to disseminate disaffection over the land. When he heard of the arrival of such books, he stated to the students that he could not permit them to have a place in their library, or to be circulated among them. Though attached to liberal principles, he was unwilling that his students should engage as disputants or partisans in the political contests of the day. It was in meekness, truth, and righteousness, that he wished them to go forth as does the Captain of salvation. The selection made by the students of books for the library was submitted to him for his approval; and his opinion was given so wisely, and so mildly, that when unfavourable to any book it was never resisted. As a proof of his amiable modesty it may be mentioned, that when any ministers venerable for age or wisdom visited the institution, he urged them to give, ere they went away, some counsels to his pupils. I have seen this done, at his entreaty, with much judgment, delicacy, and kindness.

The interest felt by the wise and pious of other churches in the prosperity of the institution under his care was sometimes intimated to him in a very gratifying manner. It is with pleasure I select, as a specimen of this interest, a letter of the venerable Dr. Erskine, a man of primitive sanctity of character, and distinguished by a profound and extensive acquaintance with theological literature, a truly amiable humility, and a liberality of feeling which made him regard Christians of every party and of every country as his brethren:—

Laurieston, 11th Sept. 1799.

'REV. SIR,

MR. OGLE acquainted me two day ago, that my Sermons being out of print, he wished I could spare him two copies, and particularly one for your students who desired to have it in their library. I informed him I had only three copies, which are intended for friends at a distance. I have since happily got a copy in another shop, which I beg you will accept with best wishes to you and the young men under your care. I am, Rev. Sir,

Your affectionate Brother and Servant,

JOHN ERSKINE.'

In this charge Dr. Lawson continued to officiate till his death, with the entire confidence of the church with which he was connected; whose ministers and elders voted him, not long before he died, a present of one hundred pounds sterling, as an expression of their high estimation of his services. In the meeting of Synod in April 1820, when his death was announced, the Rev. Mr. Greig of Lochgelly, who had lived in the most intimate friendship with him for more than fifty years, proposed that the Synod should insert in their minutes an expression of their high estimation of his worth and services. It was left to Mr. Greig to prepare it, and after being read and approved it was engrossed in their records, and a copy of it follows:—

'In recording the decease of the Rev. Dr. Lawson, the Synod find themselves called on to express in their minutes the peculiar and important obligations which they and the people of their charge are under to the Head of the church, for the prolonged and valuable services performed by this worthy and venerable member of their body as their Professor of Divinity; to whom under God most of the ministers of this Synod are much indebted for their knowledge of the Gospel of the blessed God, and their qualification for preaching it to their fellow men; and the impression of whose amiable and venerable character for piety, for knowledge of the word of God, for sacred literature, and for every excellence which can adorn the man, the Christian, and the Professor of Divinity, they wish ever to retain, and to cherish as an excitement to the faithful discharge of the duties of their office.'

How valuable is such a tribute from such a man! and still more does it appear so when thus sanctioned. Of Mr. Greig it is but justice to say, that he was distinguished by uncommon vigour of intellect, commanding energy as a preacher, great probity of character, and by a close walk with God.

B

It will be felt as a very interesting part of this Memoir, to state what Dr. L. was in his family, and as a friend. It is most gratifying to his family to reflect how he 'counted the Sabbath a delight, the holy of the Lord and honourable.' He used to remark—that he would like to see the Jewish custom universal, of beginning the duties peculiar to the Sabbath at six o'clock on the Saturday evening; and in his own house he made it to be devoted to books or conversation of a serious cast. So different was his conduct from the common practice of indulging longer in sleep on the Sabbath morning than on others, that he rose earlier, and made his family do so; and his domestic instructions and prayers were never hurried over, but discharged as a duty felt to be pleasing as well as solemn. Of *Fisher's Catechism* he had a very high opinion, made his young people read portions of it again and again with great care, and meditate on them, and he then examined them as to their conceptions of its meaning, and the impressions which it should produce. There was a circumstance in his family instruction which showed his admirable skill, and which rendered it most delightful to the young: with his questions and counsels he mingled appropriate anecdotes, exhibiting the pleasures of religion, God's care of his saints, the beauty of early piety, the happiness of the family whose God is the Lord, how the fear of God operates as a preservative from sin, what God has done in honour of his own day, and what consolations and hopes the promises of the Gospel have yielded in sickness and death.

The daily reading of the Scriptures was one of his counsels, and also to commit a portion of them daily to memory. Texts of Scripture you will find your best wealth; and the judgment, the memory, and the heart should be their treasury. One of the schemes of doing good in our day has been, recommending the formation of societies, whose members are pledged to commit one verse of the Bible, or more, every day to memory. Perhaps this is giving too much parade to an exercise of secret piety, but the practice itself is excellently calculated to enrich the mind, to improve conversation, and to guide the steps.

The conversation which he maintained in his family was worthy of his character for wisdom and goodness. While some studious men have maintained a gravity before their children gloomy and reserved, as if they would degrade themselves by unbending; and while others have indulged in a playfulness and levity which lessened their authority, and produced disturbance in their serious moods, and dislike to their solemn counsels; he opened the minds and won the hearts of his children, by appropriate anecdotes, of which his store was inexhaustible, and his introduction most happy.

His two sons whom he lived to see ordained to the holy ministry, were objects of his pious solicitude in their studies and labours. Many were the prayers, counsels, and charges which he devoted to this great object, that they 'might show themselves approved unto God, workmen that needed not to be ashamed, rightly dividing the word of truth.' It is a striking fact, honourable to his memory, to the judgment and feeling of his congregation, and to the talents of his sons, that they were both called to succeed their father in his pastoral charge.

He was repeatedly visited with bereavements in his family, and in such affecting circumstances his piety was manifested in a very interesting way. The death of the wife of his youth, and of one of his sons by his second marriage, a most accomplished young man, and whose future course of piety and utility was anticipated in many a fond hope, were felt by him very painfully; and over the graves of other promising children he was likewise called to mourn. Some have supposed that on men devoted to study, such bereavements fall lightly; but by them they are felt with peculiar keenness: while to other losses they may feel comparative indifference, at the death of friends their hearts bleed most profusely. Amidst the languor of study they are cheered by their sprightliness, or cherished by their care; to them they cling with an affection which is never solicited by the world's gayeties, and which feels in their removal as if 'the light had become dark in their tabernacle,' and that they must follow them in the path to their long home. I shall give a few extracts from some of his letters after such trials, which will be useful to mourners, while they show how deeply these were felt, and how piously they were improved.

'The death of children puts a final period to all that we can do for them, but our grief on this occasion is effectually counterbalanced by the consciousness that we have earnestly endeavoured to do for them what lay in our power whilst they were with us; especially when we have good reason to hope that our prayers for them have not been rejected, and that Divine Mercy led them safe through life and death to a world from whence they would not for a thousand worlds return. I have lost for the rest of my time in this world some children whose faces I always beheld with pleasure; but I hope, young as they were, they were better fitted for leaving this world than I am. We are authorized by Scripture, without expecting a revelation from God respecting their state, to rejoice in the hope that they are sleeping in Jesus; and, living with Him, shall be brought with him at the great day of his appearance.'

The following is an extract from a letter to one of his sons, in whose house, and at a distance, his sister was dying. When beloved friends in distress are at a distance, the heart is often agitated with fears, anxieties, and regrets which work more painfully than if we were near them. Fancy, strongly excited, paints the scene in darker colours than reality; and the heart is ready to repine that our hands can take no share in the ministrations of kindness and sympathy, and that to us their last looks and tokens of love are denied. In the quotation which follows, resignation hath its perfect work amidst nature's strongest feelings.

'My heart is grieved because you have not been able to give a more favourable account of my beloved daughter's health; but I have better reason if possible than Eli to say, 'It is the Lord, let him do what seemeth him good.' In the threatened destruction of his two wicked sons, he trembled at the thought of their awful condition under the wrath of God. I have reason to hope that our dear J. is suffering under the hand of a gracious Father, to make her a partaker of his holiness, and to prepare her for eternal happiness. It must give you great pain to witness the sufferings of a sister so justly dear to you, but it will give you pleasure many days hence to remember that you had the opportunity, and did not suffer it to pass unimproved, of consoling her mind, and suggesting useful directions to her. May God bless all your endeavours to tranquilize her, and to prepare her for the event!'

After her death he thus writes: 'My beloved J. is gone from the world, but she will never be forgotten by me if I should live a thousand years twice told. I have no cause for the least reflection on any part of her behaviour to me. I wish I had no cause for reflection on the omission of what I might have done to her. Yet I am conscious that I have endeavoured to train her up in the way that she should go, and I trust that my endeavours have not been in vain in the Lord.'

How different is such a spirit and such language from that of the ancient heathen sages under such trials, in whom we often see an affected sturdiness and indifference; or a grief, wild, audacious, and despairing. The following passage from the Christian Observer beautifully illustrates this statement:—

'Quinctilian's letter upon the death of his two sons, one of whom was a youth highly accomplished, and of great promise, is beautiful and touching. But in it he boasts of his impatience; thinks it necessary to excuse himself for having survived the stroke; denies the doctrine of a Divine superintendence over the affairs of men; accuses the gods of spite and injustice; and says his tolerance, not his love of life, will revenge his son for the rest of his days. This was all that his ethics could do to calm his mind. What will an infidel say to such a scene as contrasted with the faith and patience of the saints? Will he say that their meek endurance is the fruit of advanced philosophy? Quinctilian lived in an age enlightened by literature; but Rome was far behind Jerusalem in the sublimities of moral precept, because the true light had not radiated its horizon. And then see how Job acted, though in a ruder age, and surrounded by idolatry. Revelation cast a bright hue of heaven over all his sorrows.'

We can only find a place for a few sentences from some of his other letters on such occasions. 'God is righteous in taking from us. He is merciful in sparing to us what he has not taken. If it had pleased God to cut off the half of our families, it would have been our duty to have given him thanks that the other half was left. I bless God for the hope of seeing those whom I have lost, with greater pleasure than ever; but

I have still more reason to bless him for the gift of his own Son to such unworthy creatures as I am, that through faith in Him I may have everlasting life. J. M. has been for some time in a state of derangement. This must give great distress to his wife; and yet to be the wife of a pious man under this sore affliction is a less evil than to be placed in a like relation to a man who wants the fear of God, whatever other recommendations he may possess. Insanity will not, like unregeneracy, exclude from the kingdom of God.'

While he cherished kindly feelings to all the ministers of the church with which he was connected, there were some of them with whom he cultivated a special friendship. With Mr. Greig of Lochgelly he maintained a frequent correspondence by letters, from their first acquaintance while studying divinity, till his death. Such correspondence would be deemed very valuable by all that knew the men, from the views it would give of many important topics, of the signs of the times, and of the state of religion at home and abroad.

In writing to one of his sons he says, 'Our chief pleasure as ministers should be in doing good, and in the conscientious use of the means of doing good. It can give little pleasure to any man of consideration to be valued more than he deserves, and it need not give us great pain to be despised, or to incur the displeasure of men, if we are conscious of endeavouring to perform the duties which we owe them. I have no hope of ever seeing you or your brethren at K. I have had my time in which I was happy to visit distant friends, but every thing in this world has its end. Let your brethren know that I am glad to hear of their prosperity, and of their endeavours to perform faithful service to Christ and to their people. I am sorry that I have not been able to do more than I have done to prepare them for usefulness, but to supply my defects I hope that they will be daily learners at the school of Paul, or rather of Christ; and that they will treasure up in their minds the epistles of Timothy and Titus, which are epistles from Christ to all ministers who are called to labour in His service.'

With some ministers of the Established church in his neighbourhood he lived on terms of friendly intimacy. By Dr. Douglas, who was Minister of Galashiels for more than fifty years, a man of great good sense and public spirit, and by Dr. Hardie, Minister of Ashkirk, an accomplished scholar, and an amiable man, he was beloved and respected. On various occasions, and particularly when the degree of Doctor in Divinity was conferred on him by the Marischal College of Aberdeen, they bore the most ample testimony to the piety of his character, and to the uncommon extent of his attainments in literature. It is while merit is associated with modesty that its claims are most readily admitted; and it is when it is vain-glorious and overbearing that it is decried and opposed.

Living in the neighbourhood of Sir Walter Scott, Dr. Lawson was no stranger to the benevolence and kindness of his disposition, the stores of his mind, and the power of his fancy; yet amidst the admiration which he felt for a genius which has shed such lustre over the literature of his country, and given to the place of his abode attractions which will exist to the latest age, he showed no solicitude to engage his notice. The only time he ever was in his company was when Prince Leopold was passing through Selkirk, on which occasion Sir Walter was the person who introduced him to the Prince, and mentioned to a friend afterwards that the interview was a very affecting one. The hospitalities of Abbotsford would neither have accorded with the state of his health, nor his habits of seclusion; and he would have considered it as a waste of time, and an act of injustice, to have frequented scenes where he could neither give, nor receive enjoyment. He admired Sir Walter Scott's works, and had read with interest all that he had published previous to the first series of 'Tales of my Landlord.' Before he had an opportunity of examining that book, Dr. M'Crie's review came in his way, which influenced him so much that he would not read it. Some of the members of his family thought that he had imbibed a worse opinion of the book from the passages quoted, than he would if he had read the whole. So keenly did he feel the injustice which he thought had been done to the Covenanters, and so strongly was he impressed with the dishonour brought on the spirit of piety by the ludicrous manner in which its feelings and language were portrayed, that not all the beauty and wit by which the work is characterized could keep him from thinking of it with horror. There were various circumstances in his situation which led him to feel a peculiar regard for the memory of these worthies. The writings of the puritanical divines, which he regarded as stores of wisdom, were his favourite study; in the religious body with which he was connected, high importance is attached to the Covenants and to the struggles connected with them; their *Testimony* breathes an ardent zeal against all violence to principle and conscience; and the vicinity of Philiphaugh, where Montrose was defeated by Leslie, to the place of his residence, and the traditions current in the neighbourhood as to the battle and its results, were all adapted to strengthen his interest in the faithful of the land at that period, and his displeasure at every attempt to degrade them.

Feeling, as we do, a very high veneration for the memory of the Covenanters, we have regretted that Sir Walter Scott should have degraded his genius, by representations calculated to bring ridicule and odium on some of them, as coarse in their manners, sticklers for trifles, and delighting in tumult; but it was by his political prejudices that his judgment was warped. The time is gone when the flatteries of monarchs had power to charm; the exposure of their follies is more agreeable to the taste of the day; the vail which charity would draw is torn in pieces by the rude hand of vulgar abuse; and the attempt to deck the characters of Charles and Claverhouse with qualities to which they had no claim, has tended to sharpen the exposure of their wickedness. But it ought to be remembered what justice Sir Walter has done to the Covenanters in his subsequent volumes; how he has exhibited some of them as rising to the highest attainments in moral worth ; distinguished by all that is amiable in female character; exemplifying a generosity of the noblest order; and maintaining their integrity unshaken amidst the severest trials of human virtue. The power of moral principle manifested by him in the sacrifices and the exertions which he made for the payment of debt, contracted by becoming responsible for others, entitle him to a high place in the memory of the just. While genius and patriotism strike their harps at his tomb, let not piety hang hers on the willows ; but let it touch it to the praise of the Father of lights—of Him in whose hand it is to make great—of the righteous Lord who loves righteousness, and whose mercy endureth for ever.

There were circumstances in the conduct of his friends in which admonition seemed to Dr. L. necessary, and the following letter written to a lady of his acquaintance who had married a French Officer, a Catholic, shows with what fidelity and delicacy he could give it:—

'I wished to call upon you before you left Selkirk for a foreign country. Indisposition was one of the causes that hindered me; now I believe it is too late, I therefore bid you farewell by a few lines.

'You know the reason for which I was dissatisfied with your marriage, but I heartily approve of your following the husband you have chosen, were he to go to the end of the world. The difference of your religion from his is so far from being a reason why you should not fulfil every duty as a wife, that it furnishes a strong argument for endeavouring to fulfil them in perfection, that you may adorn your profession.

'Your husband, I hope, is too generous and too reasonable to wish you to change your religion unless you are convinced of its being false. He would certainly rather wish you to be honest in the profession of a religion which he may esteem erroneous, than a hypocrite in the profession of a religion which he esteems to be true.

'You will, however, meet with temptations to the change of that good religion which you learned from your worthy father; but I hope you will attend to the Bible, and pray daily for the enlightening and establishing grace of the Holy Spirit, that you may be kept from falling. You know the sentence pronounced against all who are ashamed of Christ and of his words; and against all who love any earthly friends, or even their own life, more than Christ. Mark viii. 38. Luke xiv. 25-27.

'I pray that you may always enjoy the pleasure of a good conscience; that, whether present or absent, you may be accepted of God; and that He may make you the delight of your husband and friends while you are in the world.'

The humility this letter manifests is truly amiable. It discovers not the least working of that irritation which many would have shown at the disregard of their opinion as to the impropriety of the connection; and while it brings forward the highest motives to stability in her profession, it points to the lessons of a father's piety, as what might counteract the influence of her new connexion in recommending an opposite creed. If the husband was a man of a liberal spirit, the generous and enlightened character of this letter would give him a favourable impression of the candour and Christian charity of the writer.

In a letter written to a nephew who had engaged in a sea-faring life, there are many excellent counsels. Our limits permit us to give only a few extracts; the whole letter discovers a great knowledge of human nature and character, and it is employed to give effect to the most wholesome admonitions:—

'I hear that you have made choice of a sea-faring life. I hope you will find that our God is the God of the sea as well as of the dry land. Those who go down to the sea, and do business in the great waters, see his works and his wonders in the deep; and often find reason to thank him for signal deliverances from perils of great waters. It was surprising, that Jonah should ever think of fleeing away in a ship from the presence of the Lord; but his eyes were soon opened, and he received a chastisement which brought him down to the belly of hell, and got an unexpected deliverance which made him an eminent type of our great Redeemer.

'Your life may sometimes be exposed to alarming danger, but the knowledge that this may often be the case will, I hope, be useful to you. Boast not of to-morrow, for thou knowest not what a day may bring forth. This may be said of us who remain on the dry land as well as you; yet seamen are still more inexcusable than other men, if they do not remember a lesson so loudly proclaimed by the raging waves, and the roaring wind; and I do not see how they can enjoy peace in their minds, unless they endeavour so to behave in the course of their lives as they would have wished to have done, when they see themselves carried up by one wave to the clouds of heaven, and ready to be plunged into the bosom of the ocean by the next.

'I hope the grace of God will preserve you from imitating any of the bad examples that may be set before you by your companions. It has been the unhappiness of many of them, that they have not received an education fitted to preserve them from yielding to the temptations to which they may be exposed; but you have been taught the fear of the Lord, and in you it will be more criminal to practise wicked deeds with them that work iniquity.'

He then warns him against being influenced by the fear of ridicule, to yield to the solicitations of sinners, or to neglect religious duties; and against that brutish folly into which sea-faring men are so apt to rush in scenes of relaxation after a long period of restraint and toil. He suggests this as one of the best maxims for the regulation of the conduct, not to do what may please us for the moment, but what may please us afterwards; and inculcates dependence on divine grace, and frequent prayer for it, as the best means of comfort and of moral security.

There is another letter which amply deserves a place in this sketch on account of its wisdom and amiable sympathy, and the peculiar circumstances of the worthy man to whom it was addressed. Mr. Young had been a fellow student, and was called to minister at Newtown in his neighbourhood. While going through his trials for ordination he fell into such a state of nervous agitation and despondence, that when the day for that service arrived, he could not be induced to submit to be ordained. I have heard him speak with much feeling of the considerate mildness and pity with which he was treated by the venerable Mr. Brown of Haddington on that occasion; of the zeal with which he defended him from the harsh remarks of some disposed to judge him with severity; and of the solemn admonitions addressed by him in a sermon he was requested to preach to the congregation ere they were dismissed. Mr. Young was soon after ordained at Kincardine, and led there for a long period a holy, useful, and contented life. In old age his mind again became clouded; he resigned his charge, retired with his family to Edinburgh, and after labouring for some time under the dark impressions of a disordered intellect, he entered into peace.

It would be most foolish and unjust to charge this gloom on religion; it arose from a constitutional tendency; and in marking his condition there is far more reason for wonder that his long course in the ministry was so steady and cheerful, amidst difficulties which might have shaken firmer minds, than that its close should have been darkened by morbid anxiety and gloomy forebodings.

The letter was written to him when Dr. L. had heard of the disturbed state of his mind, and its tone of pity and friendship is very soothing. Such a state of mind is too often treated roughly by the vigorous, the tranquil, and the gay: and often are its aberrations and tremours made the subject of ridicule: but Dr. L. felt, that while the spirit of a man unbroken may sustain his infirmity, a wounded spirit who can bear? He expostulated with him in holy kindness, laboured to restore his soul by wise counsel, and left him to the mercy of Him who will not break the bruised reed, nor quench the smoking flax:—

'As I have seldom had the opportunity of seeing you for many years back, I take this opportunity of putting you in mind, that by the long-suffering of God I still continue in the world, and may derive much benefit from your prayers. I am not what I once was, yet through God's mercy I possess many comforts, and that cheerfulness of spirit which becomes creatures to whom He is so indulgent.

'It gives me pain to hear that a man of your good sense, and one with whom the credit of religion is materially concerned, from the good opinion entertained of you as a Christian and a minister, should groan under disquieting thoughts concerning your future allotment from the hand of

God. Do you not remember the pleasant doctrine that you have taught from your youth up. You surely would not for the whole world have it thought that you call in question the exceeding riches of the grace of God, who sent his Son to die that we might live. I hope you will follow the example of David, who did what he could to dispel all gloomy thoughts from the mind, by turning his thoughts to the excellency of the mercy of God; the wonderful works which he did in the days of old; and the sure word of God. Your Bible is much larger than his, and brighter and sweeter is the light which flows from Him who came to heal the broken hearted.

'I would be much dejected were my thoughts always to dwell on myself, but, through the righteousness of Christ, grace reigns to eternal life, and in Him it finds all that justice can demand from the believing sinner. I will therefore hope in Christ; and as a penitent malefactor once said,—No man ever perished with his face turned to the cross of Jesus. The God of all comfort will, I hope, in due time drive away every gloomy thought from your mind. For your friends' sake, for your own sake, for Christ's sake, look in humble hope to the Saviour, and may you be enabled to glorify God by a cheerful reliance on his rich mercy in Christ Jesus.'

In looking over a number of his letters to his correspondents, it was delightful to mark with what simplicity and beauty the amiable qualities of his character are manifested, without the least solicitude or art. In some of them he expresses his gratitude for any attention or kindness shown to himself or to any of his family. Some good men have thought it testified their piety to keep earthly benefactors out of view, and to say that they looked not in gratitude to them, but to the Father of mercies. To him undoubtedly our eyes should be first and constantly directed, but the instruments of his bounty deserve our regard. And while some have acknowledged kindnesses in a manner savouring too much of the spirit of the world, his thanks were given in simplicity and in godly sincerity, and in a mode which evinced that he felt in their complacency, that God was lifting on him the light of his countenance, and that their favours were put by Him into their hands to bestow.

In some of them we find him pleading the cause of the blind, the diseased, or the infirm, with those who were able to assist them. He does this in a tone which shows that he remembered them that suffered adversity as being himself also in the body; and the allusions which he makes to the cross, and to the grace of Jesus, show that his compassion was excited by a divine impulse.

He makes, in his letters, some beautiful allusions to the friends and the scenes of his youth ; and though many years had elapsed since some of them had gone down to the grave, his heart kindles on the remembrance of their kindness, their genius, and their piety. Fancy brings back to the tender heart friends long since gone, in smiles sweeter than any the face ever wore, and in acquirements brightening as they rise from the darkness of the grave:—'Never was any man blessed with friendships more delightful or more useful than myself. David himself had not more reason to rejoice in his pleasant brother Jonathan, than you and I have to rejoice in our beloved A. S.* But I hope death has not imposed an everlasting termination on our friendship.'

The happy use made of the Bible in all his letters, is a proof of the delight which he had in the law of the Lord, and that in His law he meditated day and night. There is no small measure of wisdom necessary in introducing with propriety the language of Scripture, either in conversation or in letters. This is sometimes done in a manner too easy, and in circumstances too familiar; but the texts to which he refers appear as words in season, and as the voice of God elevating the views and solemnizing the feelings of men.

These letters abound with reflections and maxims important and interesting, and of these we shall give a few as specimens, regretting that our limits admit not of further indulgence:—

'The Gospel gives us its strongest consolations under those afflictions which press heaviest upon us.

'Never was friend more loved by me than he whom God has taken from me, but we will never be happy unless we can say with some degree of sincerity, "Whom have I in heaven but thee, and there is none in all the earth whom I desire beside thee." At the same time I have reason to rejoice that all my lovers and friends are not put far from me, and that the departed are not for ever removed. Oh that we possessed a large measure of that faith which is the substance of things hoped for!

'When children are removed out of the world before their parents, it is happy when they leave such a pleasant memorial behind them, that the sorrows of the mourner are mingled with joy and thanksgiving.

'I dislike to hear Christ's lamentation on the cross, "My God! My God! why hast thou forsaken me?" called his *complaint*. This seems not to accord with his resignation and patience, the voluntary character of his sufferings, nor the words which follow in the Psalm from which the language is quoted: "But thou art holy, O thou that inhabitest the praises of Israel."

'He that is animated throughout a discourse, is not animated at all.

---

* Probably, by these initials is indicated the Rev. Andrew Swanson, who died early in life, after a brief but gifted ministry. His published Sermons are still extant and highly esteemed. Although reared with Lawson under Professor John Brown of Haddington in the Secession Church, he made several changes in his Ecclesiastical relations. With a delicate allusion to this, his pious and excellent old Professor, on being informed of his death, said; 'Ay, ay, is Andrew dead? Weel, he has found a Kirk to suit him noo!' It is highly creditable also to Dr. Lawson, that the changes made by his friend and fellow-student made no change in the warmth of their friendship throughout life.—ED.

It is absurd to seem as earnest in announcing a method, as in recommending Jesus Christ.

'Mr. Bell of Wooller is gone. He has I believe left few equal and none superior among us, in those qualities which command esteem and engage love. I am persuaded that he is now with Christ. Is it not material for us to consider whether we are as likely as he to make a happy exchange when we are called from this world?

'I do not think it difficult to bear reproach as a stoic, but to bear it as becometh saints, we need the grace and the spirit of love and meekness. How can we find in our hearts to pray for pardon if we do not forgive?

'Many of our anxieties are superfluous, and those most of all which respect futurity. Many who are now in health will die this year, and many who are now looking daily for the message of departure will be preserved alive for years to come.

'A turn is given to the mind by the companions of our youth, which for the most part, has an influence on the remainder of life.

'Unhappy must the happiest of those men be, whose happiness rests on any thing so precarious as that which is but a vapour.

'I wish if possible to have every reproach cast on me to die a natural death. Boerhaave never troubled himself to confute calumnies; they were sparks, he used to say, which if you blow them, will kindle into a flame: if you let them alone they will expire.

'The present state of affairs confirms the words of Elihu, "Great men are not always wise." May they learn this, that they may show indulgence to those who differ from their present way of thinking!

'We have great reason to bless God for sound understandings; but they cannot well be called sound, if their powers are not employed in His service.

'It will be known at the great day *when* long life turned out a blessing; and *who* have, by their own folly, made it a curse to themselves.'

ANECDOTES OF DR. LAWSON.

Ere I come to the concluding part of this sketch, a few anecdotes may be introduced with good effect illustrative of his character as a minister, as a man, and as a teacher of theology.

Though he lived in a Burgh, which like other towns of that class, was frequently agitated by electioneering politics, he never took part in such contests, but gave faithful warning when he felt it necessary, against the evil tempers and the violence which they so often excite. On one occasion when the town was much inflamed, he exhorted his people not to lose sight of their Christian character amidst the contests of party; and to strive to enter in at the strait gate. His heart was so affected with the importance of eternity, and with solicitude for the spiritual welfare of his people, that he was overpowered even unto tears.

Though his audience was in general an attentive one, he observed, on one occasion, that many of them were asleep while he was preaching. He made a pause, at which they all lifted up their heads with evident anxiety. On observing this, he said, 'How strange is your conduct! You gave yourselves up to sleep while I was preaching the Gospel of Salvation; and now, when I am silent, you seem all anxious to hear!'

Of his skill in introducing local allusions, the following incident is a striking illustration. A few years before he died, he preached at Stitchel, on the Monday after the dispensation of the Lord's Supper. The text was John xxi. 18. 19. 'Verily, verily, I say unto thee, When thou wast young thou girdedst thyself, and walkedst whither thou wouldst: but when thou shalt be old, thou shalt stretch forth thy hands, and another shall gird thee, and carry thee whither thou wouldest not. This spake he, signifying by what death he should glorify God. And when he had spoken this he saith unto him, Follow me.' And it was with these words he commenced his sermon: 'Forty years ago I preached at the communion in this place. Your holy and beloved pastor discoursed on that occasion on these words, 'This beginning of miracles did Jesus in Cana of Galilee, and manifested forth his glory; and his disciples believed on him.' That was a sermon on the *first* of Christ's miracles and its blessed results, and I am now to discourse to you on some of his *last* words, and oh may it be with such happy effects! There are few in this assembly who were present at the service to which I refer, and forty years hence the greater part of us will be in eternity, and an eternity either of happiness or misery. Oh that we were wise, that we understood this, that we would consider our latter end!' This preface made the deepest impression on all present, and the whole discourse was heard with uncommon interest.

I shall give one instance out of many of his happy quotation of texts of Scripture; and in it we see the delicate kindness with which he could apologize for omissions, and the dexterity with which he could check censorious remarks. At the close of a Sacramental solemnity in Selkirk, the minister who officiated last pronounced the benediction at the end of his prayer. The people remained in the yard, and Dr. L. suggested to him to give out a psalm. Though labouring under pain, he arose and did so; and Dr. L. when the psalm was ended, addressed the people in various excellent counsels, calling them to value more highly that redemption which would be the perpetual song of heaven, and to cultivate and exercise those devout affections which should be expressed in an eternity of praise. He then said that it was usual to make the benediction the close of the service; but that the apostle Paul after having expressed the holy wishes implied in it for the Romans, felt some new matter occurring to his mind which he states to them, and then repeats it. Let us now repeat it, and may it be doubly felt in the piety it breathes, and doubly experienced in the grace and peace which it contains.

It deserves to be noticed that he lectured through the whole Bible, a task which few have been able to accomplish. For some time after his ordination he did not write his lectures, but the thought struck him that he ought to have done so, and that this portion of official duty required as much careful preparation as was bestowed on sermons. From that time he wrote them regularly. He left behind him no less than eighty considerable volumes in manuscript; and it is to be regretted that so few of them have been given to the public. If a man so gifted in memory and a ready elocution wrote with such care; and if Paul with his extraordinary endowments had his parchments containing, we may believe, suggestions for preaching, the fruits of study, and the records of experience; most inexcusable are they who lay up no stores of knowledge, and who degrade sacred subjects by the flimsiness and incoherence of their attempted illustrations.

A circumstance may be mentioned as evincing the power which God sometimes gives to moral admonition from the pulpit. Dr. L. when preaching on the eighth commandment, insisted strongly on the duty of restitution. Next morning a family from whose house a pair of shoes had been stolen some years before, found the price of them lying on the sole of the window, placed there by the unknown offender. Ministers draw the bow at a venture, but God directs the arrow to the heart.

The anecdotes illustrative of his character as a man and a Christian will exhibit

HIS HUMILITY.

In a discourse on the Sovereignty of Grace in the conversion of sinners, he made the following declaration:—'For my part I am firmly persuaded that all my hope must rest upon the richness and sovereignty of the mercy of God in Christ Jesus. I am persuaded that millions already in hell were far less criminal when they left the world than I have been. I am sensible that I can never make myself a fitter subject of mercy than I am at this moment; and that therefore I must follow to the pit those miserable wretches that are groaning under the wrath of God, unless I am plucked as a brand out of the burning. A doctrine so necessary to my hope and peace as the sovereignty of divine mercy I hope never to renounce.'

In travelling with a young friend, the conversation turned on the corruption of the human heart. The youth, who had the highest sense of his wisdom and sanctity, said to him, 'I do not think you would need to fear much though your thoughts were laid open.' Dr. L. replied, 'I could not bear that the course of my thoughts even for one hour should be exposed.' Most needful is the prayer, 'Cleanse thou me from secret faults; keep back thy servant also from presumptuous sins!'

Soon after he commenced his course as Professor, a very unpopular preacher was sent to supply his pulpit for three Sabbaths in succession. He felt the appointment as unkind, and had some reason to suspect that it proceeded from no friendly feeling. Thinking it, as he said, better to prevent complaints than to answer them, he preached a discourse to his people on each of these sabbaths. And after the preacher had left him he made the following statement: 'I never heard him preach a sermon but he told me more of my duty than I practised all my life; and while this was the case, whatever reason I had to find fault with myself, I had none to find fault with him.'

HIS MEEKNESS AND FORBEARANCE.

When in London he was asked to dine with a family where he was to meet with a minister who was at that time in high popularity. From the simplicity of his appearance and manners, Dr. H. thought him a fit subject for his wit, and treated him with rude freedom. Dr. L. felt his indignation kindled, and thought not only of repelling his insolence, but of exposing him to shame on account of the spirit he had manifested, and the claims he had advanced. But this reflection made him let him alone;—'London is the scene of his duties, what I say may injure his usefulness. His reflections can do me no harm. It will be far better for me to gain a victory over myself than over him.'

He was called to preach at the dispensation of the Lord's Supper in Glasgow at a time when the controversy in the Secession church about toleration had raised malignant feelings in the minds of many against him. He was to officiate on the Friday evening, and so tempestuous was the weather that the attendance was very small. Some person in the vestry, afraid lest he should consider that as an indication of public feeling which arose merely from the storminess of the night, kindly suggested what reason he had to disregard the slanders of ignorance and malice; upon which he repeated a sentence in Latin in which there was a double allusion to the storm and to the prejudice which had been excited;—'It is but a little cloud and it will soon blow over.' Some one expressed his surprise that he had not repelled the attacks which had been made on him, and he replied in the words of a heathen philosopher;—'Why should I kick an ass because an ass has kicked me?' When it was suggested that the epithet would be applied to the most abusive and the most despicable of his assailants, he replied, that he would be sorry if it were, and that if he thought so, he would never use the language again.

HIS DELIGHT IN THE ACCEPTABILITY OF OTHERS.

On one occasion, when two preachers had officiated in his place and that of a friend, and had been highly popular, he remarked, that 'it was not very easy to ascertain from their appearances at the hall, what measure of popularity young men will attain. If Christ be magnified, all is gained.' Envy was a feeling he despised for its meanness, and abhorred for its malignity. He spoke of it as directly opposed to the temper of the Gospel, and remarked that the passage in James condemnatory of it should be read as a question;—'Doth the Spirit that dwelleth in us lust to envy?' The phrase, 'The spirit that dwelleth in us,' is never used in Scripture for our own spirit, but for the Spirit of God.

HIS CANDOUR.

I never saw a man, said one who knew him well, who was more ready to acknowledge the force of an argument, though it had not occurred to himself. As an evidence of this it may be stated, that when a young friend had given it as his opinion that Melchizedec was only a king in Canaan; and that, as Paul was reasoning with the Jews from the Old Testament Scriptures, no man reading only the passages in Genesis and in the 110th psalm was likely to suppose him to be any thing else; he admitted the force of the suggestion, and said it would not be easily answered by those who wished to assign to him a higher character.

On one occasion while he was travelling in a stage coach, one of the passengers, supposing him to be a clergyman, expressed his surprise that a tenet so horrible as the perdition of heathens should have a place in the creed of Christians; and that any man should think that one so enlightened and so virtuous as Socrates should not be saved. To this tirade Dr. L. replied;—'God is the judge of all, and it is not for us to pronounce a sentence on any. If you and I meet Socrates in heaven, we will be happy to find him there. If he is not, sufficient reasons will be given for his absence.'

HIS SCRUPULOUS REGARD TO ENGAGEMENTS.

When at Glasgow he accepted of an invitation to dine at a friend's house, but having gone to Paisley, he met with a party there with whom he saw much that was interesting, and with whom he was solicited to spend the afternoon. The son of his friend who was with him urged him to do so, as there were persons in the party whom he might not again meet, and with whom this unexpected intercourse might be mutually agreeable; and said that his parents would be glad to see him any other day, and would be satisfied if he was happy. His reply was, 'I will keep my engagement, for you have no authority from them to release me from it; and I will not hurt any one's feelings, even though by doing so, I might gratify my own.'

HIS DELIGHT IN HIS CHILDREN.

I have heard various anecdotes which illustrate this, and which show the pleasure he took in opening their minds and engaging their affections. Let not this be thought too minute and familiar for mention. Who does not think with more interest of the heart and the character of Melancthon when he finds him relating this little circumstance;—'I was holding my little daughter in my arms in the morning, when she had only her night gown on. She observed tears stealing down my checks, and took up her skirt and wiped them away. This little act of hers has made a lasting impression on my memory and heart, and I could not but think it significant.'

HIS EXCELLENT QUALITIES AS A FRIEND.

He delighted much in the visits of his friends, though he rarely suffered intercourse with them to encroach on the time claimed by other duties; and those that knew his habits felt it would be wrong to interfere with that which was to be so well spent. A friend mentioned to me that he had travelled some miles to see him, and meant to go to Stitchel in the evening. He urged him to tarry all night, but finding him determined and the evening advancing, he said;—'If you are determined to go to Stitchel, it would be unkind to detain you, as the road is neither short nor easy.' It was mid-summer, and he added,—'but there is hardly any night at this time of the year. I often think of heaven at this season, and of the statement of the apostle John,—"And there shall be no night there."'

With his neighbour, Mr. Kidston of Stow, he maintained a very close friendship, and respected him much for his piety and holy skill in the things of God. On one occasion he had been selected as umpire in a dispute betwixt that minister and some members of his congregation, and Mr. K., irritated at what he thought his intention of deciding against him, broke out into some harsh reflections, which he ended by saying,—'but still I believe that you are a saint of God.' 'If you think me so,' was the meek reply, 'you cannot think ill of me.'

When Mr. K. died he went to his funeral, and as the coffin was kept open till near the time of interment that his more intimate friends might take a last view of his countenance if they chose, Dr. L. went into the death-chamber, and stood and looked earnestly at the corpse. When it was necessary to retire, he lifted up his arm to brush away his tears, and, saying, 'I will see him again,' turned about and went away. Next day he preached the funeral Sermon from these words,—'Moses my servant is dead;' in which he bore ample testimony to the gifts, graces, and labours of his departed brother; and addressed many solemn and suitable admonitions to the people.

AS A PROFESSOR OF THEOLOGY.

I may relate a few anecdotes illustrative of his wisdom, fidelity, and paternal kindness in this capacity; only premising that the substance of his counsels will be found in the Christian Repository for March and April 1821, under the title of 'Faults into which Ministers may fall as to the matter and the manner of their preaching.' Though he discharged his duties in this character to the high satisfaction of the generality of his brethren, there were some who, irritated at the part which he had taken in the controversy respecting toleration, wrote him a letter, in which it was insinuated that he did not attend with the necessary strictness to the religious principles of his students. To it he sent no reply, but in speaking of it to a friend said, that he felt peculiarly hurt at seeing appended to it the name of one who should have known him better. He added: 'His simplicity has been imposed on by specious pretenses. Another letter of that kind will make me resign my office.'

It was seldom that he was called to reprove any of his students; and when he did so, it was done with such solemnity as secured its effect. To two students who were whispering to each other during his lecture, he said,—'If your conversation is considered by you as more important than what I am stating, and you cannot defer it, you may proceed; but if not, you will wait till I be done.'

Mention has been made in a former sketch of the reproof which he gave to a young man for levity. I am happy I can add to the account a circumstance worthy of notice in regard to both. The youth came to make the apology which was expected; but Dr. L. who had been informed that the levity manifested was occasioned by a circumstance which rendered it excusable, stopped him while entering on his apology; expressed the confidence which he had as to his demeanour in future; and conversed with him on other subjects in the most friendly manner. How beautifully did this exhibit the spirit of the father to the prodigal son, a spirit whose exercise cherishes most sweetly the feelings of contrition, and secures most effectually steadiness in virtue.

He often urged on his students to treasure the word of God in their memories; and it deserves to be mentioned that, while himself a student, he had committed to memory so accurately the numerous texts of Scripture at the close of the various paragraphs of Mr. Brown's System of Divinity, that that excellent man used to say, that he never found a student who could repeat them so exactly; and that he never run him out but once.

In his counsels respecting prayer he recommended simplicity, earnestness, and brevity; and remarked,—'It was the saying of some man, that the devil was served by long sermons (as they led the hearers to worldly thoughts, fretfulness, weariness, and slumber); and he might have added, and by long prayers too.'

Respect and deference to elder ministers was one of his counsels:—'Attached as I am to Presbyterian parity, yet such modesty and deference is amiable in youth, and to it age has a claim.'

In a conversation with some of his students he remarked, that 'a good voice would go far with some to gain popularity; but rest assured, it will take something else to maintain it.'

The subject of mimickry was introduced: he said, where young men could bear it, it might be useful to correct improprieties. On one occasion he heard an imitation of his own manner, and said, 'Had I been early aware of its defects, I might have been able to correct them.'

His parting with his students was solemn and tender. When they went to his dwelling to take leave of him, he gave a freer vent to his feelings than he did in the public hall. A friend has mentioned to me, that in his last call on him along with two of his companions, he said, 'You do not return to your place as Joshua sent away the children of Reuben and the children of Gad, with much riches of silver and gold;

but I hope you go away with your minds stored with divine truth, and your hearts with holy affections, a treasure far better.' To one of them, then in delicate health, he said; 'You are not so well in body as your friends would wish you, but we are in the hands of a good God who knows what is to be the issue of our afflictions, and the best issue;' and his voice faultered while he said farewell.

He felt a very deep interest in the settlement, the lot, and the labours of his students when they were ordained to the ministry. As an instance of this it may be mentioned, that one morning when about to partake of some refreshment with a friend, he requested him to ask a blessing, and to supplicate, while thus engaged, God's blessing on the ordination of one of his students which was to take place that day. He said, 'I have endeavoured to remember it before the Lord in private, and if my prayers are granted, God will bless him, and make him a blessing.'

To one of his students, an intimate companion of one of his sons, he wrote a very affecting letter in peculiar circumstances. That young man, who was himself very unwell, wrote to his friend at Selkirk a letter of affectionate enquiry as to his indisposition, of which he had heard. Ere his letter reached Selkirk, John Lawson was no more; and his father replied to it as if from his departed son. The answer is written in a strain uncommonly solemn and affecting, and indicates in a very striking manner how much his mind had been conversant with things heavenly and eternal. It breathes not the language of terror and despair, like the spirit that assumed the figure, the voice, and the mouth of the departed prophet; but that of holy love and hope, like the words of Moses and Elias when they appeared in glory on the mount, and spake of the decease which Christ should accomplish at Jerusalem :—

'DEAR SIR,

'YOUR hope that I am in a better state of health than formerly is now more than realized. God has, in his infinite mercy, been pleased to receive me into those happy abodes, where there is no more sorrow, nor death, nor sin. I now hear and see things which it is impossible to utter; and would not give one hour of the felicity which I now enjoy, for a lifetime, or for a thousand years, of the greatest felicity which I enjoyed on earth.

'I still love you, and the other friends whom I left on earth, but my affection for them is very different from what it was; I value them not for the love which they bear to me, or the amiable qualities which are most generally esteemed by men, unless they love my Lord and Saviour, through whose blood I have found admission to heaven. The happiness that I wish for you is not advancement in the world, or a rich enjoyment of its pleasures; but the light of God's countenance, the grace of his Spirit, and a share, when a few years have passed, of those things which eye has not seen nor ear heard, and which it has not entered into the heart of man to conceive.

'It is not permitted to us who dwell on high to appear to our former friends, and to inform them of our present feelings; and, ardently as I desire to have you a participant of my felicity, I do not wish to approach you in a visible form, to tell you of the riches of the glory of that inheritance which I possess. Abraham tells me that the writings of the prophets and apostles are better fitted to awaken sinners to a sense of everlasting things, and to excite good men to holiness, than apparitions and admonitions of their departed friends would be, and what he says is felt to be true by all of us. I do not now read the Bible. I thank God I often read it from beginning to end, when it was necessary for me to learn from it the knowledge of my beloved Saviour; and yet, if I could now feel uneasiness, I would regret that I made it so little the subject of my meditation. You would be glad to know whether, though unseen, I may not be often present with you, rejoicing in your prosperity, and still more in every good work performed by you; in every expression of love to my God; and care for the welfare of your own soul. But I am permitted to tell you no more on this subject than God has thought fit to tell you in his word, that there is joy in heaven over one sinner that repenteth; that angels are present in Christian assemblies, observing with pleasure or indignation the good or the bad behaviour of the worshippers; and that we welcome with great joy our friends from earth, when they are received into our everlasting habitations.

'Farewell! my dear friend, farewell! but not for ever. What are all the days you have before you on earth, but a moment? I hope that the grace which hath brought me so early in my existence to heaven, will bring you all to the same happy place, after sparing you some time longer in the lower world to serve your generation, by his will, and to do more than I had an opportunity to do, for exciting your neighbour to choose the path of life. Much good may be done by the attractive example; by the prayers; and (at proper times,) by the religious converse of Christians engaged in this world.

'Farewell! again, till we meet never to be separated.

'I am your friend, more sincerely than ever,

J. L.'

To his students when fixed in scenes of pastoral duty he was always ready to give his best advice; and their applications for his counsel were received with pleasure, and answered promptly and kindly. And to those of them who did not obtain any fixed charge, he was most anxious to do justice; and when opportunity was afforded him, to excite them to labour to show themselves approved to God; and to maintain that meekness of wisdom, that patience of hope, those kindly feelings to their more successful brethren, and that diligence in study and in doing good, so difficult to be kept alive amidst the bitterness of disappointment, and strong temptations to envy.

It has happened that in two or three instances, students left his tuition, and connected themselves with other religious parties; but in none of these cases did he discover any irritation, or the slightest solicitude either about the good report or the bad report which they carried away. His wish was that the Lord might lead them in his truth, and teach them; the counsel he would suggest from it to others was, 'Prove all things, hold fast that which is good;' and the influence it should have upon himself and others he would state in allusion to the words of the apostle Paul, 'Nevertheless, whereto we have already attained, let us walk by the same rule, let us mind the same thing.'

In a sphere so retired, and in a life so studious, it may easily be supposed there would be few incidents of general interest. There were, however, some incidents the statement of which will illustrate the moral as well as the intellectual qualities of his character.

When the question of toleration was agitated in the religious society to which he belonged,—a topic on which it is so truly astonishing that men should have been so slow in receiving the light of mercy,—he felt himself called upon to recommend the great duty of forbearance, in a pamphlet of which it is only justice to say, that it is characterized by good sense, candour, and mildness. A superstitious veneration for the views of our ancestors, who, notwithstanding their struggles for freedom, civil and religious, and their sufferings by the arrogance and cruelty of their persecutors, still maintained the power of the magistrate to suppress error and heresies, (that is, every opinion which the ruling power in church or state might call so,) led many to oppose any indulgence to the sentiments of those that pleaded for statements more accordant with the genius of the New Testament, and with liberty of conscience. His pamphlet was attacked with great virulence, and his name coupled with many an odious epithet; but he committed himself to Him that judgeth righteously, and nothing could provoke him to render railing for railing. In a letter to a friend he says, in allusion to this abuse; 'I have more than once heard of things said in my name that were very remote from the truth; but I paid no regard to them, because I was persuaded they would make no impression, or very short lived, on any person whose good opinion I wished to cultivate. I had read a story when I was a boy, in an old author called Valerius Maximus, which I shall never forget, and which I consider as a rule for my conduct. Plato, hearing that one of his friends had aspersed his character, replied, 'I will endeavour to live so as that nobody will believe him.' There is no part of my character about which I am less solicitous than my reputation for integrity. I am pretty certain from my own consciousness, joined with the testimony of my father concerning my years of childhood, that since I could use my tongue I have never polluted it with a wilful lie.'

When the plan of enlarging the Psalmody was in agitation, he argued for it in the church courts in a very persuasive manner. Among other statements which he made, it is recollected how he mentioned the passages which, it was predicted, should be sung in New Testament times; and held these up as an intimation from heaven, that the praises of the Gospel church should not be limited to the Psalms of David. It is a very interesting fact, that some of the Paraphrases then adopted were made the means of cheering him in his last hour; and that in singing lines which exhibit the blessedness of the saints in death, and at the resurrection, and which occurred in the usual course of domestic worship, his family joined with him, in some of his last acts of worship on earth.*

When Prince Leopold, a man in whom the country felt so deep an interest, on account of that mournful event which blasted a nation's hopes, and left his house to him desolate,† was on a tour through Scotland, and passed through Selkirk, the Magistrates and the neighbouring gentry went out to meet him, attended by Dr. Lawson's students, headed by Dr. L. as their Professor. Dr. L. was happy in having an opportunity of paying his respects to a person descended from ancestors who had sacrificed so much in the cause of Protestantism, and expressed these feelings on being presented to the Prince by Sir Walter Scott, in very appropriate language. The Prince felt highly gratified, and remarked to Sir Walter Scott afterward, that he had received many compliments on account of the Princess, but this was the first he had received on his own account, or that of his ancestors.

In a letter to a friend who wished to hear from himself an account of what passed betwixt the Prince and him, Dr. L. writes,—'I entertain a high respect for Prince Leopold, as the descendant of Princes to whom the Protestant part of the world is much indebted. He appears to possess a degree of condescension and affability not very common in his high rank. Besides what you saw in the Papers, he asked me my age; when I told him what it was, he complimented me on the health which I seemed

---

* We do not consider it necessary, or incumbent on us, to enter on an editorial criticism or confutation of Dr. Lawson's views on the subject of Psalmody; which is so vexed a subject among Presbyterians in the United States. We shall only say, that we do not indorse Dr. L's views on that subject, as above stated. Still, we may remark, that the 'Paraphrases,' so far as they are faithful 'translations' of God's word, must be allowed to be well suited for worship, by those who consider that 'the praises of the gospel church should not be limited to the Psalms of David.' We are not one of such as hold that sentiment. Yet, happy were it for the unity of the churches of Christ to-day, if they would agree to limit themselves in their Psalmody, to the inspired Word of God, faithfully translated, as contained in the Old and New Testaments, chanted or sung, either in prose or verse. It does not appear that Dr. Lawson's sentiments went beyond this.—ED.

† Referring to the lamented death of the Princess Charlotte of Wales, the wife of the Prince, daughter of George IV., and heir of the British crown; a princess who was held in the highest esteem and love by the nation. Her death plunged the nation into universal mourning.—ED.

to enjoy. Part of my answer was, that one may enjoy as much comfort in old age as in youth, if he is a fearer of God. But my dullness of hearing unfitted me for much conversation with him. We esteem ourselves honoured when we are admitted to the converse of earthly princes, who are creatures of the dust like ourselves; why have we not a profounder sense of our obligations to the everlasting God who allows us to come to Him, even to his mercy seat? Oh that we could approach to Him at all times with the reverence and the confidence which are due to his greatness and his mercy!'

Compared with the idle and fulsome flatteries so common in the presence of the great, his address appears dignified and becoming; indicating, not the spirit or the policy of the sycophant, but the holy kindness and the due respect of a man of God.

At a time when disaffection to government was supposed to be prevalent in some districts, and when Dissenters were regarded by some alarmists with jealousy and suspicion, Dr. Lawson approved himself the friend of order, loyalty, and peace. In answer to a very gratifying communication from the Lord Lieutenant of the County of Selkirk, he sent him the letter which follows, which is highly honourable to his political principles, and to his Christian conduct and faithfulness:—

'MY LORD,
'I was highly flattered by the letter with which your Lordship honoured me, expressing the Lieutenancy's approbation of my poor endeavours to serve my king and country. I will certainly endeavour to spread the address which you was pleased to commit to me. I can assure your Lordship that whatever distinctions may be found among either denomination of Seceders, they will all be found loyal subjects. Drunkards may have their reasons for calling themselves Christians, and profane swearers for ranking themselves with gentlemen, but no man who does not wish to be a faithful subject can have any temptation to associate himself with either of the societies of Seceders. It is well known that upon any discovery of his principles, he would be turned out of either of them with disgrace. I am far from saying that they will be found more loyal than other subjects. Every honest man in the Island will contribute his support to the government that protects him. I pray God that the Nobility and Gentry may be as unanimous in support of our holy religion, as I am persuaded ministers of every denomination will be in the support of the State; I should then entertain little fears of any invader, in the assurance that God Himself would be our salvation in the time of trouble.

'I am, My Lord,
'Your Lordship's and Gentlemen of
the Lieutenancy's humble servant,
GEORGE LAWSON.'

Living so near Melrose Abbey, he often examined with delight and wonder this much admired remnant of ancient magnificence and beauty. I allude to it only for the purpose of showing the devout tendency of his mind. While tracing the various parts of its exquisite workmanship, he would contrast, as I have heard him say, what he saw with Ezekiel's temple, so minutely described in the last part of his prophecy, and made the one aid his conceptions of the other. While the antiquary marks in it only its memorials of the olden time, its roof sculptured with sacred history, the remarkable events of which it has been the scene, and the interesting pilgrims that have resorted to it; and while the poet has brought before the fancy its priests in their vestments, its choir resounding with grave sweet melody, warriors consecrating their swords at its shrine, nobles uttering their vows at its altars, the dead interred with sacred pomp within its precincts, the moon gleaming on its arches and its pillars, and the rushing of the waters by its side when 'the deep uttered its voice, and lifted up its hands on high;' to the pious it will suggest contemplations more solemn and important, and point them to that fabric which shall endure for ever, 'which is built on the foundation of the apostles and prophets, and of which Jesus Christ himself is the chief corner stone.'

During the latter years of his life he laboured under various infirmities. His habits during his whole life had been remarkably abstemious. He probably felt this necessary for his health, but he did not put the families where he was a guest to trouble in preparing what was nice and delicate for his use, for the simplest fare was that of which he would alone partake; nor was his abstemiousness marked by ought like cynical moroseness, or Pharisaic sanctimony, for he delighted to see his friends eat their bread with joy, and by his rich fund of anecdotes made the conversation pleasant and improving.

In a letter to one of his friends written by him when far advanced in life, he gives a view of the state of his mind and feelings deeply interesting.

'I certainly am become very feeble, but I have reason to thank God that I am free from sickness, and mostly from pain. I could walk but a small part of the way to the meeting house without extreme fatigue, (he was now regularly carried in a sedan chair to the church on Sabbath,) and yet I can preach for a decent length of time without much fatigue, and I believe I am as well heard as in my younger days. I am now past my seventieth year, and I cannot expect to recover the strength which I once had, but I am in the hand of a good God who has preserved me hitherto, and sometimes delivered me from very alarming sicknesses. I complain not that I share in the common lot of the old, but I bless God that I still live when so many of my acquaintances are gone down to the grave, that I still enjoy many comforts, and that I can still perform the chiefest part of my ministerial work. I might have been happier in heaven than on earth, but alas! I need all the time that has been given me to prepare to meet God in another world. May He grant that I may not after all be found unprepared, when the day comes on which I shall go whence I shall not return! It gives me pleasure to hear that the brethren in your neighbourhood interest themselves deeply in my welfare. I hope if they live to old age, they will meet with that respect from their juniors which they now pay to their senior brethren.

'We must look forward to changes in this world, but we have reason to be thankful not only for our present circumstances, but likewise for our ignorance of what is before us. I know that I must die, and that soon, but I by no means wish to know when I am to be called out of the world, or what I may be called to suffer before I leave it. My desire is to be found ready to go when called by Him, to whose sovereign pleasure it belongs to order every thing that concerns us. I often wonder that men should think so much on a world in which they are to dwell but for a moment, and so little upon that world in which they are to dwell for ever and ever. On this moment depends eternity.'

It has been felt by some ministers as a very painful circumstance, that in their old age, their debility of mind or body became such that they were debarred from the public duties of their ministry; and it has required all the power of resignation to check repining, and to bear the languor of such a period. Happy is their lot who are enabled to labour to the last in the work of Christ, and to bear the testimony of their old age to Him to whom they have devoted the kindness of their youth. Such public services cheer their spirits, and while engaged in them the Redeemer's strength is made perfect in their weakness. It has sometimes happened that the debility of aged ministers has been such, that these services have been painful to themselves, and also to others; when the voice which was to them as a lovely song is feeble and inarticulate, and the memory, once rich in the stores of wisdom, is so decayed as to make their attempts to instruct tiresome by repetitions, embarrassed and desultory; but in the case of Dr. Lawson his public appearances to the last were characterized by the variety, self-possession and readiness of his best days. He felt that they were listening to a father's voice, and his discourses had much of the tenderness and solemnity of a father's parting counsels.

It was in the advanced period of his life that a testimony of the love and veneration of his students was given him, which could not but gratify him. He was requested by them to sit for his picture, and this picture executed at full length by an artist of merit, and elegantly framed, was placed in the hall of meeting, as a mark of their affection and gratitude. His likeness has been thought by some coarse; to me the face seems to want the benignity which it still wears in my remembrance, and the paternal blandness which made his prayers and counsels to be felt by his students as the dew of their youth. The old have frequently complained of the neglect, nay, of the insolence of the young. It is not from them that fallen greatness, or the infirm in body or mind, receive much commiscration. This was the complaint of Job, 'upon my right hand rise the youth, they push away my feet, and they raise up against me the ways of their destruction.' To them the kind attention of the young is peculiarly pleasing, and here it was felt by the good man as a great blessing of his lot. His pupils felt his infirmities, adding tenderness to their respect, and solicitude to their efforts to please him. The evident nearness of the account he was to give to God, and in which their conduct must occupy a place, was an idea deeply solemnizing; and the prayer put up by his pupils in rotation attested how they felt this memento. There was not one of them who had the heart to treat any symptom of his weakness with levity; nor one of them who would not have counted it his honour and delight to have adjusted his mantle, and to have felt him leaning on his arm.

He preached till within a fortnight of his death, and his last text was Psalm lxxxii. 6, 7: 'I said, Ye are gods, and all of you are children of the Most High; but ye shall die like men, and fall like one of the princes.' It was a funeral sermon on account of the death of George the Third. It was not, like too many sermons on such occasions, a fulsome panegyric on departed greatness, but a solemn admonition to the living. While eloquence, not content with decking the throne, garnishes the sepulchre, piety feels itself impelled by the death of kings, to give effect to those lessons on the vanity of man, which are too often forgotten amidst the pomp of the world. He read out a portion of the ninetieth Psalm to be sung by the congregation, and piously applied it to himself. He felt that he had arrived at the limits of life, and that his strength was sinking to the dust; but in him it was seen, that for an old age of piety and wisdom religion has provided her sweet consolations and her reviving hope; like nature reserving its mildest lustre and its softest calm for the setting sun. During his last illness, though unable to lie in bed during a great part of it, he was uniformly patient, and full of prayer. He bade adieu to all his family one by one, and expressed his hope that they should meet again in heaven. How delightful is such a hope to a dying parent! It has sometimes been the sorest pang felt in death by the good, that they were leaving some of their family in the gall of bitterness; that their efforts for their salvation had been fruitless; nay, that had they been less indulgent and more faithful, the result might have been different; and that this might be the last time in which they should look on them with affectionate solicitude. Such reflections are sometimes alleviated by hope that they may yet be converted from the error of their ways; but still anxieties and fears will return; but to leave them with the consciousness that they are heirs of the grace of life, and in the way of salvation, renders the last farewell comparatively easy, and makes them bless God that they can carry them with them in their hearts to heaven.

Most precious to them was his last blessing, 'God be with you all!' He had felt the presence of God as the greatest blessing of his life; in it he had found guidance in all his difficulties, encouragement in all his fears, and help in all his duties; and his persuasion was that in that presence they should enjoy direction far beyond all that a father's counsel could suggest, and care beyond all that could be exercised by a father's hand. God with us, is the highest privilege of earth; being with God, is the happiness of heaven.

As to his own state, he had the firm hope of being with Christ. When the assurance of the apostle, 'I am persuaded that neither death, nor life, nor angels, nor principalities, nor powers, nor things present, nor things to come, nor height, nor depth, nor any other creature shall be able to separate us from the love of God which is in Christ Jesus our Lord,' was repeated, he replied in language expressive of his high estimation of such an assurance, and of the blessed hope with which he was cleaving to the Lord. The manner in which he expressed it evinced the holy modesty of his spirit; and it was evident from what followed, that he wished that his Lord's translating hand should find him kneeling at the footstool of his mercy.

The last words which he uttered were these, 'Take me to paradise!' a petition beautifully expressive of his faith in the Redeemer's power and grace, and how his mind was dwelling on the cross of his Lord, and on the mercy to the penitent sufferer by his side which blessed that scene. He trusted in that power and grace which had raised him from death to life, for his translation to glory; and in that merciful hand by which nature was supported, while sinking into dust, for the conveyance of his spirit to everlasting rest. To that Saviour he would look for life in death, and for felicity in heaven. How similar were his feelings at a moment so solemn, to those of Mr. Greig, the most intimate of his friends, at such a crisis some years after! who, with a voice faultering in death, said, 'I will soon be in heaven.'

Not long after, while one of his brethren was employed in prayer, and presenting that petition, 'that an abundant entrance might be ministered to him into the everlasting kingdom of our Lord and Saviour,' he entered into the joy of his Lord. A very appropriate discourse was delivered after his funeral by the Rev. Adam Thomson of Coldstream, on devout men carrying Stephen to his grave, and making great lamentation over him. In this discourse, after a very interesting delineation of the character of Stephen, and the regrets called forth by the departure of good men, the character of Dr. Lawson is sketched with skill, fidelity, and affection.

DR. LAWSON'S WRITINGS.

With regard to the writings of Dr. Lawson, it is not necessary to say much, as the favourable reception they have met with from the public attests how their merit has been appreciated. The chief of them are

Lectures on the books of Esther and Ruth, on the History of Joseph, and on the Proverbs of Solomon, and Discourses on the History of David. No person qualified to judge can read these volumes without being struck with the ingenuity and fertility of the exposition which he gives; the deep insight into the human heart and character they discover; the engaging simplicity of the style, and their practical cast. There is not the least affectation of critical skill, by which many far inferior to him in scholarship have sought to astonish the vulgar: nor does he give any countenance to the practice of converting every incident into a typical exhibition of evangelical truth. Some have indulged in this practice under the influence of an ill regulated zeal for the Gospel; and others have done so, contrary to their better judgment, from an undue deference to popular prejudice; and it requires no small courage to risk the offense which may be given by avoiding such allusions, and the imputation of the motives to which it may be ascribed. An enlightened friend of the Gospel will never aid in perverting it, or betray it to the scoffer by any low fancies. At the same time, he eagerly embraces every fit opportunity of adverting to the doctrines of grace, and to the excellencies of the Saviour; and his acquaintance with history, ancient and modern, has enabled him to enliven these lectures with many happy illustrations from incidents or characters. It is to be regretted that some preachers have degraded this practice by the low and frivolous cast of the anecdotes they have introduced, and others destroy its effect by their frequency; but in the hands of a man of taste and wisdom, an incident may be exhibited from books or from real life with the happiest results. It arrests attention, gives force to the lesson, impresses it on the memory and the heart, and is never thought or talked of without recalling the object it was intended to gain.

His Sermons to the Aged are remarkably appropriate, and written in a strain plain, faithful, and earnest. The aged are a class of persons who require peculiar attention from the ministers of the Gospel. If still careless, it is a most difficult task to rouse them to serious feeling; if awakened to see their guilt and danger, the consciousness of a life of sin is apt to drive them to despair; while their many infirmities, and the neglect with which they are treated, they are apt to consider as justifying or excusing their fretfulness. To stir up the slumbering conscience, to give hope to those agitated by remorse, and to call murmurers to contentment and praise, seem to have been his object in these sermons, and they are admirably adapted to accomplish it.

To some of these volumes Dr. L. appended Sermons, chiefly on relative Duties, which are marked by the peculiarities of his manner. He thought that such topics were less attended to in published sermons than others. To carry religion in its light, benignity, and consolation to the bed of languishing, to the house of mourning, to the fire-side, and to the scene of lowly toil, requires a skill in the word of truth and in the human heart, a kindliness of spirit, a minuteness and fidelity in admonition, and a judiciousness and delicacy in counsel, not frequently associated; but in him they were happily united, and by them God has glorified himself in the dwellings of Jacob.

He cheerfully complied with the requests which were made to him to write Essays for several of the religious Magazines of the day, and to some of them he was a frequent contributor. He sometimes selected topics which he handled in several Numbers in succession. I refer to a series of Essays in the *Christian Repository*, on Predestination, in which the objections to this doctrine are repelled in a most satisfactory manner, and with uncommon perspicuity for so dark a subject. I refer also to another series on what he calls the Popery of Protestants, in which he shows how much of the superstition, false doctrine, and evil spirit of the church of Rome are to be found among those who boast of their hostility to the man of sin. This difficult topic he has managed with great candour, fidelity, and judgment. Those false impressions which he exposes are not confined to the vulgar, who in ignorance or prejudice build wood, hay, and stubble on the foundation laid in Zion; but may be found in Masters and Rulers in Israel, who have daubed its walls with untempered mortar, and fenced it round with the restrictions of worldly policy, and the claims of secular domination. Christianity in the purity of its worship, the humility of its spirit, and the brightness of its charity, is the scheme by which its author will be glorified, its enemies put to shame, and the nations blessed.

In a Number of the *Religious Monitor*, there is a paper written by him under the title of 'Reflections of an Aged Sinner on his Birth-day,' breathing the deepest contrition of a tender conscience on reviewing the past years of a long life; that humble hope of mercy which the atoning sacrifice of the Lamb of God inspires; the most solemn dedication of the days which may be yet allotted to him by the will of Him who had fed him all his life long to that day; and a firm trust in the Angel who had redeemed him from all evil, for strength in the infirmities, courage in the fears, and light in the darkness of age.

He was led into a short controversy with the Editor of the *Quarterly Magazine* by an attack made on a Sermon of his, bearing the title of 'The Joy of Parents in Wise Children;' in which he was represented as teaching undisguised Arminianism, by ascribing an undue influence to parental culture in particular, and to the means of salvation in general. His reply was very able, and exposed in the clearest manner the misconceptions of his opponent, and the gracious character of the connexion which God has established betwixt the means and the end. The controversy was soon terminated, and had been prompted by the spirit of sectarian jealousy and censoriousness, or by the hope of adding to the circulation of that periodical.

LECTURES

ON THE

WHOLE BOOK OF RUTH.

INTRODUCTION

TO

LECTURES ON RUTH.

THE design of this book, say some, is to give us the genealogy of David. This certainly could not be the chief design either of Samuel, who is generally supposed to be the writer of it, or of the Spirit of God, in giving us this history. The genealogy of David from Judah is contained in very few verses, and we find it in several other parts of Scripture. Every part of the book affords rich entertainment and useful instruction.

What would we give for a piece of family history, equally ancient and authentic, of any of our own nation, or rather that nation, whatever it was, from whence we have derived our origin? The holy Bible was not written to gratify our curiosity, and yet what book was ever written that can equally gratify laudable curiosity about the occurrences and manners of former ages?

This book is one of those which were written by inspiration of God, and must therefore be exceedingly profitable to us, if we read it with a due attention of those instructions which it is designed to impress on our minds. It is not one of those books in which we are to look for new instructions. The religion recommended in it is that which had been already taught by Moses; but it impresses deeply upon the mind of the attentive reader many truths highly conducive to holiness, and to the happiness even of the present life.

We find in this book, that private families are as much the objects of divine regard as the houses of princes. The sacred writers that give us the history of Saul and David, give us likewise the history of Naomi and Ruth. What are the rich and great more than the mean and indigent, before God? The greater part of the kings and princes that reigned three thousand years ago are now utterly forgotten; but the names of Boaz and Ruth shall live whilst the world lasts. It is to be hoped that many other precious saints lived in these ancient times, whose names are now not heard of in this world. But the same God who caused the names of some to be recorded in that Book of Life which he hath given us for our instruction, hath recorded the names of all of them in another Book of Life, to be opened and read, at the consummation of all things, in the ears of all mankind.

That in this life we must expect changes, is another of the truths of which this book reminds us. 'Changes and war are against me,' said one of the best men of ancient times. Naomi, one of the best of women, met with such vicissitudes, that she wished to have her name changed into Marah. We all know that we are constantly exposed to changes, and yet we all need to be put in mind of it. One great part of our unhappiness is, that we forget the mutability of our present condition; and therefore, when trouble comes upon us, we behave as if some strange thing happened to us.

But a lesson more useful and more pleasant is impressed upon our minds by this book—that God does not forsake those who trust in Him at the time when they are visited with the bitterest afflictions. 'I will be with him in trouble, to deliver him.' The history before us is a comment on this promise. Many were the afflictions of Ruth and Naomi; but the Lord delivered them out of them all, and, 'according to the days wherein he had afflicted them, he made them glad.'

But what distinguishes this book from other sacred books is, the charming picture it gives us of domestic felicity in the lowest rank of life, and in persons deprived of those friends to whom men or women use to look for felicity. Naomi was bereaved, by the king of terrors, of her husband and of all her children. Ruth was bereaved of the husband of her youth, and was left childless. They both felt their griefs like women of tender sensibility; yet they were neither discontented nor unhappy. There were three things which contributed to preserve them from sinking into despondency, and that rendered them happier under their afflictions than many other persons find themselves in the most prosperous circumstances.

First, Their piety. They trusted in God. Naomi doubtless had taught Ruth the knowledge of the God of Israel before she brought her into the land of Israel; for 'she came,' as Boaz says, ' to trust under his wings,' Ruth ii. 12. In the low circumstances of both these women, they hoped in God, they submitted to his providence; and they could not be miserable in any situation in which his providence placed them.

Secondly, They loved one another with a fond affection; and where there is true love there will be pleasure, where there is mutual love there will be happiness.

Thirdly, Their behaviour towards one another was a continual expression of their mutual love. There were none of those brawlings, unkind reflections, and fits of sullenness, between them that often embitter domestic life. Naomi never complained of too little respect from Ruth, never exercised her authority with bitterness, never distressed her daughter-in-law with peevish complaints of the afflictions of her former life, or of neglect from her kinsmen, or of her other friends. 'The law of kindness was in her mouth,' and it was evident, from every part of her conduct, that she set as high a value on Ruth's happiness as on her own. Ruth, on her side, considered the desires of her mother-in-law as commands which she was happy to obey, and did every thing in her power to compensate to her the loss of her husband and her sons. So wise and affectionate was her behaviour, that the townsmen thought her better to Naomi than seven sons.

Our natural tempers will have much influence to make our lives happy or miserable. If they are happy, they will dispose us to be cheerful, and to promote cheerfulness in others. If they are unhappy, the bad effect of them will be felt by our neighbours, especially by those who are under the same roof with us. But we are rational creatures, capable of instruction and of reflection. We are all desirous of happiness; and, if we find any thing in ourselves that makes it impossible to attain happiness, is it not our wisdom to put it far from us?

Why should a disease be suffered to embitter our days and endanger our lives, if a remedy can be found?

And does not the Scripture furnish us with remedies for every distemper of our hearts? The words of God are healing words. The entrance of them gives light to the understanding, peace and purity to the heart. The naturally bad tempers of men must be changed where they produce their proper effect. The wolf and the lamb, the lion and the cow, are made to feed together where the gospel is received by faith. It must be confessed, that vestiges of our corrupt dispositions will still continue to blemish our conduct till the body of sin be destroyed; but, beholding as in a glass the glory of the Lord, we are changed into the same image from glory to glory. Nor are the virtues of the ancient saints without their effect upon the attentive reader of the Bible. Although Paul never ceases to call upon us to 'look to Jesus as the author and finisher of our faith,' yet he frequently puts us in mind likewise of the advantage we may derive from a due attention to the virtues and graces which appeared in those that have gone before us to heaven. As we all ought to walk in the steps of the faith of our father Abraham, all women, as the apostle Peter tells us, are bound to imitate Sarah in obedience to their husbands, and in meekness and goodness of spirit. Naomi and Ruth were two of those holy women, who, he says, 'adorned themselves,' as all women ought to do, 'with that ornament of a meek and quiet spirit, which is, in the sight of God, of great price.'

You are charmed with the lovely beauties of domestic harmony and affection which adorned these good women. You praise them. You would be glad to see mothers and daughters by blood or affinity, husbands and wives, mistresses and maidservants, living together in amity, and contributing, as they did, to one another's felicity. Why then do you not imitate them? Are your tempers so incurable, that there is no possibility of persuading you to prefer the glory of God and your own happiness, to the gratification of humours and passions which appear to yourselves detestable?

Read this history, not to gratify your curiosity, but to improve your hearts. Remember that you are bound, by the authority of God, to imitate the meekness and gentleness of Christ and of his saints. The grace revealed in the gospel teaches us to deny every lust of the flesh and of the mind, and to practise every lovely virtue. The power of the Holy Spirit can subdue our rough tempers, and beautify us with those graces of holiness by which the gospel of Christ is adorned; and his own Word is the great mean which he uses for fulfilling in us the good pleasure of the divine goodness. Not only faith, but every fruit of the Spirit, love, joy, peace, long-suffering, gentleness, goodness, meekness, temperance, are produced through the word of truth; and the short history of Ruth is as really a part of the word of truth, as those books which give us the history of our Lord's life and death.

The female sex may likewise learn from this book a lesson of great use to them—how they may preserve their beauty, and make themselves amiable in old age. It is the glory of those 'trees of righteousness which are planted in the house of the Lord, to bring forth fruit in old age.' It is the privilege of those women who are adorned with the beauties of holiness, that old age does not wither, but improves their beauties. Sarah's face was so lovely at ninety years of age, that her chastity was brought into danger at the court of Gerar. The daughters of Sarah, in the most advanced period of their lives, possess beauties more charming, and less dangerous. Naomi was not less lovely than Ruth, and, had Elimelech been alive, she would have been as dear to him when she was approaching to the grave, as in the day when he first received her into his arms.

The male sex, as well as the female, may derive useful instruction from this book. Consider Boaz as a master, as a friend, as a neighbour, as a man of consequence and wealth, as an honest man. In all these respects, you will find him worthy of esteem and imitation.

If young and old, rich and poor, masters and servants, do not find useful instruction in this book, the fault is their own. It is easily understood, and scarcely needs a comment for explication. But it may be useful to have some of those practical instructions which it contains set before us, that we may be assisted in meditating upon this part of the Word of God. It was, doubtless, one of those books of Scripture in which David found such delightful and nourishing food to his soul. O that the holy Spirit, who wrought so powerfully in the heart of that blessed man, would work in us the same temper! Then we would find a feast for our souls in every portion of Scripture. Our days would be a continual festival, because we could always find food ready at hand, more delightful to our taste than honey from the comb.

THE

HISTORY OF RUTH.

LECTURE I.

ELIMELECK AND HIS FAMILY GO TO SOJOURN IN THE LAND OF MOAB.

CHAPTER I. 1–5.

THE intention of this history, according to some, is, to trace the genealogy of David from Salmon, the son of Nahshon, prince of the children of Judah at the death of Moses. But this part of the genealogy of David and of Christ, could have been given us without writing a whole book. It is given us in not more than two verses by the writer of the first book of Chronicles, 1 Chron. ii. 11, 12, 15, and in little more than one by Matthew, chap. i. 5, 6.

The reading of the book is sufficient to convince us, that it was written to furnish us with the most useful instructions in righteousness. It gives us a beautiful picture of female virtue, first shining in the midst of poverty, and then crowned with felicity. Let all women read this book, and learn those virtues which will adorn them with honor and beauty. Let poor and afflicted women read this book, and learn to bear their troubles with a becoming sense of the divine agency in their trials, with patience, with meekness, with all those gracious tempers which will endear them to their friends, and furnish them with agreeable reflections at the end of their distresses.

But why should we speak at present of all these precious

advantages which may be gained from this book? Every part of it is rich in instruction, and the instruction is conveyed to us in a story, which never failed to interest any reader who was not utterly destitute of human sensibilities.

Verse 1.—*Now it came to pass, in the days when the judges ruled, that there was a famine in the land: and a certain man of Bethlehem-Judah went to sojourn in the country of Moab, he, and his wife, and his two sons.*

We are not told the precise time of the story recorded in this book. And why should we be solicitous to know what God has not put it in our power to know? One thing appears certain, that Ruth became the wife of a son of Rahab the harlot, who was famous for her faith and her works in the time of Joshua. But we have reason likewise to believe that Boaz, the son of Rahab, was a very old man when he married Ruth, for he was the grandfather of Jesse, the father of David. Between the entrance of Joshua into Canaan, and the birth of David, there intervened three hundred and sixty-six years, which are to be divided amongst four progenitors of that illustrious prince.

Now it came to pass in the days of the judges who ruled Israel, that is, in the time when Israel was not under regal government, but after the days of Joshua. The expression does not necessarily imply that a judge ruled at the time when Elimelech went into the country of Moab. It was a famine that drove him from his own country; and famines, with other public calamities, were most frequent in the intervals of the government of the judges.

There was a famine in the land. The land of Israel was a land of milk and honey, the pleasant land which God had chosen for his people Israel; and yet we often read of famines in this land. Think not that the fertility of a land is able to secure its inhabitants against famine, or that any earthly advantage is sufficient to secure us against any calamity whatsoever. All things are in the hand of God, and his creatures change their qualities or effects at his pleasure. Without him, we should die of hunger amidst plenty, we should be miserable amidst all possible means of happiness. But, through the kindness of his providence, many have been well satisfied in the days of famine, or in a waste howling wilderness.

But why does God send a famine on the land which he had chosen for his own people; upon the seed of Abraham, whom God had called out of the land of the Chaldees, to give this fertile land to his seed? There is no reason to doubt that this famine was well deserved by the sins of the people; for the Lord had promised, that as long as they walked in his law, they should enjoy his blessing on their land, on their basket, and on their store. But he had threatened famine, and many other calamities, as the just reward of their deeds if they should apostatize from him.

We have never felt famine, although we have well deserved it. We have indeed felt scarcity, and stood in fear of famine. But the Lord hath hitherto dealt wondrously with us, in supplying us with the necessaries, and many of us with the comforts of life. Let us bless God who hath hitherto preserved us from this terrible judgment. Let us be deeply sensible that, whatever we may want of the good things of this life, we have much more than we deserve. In days of scarcity, let us call to mind those famines in which the sufferers would have thought themselves happy as kings, if they could have been supplied but once in two or three days with that bread which we eat every day of our life.

And a certain man of Bethlehem-Judah went to sojourn in the country of Moab. The Jews often gave names to persons, or places, expressive of something that was true concerning them. Bethlehem, which signifies the 'house of bread,' seems to have been a place famous, even in the pleasant land, for its fertility. Yet even in this fruitful district of a fruitful country, famine prevailed to such a degree, that one of its proprietors was compelled, by the want of bread, to leave it, and seek food in a foreign country. We may reasonably conjecture, from the behaviour of Naomi, that her husband was a fearer of God. And yet he is forced to seek bread in the land of Moab, where his God was unknown. Men are commonly attached to their native soil; but none among us is so much attached to his native country, as the ancient Israelites were to theirs; those of them especially who were lovers of the religion of the God of their fathers. There is a great difference between a Scotsman going to America, and an Israelite going to dwell in the land of Moab. In many places of America, our God and our Saviour is as well known as amongst ourselves. Should you want bread at home, you would not account it a very great hardship to go to a strange land, where you might find bread to your bodies, and at the same time find provision for your souls. But you would almost perish with hunger rather than go to live among the Turks; and yet the Turks are not so great enemies to the name of Christ, as the Moabites were to the name of the God of Israel.

Some blame this Ephrathite for going to sojourn in the land of Moab. Why (say they) did he not rather bear all the hardships of famine, as well as his neighbors, rather than go to dwell amongst heathens,—amongst such heathens as the Moabites, of whom the Lord had said, 'Even to their tenth generation, they shall not enter into the congregation of the Lord for ever: thou shalt not seek their peace nor their prosperity all thy days for ever?'

It is not necessary to enquire, nor is it perhaps possible to determine with certainty, whether this Bethlehemite did right or wrong in going to sojourn in the land of Moab. Yet no man ought to be condemned, whether dead or alive, without proofs of guilt; and no certain proofs of guilt appear in the present case. Undoubtedly, the people of God were commanded not to mingle themselves with the heathens, lest they should learn their ways; but they were not absolutely prohibited to sojourn in a strange land. When imperious necessity forced David to dwell in the tents of Kedar, or in the city of Gath, or Ziklag, he was to be pitied rather than blamed.

The children of Israel were forbidden to do any servile work on the Sabbath day; and yet when the disciples were accused for rubbing the ears of corn to prepare them for food on that day, our Lord justified their conduct on the ground of necessity, and silenced his enemies by producing the example of David; whom these hypocrites themselves did not blame for eating, when hunger compelled him, that show-bread which it was lawful for the priests only, in ordinary cases, to eat. And have we not read what David did in another case, how he sent his father and mother to the king of Moab, to dwell with him, till he knew what God would do for him?

It is not certain that none but this Bethlehemite went at this time to sojourn in Moab. We read of Israelites that dwelt in Moab, and attained high stations in it, although we cannot tell at what period, 1 Chron. iv. 22, 23. Nor can we tell what connections might be formed amongst individuals of Israel and of Moab, when both nations were under one lord, Judges iii. 14. If Naomi's family were like herself, they could not but conciliate the regard and love of all that knew them, whether Moabites or Israelites. A sweet temper disarms the fierceness of savages.

It seems probable that this family lived under, or near the time of Ehud's administration, although we cannot certainly tell why they chose rather to go to the land of Moab than to any other country. One thing is evident, that there was plenty of bread, and to spare, in the land of Moab, when little was to be had in the land of Israel. What shall we say to this? Were the Israelites greater sinners than the Moabites? or were they less favored by that God who causeth the corn to grow up out of the earth? Neither of these conclusions would be just. The Moabites were great sinners, for they were apostates from the religion of their father Lot, and worshippers of Chemosh. But God then suffered all nations to walk in their own way, except his chosen people. 'Them only he knew of all the families of the earth, therefore he punished them for their iniquities.' Because God was gracious to them, he would not suffer them to walk in their own ways, that he might turn them again to himself.

Many times was Israel afflicted by various calamities, but 'Moab was at ease from his youth.' Was Moab, then, happier than Israel? No, in no wise. He was miserable. 'He was at ease from his youth, and he settled on his lees, neither did he go into captivity, therefore his taste remained in him, and his scent was not changed. Therefore, behold the days came at last, that the Lord sent wanderers that caused him to wander, and emptied his vessels, and brake his bottles.' Elimelech went to sojourn in the country of Moab; not to dwell there longer than necessity compelled him. He chose rather to dwell in the Lord's land than any where else; but who can endure the rage of hunger? We cannot always dwell where we wish, but if at any time we are forced to sojourn at a distance from the place where God's name is known and preached, our hearts ought to be left in the sanctuary. David was sometimes compelled to sojourn in the tents of Kedar, but he ever loved the habitation of God's house, and his heart was poured out within him when he thought of the pleasures of the sanctuary.

He, and his wife, and his two sons. It is possible that if he had wanted a family, he might have been able to live at home. In times of extreme scarcity, a family may be as a heavy burden upon the minds of the poor, who know not how to satisfy the appetites of their little ones, and cannot open their understandings to make them sensible of the necessity of wanting what cannot be had. Our Lord speaks of times when it is miserable to be with child or to give suck; and Paul tells married persons, that they ought, in times of distress, to look for troubles in the flesh. Beware, however, of dissatisfaction with the providence of God, which has given you families. Amidst all the anxiety that you feel about the means of their subsistence, would you be willing to lose any of them? Would you not rather rise early and sit up late, and eat the bread of sorrow, in laboring for their subsistence?

The man's wife, with his two sons, went with him. We are not told whether Naomi was willing to go to a strange land, but we have reason to believe that she was willingly obedient to her husband. She was one of those wives whose law is their husband's will in all things wherein the laws of God leave them at liberty. These are the women who are qualified to give and to receive happiness in the married state. But those men are brutes, rather than husbands, who put the temper of such wives to a severe trial, when irresistible necessity does not compel them. It was necessity that compelled the Bethlehemite to remove his family to the land of

Moab. His wife saw the necessity of the case, and therefore she did not think of returning, when she was become her own mistress, till the necessity was removed.

Verse 2.—*And the name of the man was Elimelech, and the name of his wife Naomi, and the names of his two sons Mahlon and Chilion, Ephrathites of Bethlehem-Judah. And they came into the country of Moab, and continued there.*

The mention of the names of the father, mother, and sons, gives an air of truth to the narration, and tends to interest us in their fortunes. When we know the names of persons, we seem to ourselves to be in some degree acquainted with them, and therefore when we hear of any remarkable event befalling any person, we wish to know his name, although we can have no opportunity of ever seeing him.

We are not told of what lineage this family was, but we learn afterwards that they were nearly related to the noblest of the families of Judah. Chilion and Mahlon were almost the nearest of the kinsmen of Boaz, who was the son of Salmon, the son of Nahshon, prince of the tribe of Judah in the days of Moses. Greatness will secure no families from poverty and want. Many who once rode in their own chariots, have been compelled to subsist on the bounty of others.

The family were Ephrathites of Bethlehem-Judah. 'Bethlehem was not the least among the cities of Judah.' It was the city of Boaz, the city of David, the city 'out of which came forth to God that Ruler of Israel, whose goings forth were of old from everlasting.' What city ever deserved so well to be renowned, except Jerusalem, where God long dwelt; where Jesus himself preached; and from whence his word of grace went forth to the nations?

And they came into the country of Moab, and continued there. In the former verse, we are told that they *went to sojourn in the country of Moab*. They set out from their own country with a design to sojourn in the land of Moab. Here we learn that they actually accomplished their purpose of going into the country of Moab, and there they continued longer perhaps than they wished or intended. They hoped that in a year or two they might find it convenient to return to the land of

Israel. When we go from home, it depends entirely on the will of God whether we shall arrive at the place of our destination. When we are in it, it depends no less on the divine pleasure whether we shall ever again see the place from which we went out. 'A man's heart deviseth his way, but the Lord directeth his steps.' Beware of bringing upon yourselves the punishment that came upon the proud king of Babylon, because he did not glorify that God in whose hand his breath was, and whose were all his ways. Do you say, that to-morrow you will go into such a city, and buy, and sell, and get gain? Say rather, If the Lord will, we shall live, and go into that city. In Him you live, in Him you move, in Him you have your being.

Verse 3.—*And Elimelech, Naomi's husband, died, and she was left and her two sons.*

'What is our life? It is a vapour which appeareth only for a little while, and then vanisheth away.' Elimelech went only to sojourn in the country of Moab; but the same reasons which compelled him to go to that land, compelled him to continue in it, till a stronger necessity compelled him to go the way whence he was never to return. Amidst all your trials, remember that the greatest of all trials is approaching, and perhaps nearer than you imagine. Do you fear that you shall want bread in times of scarcity? Perhaps before they are at an end your lives may end. Are you obliged to leave your native fields? The time is fast approaching when you must leave the world. Why should dying creatures be perplexed about things that they may never need, and at most cannot enjoy long? Death will soon level the distinction between the most affluent and the most indigent of the sons of men; and, therefore, let the rich enjoy their portion in this world without abusing it, or placing their confidence in what must be theirs but a very short time. And let not the poor be greatly dejected by the want of what they cannot long need. If we can procure but 'food and raiment, let us therewith be content; for we brought nothing into the world with us, and it is certain that we can carry nothing hence.'

And she was left, and her two sons. It was, no doubt, a grief to Elimelech, if he felt the approaches of death, to leave his wife, and his two young sons, in a strange land, in a land of heathens, poor, and, for aught we know, almost friendless. When you choose your place of abode, if you have families, or may have families, let this be one principal consideration, where you will leave them if God should call you out of the world. What cheerless prospects must present themselves to the view of a good man leaving a young family in the midst of neighbors that have never heard of the grace of God, or never paid any regard to what they have heard!

She was left of her husband with two sons. How much was this good woman to be pitied! She was left in a state of indigence. Her sons, very probably, were come to that time of life in which they might be of some use to her; but she had lost that friend in whom her hope rested for the support and government of her family in its distressed and dangerous condition. I call its condition dangerous, not because they were in a country of enemies to their nation, although the Moabites were seldom the friends of Israel, but because they dwelt in a land devoted to the worship of Chemosh. Without the comforts of religion, Naomi's heart must have died within her; yet in a short time afterwards, the Lord added new affliction to her former griefs.

Verse 4.—*And they took them wives of the women of Moab; the name of the one was Orpah, and the name of the other Ruth: and they dwelt there about ten years.*

Many blame these young men for marrying wives of the daughters of Moab; and certainly they were much to be blamed for marrying them, if they had not credible evidence that these young women were convinced of the folly of worshiping Chemosh, and cordially disposed to join with their husbands in the worship of the God of Israel. When Ezra was informed that the holy seed had mingled themselves with the Moabites, and with other idolatrous nations, by marrying their daughters, he was filled with almost inconsolable grief. Nothing but the expulsion of the strange wives could dispel his anxious apprehensions of the wrath of God, merited by the conjunction of the men of Israel with the people of these abominations.

If Mahlon and Chilion had good reason to think that their intended wives were sincere proselytes to their religion, they deserve no blame, but rather praise. But whether they were justifiable or excusable, or neither the one nor the other, it is perhaps impossible for any man to determine, because we have not sufficient knowledge of the circumstances of the case. Certain it is, that Salmon did well in marrying Rahab, who belonged to a worse race of people than the Moabites, for she renounced the idols and abominations of her country, and showed her faith in the God of Israel by her works. Perhaps the example of Salmon, to whom this family was related, induced them to venture upon this alliance with strangers. But why should we pronounce a sentence against any man, when we are neither called to be his judges, nor furnished with means for judging?

This we know with certainty, that whether Elimelech did right or wrong in going with his family into the land of Moab, which led the way to their marriages, and whether the sons of Elimelech did right or wrong in contracting these marriages, the providence of God, by what it did, was accomplishing its own gracious purposes. Ruth was one of God's elect. She was to be brought to the knowledge and love of the truth by her connection with the family of Elimelech. The happiness which she gained, was a good compensation for all the distresses which this family had endured—for all that the land of Israel had suffered by a ten years' famine. Little did the pious remnant in Israel know, when they were deploring the miseries of the poor, that the famine was to be subservient to the salvation of a precious soul in the land of Moab.

They dwelt about ten years in the land of Moab. It seems that Naomi could not return sooner on account of the famine. What a dreadful scourge was this famine of ten years! We need not think it strange that Elisha sent away his friend the Shunamite to sojourn in a strange land, when there were to be seven years of famine. Every year in the course of this famine must have made a very great accession to the miseries of the poor, or rather of the whole people. We find that a second year of dearth is likely to be worse than the first, although the price of provisions is not so high, because money is more scarce. What would seven or ten years of scarcity be, although they should not amount to a famine? Blessed be God, who has not year after year turned the rain of our land into powder and dust!

Verse 5.—*And Mahlon and Chilion died also, both of them; and the woman was left of her two sons and her husband.*

Poor woman! what will she now do, bereaved of both her sons, after her husband? Might not one of them at least have been spared for her comfort? Let us not speak in this manner, lest we should seem to charge God with folly. God's thoughts are not as our thoughts. If God loved this woman, we think that he would have left her one or another, at least, of her family, if not all of them. Yet all of them die, and leave her desolate in the land of Moab, far from all their relations that were yet left in Bethlehem! The love or hatred of God is not to be estimated by our feelings, or by our reasonings, unsupported by the Bible.

Naomi might probably think that she was one of the most unhappy women in the land, when necessity compelled her to leave the land of Israel. When she afterwards lost her husband, she might think that then only she began to be miserable, and that she greatly erred when she thought herself unhappy before this calamity befel her. But when she afterwards lost first one and then another of her sons, new thoughts would come into her mind. Then she might suppose that she had complained too heavily of the loss of her husband, and was not duly thankful to God for sparing her sons. Now at last, and not before, she might think that the Lord dealt bitterly with her, and had made desolate all her company. When heavy calamities befal you, beware of speaking unadvisedly with your lips. Beware of gloomy and impatient thoughts. Say not that God has bereaved you of all earthly comforts, when he has reduced you to poverty, if your friends are preserved alive. If some of your nearest friends are cut off by a stroke, still you must not say that nothing is left to sweeten life, when others are left whom you love. It is presumptuous in mortals, in sinful mortals, to think or talk as if the Lord had forgotten to be merciful.

Naomi's thoughts of God's dealings with her upon earth are now very different from what they were when these two things came upon her, the loss of children and widowhood. All these things appeared then to be against her. But now she knows and sees that all these things were fruits of the love of God. Amidst your perplexing thoughts about the occurrences of life, it will be profitable to consider what you will think an hundred years hence of these adversities which now spread such a dismal gloom upon your spirits. Blessed are the men who firmly believe that God is wiser than themselves, and who act according to that belief by a patient resignation to God under every trial. They will see at last, and they believe at present, that 'all the paths of the Lord are mercy and truth to such as keep his covenant and his testimonies.' At last it will be found, that we could not, without great loss, have wanted any of those trials of faith which once were ready to overwhelm our spirits.

LECTURE II.

NAOMI'S RETURN TO HER OWN COUNTRY.

CHAPTER I. 6–10.

Verse. 6.—*Then she arose with her daughters-in-law, that she might return from the country of Moab: for she had heard in the country of Moab, how that the Lord had visited his people in giving them bread.*

NAOMI would, no doubt, often say within herself, Woe is me that I dwell so long in the country of Moab; that I sojourn year after year amongst the worshipers of Chemosh! Yet she found herself under the unhappy necessity of continuing among them till she could entertain the prospect of being able to live in her own country. It was David's most earnest desire, that he might dwell all the days of his life in the house of the Lord; yet, more than once, he found it absolutely necessary to dwell amongst heathens. But as soon as God opened to him the way to return to the Lord's land, he gladly and thankfully improved the opportunity.

Naomi justly thought that the Lord called her back to Bethlehem, when she heard that he had visited his people in giving them bread. She might now entertain rational hopes of finding the needful supports of life in her own land. She could not hope to make the figure at Bethlehem which she did in the days when the candle of the Lord shined upon her head, when her husband was yet with her, when her children were about her, when the family estate supplied it with the means of keeping a plentiful table; but she might hope, by the labor of her hands, and the kindness of her friends, to live in a manner suited to the circumstances in which divine providence had now placed her. It is not pleasant to flesh and blood to be reduced to a dependent condition. But humbling dispensations of providence ought always to be attended with a correspondent humility of spirit, unless we desire misery as our portion, and, what is still worse, to be found fighting against the Almighty. His will must be done; and, if our will stand in opposition to his, it must bend or break.

She had heard in the country of Moab, that the Lord had visited his people. In the land of strangers, she was always anxious to hear what was passing in the land of Israel. She still took an interest in that country for her own sake, for her friend's and brethren's sakes, for the Lord's sake. Although she was dwelling in a land well supplied with bread and wine, (Isa. xvi. 9, 10.) yet she felt deeply for the poor Israelites in their own land who were punished with hunger. She mourned for the long continuance of the famine, and was filled with joy in the midst of her sorrows, when she heard that the Lord had visited his people in mercy. Thus Nehemiah, at the court of Shushan, was ever careful to be informed of what was passing in the land of Judah. He was rich and great, and enjoyed the favor of the greatest prince in the world; but his happiness could not be complete unless he heard that his people were happy.

The Lord visited his people in giving them bread. 'Thou visitest the earth, and waterest it,' says David, 'thou greatly enrichest it with the river of God which is full of water, thou preparest them corn, when thou hast so provided for it.' The Psalmist teaches us to consider every fertilizing shower from heaven, as a kind of visitation from that God who keeps the clouds in his hand, and 'turns them about by his counsels, to do whatsoever he commands them upon the face of the world, in the earth.' When Naomi heard that plenty was restored in the land of Israel, she saw that the Lord had visited his people, and brought with him a rich present of suitable supplies for their necessity. She had seen, that even the land flowing with milk and honey could not supply its inhabitants with the necessaries of life, unless God were pleased to 'hear the heavens, that the heavens might hear the earth, and the earth hear the corn and the wine and the oil, that they might hear his people.'

If God after nine years of scarcity, should return to us in mercy, and give us abundance of bread to eat, would we not confess that we could never be sufficiently thankful to God for his undeserved bounty? But have we not still greater reason to be thankful, when scarcity is hardly felt in one year out of ten? Why should we need cleanness of teeth to make us sensible of that bounty by which we are fed every day of our lives? If you were in a dependent condition, and one of your friends should supply you once in a week with provisions for your table, would you not reckon yourselves highly indebted to his goodness? But would it not be esteemed by you an higher act of kindness to make a settled provision for your subsistence, that you might never want what is needful? If rare mercies from God are acknowledged with thankfulness, (and who can be unthankful for them?) what praises are due to him for mercies showered down upon us every day in our lives!

Then she arose with her daughters-in-law, that she might return from the country of Moab.—

Verse 7.—*Wherefore, she went forth out of the place where she was, and her two daughters-in-law with her; and they went on the way to return unto the land of Judah.*

One of these young widows, we have reason to think, was still a heathen. And yet (let many Christians blush!) she, as well as her religious sister-in-law, behaves in a dutiful and respectful manner to her husband's mother. May we not say, that the daughter who behaves undutifully to her mother, and even the daughter-in-law who is an adversary to her mother-in-law, hath denied the faith, and is worse than an infidel? If your parents, by nature or marriage, were rich, you would treat them with respect, because you would hope to share in their prosperity; but Naomi was poor, and a stranger in the land of Moab, and yet her daughters-in-law treated her with kindness while she lived near them, and would not suffer her to leave the country without accompanying her in the way, and doing her all the service they could. Their husbands were dead. Their relation to Naomi might seem to some to be utterly dissolved; but their love was strengthened rather than abated. And why should it not? Are we to withdraw our affections from our friends because the Lord hath afflicted them? The death of husbands or wives will not put an end to the friendship of those who are allied by marriage, unless there has been bad behaviour on the one side, or an ungenerous spirit on the other. That which loudly calls for sympathy, can never be a good reason for coldness.

Verse. 8.—*And Naomi said unto her two daughters-in-law, Go, return each to her mother's house; the Lord deal kindly with you, as ye have dealt with the dead, and with me.*

Orpah and Ruth were greatly attached to their mother-in-law, although their own mothers were still alive. They did not stand in need of Naomi's friendship, but she needed theirs. Her afflictions and desolate condition endeared her so much to them, that they seemed to pay more attention to her than to their own mothers; and, on some accounts, she was better entitled to their sympathy. She seems to have travailed in birth with them, that the promised Christ might be formed in them, and probably she was in truth the spiritual mother of Ruth.

Go, return each to her mother's house. Whether their fathers were still alive, or whether their mother's house is mentioned because their intercourse in the house of their parents would chiefly be with their mothers, we cannot tell.

The Lord deal kindly with you! She blesses them when she sends them away, not in the name of Chemosh, but in the name of Jehovah the God of Israel; and thereby insinuates, at a time which they could never forget, and in words which were likely to be often present to their minds, that not the gods of Moab, but the God of Israel, was the eternal fountain of blessings, from whom every good and perfect gift was to be expected. Our speech ought to be always seasoned with salt, but there are particular seasons when our words ought to be ordered in consummate wisdom. The words of parting friends, who are likely never again to meet, make an impression never to be erased. Who knows what good may be done by such words, when they breathe at once the fervour of piety and of charity? They are like dying words, for our friends are then dead to us when we see them no more.

The Lord deal kindly with you, as ye have dealt with the dead, and with me. It seems these two women had been good wives to their husbands, although their husbands were poor men and strangers. If they had assumed more power over their husbands than they ought, they would probably have been supported by their relations and countrymen. But they always dealt kindly with them, and endeavored to render their condition in a land of strangers comfortable and pleasant. Nature itself, you see, teaches wives to deal kindly with their husbands, for Moabitesses were taught by it to deal kindly with those that married them. Beware, ye who call yourselves Christians, of behaving worse than women that never heard the duties of wives enforced by such powerful motives. 'Submit yourselves unto your husbands as unto the Lord; for the husband is the head of the wife, even as Christ is the head of the church, and he is the Saviour of the body. Therefore, as the church is subject unto Christ, so let the wives be to their own husbands in every thing.'

You know not, husbands and wives, how long you may dwell together. Death may soon come, and will doubtless, sooner or later, come and tear away the one of you from the other. When that event shall take place, how will you wish to have behaved? Behave at present as you would then wish to have behaved, for then you will not be able to bring back the present time. Many great miracles have been wrought by the power of God, but it never did, nor ever will, recal the time that is past. How comfortable was it to Orpah and Ruth to hear Naomi say, Ye have dealt kindly with the dead! And how comfortable was the reflection to them through life, that she had reason to give them this commendation!

As ye have dealt with the dead, and with me. These amiable women extended their kindness from their husbands to their mother-in-law, the only friend of their husbands to whom they could shew kindness. It is commonly supposed, that a widow may hope to live amongst us more comfortably with a son-in-law, than with one of her own married sons. This observation often holds good, but not to our honor. Why should not daughters-in-law behave like daughters? If husband and wife are one flesh, your husband's father is your father, your husband's mother is your mother. Why should Moabitesses behave better than many Christian wives, and merit commendations which cannot, without flattery, be given to those who have such superior advantages for knowing and for practising their duty? I say not this to shame you. I know that there are some to whom no reproof of this kind is due. But are there not others who behave less affectionately to their own mothers than did Orpah and Ruth to the mother of their husbands?

And with me. When I speak of the unkind behaviour of some wives to the mothers of their husbands, let me give to every one her portion of reproof. The blame of unkindness does not always lie on one side. If there were more Naomis, there might be more Orpahs and Ruths. Naomi was disposed to take in good part the conduct of her daughters-in-law, and to express a grateful sense of the attentions that were paid to her. Some old women look upon every instance of kindness from their daughters, or their daughters-in-law, as a debt for which they owe them no thanks. Others are so sullen, so suspicious, so fretful, that there is no possibility of pleasing them. They turn the duty of their children into a hard task, which they find it impossible to perform with satisfaction to themselves, because it gives so little satisfaction to those whom they wish to serve. True, your children are bound to honor you, but they are not bound to comply with all your humours. They are bound to be the comforters of your old age; but how can they comfort you, if you refuse to take comfort in all that they can do to please you? They do no more than their duty when they endeavor to gild the evening of your days by their dutiful behaviour; but are you not bound to show a grateful sense of their care to perform their duty? You see that Naomi thanked and blessed her daughters-in-law for the kindnesses which they had showed to herself, as well as for their endeavors to contribute to the happiness of her sons.

Verse 9.—*The Lord grant you that ye may find rest, each of you in the house of her husband!* *Then she kissed them, and they lifted up their voice and wept.*

Naomi did not wish her daughters-in-law to continue through the remaining part of their lives unmarried. She was far from thinking that their entrance a second time into the bond of marriage, would be in any degree inconsistent with all due respect for the memory of their first husbands. If ever they should again enter into this state of life, as she hoped they would do, she wished them all that happiness which they might have expected to enjoy if the Lord had been pleased to spare the lives of her sons.

There are seasons, in which unmarried persons and widows will act wisely if they continue as they are; but there are other times, in which it is in general better for the younger widows, as well as unmarried women, to marry. We cannot, indeed, fix a rule which will include all without exception, because that may be good for one which is not good for another, whose dispositions or circumstances require a different conduct. There are some who err by marrying when they ought not, or whom they ought not to marry; and there are others who sin when they do not marry, as we learn from the different advices given on this subject by the apostle Paul, 1 Cor. vii. 1 Tim. v.

But whenever men or women marry, if they are wise for themselves, they will take proper measures to find satisfaction in that new state of life; and one of the chief means to be used for this purpose is prayer to God. *The Lord grant you that each of you may find rest in the house of her husband.* 'A prudent wife is from the Lord,' and a kind husband is from the Lord also; and, if in any thing, surely in this most important step of life, we are to ask counsel from the mouth of the Lord, and to implore his blessing. Let it be, however, remembered, that if you are sincere in seeking the blessing of God upon this relation, you will follow the directions of his word in making your choice. Have you not a husband or wife at present? judge for yourselves whether you ought, or ought not to marry. 'Marry whom you will, only in the Lord.' Do you seek rest in the house of a husband, or comfort with a wife? remember what God says concerning the virtuous woman, Prov. xxxi.

and what he says in many places of his word concerning the character of the man whose conduct he approves, and to whom he will give his blessing, Prov. iii.

If it is to be wished that wives may find rest in the houses of their husbands, it must be the duty of husbands to do what they can to procure them rest, not only by endeavouring to provide for them what is necessary for their subsistence and comfortable accommodation, but by such a kind behaviour as will promote their satisfaction and comfort. Men and women may have affluence without rest, and rest without affluence. But let women also contribute to procure rest for themselves by frugality, by industry, by such behaviour to their husbands as will merit constant returns of kindness.

Then she kissed them, and they lifted up their voice and wept. They wept because they were to part, never again to meet, all of them, together in this world. They had been happy in one another, and one of the sorest afflictions incident to this life, is the everlasting separation of those who are mutually dear. But why do we say everlasting separation? There is no everlasting separation of Christian friends. Little was known of what we know concerning the future state, by these friends of whom we are speaking, and there was little ground of hope that they would all meet in that state, if they had known it; for it does not appear that Orpah was willing to take up her cross, and deny herself, to serve the God of Israel. We that are Christians have the happiness to know with certainty, that our separation from our friends in Christ will not be eternal, though it may be long. Because it may be long, we mourn; because it is not to be eternal, we do not mourn as they that have no hope.

They lifted up their voice and wept, not only at the thought of their long separation, but at the recollection which rushed into their minds at this time, of many endearing, of many sorrowful, of many joyful circumstances of their past lives. For such is the precarious and changeable nature of worldly felicity, that even the sweetest joys of life often make way for the most piercing griefs. Our remembrance of pleasures enjoyed, and to be enjoyed no more, spreads a dismal gloom over those pleasures that we might yet enjoy. We cannot be made happy by a rich abundance of those things which give happiness (such as the world can give) to others, because we are bereaved of those things in which we placed too much of our happiness.

This world is a place of mourning to all, but to some more than others, by the afflictive changes which darken many of their days. Let us all seek to be found in Him whose office it is to 'comfort all that mourn.' Sorrow is turned into joy by him who is 'the Consolation of Israel.'

Verse 10.—*And they said unto her, Surely we will return with thee unto thy people.*

We have no reason to doubt the sincerity of both these women in this extraordinary profession of attachment to Naomi, although one of them was easily diverted from her purpose. There is a great difference between the same mind at different times. Orpah's intention of going with Naomi, included an intention of serving Naomi's God, and of relinquishing the gods of Moab; for it is not likely that she thought she would be permitted to practise the worship of Chemosh in the land of Israel. We may therefore observe from this place, that you ought not to mistake every purpose of being truly religious, as a sign of true grace. If you turn to God from sin, with full purpose of, and endeavour after, new obedience, you are true penitents; but this full purpose is attended with habitual performance. 'Bring forth fruits meet for repentance,' if you desire to be esteemed true children of Abraham. If, like Orpah, you promise and intend to perform, but return to your former course of life, your 'goodness is like the morning cloud, and like the early dew, that goeth away.'

Surely we will return with thee unto thy people. They knew but very few of Naomi's people; but from her own behaviour, and the behaviour of her family, they judged that they were people with whom it would be happy to live. Let us all endeavour so to live, as to give strangers to religion favorable ideas of those who profess it. The lewd conduct of nominal Christians has done unknown mischief in the world. If all Christians were attentive to the cause of Christ in their conversation, stumbling-blocks would be removed out of the way of the inconsiderate, and the mouths of malicious enemies would be stopped. 'Many, seeing onr good works, would glorify our Father who is in heaven.' 'Whatsoever things are true, and honest, and just, and pure, and lovely, and praiseworthy, think on these things,' if you desire to enjoy peace in your own minds, or to be useful to others around you.

May we see more and more of the accomplishment of the prayer of our Lord Jesus, that all his followers 'may be one in the Father, and in the Son; that the world may know that he is sent by the Father!'

LECTURE III.

THE SAME SUBJECT CONTINUED.

CHAPTER I. 11–15.

Verse 11.—*And Naomi said, Turn again, my daughters: why will ye go with me? Are there yet any more sons in my womb, that they may be your husbands?*

Turn again, my daughters. Naomi does not call them her daughters-in-law, but her daughters. They deserved to be addressed by her in this affectionate language. They were as dutiful and affectionate to Naomi as if she had borne them.

Turn again, why will ye go with me? We ought not, without good reason, to leave the land of our nativity. We are not bound to live all our days in one place or in one country, but we ought not to change our condition or country without being able to give a good reason for it. There is no part of the world which the curse of God hath not reached; and if we hope, by leaving our native land, to leave the miseries of life behind us, we will be miserably disappointed. Naomi had formerly too good reason for coming into the land of Moab, and she had now a very sufficient reason for leaving it; but it was highly proper that her daughters-in-law should consider, before they accompanied her to Bethlehem, whether their reasons were as good as her's. 'As a bird that wandereth from its nest, so is a man that wandereth from his place.'

Are there any sons in my womb, that they should be your husbands? Before the law was given by Moses, it appears to have been customary in some parts of the East, that the wife of a man who died childless should become the wife of his brother; and therefore Judah doomed his daughter-in-law to the fire as an adulteress, when he heard that she had committed whoredom in the house of her father, where she was ordered to continue till Shelah, the son of Judah, was marriageable. But Orpah and Ruth could have no prospect of second marriages in the family of Naomi. She was now childless, and could have no prospect of other children to supply the place of those she had lost.

Verse 12.—*Turn again, my daughters; go your way; for I am too old to have an husband. If I should say, I have hope; if I should have an husband also to-night, and should also bear sons;*

Turn again my daughters; go your way, for I am too old to have an husband; or, if I should have an husband, I cannot expect to have any more sons; or, if I should have both an husband and sons, they would be too long in growing up to maturity for becoming your husbands. Naomi would have preferred these two young widows to all other women as wives for her sons, if any sons had been left to her. But all her sons were gone to the land of forgetfulness, and she was not foolish enough to think either of a husband or sons at her time of life. She did not indulge romantic hopes, as too many do, of what would never happen. There are some who, in a bad sense, hope against hope; but their hopes, built upon a foundation of sand, deceive them, and end in deserved misery. Naomi did not allow herself to form such visionary expectations as would end only in disappointment. The hand of the Lord had gone out against her, and robbed her of her best friends, and she would not, like the foolish Edomites, say, 'The bricks are fallen down, but we will build with hewn stones; the sycamores are cut down, but we will build with cedar.' It would add greatly to our happiness, if we could believe and improve that fundamental principle of our religion, 'If God make peace, who can make trouble? but if he hideth his face, who can behold him; whether it be done against a nation, or against a man only?'

I am too old to have an husband. She would not so much as think of another husband in her advanced period of life. The apostle Paul seems to take it for granted, that a woman would scarcely be found at sixty years of age, or upwards, who would think of marriage; and therefore, in giving directions about those female servants of the church who could not conveniently perform the duties required of them if they were married, he says, 'Let no widow be taken into the number under sixty years of age.' Why? Because the younger widows, if they were taken into the number, might marry.

I am too old to have an husband; but if I should have an husband, can I hope to have children? Sarah bore a child when she was ninety years of age. But it would be presumptuous to expect miracles in the ordinary course of providence.

Some people cannot think without envy, of happiness enjoyed by others which themselves cannot hope to enjoy, as if the pleasures of others were their punishment. But Naomi wished to each of her daughters-in-law rest in the house of an husband, although she herself was to continue a desolate and poor widow. And she hoped it would not be a long time till she heard that both of them were happy in another change of life. I fear few of us are possessed of the generous charity of the apostle Paul, who could say, 'We are glad when we are weak, and ye are strong.'

If I should say that I have hope; if I should have an husband also to-night, and should bear sons,

Verse 13.—*Would ye tarry for them till they were grown? Would ye stay for them from having husbands? Nay, my daughters; for it grieveth me much for your sakes, that the hand of the Lord is gone out against me.*

Extremes in every thing are to be avoided. Some, too precipitately, rush into the married state. They do not duly deliberate about this important step of life. They do not consult with those friends who have a right to give their mind, and they do not take time to consult with God, 'from whom every good gift cometh.' But others are too dilatory about entering into the married state. The bad effects of undue delay of marriage have often appeared in the licentious conduct of the young. It was the desire of Naomi, not only that her daughters-in-law might find rest, each of them in the house of an husband, but that they might find it while the years of their youth yet continued with them. Suppose the possibility that she might yet have children, *would ye tarry for them till they were grown? Would ye stay for them from having husbands?*

Nay, my daughters; for it grieveth me much for your sakes that the hand of the Lord is gone forth against me. She was grieved for her own sake that the hand of the Lord was gone out against her, and yet she would have borne it much more easily if she herself had been the only sufferer. That she was a widow, and childless, appeared hard to her; but it distressed her no less to think that her amiable daughters-in-law were become widows in the days of their youth, especially when she thought, as she was disposed to do, that their affliction was the effect of a quarrel that God had with herself.

This is a great aggravation of the afflictions of many parents, that their children are involved with themselves. They could bear poverty, they could bear reproach, they could bear death itself, had they none who depended on them for bread and for respectability in the world. But it appears hard to them, that their innocent babes, or their affectionate children in a more advanced period of life, should suffer along with them. Under this covert, we are too apt to hide from ourselves our impatience under the dispensations of divine providence. God has the same right to rule over the fruit of our bodies as over ourselves, and to allot to them their share of the good or the bad things of this world.

It is bitterest of all, when we have reason to think that our sins have provoked God to punish us in the persons of our friends, or to inflict those strokes which our friends must feel as heavily as ourselves. Let us beware of ever exposing ourselves to such heart-piercing reflections by conduct that may bring down God's displeasure upon our families. Let us humble ourselves under the mighty hand of God, and commit to his disposal our families as well as ourselves. David procured the death of his little child, and threatenings of heavy judgments upon others of his family, by his sin. But let us remember what method David took to recover his peace of mind, and, if we are in like circumstances, follow his example; 2 Sam. xii. Psalm li.

God's people may sometimes, without good reason, think that the hand of the Lord is gone forth against them, in the calamities which befal their families or friends. David had good grounds for humbling himself under the hand of God gone forth against himself in the disasters that befel his family; but Job had no reason to think that his children were taken away by God either for their own or their father's transgression. Satan 'moved the Lord against that good man to destroy him without cause.' Our afflictions are hard enough to be borne by us, without the addition of groundless reflections against ourselves. At the same time, the error is much more common of insensibility to the divine displeasure, when it has been really kindled by our sins, than of vexing ourselves with unjust suspicions of God's anger. But it will be our wisdom to guard against mistakes fatal to our peace of mind, as well as those which indicate an unhumbled spirit. Nothing is more unlike a saint than stupidity under divine corrections, whether they come upon us in our own persons, or in the persons of our friends; but few things are more unfavorable to the progress of holiness than groundless jealousies entertained and cherished concerning the dealings of divine providence in the management of our concerns.

There is one thing that still remains to be considered concerning this parting speech of Naomi to her daughters-in-law. Why did she dissuade them from going with her to the land of Judah, where the true God was well known; and persuade them to return to a country of abominable idolaters, where they would be carried down the stream of general practice into the abyss of perdition? 'Because of such things' as are commonly practised by the heathen, 'the wrath of God cometh on the children of disobedience.' Ought not Naomi, then, to have rather endeavoured to pluck her beloved daughters as brands out of the burning, by alluring them into a land where the method of salvation was known, and where the means of grace were enjoyed?

We are not bound to justify all that Naomi spake or did; and we ought not rashly to condemn her, because we know only a few of the things that she spake to her daughters-in-law. But, in charity to that good woman, we ought to believe, that, for years past, she had been endeavoring, by her practice and her converse, to recommend to her young friends the worship of the God of Israel. If they were truly turned from the error of their ways, nothing that is here said was likely to drive them back to their own country. But if they were not, why should they go forward with her into her country, where she could not support them, and where it was possible that, from the behaviour of Naomi's countrymen to such destitute strangers, they would rather contract prejudices unfavorable to their religion, than cordially join in their worship? They might have been disgusted even with Naomi's own conduct, if she had not fairly told them what inconveniences they were to encounter in going to her land, and to her people. We ought, by all prudent methods, to gain proselytes to a religion which we know to be divine; but we are to catch none by guile. When Paul says, 'Being crafty, I caught you with guile,' he spake not in his own person, but in the person of an objector to the account he was giving of his own conduct. Far from allowing that he caught them with guile, he proves the very reverse to have been the case; for he 'renounced the hidden things of dishonesty, not walking in craftiness, nor handling the word of God deceitfully.'

Our Lord very plainly told his followers what they were to expect in his service. To a man who expressed his intention of following him, he said, 'The foxes have holes, and the birds of the air have nests, but the Son of man hath not where to lay his head.' We may however observe, that Christ usually administered proper antidotes against the fears which the doctrine of the cross might excite in the minds of his hearers. When he told them that they must 'deny themselves, and take up their cross and follow him,' he told them likewise, that 'those who lost their lives for his sake should find them.' It may be doubted whether Naomi, in the dejection of her spirits, did not overlook the powerful consolations which might have encouraged her young friends to follow her into the land of Israel, and would have more than compensated all the inconveniences to which they would have been exposed in a strange land. She honestly told them that they could not reasonably expect outward prosperity if they should accompany her. But might she not have reminded them of those spiritual advantages, which made the condition of the poorest Israelites unspeakably more advantageous than the happiest state of those heathens who knew not God? Doubtless she had often spoken of those privileges to them in former times; but as yet they had not learned their nature, and perhaps Naomi now despaired of ever being able to give them a perfect idea of it.

Verse 14.—*And they lifted up their voice and wept again: and Orpah kissed her mother-in-law; but Ruth clave unto her.*

Again they lift up their voices and weep when Naomi had represented her own destitute condition, and the little encouragement she could give them to go with her to her native land. They were also pierced with a deep concern for the afflictions which she had suffered, without any prospect of seeing them redressed in the manner they could have wished. But there is always a mixture of pleasure with the tears which flow from compassion and charity. Those men are not to be envied, but pitied, who feel not for the woes of their friends.

Naomi had already kissed both her daughters-in-law. Orpah now kisses Naomi and leaves her. We can scarcely avoid thinking, when we read this history, of the young man whom our Lord loved, although he would not follow him. The young man was amiable for his natural dispositions, and for his discreet behaviour; but, alas! he could not think of parting with all that he had for Christ. Orpah, in like manner, would have gladly accompanied Naomi to her people, could she have enjoyed with her those accommodations that appeared to her necessary for her earthly felicity. She kissed Naomi because she dearly loved her, but she did not love the God of Naomi so as to 'forget her father's house, and her own people,' to serve Him. Think not that an amiable natural temper, or an affectionate behaviour to your parents and friends, are either sufficient indications of true religion, or compensate for the want of it. The young man whom Jesus loved went away sorrowful from Jesus; but his sorrow at leaving him did by no means atone for the deaf ear which he turned to his religious instructions. Nature, in its highest endowments and improvements, is infinitely below grace. There are some believers in Christ, whose natural tempers are never refined to such a degree as we might expect from their religious principles; yet they shall dwell for ever in the region of love. There are other men, whose natural tempers are affectionate and humane. Perhaps they are improved by all the advantages of a polite and learned education. Thus they acquire an uncommon degree of respectability in the world, and yet continue destitute of faith in Christ and love to God. With all their attainments, they are still in a miserable condition. The love and esteem of men will not secure them from the wrath of that God whose service they neglect; and whose Son, the only Saviour, they despise.

Orpah kissed her mother-in-law, but Ruth clave to her. And Ruth's attachment to her was worth ten thousand of Orpah's kisses. The young nobleman in the gospel treated our Lord with high respect; but all this availed him nothing, for he would not sell his possessions at Christ's command, and become a follower of Jesus. Happy were the apostles who continued with him in all his temptations. They left all and followed him. What they left was little, but that love which disposed them to leave all was highly valued by him, and they received an hundred fold of recompense even in this world.

Verse 15.—*And she said, Behold thy sister-in-law is gone back unto her people and unto her gods: return thou after thy sister-in-law.*

It was doubtless Naomi's grief, that a young woman whom she loved, and who loved her so dearly, went back, not only to her people, but to her gods. Naomi, it is probable, knew her too well to be mistaken in the suspicion she had formed of her conduct. If her husband, when he married her, had no better reason than Naomi now had to judge favorably of her religious sentiments, he was greatly to be blamed for taking her into his bosom. But love may easily deceive a man who is clear-sighted in ordinary matters. Jacob, in all probability, did not find it so easy a matter as he expected, to reclaim Rachel from the worship of her father's images.

She is returned to her people and to her gods. Naomi doubted not that she was returning to her gods, although she said nothing of them when she left her mother-in-law. Perhaps she was not even thinking of her gods; but her return to her people was, in effect, a return to her gods. If she had intended to have nothing more to do with her idols, she would have fled from the temptations to idolatry which surrounded her on every side in the land of her nativity, and amongst her kindred.

There are too many, even of the professors of the true religion, who have no other reason for professing it, but the public profession of it amongst the people to whom they belong. Were they inhabitants of Greece, they would profess either the Turkish or the Greek religion, for the same reason that induces them to be Protestants in Great Britain. Beware of thinking that the best religion in the world will save you, if you do not receive the truth in the love of it, and in the love of it not chiefly for your fathers' and brethren's sake, but for its own sake, and for the sake of its glorious Author.

Return thou after thy sister-in-law. Example has a mighty influence, the example especially of dear friends with whom we have long lived in habits of intimacy. If Orpah had gone with Naomi, Ruth and Orpah would have kept one another in countenance. As matters stood, Ruth was likely to be esteemed by all her former friends the greatest fool in the world. Did not Orpah leave her mother-in-law, although she loved her with as warm affections as any mother-in-law could expect? But she was not so unwise as to leave all her other friends for a single friend connected with her by a relation which was now extinguished. Ruth loved her mother-in-law with an unreasonable and romantic fondness. When Orpah, in her sight, had the good sense to leave her, and to return to much nearer friends, Ruth still kept her foolish resolution to go to a country which she knew not, with an old woman, who, instead of being able to support her, must depend on the labor of this poor young woman. Such might be the reflections of those who knew not the springs of Ruth's conduct. But Ruth had sense enough to know, that neither the example nor the opinion of other people, ought to be the rule of her own conduct. 'It is a small thing for us to be judged of man; but he who judgeth us is the Lord.'

Here again it may be asked, Did not Naomi cast stumbling-blocks, as well as Orpah, in the way of Ruth? Was it not a sufficient temptation for this young woman to see Orpah returning to her gods? Why does Naomi enforce the temptation, by exciting her to follow the example? Does not Solomon give a much better advice, when with great earnestness he exhorts us to 'keep out of the path of evil doers,' Prov. iv. 14, 15.?

Naomi did not, certainly, wish that Ruth should return to her gods; and if she did not wish that she should return to her gods, she could not wish that she should lay herself open to temptations, such as those to which Orpah was now exposing herself. Ruth, therefore, who knew Naomi's zeal for the Lord God of Israel, would not understand her words as an advice to follow Orpah's example, but rather as a trial of her sincerity, and a modest reference of the important point to her own choice, whether she would go with Orpah to her friends and her gods, or come with Naomi to the land of Israel, and worship the God of Abraham and of Lot. We ought to be zealous for the Lord God of Israel, and to do what we can to turn sinners from the error of their ways; but we cannot compel the inclination or the judgment of our friends. Christ himself did not seek any followers that would not *willingly* comply with his injunctions. 'If any man is *willing* to come after me, let him deny himself.' He, who works in men to will and to do, will accept of no man's doings where the will is not engaged. Matt. xvi. 24. Gr.

When Jesus said to a man who would have followed him, 'The foxes have holes, and the birds of the air have nests, but the Son of man hath not where to lay his head,' he did not intend to dissuade any man from following him, but to let men know that they ought, before they profess themselves his followers, to consider what they may expect in his service, and whether they are prepared to bear the cross without repining, when God calls them to endure it.

When he said to Judas, 'What thou dost, do quickly,' he by no means authorised Judas to execute his wicked design of betraying his Master, but rather to awaken his conscience to a sense of the danger and baseness of his intentions, by placing the intended crime before his view, and fixing his mind upon it as a crime presently to be committed; for those evils which are considered as present may strike horror, although they were far from appearing dreadful at a distance. So Naomi, in the words before us, rather warns Ruth of the danger of returning, than exhorts her to return: *Return thou to thy people, and to thy gods.* After what Ruth had learned of the God of Israel, she could not bear the thought of returning to the gods of Moab; and, therefore, she would rather expose herself to every possible inconveniency and hardship in the land of Israel, than return to her own people. Let blinded idolaters 'walk in the name of their gods; we will walk in the name of our God for ever and ever!' Never will we be so mad, if we have any true knowledge of the glory of God, as to leave the Fountain of living waters, to make to ourselves cisterns, which will prove but broken cisterns that can hold no water. The folly of apostasy will not damp, but invigorate our zeal, for why should we follow the example of those who 'begin in the spirit and end in the flesh?'

LECTURE IV.

RUTH'S STEADFASTNESS TO HER RELIGIOUS PROFESSION.

CHAPTER I. 16—18.

Verse 16.—*And Ruth said, Intreat me not to leave thee, or to return from following after thee: for whither thou goest I will go, and where thou lodgest I will lodge: thy people shall be my people and thy God my God.*

Ruth clave unto Naomi, when Orpah kissed and left her. How firmly she clave to Naomi, we learn from her own words:—

'Do not intreat me (or do not press me) to leave thee, or to turn aside from following thee.' Dearly as Ruth loved her mother-in-law, and pleasant as her words had usually been in her ears, she was greatly distressed with what Naomi had now said. She could not really intend to persuade her beloved daughter-in-law to return to the service of Chemosh; but Ruth could not bear the slightest appearance of temptation, especially from the lips of one who was so dear to her; nor could she easily bear the appearance of any suspicion concerning her steadfastness in the faith and worship of the God of Israel.

Ruth assures Naomi, that it would serve no purpose to remind her of the inconveniences which she might expect to encounter. She had already formed her resolution, and it was so firm, that no considerations could induce her to alter it. Why, then, should any more be said on the subject? It might make her very uneasy, but her purpose could not be altered.

Whither thou goest I will go, and where thou lodgest I will lodge. Should Naomi go to the end of the world, she would go with her. How much more when Naomi was going to the land of Israel, where the God whom she had chosen for her God was known and served. The land of Israel was likely to afford but poor accommodation for Naomi, and but poor prospects for a Moabitish stranger who attended her: but it was the country of her beloved friend; it was the Lord's land; it was a land where she would be freed from those mighty temptations to idolatry which were so formidable to her in her own land; and where she would enjoy religious privileges, no where else to be enjoyed in the world.

Where thou lodgest I will lodge. The company of Naomi in a cottage would be more pleasant to her than that of any of the Moabitish ladies in a palace. 'Better is a dinner of herbs where love is, than a stalled ox and hatred therewith.' Better is the company of a poor saint in a prison, than the society of the rich and great in their splendid dwellings, if they take no delight in God, and in the remembrance of his name.

Thy people shall be my people. At this time Naomi's people must have been a very poor people after so many years of famine; but they were Naomi's people, and they were the people of the Lord of hosts. If we desire to serve God, his people must be our people. If we love Christ, we must cultivate fellowship with those whom he acknowledges as his faithful followers. If his name be dear to us, we will entertain a high value for those on whom this worthy name is called. If we acknowledge him as our Lord and Saviour, we must associate ourselves with his loyal subjects, the objects of his love and care, the partakers with us of his salvation.

And thy God my God. We are not to infer from these words, that Ruth chose the god of Israel for her God, merely or chiefly because he was Naomi's God. She had not so learned the God of Israel from her pious instructress. If she had chosen her God merely from respect to her earthly friends, why did she leave the God of her father and mother? Boaz was better informed concerning the moving springs of Ruth's conduct than we can pretend to be, and he attributed her voluntary exile from her own country to a principle of true piety. 'A full recompense,' he says, 'be given thee of the Lord God of Israel, under whose wings thou art come to trust!'

'Thy God *shall be*,' or 'thy God *is* my God.' She knew that there was no God in all the earth like the God of Israel, the only living and true God. She was instructed by Naomi, and she had probably been instructed likewise by her husband Chilion, that their God did not exclude the poor Gentiles from his covenant. They were indeed well qualified to teach her this necessary and important truth, because Rahab, the Canaanitess, that illustrious proselyte to their religion, was married into their own family. If Rahab was received by God into the number of his people, why may not Ruth also, the Moabitess, claim and expect a share in the blessings of his covenant? She appears not to have called in question her right to trust in him as her God; and she devotes herself to him as one of his people, and thereby sets us a good example of faith and obedience. The Lord requires us, in the first commandment of his holy law, to know and acknowledge him as the only true God, and our God. If Ruth, a Moabitess, one of that nation who were to be excluded for ten generations from the congregation of the Lord, is not afraid to subscribe with her hand unto the Lord, and to call him her God, why should we, from a pretended humility, call in question our right to say unto the Lord, 'Thou art our God?' Or, why should we prefer any other portion, or any other Lord to him? Ought we not to say, as Jeremiah teaches us, 'Truly in vain is salvation hoped for from the hills, and from the multitude of mountains. Truly in the Lord our God is the salvation of Israel. Behold, we come unto thee, for thou art the Lord our God!' Or, as we are taught by Israel, 'O Lord our God, other lords besides Thee have had the dominion over us; but henceforth by Thee only will we make mention of thy name!' Isaiah xxvi. 13.

Verse 17.—*Where thou diest will I die, and there will I be buried. The Lord do so to me, and more also, if ought but death part thee and me.*

Ruth was still but a young woman, and yet she thought of the day of her death; and the thoughts of that day perhaps contributed to fix her resolution of cleaving to Naomi. It is best to live with those whose death we wish to die.

Ruth supposed it likely that Naomi would die before her. This consideration was unpleasant to one who was forsaking all other friends to go with her. If she had lost one or several friends in the land of Moab, other friends would have been left; but if she went with Naomi to the land of Israel, she knew of no other friends. The death of Naomi, who was as mortal as her husband and her sons, might soon leave Ruth a friendless stranger. She is willing, however, to take the risk. If Naomi should die, she had no intention of returning to the country from whence she set out. When Naomi's friends died in the land of Moab, she returned to the land of Israel; but when Naomi dies, Ruth will not return to the land of Moab. The land of Israel is henceforth to be her country. She will not return to those friends that will exert all their influence to bring her back to her ancient gods. She will continue till she dies in the land of Israel, however friendless and unprotected, and will have her grave in the same place with Naomi, with whom she hopes to live in a better world.

God do so to me, and more also, if ought but death part thee and me. What might happen before death she could not say. Her prospects were but dark, and yet she is fully determined to abide with Naomi. Neither poverty, nor the contempt usually thrown upon strangers, nor any of the wrongs to which an unprotected woman in a strange land might be exposed, would induce her to separate from such a beloved friend, or to leave the country where the only true God was served.

God do so to me, and more also. 'God inflict upon me punishments too awful to be named, and punishments still more dreadful than any that thou canst suppose, if ought but death part betwixt thee and me.' Ruth solemnly swears that she will still cleave to Naomi, and to the God whom Naomi served. Thus David bound his soul by an oath to keep all God's righteous judgments. Thus we all ought to lay ourselves under the most sacred engagements to cleave to the Lord as our God, and to walk in his ways. Can we be too firmly engaged to the service of Him, whom to serve is liberty and happiness?

When we consider how firmly Ruth had resolved to cleave to Naomi, and to the God of Israel, ought we not to consider, whether we, who enjoy so vastly superior advantages to Ruth, are determined with equal firmness to continue in the faith, in the profession and in the practice, of our religion? Ruth was instructed only by one, or a very few private Israelites, in the knowledge of religion. She never had enjoyed an opportunity of attending upon any of the public ministrations of the priests or Levites. If she had ever seen the Bible, and learned to read it, that Bible consisted only of seven at most of the many books of Scripture which are put into *our* hands; yet she sacrifices all the pleasures—all the friendships—of her youth, all the hopes of better days in her own country, to that holy religion which she professed. What may be expected of *us* who have so long enjoyed the benefit of the church-administrations which Christ hath appointed for the conversion of sinners, and the establishment of saints; and who, from children, have been accustomed to read the Scriptures? We are under no necessity of leaving our native country and our friends, to enjoy the institutions of the gospel, or the fullest liberty of worshiping God in a manner agreeable to his own direction. If we are unsettled in our religious principles and practice, we cannot make the excuses that many might have made, who nevertheless were far from taking advantage of them to excuse a conduct that would admit of no excuse; for what excuse can be made for postponing the care of our souls to any thing in this world? If ten thousand deaths, or if circumstances of misery worse than any kind of death, were to be suffered by us for our religion, would it consist with true wisdom to purchase an exemption from such temporary sufferings at the price of everlasting destruction from the presence of the Lord? Yet still more inexcusable are we, if, without the temptations of any extraordinary inconveniences in this world, we prove unfaithful to our religious profession.

That we may cleave with purpose of heart to the Lord, it is necessary that our hearts be renewed by the grace of God; for never will we be true followers of them who left all and followed Christ, unless we are delivered from the remaining power of that attachment to the things of the present world, which renders so many professors of religion unstable in all their ways. If God put his fear into our hearts, we will not depart from him, Jeremiah xxxii. 40. If we are left to the natural impulse of our own hearts, however amiable our natural dispositions may be, we will follow the example, not of Ruth, but of Orpah, who kissed and left Naomi, Heb. xiii. 9.

Perhaps some may allege that Ruth, with all her firmness to her religious principles, forgot a part of that duty which the light of nature taught her. Why did she not show some attachment to her own mother, as well as to her mother-in-law? Why did she leave her parents with an intention never to return, that she might go to a land which she knew not? The answer is easy. She saw that she could not return to her mother without exposing herself to very dangerous temptations. She could not, perhaps, have lived in her mother's house, without seeing daily homage paid to false gods, and meeting with daily solicitations, and more than solicitations, to join in the practice of abominable idolatries. She might soon have been given in marriage to a worshiper of Chemosh; and it may easily be judged how little such a convert as Ruth was prepared to encounter the temptations to which she might have been exposed in the house either of a mother or a husband. She therefore 'forgot her mother's house and her own people.' With a disinterested spirit, she embraced and held fast that religion which she had been taught, not only by her mother-in-law, but by the Spirit of God. Unless she had been drawn by that divine power, which alone can change the hearts of men, she would not have come to the Lord's land, and to God himself as her exceeding joy. We are not called, in the literal sense of the words, to 'forsake our father's house and our own people;' yet in the spiritual sense it is absolutely necessary. We must be ready to part with every thing for Christ, if we desire to be Christ's disciples; for if any man come to him, 'and hate not father, and mother, and brothers, and sisters, yea, and his own life also, he cannot be one of his disciples.'

Whilst we consider the steadfastness of Ruth's religious principles, we cannot refrain from admiring likewise her fervent love to Naomi, and contemplating the happiness which both of them enjoyed in their mutual friendship. If earthly felicity seems a proper subject of envy, who would not envy this happy pair of friends, rather than Haman in all his grandeur, or Solomon in all his glory? And yet who were ever poorer than Naomi and Ruth?

Live in love and peace with all men if you can, especially with all Christians, and with none more than with those of your own house. But if you desire to enjoy the sweets of such domestic friendship, imitate the piety, the modesty, the gentleness, the patience, the meekness of these good women. Be careful especially of your tempers in the time of affliction. There are some who seem at times to overflow with good-will and kindness to their friends, but at other times, especially times of affliction, they are such sons or daughters of Belial, that it is almost impossible to live in friendship with them. Such was not Naomi. She was always disposed to take the heaviest share of her family afflictions, and to make them as light to her friends as possible. When her heart was wrung by sorrowful reflections, she spake kindly to them, and showed a warm regard to their interest. The law of kindness was ever on her tongue; and the complaints that were extorted from her were not of that sullen kind which provoke indignation, but expressive of that resignation, and that tenderness of heart, which excite compassion mingled with esteem.

Verse 18.—*When she saw that she was steadfastly minded to go with her, then she left speaking unto her.*

The words of Ruth evidently proceeded from her heart, and produced full conviction in the mind of Naomi, that her beloved daughter-in-law would trouble her with no sullen reflections on her change of condition, whatever new hardships might befal her in the land of Israel. Naomi, therefore, was fully satisfied, and added not a word more on the subject. She saw that it would give pain, and do no good; and why should any man speak a word that gives pain to his neighbor, unless that pain has some advantage attending it, or likely to attend it? Words should be like food or medicine. Words of reproof or alarm may sometimes be no less useful than those drugs which are unpalatable but salutary. But should a wise man use any kind of language, especially disagreeable language, that can do no good?

When Ruth had given Naomi as good proof as she could

give her of her settled determination to cleave to the God of Israel, Naomi is fully satisfied, and gives her no further trouble. Thus ought we to rest satisfied with those credible professions of faith in Christ, and steadfast adherence to his truths and ways, which are required from those who are admitted to the communion of the church. Such professions are necessary to establish that confidence which church-members ought to have in one another; and when they are made, we are deficient in that charity 'which believeth all things,' if we give place to groundless surmises concerning their sincerity. They may in the end prove insincere, for aught we can tell; but to form suspicions of them till good ground is given for them, discovers, not a godly jealousy over our brethren, but a proud censorious spirit which the laws of Christ condemn.

By her noble profession of stedfast adherence to the religion of Naomi, Ruth gained this advantage, that nothing more was said to her about returning to the gods of Moab. If we desire peace and quietness in the ways of God, let us openly avow our purpose of heart to cleave to the Lord, and make it evident in the course of our profession and practice that we are sincere, and resolved to be stedfast. When the friends of Christ see evident signs of our attachment to the good cause in which we are engaged, they will treat us with confidence, and be ready to strengthen our hands by the various offices of Christian communion. When his enemies see our Father's name written on our foreheads, they will desist from those solicitations to turn from our profession which they see to be fruitless. 'If it be possible, as much as lieth in us, let us live peaceably with all men;' but let us not seek peace with the ungodly, by dissembling our attachment to those truths which they disbelieve, or those duties which they despise. If they will not live peaceably with us unless we become their servants, and forfeit the character of faithful servants to Christ, their enmity will be better than a friendship bought at an expense so unwarrantable. But for the most part, wicked men themselves despise an unstable Christian, and cannot divest themselves of an inward reverence for the man whose professions and practice are uniform and self-consistent.

LECTURE V.

RUTH'S ARRIVAL WITH NAOMI AT BETHLEHEM.

CHAPTER I. 19-22.

Verse 19.—*So they two went, until they came to Bethlehem. And it came to pass, when they were come to Bethlehem, that all the city was moved about them; and they said, Is this Naomi?*

THERE is a great difference between the making, and the accomplishing, of a good resolution. There are some who resolve well, but they defer the accomplishment of what they have resolved till a more convenient season, which never comes; or they begin well, but they stop short in their course. Ruth not only resolved to go to the land of Israel with Naomi, and there to continue for life, but goes along with her till she comes to Bethlehem, and there dwells without ever wishing to return. She did not so much as ask leave from Naomi, before they left the country of Moab, to go back to bid farewell to her father and mother. Doubtless a woman so pious and affectionate as Ruth, must have loved and honored her parents, and have thought with regret of leaving them for ever; but had she returned to take leave of them, they might have persuaded or forced her to continue at home; and to continue at home appeared to her too hazardous to her soul. She therefore went along with Naomi, travelling no doubt on foot, and meeting with but indifferent accommodation on the road. At last, however, they come to the ancient habitation of Naomi in safety; for the Lord, by his good providence, guarded them amidst the dangers of their journey, and brought them to their city of habitation.

The appearance of Naomi with Ruth the Moabitess, excited

much surprise at Bethlehem. It is probable the inhabitants of that city never expected to see her more. She had been ten years absent, and they knew not that she was still alive. She was now to her former acquaintances almost like one who had returned to them from the land of forgetfulness.

The great alteration in her condition would likewise excite their surprise. She went out with her husband and two sons, and returned only with a stranger, whom none would expect to see, a young woman of the land of Moab. Many alterations take place in families within the space of a few years, but these alterations are the less observed that they are made by slow degrees. First one dies, and then, when he is forgotten, a second, and a third. This is the common course of things; but if two or three should die out of a family at the same time, all the neighborhood would be struck with astonishment; all the friends of the survivors would be filled with compassion. Such did the case of Naomi appear to her acquaintances, who now, for the first time, seem to have been informed of the change in her condition.

If you consider what changes have befallen many of your neighbors within the last ten years, you will be struck with a sense of the mutability of all human things. Many have within the compass of that time lost their father, their mother, some of their children, their friends whom they most loved of any thing upon earth. If you have lost such friends, God has been loudly calling you to 'set your affections on things above, not on things on the earth.' If you have not, remember that your earthly comforts are as uncertain as those of your neighbors. The next ten years may leave you as desolate as the last ten years have left any of your friends. Your husbands, your wives, your children, are as liable to the stroke of death as theirs. Whilst you pity them, learn to provide consolation for yourselves for the time when you will need it as much as they. Naomi now appeared in a very different condition from that in which her neighbors had formerly known her. But those who knew her piety would not think her miserable. She had lost her husband, but not her God. She might have still said, 'Although my husband is dead, and my children are dead, I know that my Redeemer liveth. The Lord liveth, blessed be my rock! and the God of my salvation be magnified!' Naomi, however, at meeting with her old acquaintances, had her soul harrowed afresh by the recollection of her former enjoyments, which were now lost to her for ever.

Verse 20.—*And she said unto them, Call me not Naomi, call me Mara; for the Almighty hath dealt very bitterly with me.*

Naomi now saw many of the former acquaintances of her husband and her sons. These acquaintances would expect to hear of all that had befallen them in the land of Moab, and would speak of many things that tended to revive the remembrance in Naomi's mind of the pleasant days she had passed in their society. Her heart bled at the recollection. No wonder that her words, on this occasion, express a bitterness of heart that attracts our pity; but it is the bitterness of grief, not of impatience. She is very deeply humbled under the mighty hand of God, but does not fret at the dispensations of his providence.

Call me not Naomi, but call me Mara. Naomi signifies *pleasant*, Mara signifies *bitter*. Naomi's name, when it was mentioned by her friends, added to her grief, because it brought to her mind all the pleasant things which she had enjoyed in the time of her prosperity. It is very probable that, in former days, either she herself, or some of her friends, might observe how well her circumstances suited her name. As she was a woman of a pleasant disposition, she gained the love of her husband, her sons, her neighbors; and life is pleasant to those who enjoy the friendship of all around them, especially as they are disposed to make themselves happy, when happiness is in their power. But the recollection of the delightful days she had spent in the bosom of her family and in the visits of her friends, was more grievous to her. Her earthly happiness was fled and gone. She could not now be happy in a town, which was emptied of those things that made it formerly delightful. She could not communicate that pleasure to her acquaintance which she once did. She could not now wear that cheerful air which once beautified her countenance. She could not mingle in cheerful converse. She had it not in her power to endear herself by acts or by words of kindness, as in former days. She might very probably think, in this burst of grief which broke forth at the sight of her old acquaintances, that her very name would be a source of perpetual affliction, and that she would not be able to hear it pronounced without a constant renovation of what she now felt. 'The heart knoweth its own bitterness;' and there are little circumstances unknown and unfelt by others, that exasperate the sorrows of the afflicted in a very great degree.

Call me not Naomi, but call me Mara. We excuse these words from the time when they were spoken. They were dictated by passion rather than by judgment; not indeed by the passions of anger and discontentment, but by the passion of grief, and of grief excited by the best and loveliest affections. She thought it impossible that her days should ever again be pleasant, because Elimelech, and Mahlon, and Chilion, were no more to be her companions. But we ought not so to lament the comforts we have lost, as to think that all our future days must be spent in bitterness. Has God taken away from us every thing that can render life comfortable? Has he written such bitter things against us, that our eye can never more see good? Let us mourn for our departed friends. 'By the sorrow of the countenance, the heart is made better.' Yet, when they are taken away from us, let us not say, 'Our gods are taken away, what have we more?' God can give us joy for mourning. He can even turn our mourning, and the cause of our mourning, into causes of the most heart-felt joy. 'Mine eye shall no more see good,' said Job in the day of his griefs; but he was happily disappointed, for he saw more good after his afflictions, than he had ever seen before them.

Whatever evils befal us in life, let us not forget from whence they come. 'Out of the mouth of the Most High proceedeth not evil and good.' It is He that 'killeth and maketh alive, that bringeth down to the grave and bringeth up.' Of this Naomi was sensible. 'Call me Mara, for the Almighty hath dealt very bitterly with me.' Had her husband and her children died by the hand of violence in a strange land, she would have seen the agency of divine Providence in the injuries of wicked men. But, as matters stood, she had none to blame for the calamities that came upon her, unless she thought, as she was likely to do, that she had brought her calamities upon herself by sin. There was no hand of man laid upon her beloved friends. Their death was caused by the visitation of the Almighty, who can do no injury to any of his creatures.

The Almighty hath dealt bitterly with me. If all our afflictions come from the Almighty, it is in vain, as well as impious, to contend with him that smites us. Shall the potsherds of the earth strive with their Maker, who has all power to do with them as he pleases? He cannot be effectually opposed, and He can do nothing that is wrong. Weak mortals may injure their fellow-creatures for their own advantage; but what profit can it be to the Almighty, that he should oppress the work of his own hands? 'Yea, surely, God will not do wickedly; neither will the Almighty pervert judgment. Who hath given him a charge over the earth, or who hath disposed the whole world? If he set his heart upon man ; if he gather unto himself his spirit and his breath, all flesh shall perish together, and shall turn unto dust.' And what can we say if the Almighty should thus display his sovereign power? 'Is it fit to say to a king, Thou art wicked; and to princes, Ye are ungodly? how much less to Him that accepteth not the persons of princes, and regardeth not the rich more than the poor; for they all are the work of his hands?'

This name, which we render *Almighty*, is by many understood to signify, the all-sufficiency of God. He is able to do what he pleases, and there is an abundant and overflowing fullness with him to supply all our wants, and to satisfy all our desires; and therefore, when, by the strokes of his hand, we are deprived of the sweetest of our created enjoyments, it will be our wisdom, instead of fretting at our losses, to seek a compensation for them in the enjoyment of himself. Out of his riches in glory, by Christ Jesus, he can supply all our wants. In the enjoyment of his favor, which is better than life, we may find abundant satisfaction when all things look black and dark around us. Have we lost father, mother,

children, friends? He is a thousand times better than they all, to those who choose him for their portion; Hab. iii. 17, 18.
The Almighty hath dealt very bitterly with me. It is natural for mourners to aggravate their own afflictions, and to call on all their neighbors to 'behold and see if there be any sorrow like unto their sorrow which is done unto them, wherewith the Lord hath afflicted them in the day of his fierce anger.' Naomi had better reason than most persons, to think that the Almighty had dealt very bitterly with her, when she had not a single child spared to her in the fall of her family; yet Job was afflicted with heavier strokes, and after all could praise the Lord, saying, 'The Lord hath given, and the Lord hath taken away; blessed be the name of the Lord! Shall we receive good at the hand of the Lord, and shall we not receive evil also?'

It is undoubtedly our duty to consider the divine dispensations towards us with attention, and to feel the scourge with which God is pleased to wound us. He will not lay upon man more than is meet; and therefore it is unsafe to be regardless of any of those heavy circumstances, by which he is pleased to embitter our earthly condition. If they are all designed for the accomplishment of some purpose concerning us, we must endeavor to answer God's designs, that we may not bring upon ourselves heavier calamities than we have yet felt. We may, however, err, by thinking our calamities heavier, when they are compared with other men's calamities, than they really are. Into this mistake, persons of a sorrowful spirit are ready to fall, to the no little damage of their souls. They may be full of complaint, when they have reason to be thankful that their situation is not worse. They may deny themselves that comfort which God is pleased to allow them, and disable themselves from giving glory to God in the fires, by that cheerful patience which is at all times our duty.

Do you ask how you may keep clear of both extremes? That you may be preserved from the unhappy effects which may result from too slight thoughts of divine correction, consider how loudly God calls you, by various circumstances of affliction, to consider your ways. How inexcusable must you be, after all God's dealings with you, if you are found indulging any of those corrupt affections which you are called to mortify, or neglecting any of those duties to which your chastisements ought to rouse you! Jeremiah, in the book of the Lamentations, teaches the church deeply to deplore her miseries; but to what end? Not to inspire her with despondency, for he teacheth her to say, 'The Lord will not cast off for ever; but though he cause grief, yet will he have compassion according to the multitude of his mercies.' The true reason why the prophet wished his people to feel their calamities was, that they might be thoroughly awakened to comply with his exhortations: 'Let us search and try our ways, and let us turn again to the Lord. Let us lift up our hearts with our hands to God in the heavens.'

To prevent the bad effects that might result from too deep sensibility to our distresses, as if they exceeded the bounds which God is ordinarily pleased to set to his severities in dealing with his own people, it will be proper for us to consider the good as well as the evil things in our condition; fairly to compare our grounds of complaint with those of others of God's people, either in our own times or in past times; and to remember that the 'end of a thing is better than the beginning thereof.' Nor ought we ever to forget, that, whatever grounds we have for humiliation under the mighty hand of God, for confession of sins, for fasting, or speedy reformation of every thing amiss in our tempers and conduct, these do not affect the grounds of our faith in God through Christ Jesus, nor supersede the duty of glorifying the Lord in the evil day, by the patient enduring of his will, and by expressing our faith and joy in the Lord. David, in the days of his troubles, though conscious that he had provoked the divine displeasure against himself, did not despair of seeing the face of God again with joy. 'Why art thou cast down, O my soul? and why art thou disquieted within me? Hope thou in God, for I shall yet praise him.'

Verse 21.—*I went out full, and the Lord hath brought me home again empty. Why then call ye me Naomi, seeing the Lord hath testified against me, and the Almighty hath afflicted me?*

'The Lord giveth, and the Lord taketh away.' When he

gives, he is under no necessity of securing to us the possession of what he gives. We may soon provoke him, by our sins, to bereave us of all that he hath given us; but however careful we may be to please him, we cannot merit the continuance of his favours, and, without any special provocation on our part, he may have good reasons for impoverishing us, and placing us in conditions quite the reverse of those to which we have been accustomed. Millions have found reason to say in the course of their earthly pilgrimage, that once they were full, but the Lord hath emptied them. And one great reason why God so frequently changes men's prosperous condition into misery is, to teach us the folly of trusting to our present enjoyments. 'But this I say, brethren, the time is short. It remaineth that both they that have wives be as though they had none, and they that weep as though they wept not, and they that rejoice as though they rejoiced not, and they that buy as though they possessed not, and they that use this world as not abusing it; for the fashion of this world passeth away.'

That Naomi was once full and was now empty, we can easily believe. But what does she mean by saying, *I went out full, but the Lord hath brought me again empty?* Was she not so empty when she went out, that she was forced to leave her native land for bread? And had she not now at her return the prospect of finding bread in her own land? Why then does she make herself so much richer at her departure than at her return?

It is natural for men under depression of spirit to make unfair and invidious comparisons, both of their own condition with that of others, and of their own former, with their present condition. When we look back on the past period of our life, if it has been on the whole prosperous, we forget those little vexations and disgusts that mingled themselves with our enjoyments, and fondly fix our review on the pleasant things that sweetened our former days. But when we consider our present condition, if we have been afflicted by the hand of God, and felt his chastisements, we are ready to mistake the comfortable parts of our condition; and, whilst our minds are occupied with former and present pains, we fondly imagine that if we could recover all the pleasures of our former life, we would be superlatively blessed; but when this cannot be expected, we seem to be fallen into an abyss of misery from which we can never be raised up. Thus we often, by our folly, make our present days miserable, when they might be enjoyed with some degree of comfort. The lies which our fancies invent, we believe at their report, although we might easily know the deception.

But Naomi could with propriety say that she had gone out full, although her family was impoverished when she left the holy land. Although she was destitute of silver and gold, and of the conveniences, and almost of the necessaries of life, she was rich in the possession of her husband and children. At that time, when she compared her present condition with her former, she thought that she was poor; but when she now compared it with that condition in which she returned to the land of Israel, destitute of those riches which she thought far more valuable than gold and silver, she says, *I went out full*. She was now sensible that she might have been happy and thankful at that time, although it may be questioned whether she thought so when the necessity of a voluntary exile damped her spirit. Too often our vexations cause us to forget our mercies. When every thing is not agreeable to our wishes, we sink in one disquiet the sense of an hundred mercies. We are unhappy, because we want one or two of the many things which we think necessary for our comfort. God deprives us of one or two more of the ingredients of our felicity, of far more consequence than the former, and this convinces us that we had formerly much more reason to be thankful than we could then believe.

A little reflection might convince us, that we still have reason to be thankful. 'It is of the Lord's mercies that we are not consumed.'

Consider these words of Naomi, ye who have your families yet spared, although you find it difficult, in the present distress,* to provide for them. 'Is not the life more than meat, and the body than raiment?' Bless God for the life of your

---

* This discourse was delivered in a time of scarcity.

friends, when your cupboards are empty. Do not say that you are bereaved of every thing that makes life comfortable, if you enjoy the sweet society of those whom you love, or ought to love, as parts of yourselves. If you thanklessly bemoan your condition, as if God had bereaved you of all the fruits of his mercy, the time may come when you will think that you were full, although you thought yourself empty; and ought to have blessed God for what he gave and preserved, when you were giving a loose to useless wailings for what he had taken away.

But if any of you are in Naomi's condition, bereaved not only of your substance, but of your friends, which are more precious to you than your substance; amidst your humiliation of spirit under the rebukes of God, remember that the mercy of God is not clean gone. Ruth was left to the good woman when her sons were lost, and she was as good to her as ten sons. Had she not great reason to be thankful for the daughter whom she had borne in her exile? for Ruth was not only the daughter-in-law of Naomi according to the flesh, but her spiritual daughter in the Lord.

If no friends of any kind are left to you on this earth, have you not a friend in heaven? Is not Christ the friend of our race? and does he not call unto you from heaven to come unto Him, that you may find in him that rest, that satisfaction, which nothing earthly can give?

Why then call ye me Naomi, seeing the Lord hath testified against me, and the Almighty hath afflicted me? Afflictions are a testimony against men that they are sinners, but they are not always a testimony that the sufferer is guilty of some particular sins for which God chastiseth him; Job ii. 3. Yet, when our calamities are chastisements, they are testimonies of God's displeasure on account of our offences; Psalm cvii. 17. Those who are broken in their spirit, are disposed to think of their sins under their afflictions, and to acknowledge that they are testimonies against them, the fruits of a just quarrel that God carries on with them. They know that they need corrections, and confess that they have deserved all that comes upon them, and a thousand times more.

Yet we must not judge our neighbors because they are sorely afflicted; for although they well deserve all that comes upon them, we may deserve as much, and more. And if we are not corrected by God when we offend him, we are so far from having any reason to magnify ourselves against God's afflicted people, that we have reason to tremble lest we are found 'bastards, and not sons; for what son is he whom the Father chasteneth not?'

And the Almighty hath afflicted me. Naomi dwells upon the consideration that all her calamities came from almighty God. If it is God that smites us, then let us not slight our troubles, or overlook any part of the operations of God's hand; for none of his works are unfruitful works of darkness. But let us not faint when we are rebuked of him. 'It is the Lord, let him do what seemeth him good.' He who afflicts you, believers, is your God, and your Father. Learn from your Redeemer to say, 'The cup which my Father hath given me, shall I not drink it?'

LECTURE VI.

RUTH GOES TO GLEAN, AND MEETS WITH BOAZ.

CHAPTER II. 1–4.

Verse 1.—*And Naomi had a kinsman of her husband's, a mighty man of wealth, of the family of Elimelech; and his name was Boaz.*

SOME allege that all men ought to be equal in wealth; but God maketh rich, and maketh poor. He gives to some men power to get wealth, and withholds that power from others. He enables some to leave wealth to their families, whilst the families of other men are left to struggle with all the inconveniences of poverty. 'Who shall say to God, What dost thou?' or, Why disposest thou so unequally of thy benefits? 'The earth is the Lord's, and the fullness thereof.' He hath given the earth, indeed, to the children of men, but he was not bound to give to every one of them equal portions of it. If he has given us any portion of it for our necessary subsistence, we ought to be content and thankful. Still more, if he hath given us an ordinary portion of the comforts of life. If we are displeased because he has not given us so much as he has given to some of our neighbors, 'our eye is evil because he is good.' What hast thou given to God? Verify thy claim, and thou shalt be recompensed. God will be in no man's debt.

Naomi was very poor, and she had a kinsman by affinity who was very rich. Nothing is more common than for the rich to have poor, and the poor to have rich relations. Let a man exert all his activity, let his labors be attended with all the success he can wish, let him have the comfort of seeing his children becoming rich whilst he yet lives with them, yet it is not to be expected that many years will elapse till some of his posterity feel the inconveniences of poverty. Elimelech was probably, as well as Boaz, of the princely race of Nahshon; yet Boaz was a mighty man of wealth, when Elimelech was under the necessity of leaving his country to seek bread in a foreign land. Our happiness is very precarious if it is placed either in our wealth or in our children. What multitudes of Abraham's posterity are now in a wretched condition, although he abounded in wealth whilst he lived in this world! But he sought his happiness in God, and in the better country.

Boaz is said to have been *a mighty man of wealth.* The meaning is, that he possessed a very large portion of riches. But the expression may remind us of the power that is ordinarily conferred by wealth. Rich men can do much, although not so much as many think they have it in their power to do. How many excellent things were done by Job! By the wise and charitable distribution of his wealth, 'he was eyes to the blind, feet to the lame, an husband to the widow, a father to the fatherless; and many blessings of them that were ready to perish came upon him.' Yet let us not envy the rich. They have power to do hurt as well as good; and they can do themselves much more hurt than they can do to any one else. We trust too much to ourselves, if we think that we would certainly make a good use of riches if we possessed them. Even Solomon, with all his wisdom, found that his wealth was, in many instances, a snare. He did much good, but he also did much evil which would not have been in his power if he had been a poor man.

Naomi had a kinsman of her husband's. Marriage makes the husband and wife one flesh. The kinsmen of the one ought therefore to be accounted the kinsmen of the other. It is wisely ordered by the great Lawgiver, that men should not marry the nearest of their own kindred, that various families might be connected by means of this institution. Let every man, therefore, and every woman, learn to show that respect and kindness to their relations by marriage, which they owe to their relations by blood. If we admire the behaviour of Naomi and Ruth, why do we not follow their example as far as our circumstances are like theirs?

Verse 2.—*And Ruth, the Moabitess, said unto Naomi, Let me now go to the field, and glean ears of corn after him in whose sight I shall find grace.*

Ruth is again called the Moabitess. It was her honour that, when her birth and her nativity were of the land of Moab, her behaviour was that of an Israelitess indeed. There are fools who upbraid men or women of virtue with their parentage or their country. It is mentioned to the honor of Ruth, not that she was a Moabitess, but that, being a Moabitess, she was a woman of virtue and piety. It will be the condemnation of many, that, when they were born in the church of God, they behaved as if 'their father had been an Amorite, and their mother a Hittite.' It will be the praise of others, that they forgot their father's house, and their own people, to join themselves unto the Lord.

She said to Naomi, Let me go and glean. It was necessary for her to think of some way of obtaining a livelihood for herself and for her mother-in-law, who had returned empty to Bethlehem. Some women in Naomi's condition would have thought themselves entitled to a decent support from their rich relations; but the good woman did not wish to be troublesome to her friends. It does not appear that she had even spoken of them to Ruth, and Ruth knew no way of obtaining bread but by her own industry. As long as we can live by the labour of our own hands, why should we be a burden to others? This the apostle Paul declares, that 'if any man will not work, neither should he eat.'

But why does Ruth propose such a mean employment as that of gathering ears of corn wherever she could find a man that would give her leave? Should not a woman, connected by marriage with an illustrious family in Judah, have sought out a more honorable employment? It is to be considered, that the land of Israel was not a commercial country like ours, and afforded much less choice of employment to the poor. Besides, the refinements of our age and country were never thought of in those ancient times. We find that Boaz was far from being ashamed of the employment chosen by his kinswoman, if she could be said to have made a choice where choice was perhaps not in her power. She and her mother needed bread; and no time was left her for seeking out another way of life, till present wants were supplied.

'When ye reap the harvest of your land,' said God to his people, 'thou shalt not wholly reap the corners of thy field, neither shalt thou gather the gleanings of thy harvest. And thou shalt not glean thy vineyard, neither shalt thou gather every grape of thy vineyard; thou shalt leave them for the poor and stranger: I am the Lord your God.' Lev. xix. 9, 10. In these words, God gives to the poor and stranger a right to glean in the fields of the Israelites. Ruth was both poor and a stranger. The same God who gave the field to the proprietor, gave the gleanings to the poor and stranger. She had the same right to glean in the fields, which the disciples of Jesus had to pluck the ears of corn in another man's field; and even the malicious Pharisees did not question their right to do it on a labouring day, because the law had said, 'When thou comest into the standing corn of thy neighbour, then thou mayest pluck the ears with thy hand, but thou shalt not move a sickle into thy neighbour's standing corn.'

Yet Ruth, who was probably ignorant of the law, was willing to accept as a favour what she might have claimed as a right. 'Let me go and glean in the man's field in whose sight I shall find grace.' The poor are often too bold in their claims. They have a title, by the law of God, to their necessary food from the rich; yet they ought to be thankful to the rich when they are willing to allow their claim. The rich should be ready to distribute; yet they must be judges of their own ability to distribute, of the persons that have a claim upon their charity, and of the share that these claimants ought to have of the fruits of their liberality. The modest and thankful among the poor will be most cheerfully and liberally supplied; nor will they be despised for their poverty by any Christian who remembers that our Lord was once so poor for their sakes, that he accepted of the ministrations of the substance of many women from Galilee. Impudence and greediness will expose poor persons to contempt and neglect, but honest poverty will always meet with respect.

'Let me go and glean in the field of the man that will favour me with permission.' She is willing to employ herself in this mean occupation, rather than return to the land of Moab, where she might perhaps have found a more plentiful subsistence, without incurring obligations to strangers. She was a true daughter of Abraham, although she sprung from Lot. When Abraham came into the land whither Ruth had now come to dwell, there was a famine; but Abraham never thought of returning to the country of his kindred, which he had left in obedience to God. He would rather risk his own life, and what was dearer to him than his life, amongst strangers, than return to the country which God had commanded him to leave. Ruth would rather have been a gleaner of the ears of corn in the land of Israel, than a lady in the land of Moab. She had come to trust under the shadow of the wings of Naomi's God; and the meanest estate in the land where He was known was preferable in her eyes to the highest station in a land of idolaters.

Ruth does not propose that Naomi should go with her to the field. She wished her honored mother to enjoy the rest and ease suited to her time of life, whilst herself was exposed to the troubles and inconveniences of her humble occupation in the fields of strangers. Young persons should be cheerfully willing to bear fatigues and troubles for the sake of their aged parents, that they may enjoy such ease as the infirmities of age require. Let those who are in the vigour of age, if their parents are feeble, remember what their mothers endured for them in infancy or in sickness; how they willingly suffered anxiety of mind, the want of sleep, and many fatigues of body, that their beloved offspring might enjoy pleasure, or be relieved from distress. How selfish are the spirits of those young persons, who grudge toil or expense for their parents in that time of life when they can enjoy little pleasure but what arises from beholding the affectionate attachment of their children! The charities of the heart sweeten life. A young woman cheerfully laboring for aged parents, is far happier than a fashionable lady spending in idleness and dissipation the fruits of the industry of her ancestors.

David, the great grandson of Ruth, showed a like regard to

his parents with that which Ruth showed to her mother-in-law. Jesse needed no provision to be made by his children for his old age; but he found himself under a necessity of becoming an exile, to avoid the rage of the tyrant, whose hatred to the son of Jesse extended to all his friends. David was unwilling that his aged parents should share in the toils and dangers of his wandering life; and therefore he supplicated the king of Moab to afford them protection till he should know what God would do for him. In his distresses he wished not his parents to share, but resolved that they should share in his prosperity if they were spared to see it.

Verse 2.—*And she said unto her, Go, my daughter.* Naomi was blessed with the same humble and kind disposition with her daughter-in-law. Doubtless, it was a great grief to her that she could not place Ruth in a more comfortable and respectable condition among her own people; but since it was the will of God that they should live in poverty, and subsist by the humblest of occupations, she readily submits to His pleasure. Why should we repine at God's dealings with either ourselves or our friends? If God has humbled them by his providence, we ought to be thankful if he has given them a spirit suited to their lot. If he has given them little, let us be thankful for that little. If he has given them nothing, let us be thankful if he has given them hands and a heart to work. Every thing that God gives any of us, and every opportunity of obtaining what we need, are undeserved mercies from the Giver of all good.

Go, my daughter! The affection of Ruth to Naomi was not unmerited. Naomi loved and treated Ruth as a daughter. The law of kindness was in her mouth, and transfused gratitude and love into the heart of her daughter-in-law. Mothers often complain, with reason, of the ingratitude of their children; yet one of the reasons is frequently to be found at home. If there were more Naomis, we might expect to see more Ruths. Undoubtedly, children owe affection and honour to their mothers, in whatever manner they behave. The relation, independently of every other consideration, demands filial duty. But why should parents, by coldness or rudeness to the fruit of their own bodies, provoke them to break the first commandment with promise, to the prejudice of both themselves and their children? If it is the duty of children to honour their parents, it must be the duty of parents to behave in such a way as to procure honour from their children.

Some parents do much for their children, and put themselves to a great deal of trouble on their account, and after all, lose the thanks which they might have, by the coldness, the bitterness, the repulsive manner, with which they often speak to them. 'Is not a word better than a gift? but both are with a gracious man.' Our Lord tells us, that by our words we shall be justified or condemned; and there is no place where our tongues ought to be better governed than in our own houses. It is delightful to visit those families where the various members appear, from their mutual converse, intent upon making one another happy. It is painful to observe sons and daughters, fathers and mothers, wives and husbands, turning their common dwelling into a house of correction to one another.

Verse 3.—*And she went, and came, and gleaned in the field after the reapers; and her hap was to light on a part of the field belonging unto Boaz, who was of the kindred of Elimelech.*

There are some whose virtue and industry lie only in their tongues. They say, and do not. But Ruth was no less diligent in business, than wise in her resolutions. When she obtained Naomi's leave, she went forth immediately to the field, and asked leave of a certain steward whom she met with, to glean and gather after the reapers among the sheaves. This leave being readily granted her, she entered with cheerfulness upon her work, in which she continued till the heat of the day compelled her to make use of a shelter.

Although Naomi had several relations at Bethlehem, she did not desire Ruth to go to any of their fields. Not that she wanted confidence in their kindness. She was, at least, sensible that Boaz had been a kind friend before she went to the country of Moab; but she knew that her poverty gave her a right to send Ruth to glean in the field of any of the Israelites, and she seems not to have wished to appear troublesome to her relations. Those are most likely to meet with kindness from their rich friends, who are least intrusive.

It was the hap of Ruth to come into the field of Boaz; and her coming into his field, brought her into acquaintance with the man who was to be her husband, and by whom she was to become one of the mothers of our Lord. The misery or happiness of our life is often derived from accidents that appear quite trivial. 'Time and chance happeneth to all men,' and no man can tell what consequences the slightest accident may have. Connections happy or pernicious, riches or poverty, life or death, may be the consequence of a walk or a visit intended for the amusement of a single hour.

It is plain that divine Providence was her conductor to the field of Boaz. Nothing is accidental to God. When the lot is cast into the lap, the disposing, the whole disposing of it, is of the Lord. We are ever in His hands, and he can bring the richest benefits, or the sorest chastisements, out of causes from which we formed no apprehension, either of good or evil.

'The steps of a good man are ordered by the Lord, and he greatly delighteth in his way.' The same God that brought Ruth from Moab to Bethlehem, led her to the field of Boaz for her good. He led her to the land of Israel, that she might be fully instructed in righteousness. He led her to the field of Boaz, that her virtue might become conspicuous to a man who had it in his power and in his will to reward her. When Abraham's servant went to take a wife to his son from amongst his kindred, Abraham told him that the God before whom he walked would send his angel to conduct him; and the faithful servant thankfully acknowledged that he had not been amused with vain hopes. 'I being in the way, the Lord led me to the house of my master's brethren.' All who are wise enough to observe the agency of Providence in the various accidents of their lives, will find like reason with Abraham's servant to praise God for his goodness. We may indeed recollect a variety of accidents that have proved hurtful, as well as others that have turned out beneficial to us. But to those who are taught to make a due improvement of what befals them, nothing is eventually hurtful. 'There shall no evil happen to the just.' The things that are evil to others are good to them. 'All the paths of the Lord our God are mercy and truth to them that remember his covenant and his testimonies.'

Verse 4.—*And behold Boaz came from Bethlehem, and said unto the reapers, The Lord be with you! And they answered him, The Lord bless thee!*

Boaz was an old man, and he had a steward set over the reapers. Yet he came from Bethlehem to see with his own eyes how his work was performed. When our Lord says, 'Take no thought what ye shall eat or drink,' or, as the words ought rather to have been rendered, Take no *anxious* thought what ye shall eat or drink, he does not recommend indolence or carelessness about our worldly business. We must seek first the kingdom of God and his righteousness, and then all other things shall be added to us; but they shall be added to us whilst we are using warrantable means to obtain them. 'Be diligent,' says Solomon, 'to know the state of thy flocks, and look well to thy herds.' Slothfulness may be the ruin of men of princely fortunes, 'for riches are not for ever, and doth the crown endure unto all generations?'

Although Boaz was a rich man, he despised not his menservants nor his maid-servants. He did not look upon his reapers with a supercilious eye. He did not come unto them with words of pride or reproach, but with a blessing in his mouth. *The Lord be with you!* He was a good man, and there is no place where real goodness will more display itself than in a man's own family, not only to his wife and children, but likewise to his servants. A good master will be a father to his servants when they faithfully perform their work. Such even Naaman, when he was a heathen, appears to have been; and happy was it for himself that he had taught his servants to look upon him as a father. Few parents have derived such benefits from the most dutiful children as Naaman derived from the confidence and duty of his servants, when they advised him to comply with the prophet's advice.

Good men will pray for the best blessings to their neighbours around them, and especially to those of their own house.

It has been often the happiness of masters to be blessed with praying servants, and often the happiness of servants to have masters whose prayers brought down the blessing of heaven upon those who dwelt under their roof.

The Lord be with you! This was a real prayer from the mouth of Boaz. It is too common with men to say, 'God be with you!' when God is not in their thoughts. The name of God is profaned when it is used without consideration. It is reported of the great philosopher Boyle, that he never mentioned the name of God without making a visible pause in his discourse. Most certainly none of us ought to mention such an awful name without thinking of Him who is called by it, or to seek any thing from him for ourselves or others without earnest desires to obtain it, and without a becoming sense of our dependence upon him for all those good things which we wish ourselves or others to enjoy.

All good things are requested in this prayer, *The Lord be with thee!* God's presence and favor will satisfy our souls; will supply every want; will turn sorrow into joy, and the shadow of death into the morning. But without God's presence and blessing, the richest confluence of sublunary blessings will leave us wretched and miserable, poor, and blind, and naked. The laborious reapers, whose toils ended only with the sun, and were every day renewed, were happy beyond expression if their master's prayer was heard. The kings who reign over many lands know not what happiness means, if they have nothing but what earth can bestow. 'Many say, Who will show us any good?' but few know what that good is which they should constantly seek to obtain. 'Lord, lift up the light of thy countenance upon us!' and our hearts will be filled with that gladness which the men who have their portion in this life never taste, in the richest abundance of their corn and wine.

The Lord bless thee! said the reapers to Boaz. They loved their master; they were grateful for his kindness; they prayed for the same blessings to him which he requested for them. Masters often complain of the selfishness of their servants, and the complaint is often too just. But they must be very depraved men who are not faithful servants and sincere friends to such masters as Boaz. 'Even publicans,' says our Lord, 'love those who love them.'

The Lord be with you!—The Lord bless thee! Such were the petitions which the Israelites were taught by God to present to his throne, for themselves and for one another. The priests were commanded to pray for all the people in these words, 'The LORD bless thee, and keep thee. The LORD make his face to shine upon thee, and be gracious to thee. The LORD lift up his countenance upon thee, and give thee peace.' 'Grace be unto you, and peace,' &c., or, 'The grace of our Lord Jesus Christ be with you all!' is the prayer of Paul for all the churches. Christians are called to inherit a blessing, and therefore they must bless and not curse. They ought to bless even those who curse them. It is God alone who can give the blessings that we need; but we are both required and abundantly encouraged to ask His blessings, not only for ourselves, but for our friends and neighbours, our kindred and servants. He is the fountain of blessings. He sent his Son into the world to purchase for us the best blessings. He hath promised that 'men shall be blessed in Him, and that all generations shall call him blessed.' 'Ask, and ye shall receive.' Ask for your friends and dependents. You are not straitened in Him, who giveth liberally and upbraideth not. Ask his blessings when you are upon your knees in your stated devotions. Seek them by earnest aspirations when you are on your beds; when you are sitting in the house; when you are walking by the way; when you are employed in the businesses of life. Never approach irreverently to the Divine Majesty. But where the fear of God habitually governs the heart, prayer need not, and will not, be confined to stated times. Such requests as these of Boaz and his servants, if they are offered up to God in the name of Christ, meet with a gracious audience, when the most ostentatious devotions of the formalist are despised and abhorred.

LECTURE VII.

BOAZ SPEAKS KINDLY TO RUTH IN THE HARVEST FIELD.

CHAPTER ii. 5-14.

Verse 5.—*Then said Boaz unto his servant that was set over the reapers, Whose damsel is this?*
A great man's house is different from an ordinary man's. There are servants in it of different stations. Boaz was a mighty man of wealth, and he had not only reapers, but a man set over the reapers. Servants commonly need the eye of a master, or of one in the place of a master, to direct their work, to stimulate industry, to prevent or to remedy dissension. Good servants will be pleased with proper superintendence, and bad servants need it.

Although Boaz had a faithful steward to govern his reapers, he went himself to the field to see how his work went on, and he was one of those happy masters whom the servants were happy to see.

When he saw the fields covered with plenty, he no doubt thought of the goodness of God, who had now visited his people, and blessed them, after nine years of famine, with fruitful seasons. But his attention was soon engaged by a beauteous stranger whom he saw employed in gleaning the ears of corn. He asked the steward who she was, not with an intention to check, but with an intention, if he found she deserved it, to give her encouragement.

Verse 6.—*And the servant that was set over the reapers answered and said, It is the Moabitish damsel that came back with Naomi out of the country of Moab.*

The first thing required in stewards is, 'that a man be found faithful' to his employer; but it is also a good property in a steward to be humane towards his lord's servants, and towards all that have any dependence upon him for employment or favours. The man that was set over the reapers of Boaz had already showed such favour to Ruth as it was the part of a steward to do; and, by his answer to his master's question concerning her, he was a means of procuring her such favour as a steward could not confer without permission. Words fitly spoken may do much good; and indicate good sense and good dispositions in the speaker.

'It is the Moabitish damsel that came with Naomi.' She was a Moabitess, but she was well entitled to all that respect which was due to the females of Israel, when she came with Naomi from the country of Moab. The Moabites were not to enter into the congregation of the Lord until the tenth generation. Yet the children of Israel, when they came out of Egypt, were taught to respect the Moabites as the children of Lot, the friend and disciple of Abraham. They had exchanged the God of their father for Chemosh, but Boaz might reasonably pity them for their unhappy apostasy, when he considered that his own people were reclaimed from many like apostasies by such extraordinary means as had not been employed with any other nation. But whatever might be thought of the degenerate race of the righteous Lot, Ruth was entitled to high praise, when she had left the gods of Moab to worship no other god but the God of Israel.

'It is the Moabitish damsel that came back with Naomi.' Boaz was related to Naomi. He knew her worth; he pitied the unhappy reverses of her fortune; and it was to be expected that he would look with a kind eye upon that Moabitish damsel who had been her son's wife, and who testified such uncommon attachment to her mother-in-law, when the relation between them seemed to be dissolved.

It appears from these words of the steward, that Boaz had heard of this Moabitish damsel that came to Bethlehem with her mother-in-law. It is not to be doubted, likewise, that he knew the poor circumstances in which they returned. Why, then, did not Boaz, before this time, visit Naomi, and endeavour to console her in her afflictions, and to alleviate them? We cannot give a positive answer to this question. We can easily say, it was not owing to want of generosity and kindness in Boaz; verse 20. Reasons might have hitherto hindered him which are not mentioned, and which there was no occasion to mention. Perhaps Boaz, though full of good intentions, might be too dilatory in executing them. He certainly would not have suffered either Naomi, or the Moabitish damsel, to be oppressed with the extremes of poverty, whilst he was able to supply their need; but good men have sometimes been too slow in executing their good intentions.

Verse 7.—*And she said, I pray you, let me glean and gather after the reapers among the sheaves: so she came, and hath continued even from the morning until now, that she tarried a little in the house.*

The steward informs his master, that the Moabitish damsel did not presume to enter the field without leave asked and obtained. Nor did he apologize to his master for granting her the liberty of gleaning. He did nothing but what the authority given him by his master warranted him to do. As it is a sin for a judge to countenance a poor man in his cause, it would be no less criminal in a steward to bestow favors upon the poor, without the consent of his master expressed or understood. But this steward knew that Boaz did not wish any poor person to be excluded from gleaning in his fields, and least of all a poor stranger from the land of Moab, who had showed so strong an attachment to Naomi, and to Naomi's God.

'She hath continued from the morning even until now, that she tarried a little in the house.' The steward commends her industry in these words. She had continued busy at her work from the morning, till the heat, or some other cause, constrained her for a little to take shelter in a house or shed, where it is probable the reapers rested at noon. The heat of the weather in the land of Israel would render it almost impossible to continue in harvest from morning to night, exposed, without a shelter, to the beams of the sun. Ruth had spent no more time under covert, than was absolutely necessary for enabling her to return to her labours. Some of the most ancient translations differ from our copies of the Bible, and say that she had continued all day at her labour, without returning to her house, or enjoying any rest. She was a true daughter of Jacob, who was so careful of the flocks committed to him, that, without repining, he suffered himself to be consumed in the daytime by the heat, and in the night to be pierced by the chilling frosts.

'It is vain to rise up early and sit up late, to eat the bread of sorrows.' We ought to consult our health in carrying on our labours, and not to make them a burden too heavy for us to bear. When covetous desires of gain induce men to overwork their powers, they sacrifice their health to Mammon, whom they have chosen for their God. But Ruth was labouring for her mother as well as herself. Her love to Naomi would give her spirits and strength to endure the heat of the climate. A reaper or a gleaner in the field, sustaining toil or inclement weather to support her aged parent, is worthy of more praise than a victorious general, who exposes himself to all the perils of battle, if his chief view is to gather laurels for himself.

Verse 8.—*Then said Boaz unto Ruth, Hearest thou not, my daughter? Go not to glean in another field, neither go from hence, but abide here fast by my maidens.*

Boaz was glad to meet with the Moabitish damsel that came with Naomi. He had already, we may presume, intended to show her the kindness of God; and now, when Providence brought her into his presence, he addresses her in the language of kindness, 'Hear me, my daughter.' Ruth had left her father and her mother. She lost nothing. Naomi was become her mother, and Boaz now speaks to her and treats her as a father. We may, without hesitation, leave those relations that are dearest and kindest to us for God. 'He that leaveth father or mother for me,' says Christ, 'shall receive an hundred fold more in this world, fathers and mothers, brethren and sisters.' That loss must be great indeed which infinite Goodness cannot compensate.

Go not to glean in another field, neither go from hence. This prohibition is full of love. The expression signifies, that Boaz would take it highly amiss if she went to glean in any other field but his own. But it implies a promise, that she should find it her interest to glean in his field. The tenderest love may be expressed in the language of command, of prohibition, or even of threatening. Many of God's commandments and prohibitions are expressions of his excellent loving-kindness. What can be more full of grace than the first commandment of the moral law, 'Thou shalt have no other gods before me?' or Hosea's comment upon it, 'I am the Lord thy God from the land of Egypt; and thou shalt know no God but me, for there is no Saviour besides me?' When God commands us to trust in himself alone, and threatens us with his displeasure if we place our confidence any where else, does he not tell us that we shall find it our highest interest to trust in him?

Abide fast by my maidens. Young women, if they are wise, will ordinarily choose their companions from amongst their own sex. Ruth was a modest woman, and would be glad to find a virtuous woman with whom she might associate in the field of Boaz. There were men employed with them in the labours of the harvest, but Ruth had nothing to apprehend either from the male or female servants of this good man, who ruled his family in the fear the Lord.

Verse 9.—*Let thine eyes be on the field that they do reap, and go thou after them; have I not charged the young men that they shall not touch thee? and when thou art athirst, go unto the vessels and drink of that which the young men have drawn.*

Whilst Ruth was to keep by the young women, and go after them, she had no reason to dread the young men. Young men, in any station of life, are often, by their rudeness or licentiousness, the terror of modest young women; but Boaz would allow of no indecency in words or conversation amongst his servants. A good man will not only refrain from doing or speaking evil, but will restrain all that depend on him from licentious or rude behaviour. Paul will have none to be admitted to the office of elders in the church, who do not rule well their own houses. Not that it is a duty incumbent on elders only, to keep their families in due subjection, but because elders must be exemplary in every thing worthy of praise.

We are all accountable for those evils which it was in our power to have prevented.

Have not I charged the young men? says Boaz to Ruth. He knew the heart of a stranger. She might think that she stood exposed, as a sojourner from Moab, to those insults to which a stranger from Israel might be exposed in her own country. 'We have heard of the pride of Moab. He is exceeding proud;' and, as wickedness proceedeth from the wicked, insolence and abusive treatment may be expected from the proud. But if Ruth had any fears of this kind, Boaz puts an end to them. It is an office of humanity to comfort those that are cast down, and to dispel every uneasy apprehension from the modest and timorous. A man of sensibility knows, in some measure, what is passing within the breast of his poor neighbour; and will, by his words, uphold him that is falling, and confirm the feeble knees.

We do not live in a country so fruitful as the land of Israel. Our fields are not like the fields of Bethlehem or Ephratah, which received their names from the fruitfulness of the soil. Yet every place has its advantages, as well as its disadvantages. We are better stored with water than that land which flowed with milk and honey. It was no small favour to Ruth, that Boaz invited her, whenever she was thirsty, to go and drink of the water which his young men had drawn. Thirst would sometimes be almost intolerable to labourers in the field under the scorching heat of the sun in Palestine. When Ruth felt the heat of noon, she might say, as one of her descendants did on another occasion, 'O that one would give me to drink of the water of the well of Bethlehem!' But her wishes are anticipated. Her considerate friend gives her a general invitation to drink, whenever she found it necessary, of the water provided for his own servants; or, if they had any thing better than water to quench their thirst, she was welcome to a share.

Verse 10.—*Then she fell on her face, and bowed herself to the ground, and said unto him; Why have I found grace in thine eyes, that thou shouldst take knowledge of me, seeing I am a stranger?*

What had Boaz done for Ruth that she falls down on her

knees, and thanks him for his favours in language expressive of such warm gratitude? He had assured her of his protection. He had invited her to gather the gleanings of his corn, and to drink of his water. What would she have said had he invited her to partake, as he afterwards did, of all his wealth? And what thanks do we give to Him who invites us to come and buy wine and milk from him, without money and without price? Boaz made Ruth welcome to drink of the water of one of the wells of Bethlehem. Jesus says, 'If thou knewest the gift of God, and who it is that saith unto thee, Give me to drink, thou wouldst ask, and he would give thee living water; the water of which when a man drinks he shall thirst no more.'

Ruth thought herself greatly honoured by the attentions of Boaz. She was a stranger and foreigner, an alien to the commonwealth of Israel, and did not reckon herself entitled to any kindness from the people of the Lord. Perhaps she did not yet know how kindly the laws of Israel required them to treat strangers. The children of Israel had themselves been strangers for many generations in the land of Egypt; and were required to show that kindness to strangers which they would have gladly received from the people amongst whom they sojourned. Boaz, above all other Israelites at that time, might be expected to treat foreign women with favour; for his own mother had been not only a stranger, but one of the accursed nation of Canaan; and yet there was not an Israelitess entitled to more respect, for she was famous, and deserved to be famous to all generations, both for her faith and her good works.

Most men and women entertain too high notions of themselves, because they think with complacency on those qualities that seem to entitle them to consideration, but overlook those which diminish their own value. Ruth almost forgot her own virtues. She thought she had done no more than it was her duty to do, if she did so much, when she attended Naomi into the land of Israel: but she remembered that she was a stranger; that she had been hitherto a worshiper of strange gods, and might have continued so till the end of her life, if God had not sent some of his people to guide her feet into the way of truth.

Remembering what she had been, she received ordinary favours with a warm sense of gratitude. The humble are always disposed to be thankful, and therefore they are always happy. When men are swelled with such a sense of their own merit that they think themselves entitled to every thing, they will never be pleased. If you give them small presents, they will think you defraud them of their due, because you do not give them rich presents; if you give them rich presents, they think that they are entitled to all that they have received, and much more. But you can scarcely displease the humble man, because he thinks any thing better than he deserves. He enjoys peace in his own bosom, because his expectations are seldom disappointed. He acquires the good-will of all around him, because he is thankful for the smallest favours, and not dissatisfied when he meets with none.

Verse 11.—*And Boaz answered and said unto her, It hath fully been showed me, all that thou hast done unto thy mother-in-law since the death of thine husband; and how thou hast left thy father and thy mother, and the land of thy nativity, and art come unto a people which thou knewest not heretofore.*

'Let another praise thee, and not thyself.' Ruth showed no disposition to praise herself. She did not claim a right to glean from what she had done for Naomi, but wondered that such kindness should be showed by Boaz to her who was a stranger; and she hears the voice of praise from the mouth of one whose commendations were a very great honour. No saying was oftener in the mouth of Jesus than this, 'He that exalteth himself shall be abased, and he that humbleth himself shall be exalted.'

Nothing can be meaner than flattery addressed either to the rich or poor, but it may frequently be proper to praise those who deserve to be praised. Our Lord praises his disciples, when he tells them that they were the men who had continued with him in his temptations. Paul often commends the Christians to whom he wrote his epistles, although he never failed to remind them that they were indebted to the grace of God for all that was worthy of praise in their conduct or temper. Boaz commended Ruth, not to inspire her with vanity, but to animate her resolution, to comfort her dejected spirit, and to encourage her to use those freedoms which he wished her to use with himself, and with other Israelites.

'It hath been fully made known to me what thou hast done to thy mother-in-law.' Ruth little expected that her behaviour would be reported to any great man in the land of Israel. She did no more than she apprehended to be her duty to such a kind and pious mother-in-law. If her behaviour pleased God, and her own conscience, and Naomi, she was well satisfied, although no other person ever heard of it. As some men's sins are open, going before-hand unto judgment, so are the good works of others. 'Take heed,' says our Lord, 'of the leaven of the Pharisees, which is hypocrisy; for there is nothing covered that shall not be revealed, nor hid that shall not be known.' Although we are not to do our works to be seen or to be reported by men, yet we ought to provide things honest in the sight of all men that see, or that may hear of, our behaviour. Our works will all be known at the last day, and more of them, perhaps, than we think, before the last day. Let us beware of any thing in private, that would dishonour our name and our profession if it were known to the world. Ruth found, at this conference with Boaz, the truth of what one of her descendants teaches us, that 'a good name is better than precious ointment, and loving favour better than silver and gold.'

It hath been fully showed me all that thou hast done unto thy mother-in-law since the death of thy husband. Many who are connected by affinity, think that no more duties remain to be performed, when the bond of connection is broken by the death of that husband or wife on whom the relation depended. Naomi and Ruth were of a different spirit. Naomi never could forget Ruth's kindness to her son. Ruth testified her regard to the memory of her deceased husband, by her attentions to his mother. She not only did 'good, and not evil,' to her husband, 'all the days of his life,' but she did all the good she could to him when he was dead, by performing those services to his mother which he would gladly have performed, if he had been still alive. This part of her behaviour endeared her to Boaz. He was charmed with the amiable manners of Ruth, and thought himself highly indebted to her for her goodness to the mother of his friend Mahlon. The apostle John testified his affection to his departed Lord, by taking his mother to his own house, and treating her as a mother. There are kindnesses due to the dead as well as to the living; and in these, a generous spirit will be careful not to fail.

Verse 12.—*The Lord recompense thy work, and a full reward be given thee of the Lord God of Israel, under whose wings thou art come to trust!*

Ruth's kind and good behaviour to her mother-in-law deserved much praise, but there was another part of her behaviour entitled to still higher commendation. She came to trust under the wings of the Lord God of Israel. Her humanity was consecrated by piety; her kindness to her friends was sanctified by her faith in God. Those labours of love are truly acceptable to God, which proceed from a regard to his own name; Heb. vi. 10.

The living God was exhibited to the faith of his ancient people, as the God who dwelt between the cherubim that spread their wings over the mercy-seat, the throne of his grace. It was perhaps in allusion to this symbol of God's residence amongst his people, that those who sought protection from him were said to trust under the shadow of his wings. 'He that dwelleth in the secret place of the Most High, shall abide under the shadow of the Almighty. His feathers shall cover thee; under his wings shalt thou trust; his faithfulness shall be thy shield and buckler.'

By a figure less elevated, but not less significant and consolatory, our Lord teaches us the happiness of them that trust in Him, and the riches of his own grace and condescension. 'How often would I have gathered thee, as a hen gathereth her chickens under her wings!'

Ruth came to trust under the wings of the Lord God of Israel. She had heard of him in her own country, and left it to dwell in another where he was well known, and where he gave his people signal proofs of his protection. The name of the Lord was so dear to her, that she left her kindred, and her father's house, to enjoy a place amongst his people. How inexcusable are we, if we do not make the Lord our refuge, when we were born in a land blessed with the knowledge of him, baptised in his name, and trained up to know and serve him! If a Moabitess came to trust under the wings of the Lord God of Israel, how shameful was it in Israelites not to know and trust the God by whose name they were called! And 'is he the God of the Jews only? is he not the God of the Gentiles also,' who justifies the uncircumcision through the same faith in Christ by which he justified the circumcision?

The Lord recompense thy work, and a full reward be given thee of the Lord God of Israel! The Lord God of Israel is the God and Father of our Lord Jesus Christ, in whom he is well pleased. Through him he accepts our persons; through him he accepts our works, and records them with testimonies of his favour worthy of his rich grace. Our best works have no merit in them. We are but unprofitable servants when we have done all that is commanded us; but we serve a liberal Master, who takes pleasure in uprightness, and beholds our meanest endeavours to serve him with a pleasant countenance.

Those acts of kindness which we perform to men with no higher views than their or our own advantage, cannot be accepted of God as services to himself. When no regard is entertained for His will and his glory, there is an essential defect in our performances. If men are the highest object of our regard in the good things we do, from men let us expect our reward; but God is not unrighteous, to forget our works and labours of love done for the name of Christ. He will reward them above what we can ask or think.

Boaz prays to God for the gracious reward of her works of love, and by this prayer encourages her to persevere in that confidence which was to be crowned with a full recompense. 'Cast not away your confidence,' says Paul, 'which hath great recompense of reward.' To have respect to the recompense of reward, was not unworthy of the faith of Moses, or even of the faith of Christ himself, 'who, for the joy that was set before him, endured the cross, despising the shame.'

'It is our desire,' says the apostle, 'that whether present or absent, we may be accepted of him.' And we desire not only that our own works, but that the good works of our friends and brethren, may be rewarded. Boaz intended to reward the work of Ruth by his own generous treatment of her, but great as his power was, her good works went beyond it. The rewards that the richest and greatest men can confer for services done to themselves or to their friends, are not to be compared with the gracious rewards bestowed by God on the meanest of his servants, for the meanest service. 'Whosoever,' says our Lord Jesus Christ, 'bestows but a cup of water on a disciple in the name of a disciple, shall in no wise lose his reward.'

Verse 13.—*Then she said, Let me find favour in thy sight, my lord; for that thou hast comforted me, and for that thou hast spoken friendly unto thine handmaid, though I be not like unto one of thine handmaidens.*

Ruth was so far from thinking herself entitled to any recompense from God, that she thought it an act of unmerited goodness in Boaz to take any notice of her. The Lord hath respect to the lowly, and he usually gives them favour in the sight of men also. Ruth did not reckon herself like one of the handmaidens of Boaz, and Boaz thought her worthy of his bed. Happy are they who are disposed to think their neighbours better than themselves. They are free from those stings of discontent and envy which torture the hearts of the vain and proud. They preserve themselves from those variances and strifes which are the bane of social life. They endear themselves to those with whom they are connected in society. They procure many favours and kindnesses which are doubly pleasant to them, because they did not think themselves entitled to them. 'By humility, and the fear of the Lord, are riches, and honour, and life.'

'Let me find grace in thy sight, my lord; for that thou hast comforted me, and hast spoken friendly unto thine handmaid.' Pleasant words are like an honey-comb, sweet to the soul. Those words which at once indicate friendship and nourish piety, are doubly pleasant. Boaz had not only expressed his affection and esteem to Ruth, but raised her views to the Lord God of Israel, from whom he encouraged her to expect her reward. His words were no less valued by her than his gifts. Words are cheap to ourselves, and they may be very precious to those to whom they are addressed, especially to those who need our sympathy. Job, by his words, instructed many, and strengthened the weak hands. Let us follow his example; but remember that we ought to do it, not only in the words of our mouth, but in the temper of our minds and in the works of our hands. We must 'love, not in word and in tongue only, but in deed and in truth.' Such was the love of Boaz to Ruth. Such is the love of all the followers of Him who loved us and gave himself for us.

Verse 14.—*And Boaz said unto her, At meal-time come thou hither, and eat of the bread, and dip thy morsel in the vinegar. And she sat beside the reapers; and he reached her parched corn, and she did eat, and was sufficed, and left.*

All that Ruth expected or requested, was leave to glean; but she was invited, when she was labouring for herself, to eat of the master's bread, and to dip her morsel in the vinegar provided for the reapers. In the house of Boaz, there was bread enough, and to spare. His reapers were not so stinted in their provision, as to have nothing to afford to an unexpected visitant. Boaz was none of those men who say, 'Shall I take my bread and my water, which I have provided for my shearers,' or my bread and vinegar which I have provided for my reapers, and give them to a stranger? He had a large estate, and a large heart. He truly enjoyed the liberalities of Providence, because he took pleasure in distributing what God had given him.

Boaz was not ashamed to eat his morsel with his reapers. He made them happy in his company, and himself happy, by diffusing cheerfulness around him. We must not judge of Boaz by those laws and customs of society, which regulate the behaviour of such as do not wish to appear singular amongst ourselves.

He gave to Ruth of the parched corn with his own hands, and she did eat and was sufficed. Ruth wondered at his goodness to her who was a stranger, and not like one of his own handmaidens; but she was not happier in receiving than Boaz in giving, since our Lord spake truth when he said, 'It is more blessed to give than to receive.'

Let us do good to all men, especially to them that are of the household of faith, and most of all to those of the household of faith who stand in greatest need of our kindness, to whom we are bound by particular connections to show our friendship, and to those who are most disposed to be thankful to God and man for the favours they receive. At the day of judgment we will find, that every office of love performed to the meanest of the followers of Christ, has been performed to himself.

LECTURE VIII.

BOAZ' DIRECTIONS TO HIS REAPERS TO TREAT RUTH KINDLY—HER SUCCESS IN GLEANING, &C.

CHAPTER II. 15—23.

Verse 15.—*And when she was risen up to glean, Boaz commanded his young men, saying, Let her glean, even among the sheaves, and reproach her not.*

'In the sweat of thy face,' said God to fallen man, 'thou shalt eat bread.' For our sins we must toil; but, through the mercy of God, our toil is sweetened by intervals of rest, and of refreshment from food and sleep. Ruth eats her meal, and then rises to glean till the evening, when she goes home to enjoy the rest and sleep of the night, made doubly pleasant to her by the labours of the day. Let not labourers complain; but let them confess, that the toils they endure are too well deserved; and let them bless God that their days do not pass on in an uninterrupted labour.

'She rose up to glean.' In the morning she came with, perhaps, an anxious mind to the field, uncertain what reception she might meet with, either from the master of the field, or from his servants. She rose to her new labours with pleasure, when she found herself not only allowed to glean, but commended for her virtuous conduct, and recommended to the mercy of the God whom she came to serve, by the prayers of such a venerable man as Boaz. Let us hold the path of duty, whatever it is. If it is attended with toils and anxieties, comforts will spring up when we are not expecting them, to solace our labors.

Boaz did every thing that he promised to Ruth, and more than he promised. He gave a charge to his young men to suffer her to glean among the sheaves, and forbade them to reproach her for her country, her poverty, her mean occupation; or to insinuate any suspicions of her honesty, whilst she was gleaning among the sheaves.

The permission of gleaning among the sheaves would not have been granted to Ruth, if her character had not raised her above suspicion. Are you poor? take care to avoid every appearance of dishonesty. A good character is the estate of the poor. A reputation for honesty will procure you employment and bread. Are you rich? do not causelessly suspect the poor, that you may not deprive them of that which is no less valuable to them than to yourselves—a good name. It is of more importance to them than to you, because their subsistence depends upon it. Why should you deprive your indigent brother of his only resource?

Reproach her not, said Boaz to his servants. Ill-taught servants are too often disposed to sport with the feelings or the character of strangers, or of their own indigent countrymen. Why should they who are themselves in a dependent condition, add to the distress of those who are still lower in condition than themselves? It affords them amusement, perhaps, to make those uneasy who cannot avenge themselves; but would it not give them more pleasure to alleviate distress by words of kindness, than to aggravate it by scorn and petulance? Is it more pleasant to us to make our poor neighbours unhappy, than to gladden their hearts? How then dwelleth the love of God in us?

Verse 16.—*And let fall also some of the handfuls of purpose for her, and leave them, that she may glean them, and rebuke her not.*

Why did not the good man rather make her a present at once out of his floor and wine-press, than order handfuls of barley to be dropt for her gleaning? He delighted to behold her industry, and wished to encourage it. Charity, wisely directed, will not tempt the poor to be idle. Habitual idleness is not consistent either with virtue or happiness.

'Leave handfuls on purpose for her.' The servants of Boaz could not have left handfuls to be gleaned by the poorest person in the country, without dishonesty, unless their master had commanded them. When they received commandment, it would have been dishonest not to have done it. The Lord, who hates robbery for burnt-offering, will not allow servants in great houses to give away what is not theirs to the poor. They must have the permission of their masters or mistresses to do good to the poor, unless they do it at their own expense; and, having received this permission, it would be injurious both to the poor and to their masters, to withhold what is allotted to those who need.

And rebuke her not. Boaz was very careful to prevent any insult from being offered to the virtuous stranger. He no doubt knew, that masters were in some degree accountable for the conduct of their servants, and that they shared in the guilt of those faults which they did not care to prevent or to correct.

Rebuke her not, as if she used too much freedom. Wound not her feelings, by reproaches of that poverty which I wish to relieve. God gives liberally, and upbraids not. Let us be followers of him as dear children.

Verse 17.—*So she gleaned in the field until even, and beat out that she had gleaned; and it was about an ephah of barley.*

'Man goeth forth to his labour, until the evening.' The day is the season of labour, and the night of repose for our race; except that part of mankind who choose rather to follow the example of the beasts of prey, whose season of action and enjoyment is the night, because their works must be in the dark.

When you are fatigued with the labours of the day, consider that the night is not far distant, when you may hope to enjoy that delicious sleep, which is almost a recompense for your toils. Idle men, though they feed upon dainties, toss upon their beds from night till morning; but 'the sleep of the labouring man is sweet, whether he eat little or much.' Ruth, no doubt, longed to see Naomi after her conversation with Boaz, that she might gladden the heart of her beloved mother, and pour her own grateful sensations into her bosom. But there is a time for going forth to labour, and a time for returning from labour; and the wise will endeavour to do every thing in its proper season. Their reason, and not the impulse of the moment, will regulate their hours.

'In the evening, she beat out that she had gleaned, and it was about an ephah of barley;' about a firlot of our measure.* The Lord blessed her industry, by disposing Boaz to show kindness to her. Labourers are not ordinarily to expect such uncommon interpositions of Providence in their favour; but when they are able, by their industry, to procure the necessaries, and a few of the comforts of life for themselves, and for their beloved relations, it will be owing to their own thankless dispositions if they are not happy. If riches were necessary to happiness, the Almighty must have doomed to misery the greatest part of mankind. But we are the makers of our own misery, when we prescribe to the Most High what he shall do for us.

Verse 18.—*And she took it up, and went into the city; and her mother-in-law saw what she had gleaned: and she brought forth, and gave to her that she had reserved after she was sufficed.*

It is no less necessary to be careful of the fruit of our labours, than to labour with diligence. Christ himself, who could multiply bread at his pleasure, commanded the fragments of the barley loaves and fishes to be gathered up, that nothing might be lost. 'In all labour there is profit,' says the wise man; yet there are some that 'labour for the wind.' They lose what they have wrought, because they suffer it, through their carelessness, to slip through their fingers. This folly, however, is much less frequent in things relating to the body, than in those which relate to the soul. There is a greater number of persons who deserve reprehension for immoderate solicitude to secure their property, than of that slothful generation who 'will not be at the trouble of roasting what they have taken in hunting,' or of carrying home what they have reaped in the fields. Yet some need admonition to manage their worldly affairs with discretion; but it is far more needful to be careful that we 'lose none of those things which we

---

* An ephah contained three pecks and three pints.—*Calmet*

have wrought' in the service of God, for the benefit of our souls, 'but that we receive a full reward.'

Her mother-in-law saw, and saw with joy, *what she had gleaned.* Doubtless, it was a feast to the heart of Ruth to observe the pleasure which brightened Naomi's countenance, when she saw how God had blessed her industry. Young persons! be industrious, frugal, virtuous, if you desire to give pleasure to the father that begat you, and to her that bare you. In their declining years they need such comfort. If you withhold it, the time will come when the pain which you gave them will be doubled to yourselves.

And she brought forth, and gave to her that she had reserved after she was sufficed. When Boaz gave her a liberal portion of the food prepared for himself and his reapers, it was not expected that what she left should be returned, but it was to be carried home for future use; and now she brought it forth for the use of Naomi, between whom and Ruth every thing was common. The poor stranger had now, by the blessing of God, and the kindness of Boaz, bread enough and to spare. Happy changes can soon be effected by the good providence of God, in that condition which appeared forlorn. 'The Lord giveth food to the hungry,' and he gives it in such quantities, and of such a kind, and in such ways as he pleases. 'Those who trust in Him, and do good, shall dwell in the land, and verily they shall be fed.'

Verse 19.—*And her mother-in-law said unto her, Where hast thou gleaned to day? and where wroughtest thou? blessed be he that did take knowledge of thee! And she showed her mother-in-law with whom she had wrought, and said, The man's name with whom I wrought to-day is Boaz.*

The friendly converse of those members of a family, whose hearts are knit together in love, affords a pleasure which sweetens a dinner of green herbs, and renders it more delicious to the taste, than 'a stalled ox, where love is wanting.' Naomi asks of Ruth where she had wrought, that she might have the pleasure of knowing who the friendly man was that had taken knowledge of her beloved daughter. Ruth had no reason to conceal that kindness which had been showed her beyond her expectation. They enjoyed the feast of friendship, and the flow of soul, with a keener relish than the gayest and wealthiest domestic circle in Bethlehem.

Blessed be he that did take knowledge of thee! Naomi desired to know where Ruth had wrought, that she might know her benefactor, and make such recompenses to him as were in her power, by prayer to God on his behalf. Before she knows his name, she prays for blessings to him. Her heart overflowed with gratitude, and out of the abundance of her heart her mouth spake. This is one reason why we ought to do good to those especially, who are of the household of faith. They are all praying persons, and their prayers are heard by the God who loves them. 'He is a prophet,' said God to Abimelech, concerning Abraham, 'he is a prophet, and he shall pray for thee.' Abimelech thought his presents well bestowed upon a man who could pray for him with acceptance. But, through the name of Christ, all believers, though they are not prophets, have confidence towards God; 'for whatsoever,' says our Redeemer, 'ye ask in my name, I will do it for you.'

Naomi was told that the man's name was Boaz, and immediately called to mind what kindnesses her family had received from him in times past:

Verse 20.—*And Naomi said unto her daughter-in-law, Blessed be he of the Lord! who hath not left off his kindness to the living and to the dead. And Naomi said unto her, The man is near of kin unto us, one of our next kinsmen.*

Blessed be he of the Lord! Naomi had already prayed for a blessing upon him, without knowing who he was; and she prays again for a blessing to him from the Lord, when his name was mentioned. It put her in mind of former favours, which she had not forgotten, although her distresses, engrossing her mind, had hindered her from thinking of them. A grateful heart will never forget kindnesses received from men; far less will a truly thankful soul forget the former loving-kindnesses of the Lord. 'Bless the Lord, O my soul; forget not any of his benefits!'

He hath not left off his kindness to the living and to the dead. He had been a steady friend to Elimelech and Mahlon, and he still continued a firm friend to Elimelech's widow, to the mother and relict of Mahlon. Nothing is more common in the world than fickleness in friendship; but that man only deserves the name of a friend, who loveth at all times, in adversity as well as in prosperity, in death as well as in life. We sin against God, as well as against men, when we causelessly forsake our own or our father's friend. All our professions and promises are marked in His book.

One great cause of our grief for the death of our friends is, that they are removed beyond the reach of our kindness. But they are not wholly incapable of receiving testimonies of our friendship, if they have left beloved relations behind them, to whom we can show our regard. David could recompense Jonathan's kindness to himself, when his generous friend was in heaven with the angels of God. Although our Lord left our world almost eighteen hundred years ago, we can still testify our love to Him by our kindness to his brethren and sisters on earth.

'Blessed be he of the Lord; for he hath not left off his kindness to the living and to the dead.' Naomi could not reward Boaz, but she knew who could and would reward every act of kindness done to her. Her prayers to God for Boaz were worth more than all that it was either in his heart or in his power to do for her.

And Naomi said, The man is near of kin unto us, one of our next kinsmen. The relation in which Boaz stood to Mahlon was probably one of the reasons that induced him to be so kind to Ruth. God hath made of one blood all nations of men, and therefore we ought to look upon all human creatures as our brethren and sisters, the children of the same common progenitors, by the ordination of their common Creator. But those who are related to us by immediate parents, or by progenitors not far removed from us, have a special claim to our kindness. 'A brother is born for adversity.'

Yet the poor ought not to make themselves burdensome or troublesome to their prosperous relations. Naomi sought nothing from Boaz, and, till this time, does not seem to have expected new favours from him. He had formerly been kind, and she did not wish to tax his goodness by applications for new favours. God is never weary of conferring his blessings. Those petitioners are most welcome to him that come most frequently, and ask most importunately. But the richest of men may soon be impoverished, and the most bountiful may soon be wearied, by giving.

Paul thanked God in the behalf of the Philippian Christians, that their care of him had flourished afresh. Naomi considers it as a token for good, that the care of Boaz for her family was now again flourishing and bringing forth fruit. With joy she informs Ruth, that the man whose kindness so deeply affected her, was a near relation. What might they not expect from a near relation so rich and so kind? What may we not expect from him who, being in the form of God, made himself our near kinsman, that he might redeem us to God?

Verse 21.—*And Ruth, the Moabitess, said, He said unto me also, Thou shalt keep fast by my young men, until they have ended all my harvest.*

Grateful souls take pleasure in hearing and in speaking of their benefactors, and of the favours which have been done or promised them. How constantly ought we to remember, and how ready should we be to speak of, the mercies of God! He hath done great things for us, and giveth us every encouragement to hope that he will still grant us all that is good for us.

Verse 22.—*And Naomi said unto Ruth, her daughter-in-law, It is good, my daughter, that thou go out with his maidens, that they meet thee not in any other field.*

Naomi asked Ruth where she had been, and desired particular information of the treatment she had met with, that she might give her such advice as might be useful for the direction of her future conduct. Old persons may be expected to have collected, by reflection and experience, more wisdom than the young, and should be ready to communicate instruction to those that need it. An ostentatious display of their acquirements, where it can be of no use, or where there is no disposition to profit by them, would only expose them to contempt. But they hide their talents in a napkin if they do not make those wiser by what they know, who are disposed to learn, and those especially whom divine Providence hath placed under their care. Young persons, on their side, should be ever ready to listen to the instructions of the aged, and especially of aged parents, or relations that stand in the place of parents. Ruth profited much by the instructions and advices of Naomi; and it was one of the great comforts of Naomi's declining years, that she could be useful to Ruth, by giving her the counsels of experience. Let the young have their hands prepared for the service of the old; and the old may recompense them abundantly by the words of their mouths. Happy would it have been for Rehoboam, and for all his people, had he known what respect is due to the wise counsels of the aged. What numbers of young persons take rash steps in the journey of life, which cannot be retraced, because they rather choose to follow the impulse of their own passions, than to ask and follow the advices of those who brought them into the world!

It is good, my daughter, that thou go out with his maidens. Ruth had said that Boaz invited her to keep fast by his young men. Naomi perhaps meant to insinuate in this advice, that, while she accepted the invitation, she ought to consider the maidens as her best companions. She was not bound to avoid all intercourse with the young men. Boaz had taken care that none of them should behave rudely to her; but her chosen companions were to be of her own sex. Ruth needed little admonition on this subject. Boaz observes, to her praise, that she had not followed young men, whether poor or rich.

'It is good that thou go forth with his maidens,' since he invites thee to glean in his fields. Although Naomi would not be troublesome to her relations, nor solicit favours from them when necessity did not compel her, she was not so high-minded as to reject a favour that was offered. Poor persons, who have seen better days, are sometimes too nice and scrupulous in receiving obligations. It is good to be as independent in the world as our circumstances will allow; but to be absolutely independent is impossible: and to have a spirit above the acceptance of favours, when our circumstances render the acceptance of them needful, is a proud resistance of our spirits to that Providence which manages our concerns, and which manages them with wisdom and kindness when it lays our pride in the dust.

That they meet thee not in any other field. If they had met Ruth in any other field, their master might have been offended to find that his bounty was undervalued, or his sincerity distrusted, or that his kinswoman chose rather to receive obligations from another than from himself. A generous man takes pleasure in being trusted. Nothing will more displease him than want of confidence in his kindness and professions.

If we ought to express our gratitude to earthly benefactors, by showing a readiness to be obliged to them, and a firm confidence in their favour, how readily ought we to accept of the precious gifts of God, and how ungrateful is it to act as if His gracious professions and promises were unworthy of our trust! Is not the saying, that 'Christ Jesus came into the world, a faithful saying, and worthy of all acceptation?' Why then does any of us refuse with thankfulness to receive his unspeakable gift? Or why should we be found vainly searching amongst creatures for what is to be found only in God?

Verse 23.—*So she kept fast by the maidens of Boaz, to glean unto the end of barley harvest and of wheat harvest, and dwelt with her mother-in-law.*

Her mother-in-law's word was a law to her. According to her advice, she gleaned in the field of Boaz, and associated with his maidens. Obedience to parents, is obedience to Him who says, 'Honour thy father and thy mother.' We will, however, soon have occasion to observe, that there are limits to be set to this obedience. God must in all things be obeyed. The commandments and counsels of parents are to be followed, as far as they do not interfere with the will of God.

Ruth not only entered upon a course of useful, though humble industry, but she persisted in it. She did not weary of her mean occupation, but persisted in gleaning till the end both of barley and of wheat harvest. Her relation to Boaz did not inspire her with vain conceits that she was entitled to greater favour from him than a permission to glean after his reapers. Such aspiring thoughts would have greatly impaired, or destroyed at once, her virtues, her reputation, and her happiness. She was well content with her present low condition, and thankful for the small favours that were done her, and waited patiently on that God, under the shadow of whose wings she came to trust; and, in his own time, he exalted her to possess the fields which she now gleaned.

And dwelt with her mother-in-law. 'Changes and war are against me,' said Job. This language is not uncommon with those who have lost their nearest relations and most beloved friends. But few have so much reason to speak this language as that patient sufferer. Changes in his condition robbed him of every comfort. Naomi was now deprived of her husband and her two sons. Ruth was deprived of her husband. But each of them had a kind and pleasant friend left, in one another. Their religious converse, their kind attentions to one another's comfort, compensated, in a great measure, the loss of other friends. They were not so rich as they had once been; but the goodness of Providence to them in their destitute circumstances, would probably give them more pleasure, than the rich taste in their abundance. They loved one another, and dwelt together in peace and unity. And where virtuous love is found, pleasure is not absent; for 'better is a dinner of green herbs where love is, than a stalled ox and hatred therewith.'

Many are reduced to a more solitary condition than Naomi. Deprived of their best friends, they have none else to supply their place, or none from whom they can derive much comfort. But let them not repine at the providence of God, whose ways are always mercy and truth to them that love him. Although you should be forsaken by father and mother, by wife and children, remember that there is a Friend who cannot be lost. Job's children were all destroyed. He had one near relation left, whose behaviour gave him pain instead of pleasure. But his spirit was not crushed by his afflictions; for he knew that his Redeemer still lived. Seek fellowship with the Father, and with His Son, Jesus Christ, and your joy shall be full: 1 John i. 3, 4: John xiv. 20, 21.

LECTURE IX.

RUTH, AT THE INSTIGATION OF NAOMI, LAYS HERSELF DOWN AT THE FEET OF BOAZ, AND REQUESTS HIM TO CAST HIS SKIRT OVER HER.

CHAPTER III. 1–9.

Verse 1.—*Then Naomi, her mother-in-law, said unto her, My daughter; shall I not seek rest for thee, that it may be well with thee?*

Naomi was happy to find Ruth so well satisfied with her mean condition, but earnestly desired to have her placed in more comfortable circumstances. She was herself an old woman, and wished not, at her departure from this world, to leave her daughter-in-law friendless. Her thoughts were often employed in consulting how she might best promote and secure the happiness of such a beloved friend. She had now, no doubt, given up all thought of much earthly comfort to herself, except what she found in the love of Ruth. But she was full of solicitude for her daughter-in-law, that she might have no temptation to regret the sacrifice which she had made to herself and to her religion, of the pleasures of her father's house.

Shall I not seek rest for thee, my daughter? It is our common practice to insist upon the duties owing to us from our friends, and not to give ourselves much trouble about what we owe to them. There are some parents so foolish as to think that their children owe every thing to them, and that they owe nothing to their children. For this reason, they are full of complaints concerning their children's undutiful behaviour, when, if their consciences or their reason were awake, these might tell them that the fault was originally in themselves. If they had been more attentive to the happiness of their children, their children, out of grateful affection, might probably have been disposed to return the obligation.

Shall I not seek rest for thee, that it may be well with thee? For this end, Naomi wished rest for her daughter-in-law, 'that it might be well with her.' When young persons become widowers or widows, the relations of the deceased husband or wife often attend more to their interest in the deceased, than to the happiness of the survivor, although those who have left the world can receive no more benefit from them; and the best proof which they can give of their affection to the friend whom they have lost, is to show a proper attention to the happiness and comfort of the persons dearest to them whilst they were upon the earth. Naomi doubtless thought, with as much regret as other mothers do, upon her beloved son now in the grave; but she did not think it would be any advantage to his soul, or to his memory, to keep his widow unmarried. Death dissolves the marriage relation; and at the resurrection, there will be no reclaiming of husbands or wives that were left in this world; Luke xx. 35.

Naomi had no thoughts of marriage for herself, because she was too old to think of it, chap. i. 12; but she thinks of marriage for her daughter-in-law, who was not yet too old to have an husband, and to entertain the hope of children. Thus Paul, who advises persons in certain circumstances not to marry, or to renew that nuptial bond from which they are loosed, gives an opposite advice to other virgins or widows. 'The younger widows refuse,' says that apostle to Timothy. Admit them not to those offices or trusts which would render marriage inconvenient, or which would be a temptation to them to wax wanton in the unmarried state, and then to enter into marriages with such persons, or into marriages attended with such circumstances, as would bring guilt, and reproach, and danger upon them; but 'I will,' adds he, 'that the young women,' or the younger widows, 'marry, bear children, guide the house, give none occasion to the adversary to speak reproachfully.'

Naomi was not one of those old women who grudge to the younger those comforts and advantages which themselves are too old to enjoy or to relish. 'We are glad,' says Paul, 'when we are weak and ye are strong.' Thus Naomi will be glad to see her beloved daughter-in-law enjoying rest in the house of an husband, although herself was constrained by old age to live in perpetual solitude. Perhaps her daughter-in-law, when married, might find it convenient to have her mother-in-law with her; but if not, still Naomi wished her to be happily married. The comfort of her daughter-in-law was chiefly in view in the advice she gave her. And whenever any person pretends to give an advice to another, he must lay aside all considerations of himself, and have in his view nothing but the advantage of his neighbour; or, if he wishes to serve himself by his advice, let him fairly avow it, that he may preserve the consciousness of integrity. We may very honestly request a favour to ourselves, but we must not steal it by false pretences of regard to the interest of those from whom we desire it, when we have only our own in view.

Parents, in particular, ought to have solely in view the happiness of their children in those advices which they give them about entering into the marriage state. They ought to consider the happiness of their children as their own, and to choose for sons and daughters-in-law, not those persons who are most agreeable to themselves, but such as, all things considered, are most likely to render their own children happy. It is vain to hope that we shall be able to force the inclinations of our children into a similarity with our own. Gentle persuasions and serious advices may frequently be of good use. Compulsion belongs, not to a parent, but to a tyrant.

That it may be well with thee. An augmentation of happiness is that which all men and women seek in entering into the state of marriage. And marriage, contracted with due deliberation, may be reasonably expected to yield such happiness as earthly things can afford. 'It is not good,' said God, 'that the man should be alone; I will make him an help meet for him.' It is to be remembered, however, that the woman made to be an help meet for him was made in his own image, as he was made in the image of God. Both men and women have lost their integrity, and therefore married persons may expect trouble in the flesh. Thorns and briars have sprung up in all the relations and connections of life, as well as on the face of the ground. Yet the pleasure and advantages of marriage are likely to counterbalance, by many degrees, the sorrows that attend it, when the parties are equally yoked. If we are blessed with partners renewed in knowledge and holiness, after the image of our Creator, not only will our present comfort be greatly promoted, but our eternal interests likewise; and we will have reason to bless God for the happy connection, not only during the few years that we may live together upon earth, but through endless ages.

If wise persons enter into this relation that it may be well with themselves, they will consider that their partners entertained the same views. We must be over-run with selfishness, and with a foolish kind of selfishness which disappoints its own views, if we hope to receive, without endeavouring to communicate happiness. Even an Abigail could not make such a churl as Nabal happy. But half her sense and virtue might have made a man happy, whose dispositions were like her own.

Shall I not seek rest for thee, that it may be well with thee? It might serve a good purpose, if persons joined together in marriage would seriously consider these two things—whether their happiness is increased by their change of state—and whether the happiness of their partners is increased by it. If we are rather miserable than happy in this connection, there must be a great fault on one, and probably on both sides. Nor is it the less likely to be on our own side, that we are disposed to lay all the blame on the other. Most persons might find much happiness in marriage, if they uniformly persisted in endeavours to do the duty of the relation for their own part, whatever their companions in life do, and at the same time endeavoured, to the utmost of their power, to impress religious sentiments on the minds of their partners. Religion is the solid basis of morality in all its branches. 'A woman that feareth the Lord, she shall be praised,' for her conjugal and other social virtues, as well as for her piety.

Verses 2, 3, 4.—*And now is not Boaz of our kindred, with whose maidens thou wast? behold, he winnoweth barley to-night in the threshing floor. Wash thyself, therefore, and anoint thee, and put thy raiment upon thee, and get thee down to the floor; but make not thyself known unto the man, until he shall have done eating and drinking. And it shall be, when he lieth down, that thou shalt mark the place where he shall lie, and thou shalt go in, and uncover his feet and lay thee down; and he will tell thee what thou shalt do.*

Hitherto we have found nothing in Naomi's conduct that does not gain our approbation; but imperfection is the attendant of humanity in its present state, and Naomi appears, in that part of her conduct which we now consider, to have erred. Her views were good, but the means she took to accomplish them were unwise. They were, indeed, followed with success; but for the success we are to praise Boaz, or rather that gracious Providence which over-ruled ill-contrived means to accomplish its own ends. God, in his mercy, often prevents those errors in our conduct to which the darkness of our own minds would lead us, and often prevents those errors into which we fall from being attended with the pernicious consequences which would otherwise attend them.

And now, is not Boaz of our kindred, with whose maidens thou wast? A kinsman amongst us is a person with whom we reckon ourselves entitled to use some freedom; but, to understand the words of Naomi, we must remember that there were laws concerning kinsmen given to the Israelites, by which they were encouraged to expect relief from them in their distress. The kinsman was to be a redeemer to those Israelites that were in bondage. Estates sold by the poor, might be recovered by their interposition, and children might be given to the dead by the marriage of his widow with his kinsman. Naomi knew the tender affection of Boaz for his kindred, his compassion for their afflictions, his regard to the law of God. She believed that he needed only to be put in mind of the duties of a kinsman, to do every thing for Ruth that she could reasonably desire; and we are here told how she proceeded in this important business.

Behold, he winnoweth barley to-night in the threshing floor. Barley must be winnowed that it may be used; but will Boaz himself take part in such a mean employment? What should hinder Boaz from taking part in it? He lived in the days of ancient simplicity. Modern refinements and etiquette cannot give more pleasure to the fashionable gentleman, than honest industry gave to this grandson of a famous prince of the children of Judah. We do not withhold our admiration from Camillus, or Fabricius, or other famous consuls and dictators of the ancient Romans, because they held the plough with those hands which destroyed the enemies of their country.

Wash thyself, therefore, and anoint thee, and put thy raiment upon thee. Anointing the head was customary as well as washings, amongst persons of ordinary condition in the land of Israel; where they were highly expedient on account of the heat of the climate, and where they are still much practised.

And put thy raiment upon thee. Naomi does not advise Ruth to procure new clothes for the occasion, which she might have perhaps been enabled to do by the profits of her labour. Her 'adorning was not that of the putting on of apparel, but the ornament of a meek and quiet spirit.' Yet it was proper, when she went to a feast, that she should put on the best clothes in her possession. If decency of apparel is not a virtue, slovenliness is at least an approach to vice. It is our duty to treat with becoming respect our inferiors and equals, and still more our superiors, when they honour us with their kindness.

But make not thyself known unto him until he shall have done with eating and drinking. And it shall be, when he lieth down, that thou shalt mark the place where he shall lie; and thou shalt go in, and uncover his feet, and lay thee down. She was to discover nothing of her intention to Boaz when she went to the feast, but rather to avoid any particular notice, that he might entertain no suspicion of what was to follow. Concealment of intentions may be very proper, and very consistent with uprightness, in some cases. But we must beware of doing any thing that will not bear the light, or using those arts of concealment in transacting lawful affairs that may be attended with bad effects upon our character. It was perfectly consistent with uprightness in Samuel to conceal his chief intention when he came to Bethlehem to anoint David; and in Solomon, when he commanded a sword to be brought, and his guards to slay the living child about which the two harlots contended. But it was not wise or safe in Ruth to conceal her intentions from Boaz, when she came to his feast. Friendliness, and openness of dealing, is in general better policy than those arts of concealment which, if they are not evil in themselves, are often bad in their consequences.

Naomi seems to have considered Boaz and Ruth as married persons; otherwise it is scarcely conceivable what end she could propose in advising Ruth to mark where he lay, and place herself at his feet. She either did not know, or did not recollect that there was a kinsman nearer to them than Boaz, or knew that the nearest kinsman would not perform the kinsman's part to Mahlon. However good her intentions were, she greatly erred in attempting to form a connection between them in secret. Marriage transactions ought to be openly published to the world. There may be just impediments to a marriage, which neither the parties nor their witnesses know. Naomi might probably think that their ancestor Judah plainly considered Tamar as the wife of Shelah, before she was given to him. He would not have required her to be burnt when he heard of her pregnancy, if he had not considered it as the fruit of adultery. If Boaz and Ruth stood in the same relation as Shelah and Tamar, why might they not agree about living together, without any new ceremony? or, if any thing more was necessary to be done, Boaz would take the care of it upon himself, after this plain indication of Ruth's willingness to become his wife. Such were probably the thoughts of this good woman, for many even of the thoughts of the wise are vain.

Whatever apologies may be made for Naomi or Ruth, none can with any appearance of reason be made for clandestine marriages amongst ourselves. If even the wise and pious Naomi acted so unwarily, when the laws and customs of the country seemed to favour her plan, what can be said for those who wilfully violate a plain law of their country, instituted for the prevention of the most abominable crimes? What adulteries or incestuous conjunctions would be the natural consequence of the abolition of the laws requiring publicity in marriage transactions! The transgression of laws absolutely necessary for the prevention of any vice, is an attempt to remove the barriers by which it has been restrained. Important circumstances necessary to be known and attended to, appear to have been overlooked by Naomi, when she gave directions to Ruth about her marriage. If Boaz, and other friends, had been duly informed of her views, they would have secured Ruth against that danger of disgrace, or of something worse, which was evidently incurred; though God, in his mercy, prevented the mischief.

Verse 5.—*And she said unto her, All that thou sayest unto me I will do.*

Ruth, we may suppose, felt some repugnance at the thought of lying down at the feet of Boaz; but she believed her mother-in-law to be a wiser woman than herself, and better acquainted with the laws and customs of Israel. She therefore promised to comply exactly with her advice. We are pleased with her humility, her deference, and her obedience to her mother-in-law; and yet it is to be wished that she had consulted her own judgment more than she did. The holy writers often advise children to obey their parents, but their obedience must be 'in the Lord.' Faults that lean to virtue's side are still faults. As none ought to call that unclean which God hath sanctified, nothing can sanctify what is contrary to the revealed will of God.

The blame, however, if we must blame Ruth, was not so much her own as Naomi's. Let all parents, and all whose office it is to command or to advise, be careful to furnish themselves with clear views of sin and duty, that they may not cause those who pay, and should pay, a great deference to their judgment, to err out of the way of understanding. One great end of the writing of the book of Proverbs was, that we might be furnished with stores of wisdom, enabling us to give sound counsel to our neighbours. 'A man of understanding shall attain unto wise counsels;' Prov. i. 5.

Verse 6.—*And she went down unto the floor, and did according to all that her mother-in-law bade her.*

There are some who say and do not. There are some who will not say, and yet will do what they are commanded by their parents. Ruth both says and does what her mother-in-law advised her to do. Both in word and deed we ought to testify our reverence for parents, and for all that possess a just title to our obedience. Exceptions must be made, because none but God can claim an unlimited right to our submission. Ruth might err by excess of complaisance to her mother-in-law; but the errors of young persons are commonly of an opposite kind.

Verse 7.—*And when Boaz had eaten and drunk, and his heart was merry, he went to lie down at the end of the heap of corn; and she came softly, and uncovered his feet, and laid her down.*

'Go thy way, eat thy bread with cheerfulness, and drink thy wine with a merry heart, when God accepteth thy works,' and giveth thee special testimonies of his goodness. 'Every creature of God is good, and nothing to be refused, being sanctified by the word of God and prayer.' Although wine, as it is used by the sons of riot, 'is a mocker, and strong drink is raging,' yet it is a good creature of God, given to cheer the heart of man. Christ himself turned water into wine for the entertainment of a company met together at a marriage-feast.

Boaz did not think it below his dignity to eat and drink with his servants, nor did he think it inconsistent with the laws of sobriety to take a moderate share of that pleasant liquor which 'cheereth the heart of God and man.' He would observe God's faithfulness, as well as goodness, in the provision of his table, when he enjoyed the blessing of his father Judah, to whom it was promised, that 'his teeth should be white with milk, and his eyes red with wine.'

Think not that Boaz had gone beyond the bounds of moderation, when his heart was cheerful through wine. He had drunk away no part of his understanding, as you will see by his behaviour. Drunkenness is the introduction to other sensual impurities, when the devil can find means to present a suitable temptation. 'Thine eyes,' says Solomon to the drunkard, 'shall behold strange women, and thine heart shall utter perverse things.' But when Boaz found that there was a woman lying at his feet, he was ashamed, and on his guard against every appearance of evil.

'He went to lie down at the end of the heap' of wheat, in his clothes. This was another instance of the simplicity of manners in his age. Why should we wonder that people of ancient times had manners different from ours? There is no law of reason or religion that binds the men of other nations to adopt the British laws. There was as little reason why the ancients should observe those modes of conduct which are thought proper to be observed in our days.

'She rose softly and uncovered his feet, and lay down.' Neither of them was undressed. Yet we can by no means justify Naomi or Ruth. We ought to 'abstain from all appearance of evil,' and to 'make straight paths for our feet, that that which is lame may not be turned out of the way.' No woman can plead Ruth's example as an excuse for similar conduct, not only because no bad examples, even of good men or women, are to be imitated, but because the circumstances of those who might plead such example, cannot be the same, unless the Jewish laws, concerning the marriage of the near kinsman, were to be restored to their force.

Verses 8, 9.—*And it came to pass at midnight, that the man was afraid, and turned himself; and behold a woman lay at his feet. And he said, Who art thou? and she answered, I am Ruth thine handmaid; spread therefore thy skirt over thine handmaid, for thou art a near kinsman.*

Boaz was startled when he awaked out of sleep and felt one lying at his feet. He was amazed when he cast his eyes on the person who had used the freedom, and saw that it was a woman. Had he intoxicated himself at the feast, when his heart was merry with wine, he would now have been exposed to one of the most dangerous snares of the devil. But he was in full possession of his reason. What was still better, his virtue or his grace was awake to preserve him from the power of temptation. By the grace of God he kept himself, and the wicked one troubled him not.

Who art thou? he said. He could perceive by the little light he had, that it was a woman that lay at his feet; but what woman it was he could not discern, and it was natural to suppose that it must have been one of the foolish women, who came with no good intentions, to place herself so near him. We must have no fellowship with the unfruitful works of darkness, but rather reprove those who evidently sin, and call those to account whose conduct is suspicious, when they will expose themselves to our censure.

I am Ruth thine handmaid. Spread thy skirt therefore over thine handmaid. Ruth does not now hesitate to make herself known to Boaz. She tells him who she was, and solicits him to spread his skirt over her, and thus to acknowledge himself her husband. A woman may, in some extraordinary cases supposable amongst ourselves, solicit or demand marriage from a man, without violating the laws of delicacy or reserve which nature or custom enjoins. But the law of Moses allowed a woman to request marriage from the brother of her husband who died without children, and to put him to open shame if he refused to comply. Boaz was not a brother-german of Mahlon; but either the law, it appears, was in this age understood to comprehend the nearest relations, when brothers by fathers or mothers were wanting; or a custom, founded on the spirit of the law, was introduced to extend its benefits.

Women, in ordinary cases, would greatly err and expose themselves to shame, were they to show an eager desire of marriage; but they may likewise err by affected refusals of an husband, or by obstinately continuing in the single state when they ought to marry. 'I will,' says an apostle, 'that the younger widows marry.' He does not will them all to marry. There are circumstances in which they who marry not, do better than those who marry; but there are others in which they would expose themselves to needless temptations, or to useless vexations, by continuing single. In this, as in every important step of life, let men and women attend to the directions of the word of God, and acknowledge Him by prayer, and he will direct their steps in the way of peace and holiness.

'Spread thy skirt over me, for thou art a near kinsman.' The near relation of Boaz to Ruth by Mahlon, was her encouragement to seek and to hope that she should be covered with his skirt. May we not much more take encouragement from the near relation of our blessed Lord, to hope that he will not disdain to receive us into a marriage-relation? Why did he take part of our flesh and blood? Was it not that he might betroth us to himself? In his grace and pity he 'was in all things made like unto us, that he might be a merciful and faithful High Priest, to make reconciliation for the sins of the people.' He is the great pattern of conjugal love, for he gave himself for his destined spouse, 'that he might sanctify and cleanse her by the washing of water through the word, and might present her to himself a glorious church, not having spot or wrinkle, or any such thing.' Why doth he send forth his servants, the ministers of the gospel, to declare his name to us? Is it not that they may 'espouse souls to one husband, and present them as chaste virgins unto Christ?'

LECTURE X.

BOAZ PROMISES TO RUTH TO MARRY HER, IF HER HUSBAND'S NEAREST KINSMAN DID NOT INSIST UPON HIS PRIOR RIGHT. HE DISMISSES HER WITH A PRESENT TO HER MOTHER-IN-LAW, WHO EXPRESSES GREAT SATISFACTION WITH HER KIND RECEPTION BY BOAZ.

CHAPTER III. 10–18.

Verse 10.—*And he said, Blessed be thou of the Lord, my daughter; for thou hast showed more kindness in the latter end than at the beginning, inasmuch as thou followedst not young men, whether poor or rich.*

Ruth, no doubt, felt much anxiety in her mind, when she thought of the reception with which she might meet from Boaz, as the whole colour of her future life depended upon it; but his former kindness gave her hope, and she was not disappointed.

Some men meeting with such an application from a young woman, would have taken advantage of her imprudence to draw her into the snares of the devil. Others would have treated her with asperity, as a presuming wench divested of the modesty belonging to her sex. Boaz knew Ruth and Naomi too well to entertain any injurious suspicion concerning Ruth's present conduct. He saw that she was acting according to Naomi's direction, and that their views were pure, whatever might be thought of the manner in which they endeavoured to accomplish them. Actions are often to be estimated from the character of the actor. Virtuous women may be found in situations that might justly expose them to suspicion, if their former behaviour did not give them a just title to have that conduct ascribed to mistake, or to some unknown cause, which at first view appeared almost inexcusable.

Blessed be thou of the Lord, for thou hast showed more kindness in the latter end than at the beginning, to thy husband's family. She had no doubt made an excellent wife to Mahlon. Since his death, she had fulfilled all the offices of an affectionate daughter to Naomi. Her desire of becoming the wife of Mahlon's near kinsman, was considered by Boaz as an instance of her kindness to the deceased, that deserved still greater praise. Boaz was an old man. A young woman of Ruth's beauty and character might have expected an husband amongst the young men of the country, better suited to her taste, and more likely to make her happy through life, if her happiness had not consisted to a great degree in showing respect to the memory of the dead, and to the comfort of her living friends.

'Thou hast not followed young men, whether poor or rich.' Some might have supposed, that a mean and covetous spirit had induced Ruth to seek an alliance with Boaz, rather than with a man near her own age. But nothing could have been more unjust, than to entertain such an opinion of a woman of approved virtue. None but a woman fit to be a prostitute for hire, would marry a man for his riches, when she would have preferred another man to him if he had not been poor. Ruth's contentment with her low condition, her conjugal affection to Mahlon, still apparent in her filial behaviour to his mother, her modesty, her piety, were proofs that she could not act upon motives so unworthy to come into the mind of an Israelitess. An Israelitess she may with propriety be called. She was so by choice if not by birth; and from a pious regard to the God and to the people of Israel, she preferred widowhood, or the meanest connections in the Holy Land, to any prospects she could form amongst her friends in Moab.

God hath made of one blood all nations of men, to bind them in the connections of a common brotherhood. And he hath parcelled out men into particular kindreds and families, to bind them still closer in friendship with those to whom they may communicate, or from whom they may receive, the kindnesses due from men to their own flesh. Boaz, entertaining a warm regard to his own kindred, thought himself indebted to Ruth for that affectionate regard which she had showed to his friends. He gave her due praise for her behaviour, and promised that he would take care of her interests.

Verse 11.—*And now, my daughter, fear not; I will do to thee all that thou requirest: for all the city of my people doth know that thou art a virtuous woman.*

Blessings of the tongue are cheap, and very readily given by some who have nothing else to give. Boaz prays that the Lord might bless Ruth, and at the same time undertakes to do what she required, if he found it consistent with the rights of a still nearer kinsman.

He calls her his daughter, and yet is very ready to take her for a wife. Equality of age is very desirable in the marriage relation, but not indispensable. If a young woman find that she cannot love an old man, she cannot, without sinning, and without exposing herself to great temptations for the time to come, enter into that relation, the duties of which cannot be rightly performed without that conjugal affection which ought to be maintained between those who are 'no more twain, but one flesh.' Nor can parents, without unnatural cruelty, urge their daughters to marry men, to whom they cannot cheerfully promise that love and reverence which are indispensably requisite in Christian wives. But Ruth found no difficulty in the matter. She entertained a cordial love to Boaz as a good man, as the best friend of her family, and her own friend. Boaz neither thought, nor had any reason to think, that she wished from any improper motives to become his wife, for she was well known to be a virtuous woman.

If she had not been a virtuous woman, Boaz would not have thought of making her his wife. Neither beauty, were it equal to that of our first mother in her first estate, nor wit, nor any qualification, however brilliant, or however engaging, can supply the place of virtue. Without virtue, the most attractive qualities are very likely to become incentives and temptations to vice; Prov. xxxi. 30.

All the city of my people doth know that thou art a virtuous woman. This was a great recommendation of Ruth to Boaz, that her virtue was well known and acknowledged by all his fellow-citizens. All young women ought not only to behave well, but to keep at a distance from every thing that may render their character doubtful. What wise man will ever pay his addresses to a woman, however virtuous, unless she entertain a due regard to her own character? It cannot even be said that a woman is unexceptionable in virtue, when she is not duly careful of the appearance, as well as of the reality of virtuous conduct. Whatsoever things are lovely, and of good report, must be thought upon and practised by Christians of both sexes. Female delicacy requires particular attention to this rule of conduct from the weaker sex.

Although Boaz was charmed with the behaviour, and pleased with the character of Ruth, yet he would take no unfair methods to obtain her for himself. 'A virtuous woman is a crown to her husband.' But an honest man will not use unjustifiable methods to obtain the best crown which this earth can afford.

Verses 12, 13.—*And now, it is true that I am thy near kinsman: howbeit there is a kinsman nearer than I. Tarry this night, and it shall be in the morning, that if he will perform unto thee the part of a kinsman, well, let him do the kinsman's part; but if he will not do the part of a kinsman to thee, then will I do the part of a kinsman to thee, as the Lord liveth. Lie down until the morning.*

When Alexander the Great took Tyre, he was informed of a young prince who had obtained a high character for virtue, and offered him the crown. The young prince refused it, because he had an elder brother, who had a better title than himself to the royal dignity; for they were of the ancient blood of the Tyrian kings. Boaz deserves no less praise than this Tyrian prince. Such a wife as Ruth would have been preferred by Boaz to a royal diadem; yet he would not take her to himself to wife whilst there lived another man who had a preferable claim to her, if he was willing to make use of his right. We ought to 'look every man not on his own things only, but every man also on the things of others.'

And now, it is true that I am thy near kinsman. Purse-proud men are ashamed of their poor relations, but Boaz takes pleasure in being accounted the near kinsman of such a virtuous woman as Ruth. If we are ashamed of virtuous and godly friends because they are poor, we would have been ashamed to acknowledge Jesus as a friend, when he lived in poverty upon earth.

Howbeit there is a kinsman nearer than I. There are different degrees of relation, all of which have their respective duties and their respective rights belonging to them. We sin either by neglecting any of the duties of these relations, or by arrogating the rights peculiar to nearer relations. A brother or an uncle are near relations; but neither of them can claim the authority of a father, except in extraordinary cases, when particular circumstances have devolved the authority of a parent upon them. Boaz would do every thing to serve Ruth that became her nearest relation, but one; and this one thing he declined, because he had no right to do it. He would not intrude into the rights of another man, till they were voluntarily surrendered. As every man ought to abide in his own calling, so we all ought to keep our own places in society. Much of the unhappiness, and many of the sins of social life, originate in that assuming and meddling disposition, which renders some people a pest to their neighbours, and still more to themselves.

'Tarry this night, and thou shalt know whether thy nearest kinsman chooses to do the part of kinsman to thee.' Although we must not be busy-bodies, yet we act a kind part to our friends when we take an interest in their affairs, and, at their desire, understood or expressed, transact such of them as they cannot so well transact for themselves. Ruth might have gone to her nearest kinsman, and required him either to marry her or renounce his right; but Boaz saves her the trouble, and we may say of him as he said of Ruth, that his kindness in the end was greater than at the beginning. It was a great pleassure to him to 'cause the widow's heart to sing for joy.'

'Tarry this night, and I will transact the business in the morning.' Boaz would do with his might what his hand found to do. He would not cause Ruth to wait in suspense a single hour beyond what was necessary for bringing the most important business of her life to a conclusion. One of the English kings was called Ethelred the Unready, because we was always too late with his preparations to oppose the enemies of his country. O that men could know and attend to their duties in the proper season! Then would they be like trees planted by the rivers of water, whose leaf fadeth not, and whose fruit does not fail. Christ hath redeemed us from all iniquity, that we might be ever ready for every good work.

'If he will perform the part of a kinsman, well, (or, it is good), let him perform the part of a kinsman.' But if he perform the part of a kinsman, Boaz must give up all thoughts of marrying the woman who stood so high in his estimation, and in the opinion of all his fellow-citizens. True; but if he is disappointed of a virtuous wife, he keeps a good conscience. A good wife is a good thing, but a good conscience is better. If you could obtain the best wife in the world by injustice, you make a very foolish bargain.

'We are glad,' says Paul to the Corinthians, 'when we are weak, and ye are strong.' If Boaz must see Ruth the wife of another man, he will rejoice in his happiness, and in the happiness which he hoped Ruth would enjoy in his house. We should learn to rejoice with them that rejoice, when we have reason on our own account to mourn.

'But if he will not perform the part of a kinsman, I will perform the part of a kinsman unto thee.' You see he does not think the worse of Ruth for lying down at his feet. He was governed by that charity which thinketh no evil.

As the Lord liveth. Oaths are not to be sworn on trifling occasions. Boaz accounted the present an occasion of sufficient importance to justify his taking the name of God into his mouth. His word might very well have been believed without an oath; but he wished to give full satisfaction to Ruth about his intentions, that her mind might be set perfectly at ease, and that she might patiently wait the event without putting herself to any farther trouble.

It is a sign of a profane spirit not to fear an oath. It is vain, scrupulously to be afraid of an oath when we are called to swear.

Lie down until the morning. Boaz probably wished that she had not come to lay herself down; but since she was laid at his feet, he did not think it safe for her to leave him till the morning. He did not wish her to expose herself to the fears and perils of the night, nor did he think it prudent either to go with her, or to send one of his servants to attend her, in the darkness of the night, to her mother's house. In considering what is fit to be done in particular businesses, it is often necessary to attend to existing circumstances. Certain situations and circumstances may render it necessary and wise to do those things which, in different situations, it would be very unwise to do; as you see in Paul's directions about those points, concerning which the Corinthian believers consulted him by letter; 1 Cor. vii. 10.

Verse 14.—*And she lay at his feet until the morning; and she rose up before one could know another. And he said, Let it not be known that a woman came into the floor.*

Let us endeavour to do nothing that will not bear the light. But if we have done any thing that may expose us to unjust suspicions if it were known, it is not inconsistent with integrity to conceal it, provided it can be done without falsehood or dissimulation. Although Boaz was fully persuaded that Ruth came with no evil intention to the floor, and was conscious that their mutual converse was innocent, he did not know what ill-natured constructions might be put upon the conduct of either of them by some of their neighbours. 'All men have not faith,' says Paul; and we know too well that all men have not charity.

It is necessary for us at all times to cut off occasions from those who would speak reproachfully. It was necessary especially that a stranger and proselyte should be careful of her character, and above all, a stranger whom a respectable citizen might claim for a wife. If matters had been so conducted, that Ruth's behaviour had excited suspicions against her, how could Boaz have proposed a marriage with her to her nearest kinsman? It might have been supposed, that he only wished for a refusal, that he might take her to himself. But, highly as he esteemed Ruth, he would take no steps to obtain her, on which he could not reflect with pleasure.

Verse 15.—*Also he said, Bring the veil that thou hast upon thee, and hold it. And when she held it, he measured six measures of barley, and laid it on her; and she went into the city.*

This, some may say, was a strange present. Who ever laid a load of barley upon the shoulders of a young woman whom he wished to marry, as a proof of his affection? Might he not have given her rings, or nose jewels, or some Babylonish garment, rather than a load of grain fit to be laid on the shoulders of a beggar?

It may be answered, that Boaz could better judge than we, what presents were fit to be made to Ruth. Such questions will be asked by those only, whose acquaintance reaches not beyond the manners of their own time, or of their own people. If you have read the most ancient of uninspired books, you will find that it was not, in the days of old, accounted inconsistent with the dignity of heroes and kings to kill and roast their own meat. If you read the accounts of recent travellers to the East, you will find that great men think they pay a compliment to strangers of distinction, by sending them presents of provisions, even of the kind that is most common and cheap.

Lovers amongst us, it is true, do not give presents of barley to their mistresses; yet barley is more precious than any of the trinkets which the customs of modern times have introduced, as proper testimonies of regard to the objects of love. When our Lord fed a multitude with barley loaves, he multiplied them, but he did not change them into loaves of fine wheat. Ruth, and her mother Naomi, had learned by poverty to set a value upon those kinds of grain which fulness of bread, and abundance of idleness, dispose too many to despise. Those who must live on barley bread are monsters of ingratitude, if they receive not their portion of the good things of this world with thankfulness to the Author and Preserver of their being. The apostle Paul was often not so well supplied with food as the poorest of our cottagers, and yet his heart was warm with gratitude to Him who gives us all thing richly to enjoy; 1 Tim. vi. 17.

He laid it on her, and she went into the city.—She received the barley in her veil, and carried it to the house of her mother-in-law. She disdained not the present. She did not think herself too fine a lady to carry it, although she hoped soon to be the wife of 'a mighty man of wealth.' God had given her health and vigour, and she was not ashamed to use her strength in those useful employments, which may perhaps appear too mean to some of the lowest class of society amongst us. It is said of a certain Spanish king, that one of his attendants, seeing him one day employed in a piece of mechanical work, took the liberty of observing, that such employments were fitter for a carpenter's apprentice, than a king. 'Nature,' replied the monarch, 'has given hands to kings as well as to other men, and I know no law that should hinder me from using them.'

Verse 16.—*And when she came to her mother-in-law, she said, Who art thou, my daughter? And she told her all that the man had done to her.*

Naomi doubtless waited with impatience the time when Ruth might be expected to return, but was surprised to see her come at a time she was not expecting her, when the light began to appear in the heavens. The present, too, which Ruth carried, increased her wonder, which she expressed in these words, *Who art thou, my daughter?* We sometimes use a like expression, *Is this you?* when a friend pays us an unexpected visit.

And she told her all that the man had done to her. Ruth used to hide nothing that was interesting to herself from her affectionate mother-in-law; and was, no doubt, happy to inform her of any thing that would give her satisfaction.

Let no young woman deal in secrecy and concealment. Beware of doing any thing that you would not wish your affectionate mother to know; and, if you have done any thing unfit to be known, make not falsehood your refuge. Ruth had no reason to be afraid of telling her mother-in-law what passed between herself and Boaz. 'He who doth truth, cometh to the light,' for he is not afraid to have 'his works made manifest.'

Verse 17.—*And she said, These six measures of barley gave he me; for he said to me, go not empty unto thy mother-in-law.*

Ruth could not conceal the bounty of Boaz, for her heart overflowed with gratitude; and she mentions it to Naomi in language that would highly gratify the good old woman. Although Naomi had Ruth's happiness only in view, as her own connection with the world was nearly at an end, yet she must have been pleased with the attentions paid to her by her friends. You cannot restore youthful vigour to your aged friends. You cannot give them a relish for youthful enjoyments. Yet you may console them by those kind attentions to which they are well entitled from those young friends whom they love.

Verse 18.—*Then said she, Sit still, my daughter, until thou know how the matter will fall: for the man will not be in rest, until he have finished the thing this day.*

'There is a time to speak, and a time to be silent;' a time to act, and a time to sit still. Ruth had now done all that her mother thought necessary. She may now sit still, for her affairs are in the hand of one who will take care to manage them in the most expeditious manner, and to bring them to a happy conclusion.

Some cannot be persuaded to act when activity is necessary; others cannot be induced to sit still when they have done all that is fit to be done. Their anxiety keeps them in a constant bustle. They neither can be at rest, nor suffer others around them to rest. 'It is vain for men to rise up early, and sit up late, to eat the bread of sorrow,' and to refuse to their minds and bodies their necessary repose. Let us not neglect our duty about our secular as well as our spiritual interests. Slothfulness is reprobated both by reason and religion; but let us still remember our Lord's gracious injunction, 'Take no thought,' or rather, Take no anxious thought, 'for the morrow.' We ought never to say to our souls, 'Take your rest, eat, drink, and be merry;' but we have too often reason to say, 'Why art thou disquieted within me? Hope thou in God.'

Sit still until thou know how the matter will fall. Ruth might well be supposed to entertain uneasy thoughts about a business that was to determine the fortune of her future days. She did not know whether she was to be the wife of Boaz, or of her nearer kinsman. But what could she do by the indulgence of disquieting thoughts? She could not alter the laws or customs of the country. She could not do any thing more than she had already done, to procure for herself that alliance which she desired. What could she now do better than to sit still, resigning herself to the providence of God. Things that will happen, cannot be prevented by our utmost solicitude. Things not appointed will never take place, if all the care and all the toil of men and angels were jointly employed to bring them about. For 'who is he that saith, and it cometh to pass, when the Lord commandeth it not? Out of the mouth of the Most High proceedeth not evil and good.'

For the man will not be in rest, until he have finished the thing this day. Naomi knew Boaz to be a man of wisdom and activity, a generous and honest man, who would not rest till he had accomplished the business in hand. Ruth, having such a friend to transact her business, had no occasion to give herself any more trouble. A faithful friend is the most precious blessing which this world can afford. 'He that sendeth a message by the hand of a fool, cutteth off the feet, and drinketh damage'; but 'as a cloud of dew in the heat of harvest, so is a faithful messenger to them that send him,' for he refresheth the soul of his employers.

Do you profess to be a friend? Show yourself friendly in your conduct. Be not backward to engage in the concerns of your friend, when you are qualified to manage them to better advantage than he can do, or to give him friendly assistance to manage them for himself. When you have undertaken the management of any affair, make no needless delays; for 'hope deferred,' though not crushed, 'maketh the heart sick.' It was the known character of Boaz that inspired Naomi and Ruth with such confidence in his good offices. Why should you forfeit the thanks of the services you mean to do, by wearying out the patience, and perhaps disconcerting the plans, of those who trust to your friendship? Defer nothing till to-morrow that may as well be done to day, either for yourselves or for your friends. 'Who knows what a day will bring forth?' It is said of Richard II. king of England, that he lost his crown and life by being a day too late in coming to join his army in Wales.

When you have tried friends, trust their friendship as far as men can be trusted. David was not afraid to put his life into

Jonathan's hands, when Saul, for Jonathan's interest, was seeking his destruction.

Have you no friends to manage your troublesome affairs, or to direct your management of them? Say not so, as long as you are permitted to say concerning Christ, 'This is my beloved, and this is my friend!' 'Commit your works unto the Lord, and your thoughts shall be established. Be not anxiously careful about any thing; but in every thing, by prayer and supplication, with thanksgiving, let your requests be made known unto God, and the peace of God, which passeth all understanding, shall keep your hearts and minds through Christ Jesus.'

LECTURE XI.

BOAZ, IN THE PRESENCE OF TEN ELDERS OF BETHLEHEM, PROCURES THE CONSENT OF RUTH'S NEAREST KINSMAN TO HIS MARRIAGE WITH HER.

CHAPTER iv. 1-10.

Verse 1.—*Then went Boaz up to the gate, and sat him down there; and behold, the kinsman of whom Boaz spake came by; unto whom he said, Ho, such a one! turn aside, sit down here. And he turned aside, and sat down.*

'MARRIAGE is honourable in all,' but some make it dishonourable to themselves, by being unequally yoked, or by reprehensible methods of entering into the state of marriage. By dishonest means they gain the affections of their partners, or transgress the good and necessary laws of their country by clandestine engagements. Surely there is no business in life which ought to be transacted with a closer attention to the revealed will of God, than one on which so much of the happiness or misery of life depends. We are so far from acting like Christians, that we proceed upon atheistical principles, if we expect any more joy from changing our condition than God is pleased to give us. We will find satisfaction or disquiet, happiness or misery, in marriage, according to the will of our Maker; and therefore in this, and in all our ways, let us acknowledge Him, and he will direct our steps. 'If a man's ways please the Lord, he maketh even his enemies to be at peace with him.' If a man's ways do not please the Lord, he can set his friends at variance with him, and poison the streams of his felicity with bitterness, lamentation, and woe.

Boaz proceeds with candour and openness in the business of his marriage. He would not move a step in it, without letting his intentions be known to the only man that had a right to throw obstructions in his way; and transacts the matter with him in the presence of ten of the most respectable men in Bethlehem. Thus he 'provides for things honest, not only in the sight of God, but in the sight of all men.'

He goes to the gate of the city. The gate was the place of concourse in ancient times. It was the place where courts were held, and where the most important affairs were discussed. The near kinsman seems to have been called off his way by Boaz, after he took his seat at the gate. The Lord brought him to the place where Boaz wished to meet with him. Thus, when Abraham's servant 'was in the way, the Lord led him to the house of his master's brethren.' Things the most accidental to us, are regulated by God.

Ho! such a one. Did not the sacred writer know the man's name? Undoubtedly. But he seems to have concealed it from us, with the design of burying it in oblivion. The man appears to have been more solicitous than he ought to have been about the preservation of his own name, and it is suffered to perish. He would not raise up a name to Mahlon, that he might not mar that inheritance by which his own name was to be preserved. But the name of Mahlon comes down to the latest posterity, with the name of Boaz; while none can tell what was the name of the man who was so anxious to avoid any thing that might impair the lustre of his family.

And he turned aside, and sat down.

Verse 2.—*And he took ten men of the elders of the city, and said, Sit ye down here. And they sat down.*

Whether he sent for them before or after he sat down, we are not told. He did not proceed to business till he had abundance of witnesses to attest the proceedings, and of counsellors or judges to determine difficulties, if any should occur. 'In the mouth of two or three witnesses,' says the law, 'shall every word be established.' 'In the multitude of counsellors,' says the wise man, 'is safety.'

Verse 3.—*And he said unto the kinsman: Naomi, that is come again out of the country of Moab, selleth a parcel of land which was our brother Elimelech's:*

Naomi was a poor widow, and yet she had a parcel of land to sell. It was doubtless so encumbered, that hitherto she could not derive any benefit from it since her return from the land of Moab. It was her interest to sell it, that she might draw from it some help to her present subsistence; and it was highly proper that the first offer of it should be made to that kinsman, to whom the office of redeeming inheritances belonged, according to the law. 'He that hath friends must show himself friendly' when he has the power and opportunity; and, when he is in distress, may reasonably expect succour from his friends.

'This land pertained to our brother Elimelech,' said Boaz. All near relations were called brethren amongst the Israelites. By calling Elimelech their brother on the present occasion, Boaz insinuates the obligation lying upon them to deal kindly with Naomi. When she was compelled to sell the land of her deceased husband, it was to be expected that his surviving brethren would give her better terms than strangers. If they did not give a larger price, they might soften the necessity that urged her to sell, by attentions and favours of no great cost to themselves.

Verse 4.—*And I thought to advertise thee, saying, Buy it before the inhabitants, and before the elders of my people. If thou wilt redeem it, redeem it; but if thou wilt not redeem it, then tell me, that I may know; for there is none to redeem it besides thee, and I am after thee. And he said, I will redeem it.*

Boaz plainly intimates his intention of buying Elimelech's land, if his nearest kinsman found it inconvenient for himself to do it; but he felt it his duty to give advertisement, in the first place, to him who had the best right to do it if he chose. The money of Boaz was as good as his friend's money; but it might be an advantage to possess the land, although the full price were given for it, and it seemed agreeable to the Jewish law that the nearest kinsman should have his option. We must not go beyond, or defraud our brother in any matter great or small, nor do any thing that has the appearance of taking an advantage of him. When land is to be set in tack, artful and clandestine means to obtain possession of it are suspicious. The master is under no obligation to let it to the former tenant. He may have justly incurred his landlord's displeasure. He may be less qualified to make the land productive than some of his neighbours, or he may be unwilling to give a reasonable advance in the rent. But let no unfair advantage be taken of him by his neighbours. If they find themselves at liberty to enter in bargain with his master, they ought not to behave towards the former tenant in any other way than they would think it reasonable for their own neighbours to behave towards themselves in similar circumstances. Fair proceedings seldom need concealment. 'Whatsoever ye would that men should do unto you, do ye even so unto them.' We ought not to account ourselves upright men, if this maxim does not regulate every part of our behaviour.

There is none to redeem it besides thee, and I am next unto thee. There was none nearer in relation than this kinsman, but Boaz was next in degree. 'There is a friend that sticketh closer than a brother.' Such a friend was Boaz to Ruth, and yet he would not claim the rights of the nearest kinsman, but was in readiness to perform his duties, if he declined the performance. We ought to invade no man's rights, but to perform the duties belonging to every man in his place and relation. Nor are we always to confine ourselves, in performing the duty of relations, to those which in ordinary cases belong to our degree of relation. An uncle may be called, by existing circumstances, to perform the duty of a father, or a nephew to perform the duty of a son. There are some to whom it is a great loss to have near relations careless of their duty, or not well qualified to perform it. They are neglected by other relations, who would be kind to them if they did not trust the care of them to those who are more nearly connected; or perhaps they are glad to have a pretext from the nearer relationship of others, to excuse themselves from troublesome duties. Boaz was ready, either to redeem the inheritance of Mahlon, or to leave it to be redeemed by a nearer kinsman.

And he said, I will redeem it. His meaning was, that he would give the money necessary for the purchase. But, when he heard the conditions of the bargain, he declined it.

Verse 5.—*Then said Boaz, What day thou buyest the field of the hand of Naomi, thou must buy it also of Ruth, the Moabitess, the wife of the dead, to raise up the name of the dead upon his inheritance.*

When a man dies, his wife must lose his society, and the benefits of his industry; but let her not lose what she has a right to claim, her portion of the common goods, and the friendship of his relations. The rights of the widow are protected and her injuries are avenged by Him who is 'the judge of the widow, and the father of the fatherless, in his holy habitation.' Whatever necessity Naomi was under of selling the land of Elimelech, she would not deprive Ruth of her just claim upon it. He who buys the land, must marry Ruth, to raise up the name of her deceased husband.

'The dead know not any thing, neither have they any more a reward; for the memory of them is forgotten, and their love, and their hatred, and their envy, is now perished: neither have they any more a portion for ever in any thing that is done under the sun.' Yet their memory is to be respected by surviving relations; and the respect due to their memories is to be held the more sacred that they have no more a portion in any thing. When they have lost every other thing earthly, let them not be bereaved of what may still be reserved, the esteem to which their memory is entitled. They cannot hear the voice of friendship; but it was their wish, whilst they were with us, to be remembered with kindness, when they would no longer enjoy our company. And, when we must die, it would aggravate our affliction to have reason to think that our memorial will perish with us. God provided, by a law, for the preservation of the name of those who died childless. 'If brethren dwell together, and one of them die, and have no child, the wife of the dead shall not marry unto a stranger. Her husband's brother shall go in unto her, and take her to him to wife, and perform the duty of an husband's brother to her; and it shall be, that the first born which she beareth shall succeed in the name of his brother which is dead, that his name be not put out of Israel.' Deut. xxv. 5, 6.

This law was not exactly applicable to the case in question.

The next kinsman of Elimelech was, probably, not his brother-german, nor did he live in the house together with him. But a custom, founded on the spirit of the law, seems to have given the nearest kinsman a right, by proscription, to the refusal of a childless widow; and to the widow, a right to expect the nearest kinsman in marriage, unless some considerable objections, from her former behaviour, or from particular circumstances, rendered the connection ineligible.

This law was peculiar to the Israelites. Those who die childless amongst us, must continue so for ever. But we enjoy clearer revelations than the ancient church, of the felicities of the other world. We need not greatly wish to have our names registered in the records of any city upon earth, or in the genealogy of any house. It will be sufficient for us to have our names 'written amongst the living in Jerusalem'; and, if we have begotten any children by the gospel, they 'will be to us for a name and a crown of rejoicing in the day of Christ.' This honour is to all those saints who turn any sinner from the error of his ways, though not invested with the ministry of the gospel; James v. 19, 20.

Verse 6.—*And the kinsman said, I cannot redeem it for myself, lest I mar mine own inheritance: redeem thou my right to thyself; for I cannot redeem it.*

Unless we knew more than the sacred historian has thought it necessary to tell us concerning the circumstances of this near kinsman, we cannot say whether his objection to the marriage with Ruth was founded in truth and reason, or whether his dislike to the match prompted him to make use of an evasion. It is likely that he had a family by another wife, and that he was afraid of injuring it, by laying out money on a possession that would not descend to them.

Young persons should not enter into the marriage relation without serious consideration. This is still more necessary for widowers with young families. By rashness in entering anew into the married state, they may bring great disquiet to themselves, and may incapacitate themselves to do for their families what they had a right to expect. Yet it is to be feared, that too many decline the married state through distrust of divine Providence, or through unwillingness to forego some of those gratifications which the expense and care of a family would oblige them to relinquish. Paul speaks of a time, when, 'for the present distress,' it was not good to marry; and, at any time, some are in circumstances which make it expedient for them to continue in the single state. But when men find the temptations of a single life dangerous to their souls, and yet abide in it to avoid the expenses of the reduction in their style of living, which marriage would render necessary, they expose themselves to the snares of the devil, by neglecting those precautions against sin which human corruption renders necessary. What sins and sorrows to young men might often have been prevented by prudent marriages!

Redeem thou my right to thyself, for I cannot redeem it. Although this kinsman did not choose to marry Ruth, he was so honest as not to wish to hinder her marriage with another. He was unlike to some persons, who, whilst they are undetermined about marrying the objects of their attachment, use indirect means to hinder them from marrying other persons with whom they might be happy. Nothing can be a greater indication of a selfish and grovelling mind, than for a man to work himself into the affections of a young woman so far as to hinder her from listening to the addresses of others, whilst he is balancing in his own mind whether he will marry her or not, and behaves in such a dubious manner, that expectations are raised, whilst positive engagements are avoided. Let all young women guard against such insidious enemies of their peace. A man cannot be truly in love with a woman, when his self-love is so strong, that he attends only to his own comfort and interest, and cares not what pain he inflicts upon her to whom he pretends a regard.

Verses 7, 8.—*Now this was the manner in former time in Israel concerning redeeming, and concerning changing, for to confirm all things: a man plucked off his shoe, and gave it to his neighbour; and this was a testimony in Israel. Therefore the kinsman said unto Boaz, Buy it for thee; so he drew off his shoe.*

This ceremony is evidently different from that which was prescribed in the law of Moses, concerning the man who refused to marry the childless widow of his brother that had dwelt in the house with him. In that case, the widow herself was to pluck off the man's shoe, and to spit in his face as a reproach upon him for refusing to raise up seed to his brother. A distant relation was not under the same legal obligations, nor subjected to the same reproach.

Significant ceremonies are still used amongst men in transferring the property of land from one to another, as well as in many other transactions of importance. They are useful for authenticating transactions, and preventing disputes for the time to come. The kinsman of Boaz not only expressed his resignation of his right in the ears of the witnesses, but presented a visible sign of it to their eyes, that all possibility of doubt or contention might be obviated. 'Here is my shoe,' said he to Boaz. 'He who wears this shoe, has a right to buy and use the ground in question. Let this be a witness, that what was formerly mine, is become yours with my consent.'

The use of visible signs for establishing bargains may call to our minds the wonderful condescension of our blessed Redeemer, in granting us visible signs of his grace for the confirmation of our faith. As certainly as the shoe of this kinsman was in the possession of Boaz, the land which that kinsman had the prior right to redeem now belonged to Boaz. As certainly as we are cleansed by water, and nourished and refreshed by bread and wine, (the symbols of the body and blood of the Lord,) are our souls cleansed, nourished, and invigorated, by the blood and body represented by them. We may say of such visible signs of a covenant, what Paul says of oaths, that they 'are for confirmation, to put an end to all strife.'

Verse 9.—*And Boaz said unto the elders, and unto all the people, Ye are witnesses this day, that I have bought all that was Elimelech's, and all that was Chilion's and Mahlon's, of the hand of Naomi.*

Boaz was not afraid of marring his own inheritance, nor did he seek any pretexts for declining that generous bargain which the kinsman refused. It is a happy thing, not only for a rich man himself, but for all around him, when he is disposed to use his substance for the purposes for which Providence bestowed it.

When Boaz makes the bargain, he calls not only upon the elders, but upon all the people present, to be witnesses. He followed the example of his father Abraham. He never bought any land but a burial-place, and he took all possible care to obviate any contentions about the purchase to himself and to his heirs. 'The field of Ephron, which was in Machpelah, which was before Mamre, the field and the cave which was therein, and all the trees which were therein, were made sure unto Abraham for a possession in the presence of the children of Heth, before all that went in at the gate of his city;' Gen. xxiii. 17, 18. 'A good man will guide his affairs with discretion.'

I have bought all that was Elimelech's, and all that was Chilion's and Mahlon's. You see how changeable earthly property is. Men think they can secure it almost against death. By purchasing land, and using legal methods for transmitting it to the offspring of their own bodies, they can possess it in the person of their second selves, after they go down to the grave. But although you have both children and friends, you can be secure of no dwelling, but the house appointed for all living; of no larger estate, than that quantity of ground which is sufficient to cover your bodies. In the course of ten years sojourning in the land of Moab, Elimelech and all his sons died, and now his estate came into the possession of Boaz. Here you have no continuing possession. Seek a place in the better country. All believers in Christ receive a kingdom which will not pass to others; but 'the world passeth away, and the lust thereof.'

Verse 10.—*Moreover, Ruth, the Moabitess, the wife of Mahlon, have I purchased to be my wife, to raise up the name of the dead upon his inheritance, that the name of the dead be not cut off from among his brethren, and from the gate of his place; ye are witnesses this day.*

Boaz was now, in all probability, far advanced in years, and yet he scruples not to bring a wife, and even a young wife, into his family. It is certainly not, in most cases, advisable for an old man to marry a young wife; and yet we must not reproach men for doing what the law of God does not forbid. It is probable that Abraham married a wife when he was old; Gen. xxv. 1. A woman past the flower of her age is not prohibited by the apostle to marry, provided she marry in the Lord. Men and women must judge for themselves in cases where the law is silent. 'Be ye not unequally yoked,' is a law which prohibits the marriage of believers with unbelievers, or of virtuous with profane persons. It may be extended, in the spirit of it, to other inequalities which might render the marriage state uncomfortable or ensnaring to either of the parties; which a very great inequality of age would in most cases do. But it could not have been applied to the case of Boaz, although it had been found in that part of the Bible which was given to Israel. The inequality of age was so richly compensated by similitude of disposition and mutual attachment, that it made little or no abatement of happiness to either party.

Moreover, Ruth, the Moabitess. He was not ashamed of her extraction. She was a descendant, not of Abraham but of Lot, according to the flesh; but she deserved so much the more respect when she was a daughter of Abraham and Sarah in faith, in well-doing, in patience, and in courage. She forgot her own people, and her father's house, and the eternal King greatly desired her beauty.

The wife of Mahlon have I purchased to be my wife. Ruth was a widow, but not the less desirable for a wife on that account in the esteem of Boaz. From the duty she performed to Mahlon, living and dead, he concluded that she would make the best of wives to himself. She had this advantage above virgins, that her own works, as a wife and as a widow, praised her in the gate, and all the children of his people knew that her virtue had stood the test of many trials.

'I have purchased her to be my wife,' or acquired a just right to her. It was necessary for him to redeem her estate, that he might marry her; but he made an excellent bargain, although the land was to go to the legal posterity of Mahlon, for 'the price of a virtuous woman is above rubies.' Houses and lands are the inheritance of parents, but 'a prudent wife is from the Lord.'

To raise up the name of the dead upon his inheritance, that the name of the dead be not cut off from among his brethren, and from the gate of his place. Although the happiness that Boaz expected to enjoy in his connection with a woman so virtuous and amiable, could have been a sufficient inducement to him to marry Ruth, yet it was not his only motive. He made no vain boast of his kindness to Mahlon when he expressed his desire of perpetuating the name of the dead. It was for the sake of the dead that Ruth desired him to take her into the marriage relation, and he showed all that readiness to comply with her desire which could consist with the rights of a nearer relation. It is mean and dishonest to pretend that you do any thing for the benefit or credit of your friends, when you are actuated only by self-love. 'He that boasteth of a false gift, is like clouds and wind without rain.' It is base to boast of your friendly offices to others when vanity dictates your words; but Boaz professed his friendly intentions to the dead with a view to the credit of him whose place he was to occupy.

But how did Boaz know that his marriage with Ruth would keep up the name of the dead in his inheritance? He certainly was not ignorant that God alone is the creator of man, and that the fruit of the womb is from him. But he believed that God would give him seed by Ruth, because he was taking that method which God had authorized for raising up children to the dead. He married Ruth in the faith that God would make his own appointed means effectual, if he saw it good, for the end in view. Although the letter of the law (Deut. xxv.) did not require him to raise up seed to Mahlon, he acted on the principle on which the law was founded. His expectation of seed by this marriage is the more observable, as Ruth had been hitherto barren, and Boaz himself was well stricken in years. Perhaps we should not err, if we alleged that, like his father Abraham, he received a son by faith; although his faith had not the same difficulties to surmount.

The men of ancient times seem to have entertained more ardent wishes than the people in our days, to have their names preserved after their death by real or legal descendants. A name after death will be of little use to us, if we are not found 'written amongst the living in Jerusalem.' It is certainly however our duty, to endeavour to leave a good name behind us, by doing those works that will deserve it. 'The memorial of the righteous is everlasting.' 'A good name is better than precious ointment; and the day of death (to persons entitled to a good name) is better than the day of their birth.' Christ requires us to make our 'light so to shine before men, that they, seeing our good works, may glorify our Father which is in heaven.' When our works commend themselves to the consciences of men, they will glorify God on our account, not only whilst we are yet alive, but as long as our names and virtues are remembered. Remember your rulers and other good men, now with God, who once conversed with you on earth; and follow their faith, 'considering the end of their conversation,' and then it may be expected that some will follow your faith, when you have obtained the end of it—the 'salvation of your souls.'

LECTURE XII.

RUTH'S MARRIAGE, AND THE BIRTH OF OBED.

CHAPTER IV. 10-22.

Verse 10.—*Ye are witnesses this day.*
Verse 11.—*And all the people that were in the gate, and the elders, said, We are witnesses. The Lord make the woman that is come into thine house like Rachel and like Leah, which two did build the house of Israel; and do thou worthily in Ephratah, and be famous in Bethlehem.*

Ye are witnesses this day. It was highly proper that Boaz should call the elders and the people to bear witness to the purchase of Elimelech's land. It was still more necessary to have witnesses of his marriage-contract. Many of the female sex have been rendered miserable for life by a clandestine entrance into the marriage state. Publicity in engagements of such importance is necessary to the prevention of general licentiousness of manners. And those who break the good laws necessary to prevent immorality, contribute their endeavours to promote the interests of Belial, in opposition to the interests of the kingdom of Christ.

We are witnesses, said all the people. They gladly came forward to bear their part in that generous transaction, by which the family of Elimelech was to be rescued from oblivion, and, in some sense, raised from the grave in which it lay buried. It was a grief to the people who entered in by the gates of Bethlehem, that a family once honoured amongst them, was now on the point of extinction; and with joy they declared themselves the witnesses of a marriage which gave them hopes that it would be again built up amongst them.

The Lord make the woman that is come into thine house like Rachel and like Leah, which two did build the house of Israel. The fruit of the womb was greatly desired by the ancient Israelites. It was one of the blessings promised to them in the Sinai covenant, if they obeyed God's testimonies. 'I will have respect to you, and make you fruitful, and multiply you, and establish my covenant with you.' The children of Judah would value this blessing the more, in the hope of giving birth to the Messiah, who was to spring from Judah. The men of Bethlehem did not yet know that their city was to be honoured above the other cities of Israel, or that the family of Nahshon was to be honoured above all the families of Judah, by giving him birth; but they cordially prayed that Boaz might be blessed with a numerous progeny, as the fruit of his marriage with Ruth.

The Lord make the woman that is come into thine house like Rachel and like Leah, the general mothers of Israel. Leah was more fruitful than Rachel. She was the mother of the men of Bethlehem. She was the elder sister; and yet they put the name of Rachel before hers, because she was the wife whom Jacob chose, and who had the best right to the bed of the patriarch. Perhaps they might have another reason for mentioning Rachel with distinction. Her history was a standing memorial of the power of God, in giving or withholding the fruit of the womb. She was for a time barren; but God, in answer to her prayers, gave her two sons, who were to be the fathers of a great multitude of descendants. The blessings requested for Boaz correspond to the prophecy of Jacob concerning the posterity of Joseph: 'In thee shall Israel bless, saying, God make thee as Ephraim, and as Manasseh!'

Like Rachel and like Leah, who built the house of Israel. Why is it said that Rachel and Leah built up the house of Israel? Did not Bilhah and Zilpah share with them in this honour? Yes. But the children of Bilhah were accounted the children of Rachel, and the children of Zilpah were Leah's children. This is a comfort to the poorest mother amongst us, that she possesses undivided the comfort of her relation, both to her children and to her husband.

The Lord make the woman that is come into thine house like

Rachel and like Leah, which built the house of Israel. Boaz brought the woman into his house to build up the house of Elimelech, but his townsmen prayed and hoped that this worthy action would be rewarded by the enlargement of his own family. He that does good shall receive blessings from men, and shall be well rewarded by God. 'To him that soweth righteousness shall be a sure reward.' And he may expect a reward in kind, if God sees it will be good for him. 'The Lord give thee seed of this woman,' said Eli to Elkanah, 'for the loan which thou hast lent unto the Lord.' 'He that forsaketh father and mother, and other relations, for my sake,' says Christ, 'shall receive an hundred-fold, fathers, and mothers, and brothers, and sisters.' Nothing is lost, but every thing is more than saved, that is from proper motives bestowed on those men to whom God gives a right to our benefactions.

And do thou worthily in Ephratah! He had done worthily, and they hope and pray that he may still do worthily. It is not enough for us to have done what is good; we must still continue to do what is well-pleasing to God. Are there not twelve hours of the day? none of them are intended for sleep. Let us work during the hours of day the work of our divine Master, and it will be pleasant for us to fall asleep, and to rest from our labours. Boaz was now an old man. He must still do worthily. Although he cannot, perhaps, do what he was once able to do, he may do works no less useful to men and pleasing to God. 'The trees planted in the house of the Lord, and flourishing in the courts of our God, shall bring forth fruit in old age.'

And be famous in Bethlehem! He was already highly esteemed, and they wished his fame to continue and increase by well-doing. A great name is not greatly to be coveted, but 'a good name is better than precious ointment.' The possession of a good name, acquired by doing worthily, fits us for doing much good to men, and for answering the end of our life in glorifying God; 1 Peter ii. 12.

Ephratah and Bethlehem are two names for the same town. It is situated, as the name signifies, in a fertile spot of the earth. It more than doubly deserved this name, when 'the man whose name is the Branch' grew up out of this place; that blessed man who 'gave his flesh to be the life of the world.'

Verse 12.—And let thy house be like the house of Pharez, whom Tamar bare unto Judah, of the seed which the Lord shall give thee of this young woman.

Who could have expected that Pharez, the son of Judah, should be blessed with an offspring so numerous, that in him should Israel bless, saying, 'The Lord make thee like Pharez in the fruit of thy body'? Pharez was the son of Judah by his daughter-in-law. The punishment denounced against some incestuous practices is, that the persons guilty of them should be childless; Lev. xx. Judah's sin was not intentional incest, but exceedingly blameable; and yet God, who is rich in mercy, made him, by Tamar, the father of a numerous seed, of which were many illustrious saints and heroes, and of which was Christ himself according to the flesh. When Er and Onan died, and no sons were left to Judah but Shelah, whom he was afraid to give unto Tamar, he would probably despair of ever having a great name amongst the tribes of Israel. But though his beginning was small, his latter end greatly increased. Benjamin had ten sons, and yet his tribe was the least of Israel. Judah had only three sons left after the destruction of the two oldest, and the birth of two of them was his shame and sorrow. Yet 'Judah was he whom his brethren praised' for the multitude and the glory of his race.

The Ephrathites discover great ardour in their prayers for a numerous family to Boaz. We know that their prayers were answered in the glory of many of his descendants; 1 Chron. iii, and in their great number.

Whom Tamar bare unto Judah. We all know that she was a Canaanitess, and that she brought upon herself, and upon Judah, much guilt; but God pardons iniquity, transgression, and sin. Her name was perhaps mentioned by the Ephrathites, because she was of heathen extraction, and of a race of heathens of a worse name than the countrymen of Ruth. That God, who made a Canaanitess whose name was blackened by the vices common in her nation, the mother of many in Israel, might be expected to bestow a like blessing upon the virtuous Moabitess.

Which the Lord shall give thee of this young woman. The ancient Israelites used to speak of their children as a gift bestowed upon them by God, and a gift much more precious than gold or lands. There are thankless men, who account their children a burden. Large families, indeed, may expose poor men to much toil, and to much anxiety in thinking what they shall do to find provision for so many eaters; but 'the Lord will provide;' and hath commanded us to cast all our care upon him, because he careth for us.

Of this young woman. Ruth was yet young, although her husband, whom she married in her youth, was in his grave. This is one great advantage of equality of years in the married state, that the parties may hope to live together for a greater number of years, than those who marry husbands or wives much older than themselves. But this hope, like all others not founded on the word of God, is precarious. More persons die in youth than in old age. Boaz, it is probable, lived longer with Ruth than Mahlon had done.

Verse 13.—*So Boaz took Ruth, and she was his wife; and when he went in unto her, the Lord gave her conception, and she bare a son.*

He took Ruth, and she became his wife. He did not rashly promise to spread his skirt over her; but that conditional promise which he made was faithfully, and with all convenient speed, performed. It is much better to be speedy in performing than in promising. We may easily ensnare ourselves by well-meant words. Works are the surest proof of real kindness.

And the Lord gave her conception. These words of God to Eve, 'I will greatly multiply thy sorrow and thy conception,' were a merciful threatening. God remembered mercy to our race, when he denounced the just punishment of our sin. Men's brows were to sweat with toil, but in the sweat of their brows they were to eat bread. Women were to feel bitter sorrows, that they might learn how evil and bitter a thing it was to sin; but they were to enjoy the comfort, in their sorrows, of conceiving and bearing children. When it is said that the Lord gave conception to Ruth, it is not a punishment but a mercy that is spoken of. She felt the sorrows of other women, but she blessed God for these sorrows that were to bring her the joys of a mother in Israel.

It is not said that she bare any children to Mahlon, the husband of her youth; but to Boaz she conceived, and bare a son, for the Lord gave her conception. 'He makes the barren woman to keep house, and to be a joyful mother of children: Praise ye the Lord, who forms our bodies fearfully and wonderfully,' and who creates the spirit of man within him.

Verse 14.—And the women said unto Naomi, Blessed be the Lord, which hath not left thee this day without a kinsman, that his name may be famous in Israel.

The birth of Obed brought gladness not only to his mother and father, but to Naomi and all her neighbours. They loved her, and therefore they rejoiced in her joy. It was the praise of Naomi that she gained their love, by the virtue, the piety, the mildness of her manners; and those who behave as Naomi behaved, will, for the most part, gain the affections of some of their neighours. If the poorest women are destitute of friends, let them examine their own conduct, and they will probably find that the fault is partly in themselves. That place must be very destitute both of piety and virtue, where an unblemished conduct, joined with sweetness of manners, will procure the affection of few or none.

Our joy in the prosperity of our friends and neighbours should be expressed in thanksgivings to God, the giver of all good. *Blessed be the Lord!* said Naomi's neighbours, *who hath not left thee this day without a kinsman.* Paul expected that many thanksgivings would be presented to God on account of the mercies bestowed upon himself, and he abounded in thanksgiving to God on account of the mercies bestowed on his friends.

Blessed be the Lord that hath not left thee this day without a kinsman. Whatever joy men give us, praise is due to God who makes them the instruments of his benefits. In the goodwill of Boaz, as well as in the birth of his child, Naomi's neighbours saw reasons to bless the Lord for his goodness. Her nearest kinsman would not perform the duty of the kinsman; but God left her not without a kinsman. When one friend behaves in an unfriendly manner, God can easily find us, or make us, a better friend. Let us never be dejected by the unkindness of those from whom we expected favours. All hearts are in the hand of God. When David found no favour with his own father-in-law, the king of Israel, he found much favour with the king of Gath, many of whose people he had killed in the quarrels of the king of Israel.

He hath not left thee without a kinsman, that his name may be famous in Israel. What fame would be acquired in Israel by the kindness of Boaz to Ruth and Naomi? Was it to be hoped that his goodness and bounties to them would be known and praised amongst all the tribes? It is natural for men to think that the actions which they admire, should be known and admired by all. The hopes of these good women were perhaps more sanguine than the case could justify; and yet they were more than realized. The name of Boaz became famous through all Israel, and will continue famous among the Gentiles also while the world lasts, because it is mentioned with honour in the book of God. Both bad and good actions are often published to a greater extent, and continue longer to be known, than the doers or any of their friends expected. Single actions have often become the seed of everlasting praise or censure in the world. Little did the woman, who poured the box of ointment on the head of Jesus, expect, that, whereever the gospel was preached, that which she had done would be 'spoken of for a memorial of her throughout the whole world.' Our good or bad actions never die. They are written in the book of God. Our bad actions may, indeed, be blotted out by pardoning mercy. If they are not forgiven, they will appear to our shame in the next world, and perhaps in the present. If our good actions are not remembered by men, they will be brought to remembrance by the Lord. The nearest kinsman of Naomi lost an opportunity of being renowned in Israel, because he would not raise up seed to Mahlon. The name of Boaz will live in the church, and what he did will, at the last day, be published before men and angels.

Verse 15.—*And he shall be unto thee a restorer of thy life, and a nourisher of thine old age; for thy daughter-in-law, which loveth thee, which is better to thee than seven sons, hath borne him.*

'For thy daughter-in-law hath borne to him (a son).' So some understand these words, and refer them to Boaz. Our translation is indeed the obvious meaning of the words, and agrees with others of the most celebrated versions. The verse seems, according to this way of reading it, to express the hope of Naomi's neighbours concerning the son that was now born to Ruth; that he would be a comfort to Naomi's declining years, and would, by his virtues, by his kind attentions to Naomi, as well as by the tender affection which Naomi would bear to him as the only remnant of her family, make her last days as pleasant as her former had been sorrowful.

Boaz was already, and, they hoped, would continue to be, the nourisher of her old age, and the restorer of her life. What he was, they expected his son would be. Good men have not always the comfort of seeing their children walk in their ways. But it is very natural for friends and kind neighbours to hope well of the children of those, who they know will be careful to train them up in the nurture and admonition of the Lord.

Blessed be the Lord, who hath not left thee without a kinsman, that his name may be famous in Israel. Some refer these words, not to Boaz, but to his son, of whom the following words are spoken. But the word which we render *kinsman*, is generally, if not universally, to be understood in a sense not applicable to the child; and there does not appear any absolute necessity to understand the same person as the subject of discourse in both these verses: 'And he shall be to thee a restorer of thy life;' or, 'Thou shalt have a restorer of thy life, and a nourisher of thine old age.' The God, they thought, who had showed her so much mercy, in giving her a kinsman-redeemer, had now given her a new proof of his goodness in the son that was born to him. The sight of him was already a renewal of her life, and they fondly hoped that her grey hairs would go towards the grave with joy, from the good behaviour and kindness of Obed. Nothing earthly is certain. Naomi had been already greatly disappointed in her hopes concerning her family. She had bitterly lamented the change in her condition, when she came a poor desolate widow to Bethlehem. Her spirit sunk within her, when she compared her former with her present condition. But now God smiled upon her by his providence. She had as good reason, at least, as her neighbours, or as any old person could have, to hope that her last days would be comfortable.

The time of old age is a time of heaviness to a great part of mankind. It is the time of which it is ordinary for men to say, they have no pleasure in it. For this reason, the children, or grand-children of old persons, ought to do all they can to sweeten to them the bitterness of that period. If you could restore again the life of your dead parents, would you not do it with joy? You cannot bring them again from the grave, where 'the worm is spread under them, and the worms cover them.' But you may give them new life before they go to the grave, by your dutiful and religious behaviour. 'Now we live,' said Paul to the Thessalonians, 'if ye stand fast in the Lord.' Their steadfastness in faith was life to Paul. Such a life the women of Bethlehem expected would be given to Naomi, by the child born to her by Ruth. How little do those deserve life, that will not suffer those who gave them life to live with comfort! No punishment is reckoned too severe for them who are murderers of their fathers or of their mothers; but what is life, without comfort, but a lingering death? and nothing so effectually destroys the comfort of the aged, as the bad behaviour of children. If any thing can restore that pleasant life which they enjoyed in youth, it is the sight of virtuous, dutiful, and happy descendants.

He shall be the restorer of thy life, and the nourisher of thine old age. He was to be the nourisher of her old age, not merely by supplying her wants, but by those kind regards which give far more pleasure to the mind than food gives to the taste. 'Pleasant words are like an honey-comb, sweet to the soul, and health to the bones.' But pleasant words are doubly pleasant when they come from the mouth of a beloved child.

Naomi was not the mother of this child, nor even his grandmother, in the common sense of the word; but she was his grandmother-in-law, and therefore had the same title to dutiful behaviour from him as other mothers or grandmothers. It is not to immediate parents only, but to remote parents likewise, whether they be our relations by blood, or by law, or by parental offices, that we owe filial regard. 'But if any widow have children, or nephews,' says Paul, 'let them learn first to shew piety at home, and to requite their parents, for that is good and acceptable before God.' Grandchildren are here meant by nephews. The word has changed its meaning since our translation of the Bible was made. Yet other aged relations are likewise entitled to that honour and duty which their degree of relation demands, especially when they want nearer relations. When rich friends want heirs of their own bodies, we hope to profit by them when they die. If they are poor, should they not derive some advantage from us whilst they live? If it is not in our power to supply their wants, it is in our power to pay them the respect due from the nearest of their kinsmen.

Although Naomi was not a relation by blood to the young child, she was his relation by a friendship that sticks closer than that of blood. Dearly she loved Ruth, and Ruth loved her with no less warmth of affection. 'Ruth, thy daughter-in-law, which loveth thee, which is better to thee than seven sons hath borne him.' 'Thine own friend, and thy father's friend, forsake not,' says Solomon. He speaks as if we were bound to regard our father's friend no less than our own. Naomi could not but love with a fond affection the child of Ruth. This consideration, independently of her own legal relation to the babe, must have endeared him to her heart. But he must have been endeared to her likewise as the son of Mahlon, no less than if he had been the offspring of his own body, as love to that deceased husband was one of Ruth's great inducements to desire that marriage of which he was the fruit.

Thy daughter-in-law, which is better to thee than seven sons, hath borne him. Children of the youth are compared by the Psalmist to arrows in the hands of a mighty man, and that man is said to be blessed who hath his quiver full of them. Seven children were esteemed by Hannah one of the richest of earthly blessings. 'She that is barren hath borne seven, and she that hath borne seven languisheth.' But the good behaviour, the filial affection, and dutiful conduct of children, is a far greater comfort to the parents than the number of them. Naomi had only two sons, both of whom were dead, and yet she was as happy in Ruth, as other women were in the enjoyment of seven children. Great were her afflictions, but her happiness was likewise great, and it was not lost to her in the remembrance of those children that were not. Those persons are not always the least happy, who have experienced the bitterest trials. Their comforts may counterbalance or exceed their afflictions. If we are wise, we will not think more frequently or more intensely on what we have lost, than on what we have; and if the comforts left to us are few in number, we will consider whether the value of them does not make abundant compensation for their paucity. God has taken from you many children, and perhaps left you but one, whilst he has spared the whole family of some of your neighbours. But if your one son, or daughter, excels in virtue, you may find more pleasure in your one child than your neigbours find in all of theirs. A certain Duke of Ormond, who lost a virtuous son, the Lord Ossory, said, that he would rather be the father of the dead Ossory, than of any living nobleman in England. Naomi would rather have been the mother-in-law of Ruth, and the grandmother-in-law of Obed, than the mother and grandmother by blood of any woman and child in Bethlehem, or in Israel. Her soul was melted at the remembrance of Mahlon and Chilion, but it was cheered by the virtue and happiness of Ruth.

Verse 16.—*And Naomi took the child, and laid it in her bosom, and became nurse unto it.*

The infants of our race are feeble and helpless beyond most of the young of the animal creation; but divine Providence has not left us without a protector for our years of infancy. 'Why did the knees prevent us? Why the breasts that we should suck?' Because a gracious God infused maternal love into the hearts of our mothers. Why did we find tender compassions in the breasts of those women who assisted our mothers to rear us up to a firmer age? All the care employed about us in these first years of life, we owe to Him who took us safely from the womb. That love of children which naturally arises in the minds of those who have the care of them, is wisely appointed as a recompense for their pains. Naomi laid the newborn babe in her bosom, and became the nursing mother. She did not reckon it a burden, but a delicious pleasure, to have the care of that precious infant which was now the only remnant of her family.

Some make themselves unhappy, by viewing only the gloomy circumstances of what befals them; and others live content and thankful to Providence, under many adversities, because they view every thing in its most favourable light. Naomi's sorrows would have fretted her mind, had she considered the child of Ruth only as the son of a distant relation, by one from whom she once expected heirs to her own family. A peevish woman in her place would have said to herself, This child is my son's only in name; whatever right he may possess to our estate, there is no natural relation between him and Mahlon. But Naomi loved the child, not only for the sake of Ruth and Boaz, but for her son's sake, whose name was called upon him. She expected from him, in maturer years, all that tenderness of regard which a dutiful child can have to his mother, and felt an exquisite pleasure in those painful offices which the feebleness of infancy requires. Such was her attachment to it, that her neighbours spoke of it as if it had been her own child.

Verse 17.—*And the women, her neighbours, gave it a name, saying, There is a son born to Naomi; and they called his name Obed. He is the father of Jesse, the father of David.*

It belonged to the parents to give new-born children their names. The first child born into the world received his name from his mother. John Baptist received his name from his father, when other friends wished to give him a different name. Jesus received his name from both his real and supposed parent, by the direction of an angel. The neighbours of Naomi gave a name to the child that was born to her, and both she and the parents acquiesced in their wishes. It adds greatly to the pleasure of life, when neighbours are real friends, and when the freedoms of friendship are taken kindly on both sides.

Obed signifies a servant. The reason why they gave this name to the child seems to have been, that they hoped he would cherish Naomi, and be obedient to her will in all things as a servant. Children ought to serve their fathers all the days of their life; and in childhood especially they ought to honour and be ready to serve, not only their parents, but other friends of mature age. Little hope is to be entertained of those pert children, that will rather do what they please than what they are commanded or required to do, by those to whom nature has given authority over them. The women of Bethlehem could not believe that the son of Boaz and Ruth would be one of those unnatural children, who refuse to their parents, immediate or remote, that honour to which they are entitled. 'The eye that despiseth his father, and refuseth to obey his mother, the ravens of the valley shall pick it out, and the young eagles shall eat it.' 'Honour thy father and mother,' and all that stand in the place of parents to thee, 'and thy days shall be many.' We have no reason to doubt that Obed fulfilled the hopes of the women of Bethlehem, and the following genealogy gives us reason to think that he lived very long upon the land which the Lord his God gave him:

He is the father of Jesse, the father of David. If there is no omission of names in the following genealogy, Obed's grandfather was one of the princes who came into the promised land with Joshua; and his grandson, David, lived within four years of the time when the temple of Solomon began to be built. We are told, 1 Kings vi. that the temple began to be built four hundred and eighty years after the coming up of the children of Israel from the land of Egypt. Four hundred and thirty-six years must therefore have intervened between the entrance into Canaan, when Nahshon, the father of Salmon, was dead, and the death of David, who was the fifth from him in descent.

Verses 18-22. *Now these are the generations of Pharez: Pharez begat Hezron, and Hezron begat Ram, and Ram begat Amminadab, and Amminadab begat Nahshon, and Nahshon be-*

gat Salmon, and Salmon begat Boaz, and Boaz begat Obed, and Obed begat Jesse, and Jesse begat David.

As this genealogy terminates in David, it appears to have been written in his time. Although he was anointed with holy oil, he was not ashamed to have it known that his great-grandmother was a Moabitess, and that she had once been a gleaner of corn after the reapers. The family of David was of princely extraction, and yet several of them seem to have been remarkable for their humility. Salmon married Rahab the Canaanitess. We have seen how Boaz married a poor Moabitess, and was content with the name of Obed for his son. David was the greatest and best of them all, and no less eminent for his humility than for his other virtues. 'What am I, and what is my father's house, that thou hast brought me hitherto?'

From this pedigree of David, we may guess for what reason he committed his father and mother to the king of Moab. Jesse's grandmother was a Moabitess. It is not, however, probable that his parents were well treated by that prince. When he was forced out of the land of Israel, he chose rather to go to Gath, whose mightiest champion he had killed, than to go to the land of Moab.

Ruth not only became a mother in Israel, but the mother of the best and greatest men in Israel. I question whether there ever was a line of kings of whom such a large proportion were both good and great men as the line of David.

Infidels have no just pretence for alleging that it was impossible there could be so few generations as five between the departure from Egypt and the building of the temple, at the distance of four hundred and eighty years. The life of man was, indeed, shortened before the days of David, and even from the time of Moses, to its present period. What then? 'Is the arm of the Lord shortened?' He can, if he pleases, give as many years to us as to Methuselah. It is very probable that many of our Lord's ancestors were eminent for corporeal vigour and longevity as well as for better qualities.

But how are infidels sure that there were no more generations than five? Five only are mentioned here and in other places of Scripture, where we find the names of these illustrious men. But it is well known that the Jews did not reckon themselves under any necessity to omit no names in their genealogical tables. Four kings are omitted in Matthew's genealogy of our Lord. I mention their dignity as an evidence that the evangelist, although he had not been infallibly guided by the Holy Ghost, could not be ignorant of their history and lineage.

It was the glory of Ruth to have David, 'the man who was raised on high, the anointed of the God of Jacob, the sweet singer of Israel,' mentioned amongst her descendants. The lineage of this good woman here ends in this greatest and best of kings; this eminent pattern set before all kings that are blessed with the knowledge of God, for their model.

But it is a far greater glory that we find not only her husband's name, but her own, expressly mentioned amongst the ancestors of our Lord. A rich recompense was given her by the Lord God of Israel, under whose wings she came from the land of Moab to trust. Yet we have no reason to envy her glory amongst mothers. We are related to Jesus by a more endearing and a closer connection, if we do the will of his Father. 'He that doth the will of my Father which is in heaven, the same is my mother, and sister, and brother.'

DISCOURSES

ON THE

WHOLE BOOK OF ESTHER.

INTRODUCTION

TO

DISCOURSES ON ESTHER.

EVERY word of God is precious. Let no man, therefore, pretend that there are some parts of the Bible from which he can derive little instruction. The blame is in yourselves, if you do not find treasures more precious than gold, in that inexhaustible mine of sacred knowledge, the Holy Scripture.

But you will perhaps say, We find little mention of the name or attributes of God, and still less mention of Christ and of salvation, in some books, or portions of books, in the Old Testament. In the whole book of Esther, for instance, the name of God does not once occur. Can that book come from God, or give us instruction in the knowledge of Him, that does not once make mention of his name?

The first question here to be considered is, Whether we have any good proof that this book is a book of God? If we have not, let us hold it only in that estimation which it appears to us, after reading it, to deserve. If we have, we ought to be assured, that it is 'profitable for doctrine, for reproof, for correction, for instruction in righteousness;' and, in short, that it is every way worthy of its divine Author, and of the gracious design for which he caused his Word to be published to the sons of men.

That it is divinely inspired, you know and confess. You

have the same reason, indeed, for believing that it comes from God, that you have for believing the divine inspiration of the other books of the Old Testament. To the Jews, says Paul, were committed the oracles of God. From the Jews, who lived in the days of Christ and of his apostles, we are authorised to receive as authentic whatever books were acknowledged by their church as parts of the divine oracles. They have put into our hands the book of Esther, as well as the books of Moses: And although some have pretended, that the Jews treat this book with less respect than their other Scriptures, because the name of God is not found in it; yet learned men, better informed on the subject, assure us, that no book of Scripture, after the books of the lawgiver, is held in higher estimation by the Jews, than the book of Esther.

Is the name of God not in this book? If 'the wonderful works of God declare his name to be near,' it is written in large characters in the book of Esther; which gives us an account of one of the most wonderful interpositions of God in ancient times, for the salvation of his people.

Is the name of our Lord Jesus Christ not to be found in this book? Are we not taught very plainly by Moses, and the prophets who followed him, that the Son of God, the Angel of his presence, in whom his name is, was the Saviour of Israel in every age? Exod. iii. 2, 6, 15; Gen. xlviii. 15, 16; Psalm lxviii. 17–20. Compare Eph. iv. 8–10. Was he not, then, the Author of the great deliverance wrought for his people in the days of Esther? and do we not learn the glory of his grace, and wisdom, and power, from this work of his hand?

For what end did God cause his ancient oracles to be written? Asaph informs us, Psalm lxxviii. 5–8. And do we find any of the books of the Old Testament better fitted for the important purpose there mentioned? Do we not learn from this book, if we are not absolutely unteachable, to 'set our hope in God, and not to forget the works of God, but to keep his commandments?'

But let us read this book with attention. Let us consider the instructions plainly conveyed in it to our minds. Let us meditate upon the glorious works recorded in it. Let us supplicate God to open our eyes, that we may see the wonderful things of his law. Then shall we know whether this book is from God or not. In the mean time, we need not trouble ourselves with the question, Why the name of God is not to be found, in the letters of it, in this book? It is found in it in such a form, as will strike with admiration, and inspire with holy affections, all who have learned that 'the Lord is known by the judgments which he executes.'

DISCOURSE I.

AHASUERUS'S FEAST.

CHAPTER I. 1–9.

Verse 1.—*Now it came to pass in the days of Ahasuerus, (this is Ahasuerus which reigned from India even unto Ethiopia, over an hundred and seven and twenty provinces;)*

IT is the opinion of those who seem to have considered the matter with most attention, that the Ahasuerus here mentioned was Artaxerxes Longimanus, one of the most humane and most prosperous of the kings of Persia, of a quite different character from the Ahasuerus spoken of in the fourth chapter of the book of Ezra.

This prince was lord of a great part of the world. He reigned over an hundred and twenty-seven provinces, some of them large enough to have made powerful kingdoms. What rich gifts hath God often bestowed on men who know him not! Think not, however, that God is more liberal to his enemies than to his friends. Some of the vilest of men possessed all the great and large dominions of the Persian empire. But if God has bestowed on you the least measure of true faith, of unfeigned love, of unaffected humility, he hath bestowed on you treasures of inestimably greater value than all the possessions of Artaxerxes Longimanus, or of Nero. It would be unreasonable and impious to think, that his donations to such men as the last mentioned prince, the disgrace of thrones, could bear any proportion in value with his gifts to the poorest and meanest of the objects of his special love. The richest of earthly blessings are but curses to those who are not enabled to make a good use of them. Some of the objects of the love of God in Christ Jesus are naked, and destitute of daily food, till they are supplied by the hand of charity; but they are 'blessed with all spiritual blessings in heavenly things in Christ.'

Ahasuerus reigned from India even to Ethiopia: A vast extent of country, much larger than the dominions of David or Solomon, when they reached 'from the river to the ends of the earth,' or of the land. Why, then, did God so often speak of the vast extent of dominion given to these princes, as a testimony of his special favour, when he has given much larger dominions to many who called not on his name? The extent of the dominions of David and Solomon was a pledge of his kindness to them, as kings of his own people, to whom God showed forth his covenant-faithfulness, not only in giving them the large inheritance promised to their fathers, but in making them 'the head, and not the tail,' among their neighbours. David and Solomon were blessed in the great extent of their dominions, because the sphere of their usefulness and virtues was thereby enlarged. A curse is mingled with all the prosperity of sinners, because they know not how to use or to enjoy, but are disposed, by their corrupt tempers, to abuse every thing which they possess. But it is chiefly to be observed on this subject, that the extent of the dominion given to David and Solomon is to be considered as a shadow of the vast extent of dominion which was to be given to the true Son of David, whom all people, and nations, and languages, were to obey. Ahasuerus reigned from India to Ethiopia. David, in the person of his glorious Son, was to be 'the head of all the heathen,' of all the nations 'from the rising of the sun to his going down.'

Verses 2, 3.—*That in those days, when the king Ahasuerus sat on the throne of his kingdom, which was in Shushan the palace, in the third year of his reign, he made a feast unto all his princes and his servants; the power of Persia and Media, the nobles and princes of the provinces, being before him:*

This prince did not sit quietly on the throne of his kingdom in the beginning of his reign. By the wicked artifices of Artabanus, who had killed his father, he was persuaded to kill his own brother, Darius; and he was under the necessity of disputing the throne with another brother, whom he subdued, after detecting and punishing the wickedness of Artabanus, who wished to destroy him, and seize his throne. When he obtained the peaceable and secure possession of his throne and kingdom, he made a feast, that his princes and servants might rejoice with him.

'A feast is made for laughter:' And we do not blame the prince for calling his ministers and princes to celebrate a festival on an occasion happy for himself, and for his kingdom. Yet it would have been more honourable for him to have feasted less, and to have testified his joy in thanksgivings to Him 'by whom kings reign'; and at the same time his grief, that the death of two brothers should have been found or supposed necessary to his own security, and to the peace of the empire. It can scarcely be supposed, that a prince so humane would ever entirely forgive himself for the death of his elder brother, when he found that there was not the least ground for those reports which induced him to consent to his destruction. 'But the heart knoweth its own bitterness;' and often the policy of the great obliges them to conceal it under the appearance of joy.

Verse 4.— *When he showed the riches of his glorious kingdom, and the honour of his excellent majesty, many days, even an hundred and fourscore days.*

Many days, even an hundred and fourscore days! What intolerable feasting was this! Did not the king see that he was turning a pleasure into a burden too heavy to be borne? Who would not rather be condemned to work in the gallies for a whole year, than to perpetual feasting for the half of that time? Solomon said in his heart, 'Go to now, I will prove thee with mirth; therefore enjoy pleasure.' But (possibly before half a week elapsed) he said, 'This also is vanity.' He 'said of laughter, It is madness; and of mirth, What doth it?' I believe all those princes, who had the honour to partake of Ahasuerus's feast, said so in their hearts, whatever language flattery might dictate to their lips.

Epicurus himself, who placed happiness in pleasure, enjoined temperance as a necessary means of pleasure. An author of our own nation justly observes, that, when a great multitude of alluring dishes are set upon a table, a wise man may see palsies, apoplexies, and other grievous or mortal distempers, lurking amongst them. What disorders of the head, of the stomach, of the bowels, of the spirits, must have been the effect of an half year's gormandizing and drunkenness (for the Persians piqued themselves in their strength to drink wine, and mingle strong drink)! Dearly did they pay for their entertainment.

Poor men, who are unable to provide for themselves any thing beyond the bare necessaries of life, are apt to envy those who have it in their power to fare sumptuously every day. Be persuaded, if you desire to be content with your condition, that happiness does not lie in the abundance of the things which a man possesseth, or in the rich entertainments which he is able to furnish out for himself or his friends. A person of quality * observes in his works, that 'the rich, if they do not in many things conform to the poor, particularly in temperance (sometimes even abstinence) and labour, will be the worse, and not the better, for their riches.' This remark he makes as the result of his own large compass of observation; for he had been frequently in foreign countries, and had an extensive acquaintance with the great. Could not Jesus have furnished out as elegant an entertainment for those whom he fed by miracles, as Ahasuerus to his noble guests? And yet he fed them only with barley-loaves and fishes. Could not God have brought wine, as easily as water, out of the rock for the refreshment of his people?

But, do you think that you would be really happy, if you were admitted to a banquet as rich, and of as long continuance, as that of Ahasuerus? Well, you shall have a feast far richer, and of far longer continuance, if you will believe the words of Solomon, and follow his directions: 'He that is of a merry (or cheerful) heart, hath a continual feast.' 'Wisdom hath builded her house, she hath hewn out her seven pillars, she hath slain her oxen, she hath mingled her wine.' Surely the feast which wisdom hath provided, the eternal, the personal Wisdom of God, is as much richer than this magnificent feast of Ahasuerus, as the heaven is higher than the earth. True, you will say;

---

* Sir William Temple.

of this there can be no doubt: but where are the happy men that are invited to the feast?—You are invited. You shall partake of this precious entertainment, if you do not turn a deaf ear to the voice of the eternal Word: 'Whoso is simple,' says the Wisdom of God, 'let him turn in hither: Come, eat of my bread, and drink of the wine which I have mingled; Prov. ix. 4, 5.

When he showed the riches of his glorious kingdom, and the honour of his excellent majesty.—Poor man! little did he know wherein true riches, and glory, and royalty consisted. Happy were those kings that lived in Solomon's days, and heard his wisdom. If Ahasuerus had enjoyed this advantage, he would have learnt, that the land is to be pitied 'whose princes eat in the morning,' and that the land is happy 'whose princes eat in due season, for strength, and not for drunkenness.'

It is said of the father of Louis XV. King of France, that when his preceptor one day was speaking of this feast of Ahasuerus, and wondered how the Prince of Persia could find patience for such a long feast, he replied, that his wonder was, how he could defray the expense of it. He was afraid, that the provinces would be compelled to observe a fast for it. On another occasion, the same prince said, that he did not understand how a king should taste unmingled joy at a feast, unless he could invite all his subjects to partake; or unless he could be assured, at least, that none of them would go supperless to bed. Had this prince lived to reign, and retained such sentiments, he would have taught his people, by their happy experience, wherein the true glory of a king consists.

Verse 5.—*And when these days were expired, the king made a feast unto all the people that were present in Shushan the palace, both unto great and small, seven days, in the court of the garden of the king's palace:*

This generous prince did not despise the poor of his people; but wished them to taste, for once, of his bounty. For small and great, in the royal city, he ordered a feast of seven days to be prepared. All that were wise among them would think seven days enough, or too much, to be spent in eating and drinking. Job thought one day at a time was rather too much than too little, to be employed in feasting. In the days of his sons' feasting, he was afraid that in their mirth they might lose their reverence for God, and provoke him to anger against them; and therefore, while they were eating and drinking, he was praying for them, that they might be preserved from sin. Christ himself sometimes attended feasts in the days of his abode on earth; and therefore it cannot be unworthy of his followers, on proper occasions, to partake of a feast. But, whatever heathens might do, let the followers of Christ endeavour, on festival or on other occasions, to behave as Christ did.

As the king of Persia could not furnish a house for so many guests as were invited to his entertainment, pavilions were prepared for them in the palace-garden.

Verse 6.—*Where were white, green, and blue hangings, fastened with cords of fine linen and purple to silver rings, and pillars of marble: the beds were of gold and silver, upon a pavement of red, and blue, and white, and black, marble.*

Learned men are not agreed about the exact meaning of the words which we render 'red, and blue, and black marble.' Certain it is, that every thing on this occasion was suited to the state of the king, and fitted to give high ideas to the people of his riches and magnificence. The guests would reckon themselves happy to be admitted to the view of such splendour, and to take their seats on beds of gold and silver. Yet it is questionable, whether their pleasure would be very great at the end of the first, or of the second day. Every day we behold a more glorious scene in the canopy of the heavens, spread over our heads. The roses and the lilies which adorn our gardens, are more beautiful than any of the productions of art which royal wealth can call forth. 'The earth is full of God's riches. The heavens show forth his glory.' Those who delight to have their eyes and their minds at once entertained, can be at no loss, though they are far from royal palaces, when the earth displays her beauty, and the stars their glory.

An ancient father, when he first set his foot in Rome, at that time the mistress and the wonder of the world, made this pious observation: 'If an earthly kingdom is so glorious, how glorious must the New Jerusalem be!' If you account those men happy who were feasted in the royal gardens of Shushan, how blessed must those be, who are admitted to an eternal feast in Christ's Father's house! Gold, and silver, and pearls, are but poor emblems of its celestial splendour.

Verse 7.—*And they gave them drink in vessels of gold, the vessels being diverse one from another, and royal wine in abundance, according to the state of the king.*

A certain king, asking a philosopher's advice how he should behave, was counselled by him, 'always to remember that he was a king.' Ahasuerus remembered that he was a king in his feasts. His wine was royal; his wine-vessels were of gold: every thing was 'according to the state of the king.'

Blessed are they that shall drink new wine with Christ in his Father's kingdom! Every thing there is according to the state of the King of kings. His entertainments are worthy of his infinite grandeur and love. If all wise princes make it their rule to be like themselves in every thing they do, it is not to be feared that God will ever deny Himself.

Verse 8.—*And the drinking was according to the law; none did compel: for so the king had appointed to all the officers of his house, that they should do according to every man's pleasure.*

None was compelled to drink less or more than he pleased. The king's officers had positive orders to leave all his guests, poor or rich, to please themselves in the quantity or quality of the wine. This heathen prince behaved better than many Christian landlords; if we can call those men Christians, who tyrannize over the will and consciences of their guests, by forcing them to make themselves brutes, and to expose themselves to the damnation of hell. Are not men made brutes, when they are compelled, by importunate solicitations, to drink away their reason? Is not drunkenness one of those 'works of the flesh which bring the wrath of God on the children of disobedience'? What Habakkuk says to the king of Babylon, in figurative language, is true in the literal sense: 'Woe unto him that giveth his neighbour drink, that puttest thy bottle to him, and makest him drunken also, that thou mayest look on their nakedness;' Hab. ii. 15.

Wise men will not be forced by any consideration to eat or

drink more than the laws of temperance allow. They will not be teazed to destroy their own health, or their souls, by drinking the healths of the greatest men in the nation. The man who would compel them to wound their own souls, by sinning against God, they will view in no better a light than a barbarian, who puts a sword into their hands, and requires them to sheathe it in their own bowels.

It was the law of the Persians, that no man should be compelled to drink more than he pleased; and the king ordered this law to be observed in his feast. Did an absolute prince pay such regard to the laws of his country, and to the liberty of his subjects? and shall not Christians pay an equal regard to the laws of their religion? Are these laws less obligatory upon us at feasts, than on other occasions? Shall we requite the liberal Giver of all good things with insults on his authority, at the very time our table is covered by his bounty? No; in eating and drinking, and in every thing we do, we should remember the chief end of man.

In one thing we ought to go farther than the Persian prince. He would suffer no man to be compelled to drink: We should suffer no man to drink too much in our houses without compulsion; otherwise, we are accessory to the guilt and ruin of our neighbour. If we saw him, through heedlessness, in danger of falling over a precipice, and breaking his neck, would we not reckon it an act of charity to hold him back by force? If we saw him about to swallow some deadly poison, would we not seize upon the vessel which contained it, and cry aloud to him to do himself no harm? Perhaps we may be made the song of fools for refusing to drunkards the means of gratifying their intemperate appetites. But better to be the song of fools, than to offend God by neglecting to strive against sin. If we exercise liberality when it is our duty, we are in no danger of being reputed misers for exercising our authority in our own houses, in matters wherein it ought to be exerted.*

---

* Dr. Lawson lived at a time long before the modern *Temperance Reformation* originated. In his day, a moderate indulgence in the use of intoxicating beverages on festive, and indeed we may say on ordinary,

Verse 9.—*Also Vashti the queen made a feast for the women, in the royal house which belonged to King Ahasuerus.*

The King did not grudge to his queen, and to the women of Shushan, the pleasures which he allowed to himself and to his male subjects, as far as they could be enjoyed without indecency. It would have been dangerous to morals, and inconsistent with received usages, for the queen and the ladies of Shushan to have associated with the other sex in their banquet; but they had a feast by themselves, in which they doubtless respected the laws of decorum and temperance.

It has been justly accounted an instance of grievous tyranny amongst the nations of the East, that the women are excluded from society with men. But every thing may be carried to excess. How many mischiefs does the unrestrained intercourse of the sexes occasion in many public diversions! Let not women be locked up in their chambers, as if they were criminals that must be held under close restraint; but let them not use their liberty for an occasion to the gratification of idleness, or a spirit of dissipation. Let them beware of that society that would corrupt their morals, or stain their character. Let them keep at a distance from those scenes of riot and festivity, where 'foolish talking and jesting, which are not convenient,' are likely to be heard. They are not obedient to Christ, speaking by his apostles, if they are not 'keepers at home,' and if 'shamefacedness and sobriety' are not better 'ornaments' in their estimation 'than gold, and pearls, and costly array.'

---

occasions, was considered fitting and proper; and conducive to health, as well as essential to hospitality, even by Christians and ministers of the Gospel. And they practised according to their light. Yet it is instructive to note, that the essential principle of the modern Temperance reformation is recognised and enforced in this passage by our author. The only difference is, that that principle is now extended by us in practice. Our author here inculcates the obligation of 'refusing to drunkards the means of gratifying their intemperate appetites'; *we* now go farther, in accordance with our increased light and knowledge, and insist on the duty of ourselves abstaining from, and withholding from others, the means of *forming* intemperate appetites. *We* know (what our fathers did not know,) that intoxicating drinks are 'deadly poison' in their own nature and effects to all who indulge in their use; and woe will be unto us if we do not obey the superior light we enjoy.—ED.

DISCOURSE II.

THE DISOBEDIENCE AND DIVORCE OF VASHTI.

CHAPTER i. 10-22.

Verses 10, 11.—*On the seventh day, when the heart of the king was merry with wine, he commanded Mehuman, Biztha, Harbona, Bigtha, and Abagtha, Zethar, and Carcas, the seven chamberlains that served in the presence of Ahasuerus the king, to bring Vashti the queen before the king with the crown-royal, to show the people and the princes her beauty; for she was fair to look on.*

'WINE is a mocker, strong drink is raging; and whosoever is deceived thereby is not wise.' Ahasuerus formerly behaved like a king. His wine, and the vessels in which it was drunk, were royal, according to the state of the king; but now his behaviour is like one of the vain fellows. He boasts of the extraordinary beauty of his wife. In defiance of the laws of decency, he will now have her brought into a drunken assembly of princes and peasants for a public show. What is it that has thus degraded the great king? An honest peasant, that knows how to guide his affairs, and to govern his family with discretion, is more truly royal than Ahasuerus, exposing his shame before his people. Wine has transformed him from a king to a clown, or something below a clown. It is said, that the Spartans used to compel their slaves to intoxicate themselves, that they might show them in their cups to their children, and thus produce in their minds a perpetual detestation of this worse than beastly vice. You have no occasion to bring drunken men into the presence of your children. Scripture gives you pictures of this vice, sufficient for your admonition and theirs. It is plain, from the instance before us, that a sober slave is more respectable than a drunken king.

'The crown of the wise is their riches; but the foolishness of fools is folly.' The foolishness of rich and great fools is folly in its exaltation. The great king sends not a menial servant on the foolish business of bringing Vashti before him; but he sends seven of his high lords, in all the pomp of state, to conduct the queen; and she must come with the crown-royal upon her head, that not only Vashti, but royalty itself, might be disgraced in her person, when she was made a gazing-stock to the people with her royal ornaments.

She was fair to look upon;—and all the princes and the people must, for once, be gratified with a sight of her charms, that they might admire the king's happiness in the possession of such unrivalled beauty. Vain man! Did he not know, that the most glorious beauty of the human face is but a fading flower? Still less did he know, that this beauty, in a day's time, would be no longer his property, and that he would lose the possession of it by his own folly. Let those who have wives, however beautiful, be as though they had them not; for the fashion of this world passeth away.

Verse 12.—*But the queen Vashti refused to come at the king's commandment by his chamberlains: therefore was the king very wroth, and his anger burned in him.*

Learn from this part of the history, that 'favour is deceitful, and beauty is vain; but a woman that feareth the Lord, she shall be praised.' A beautiful woman, destitute of virtuous principles, will, by the frowardness of her temper, and her rebellion against those whom she is bound to obey, discover a soul more deformed by pride and selfishness, than her body can be beautified by nature and art combined: but a woman that feareth the Lord will cultivate humility and self-denial. She will show a ready disposition to give honour and obedience to whom honour and obedience are due; because she makes the will of the Lord the rule of her conduct.

Vashti had good reason to beg to be excused from appearing in a company where too many were merry with wine; and it is probable, that if she had sent her humble request to the king to spare her modesty, he might have recalled his orders. The king's word was not, like the laws, sealed with the king's seal. But Vashti gave a flat and unqualified refusal to the king's orders, announced by his honourable princes. She very probably thought she was supporting the decorum of her sex. But in the judgment of the king's wisest counsellors, she was exposing herself by her disobedience to just punishment; and she was really acting under the influence of pride, covered with the appearance of modesty. The king's command was foolish; but her disobedience was not wise. She was in no danger of being insulted by indecent words, or wanton glances, in the presence of her royal husband, whose frown was death to his subjects. She thought she was supporting the honour of her sex. But did she not see that she was affronting her husband, and her king, not only before his chamberlains, but before all his people? If he suffered his own family to trample upon his authority, his respectability amongst his other subjects must have been greatly lessened. The queen is the first subject in the kingdom; she ought, therefore, to go before all the other subjects, in showing a becoming deference to the king's pleasure. In like manner, the wives of other men who have servants or children to govern, are utterly inexcusable, if they do not, by such obedience as is required from wives, render the authority of their husbands respected in the family. This is a matter of such importance, that Paul will not allow those men to be chosen to rule in the church, who have not the power to govern their own houses: 'For if a man,' says he, 'know not how to rule his own house, how shall he rule the church of God?'

I will not come, said Vashti; and all the persuasions of the great men sent to conduct her could not prevail upon her to give satisfaction to the king. She is too often imitated by women who have promised obedience to their husbands. They will allege, that the meaning of their promise was, that they were to obey their husbands in all reasonable things. If by reasonable things they meant things in which they could give obedience with a good conscience, the limitation would be very proper. But a more frequent meaning which they have for the expression is, things which please their own humours. If these only are the matters in which they are disposed to yield obedience, the promise ought never to have been made; for whenever they conform themselves to their own humour, rather than to the known will of their husbands, they break a solemn promise; and thus, in the course of their lives, heap guilt upon guilt by many violations of the covenant of their God.

Let us not, however, overlook another observation suggested by the words before us, for the admonition of husbands. If they expect due obedience from their wives, let them be always reasonable in their commands; otherwise, half the guilt of the disobedience of their wives will remain with themselves. You see, that all the authority of the greatest king in the world could not make Vashti obedient to a foolish command. She will rather encounter the king's wrath; and 'the wrath of a king is like messengers of death.' She will rather risk the loss of her royal dignity, than come into a drunken company, at the order of Ahasuerus himself. Never impose a burden upon your wife, which either female delicacy, or her particular temper, which you ought to know, will render too heavy for her to bear.

Therefore was the king very wroth, and his anger burned in him. —He was confounded and shocked at the unexpected disappointment. He hoped to show to all his princes and people in Shushan how happy he was, and only showed them his misery. He boasted of his wife's beauty; and she showed how little respect she entertained for her husband and her king. When he expected the readiest obedience, he met with avowed rebellion. The person most indebted to him in all his dominions, was the first to set an example of opposition to his will.

Let husbands and wives remember, that there are no persons in the world from whom they have received more decisive testimonies of esteem and affection, than from one another; and therefore, that there are no persons from whom any instances of disrespect will be taken in worse part, unless they have obtained a great command of their temper. Husbands! provoke not to anger your wives, who have placed such confidence in you, that they have given you themselves. Wives!

do not dishonour those husbands, who have chosen you from among all the rest of your sex, to commit to you the care of their comfort and their honour.

Beware of being too easily provoked by the behaviour of your husbands or wives. They have not treated you, you say, as they ought to have done. It may be so. But, perhaps, if you duly consider your own conduct, you may find that a part of the blame is your own. Was Vashti ever wont to treat Ahasuerus as she now did? No. He had never treated her before as he now treated her, and her resentment was kindled at the indecent proposal of being made a spectacle to all the people in Shushan. She could not be justified; but if Ahasuerus had considered how much of the blame lay upon himself, he might have moderated his anger, and turned a great part of it upon himself.

Verse 13.—*Then the king said to the wise men, which knew the times, (for so was the king's manner toward all that knew law and judgment:*

It was a good advice given to Augustus Cæsar by the philosopher Athenadorus, when he found himself angry never to speak or act under the influence of this passion, till at least he had repeated the Greek alphabet. By the time when he had done so, the philosopher thought his passion would be so far calmed, that his judgment would have liberty to operate. Ahasuerus was wise in taking the advice of his wise men, when his anger burned within him, before he would inflict any punishment on Vashti. He would have acted still more wisely, if he had delayed the matter till his passion was abated, and till he considered how much himself was to blame.

'In the multitude of counsellors is safety,' says Solomon. Not only kings, but also private persons, often need wise counsels, especially when they are hurried away by their passions. But our loss is, that at such times we are more unfit than usual to receive counsel. Anger has been justly said to be a short madness; and yet we never think ourselves so wise as when this fit of madness is upon us.

Every man is not fit to be a counsellor. Ahasuerus took advice with his wise men, who knew the times, and who knew laws and judgment. 'Times' sometimes signify the events that fall out in different periods; 1 Chron. xxix. *ult.* Those who in this sense know the times, are eminently fit to give good counsel, because, from what has been, and from what has been done, we may form a good conjecture of what is likely to be, or to be done; Eccles. i. 9, 10. But by men that know the times, it will perhaps be better to understand those who know what is fit to be done on any occasion. The princes of Issachar, in the days of David, are said to have been 'men who knew the times, what Israel ought to do.' No kind of knowledge is more important than the knowledge of the times, and of the duties proper to them. 'Because man knoweth not his time,' says Solomon, 'he is like fishes taken in an evil net, and like birds caught in a snare, when it falleth suddenly upon them.' Our Lord greatly laments the ignorance and inconsideration which made the people of Judea, in his days, careless about the signs and the duties of the times. 'O that thou hadst known, thou at least, in this thy day, the things that belong to thy peace!'

For so was the king's manner toward all that knew law and judgment.—It was customary with the king to treat with high respect men of knowledge in the laws, and to consult them in the management of his affairs. Happy is the land that is governed by kings who trust not to their own understanding; who highly respect the laws, and make use of wise men learned in the laws, as their counsellors! Such was Solomon's disposition. Although he was the wisest of men, he had old counsellors, whom he consulted in all his affairs. And it was the folly of his son Rehoboam, by which he brought unspeakable mischief on himself, and upon his people, that he forsook the old counsellors who had stood before his father, and hearkened to those young counsellors, that paid much more regard to their own passions, and the king's, than to laws and judgment.

It was one great loss, however, to the Persians, and to all the heathen nations, that they were unacquainted with the laws of the Bible. There were, doubtless, many good laws among them; but there were bad laws likewise; such as that made by Darius, that no god or man (save the king only) should have any supplication presented to him, for the space of thirty days. It was the distinguishing advantage of the people of God, that their laws were the perfection of wisdom; Deut. iv. 6-8. Let us make the laws of God the subject of our meditation day and night; so shall we attain more true wisdom, than the wisest heathen sages by a thousand years of the most diligent study. The laws of the Bible will direct our own feet in the paths of peace, and enable us to give the best counsels to our neighbours. 'Have not I written to thee,' says one of the inspired writers, 'excellent things in counsels and knowledge, that I might make thee know the certainty of the words of truth; that thou mightest answer the words of truth to them that send unto thee?'

Verse 14.—*And the next unto him was Carshena, Shethar, Admatha, Tarshish, Meres, Marsena, and Memucan, the seven princes of Persia and Media, which saw the king's face, and which sat the first in the kingdom;)*

The kings of Persia did not suffer themselves to be seen by their people promiscuously. They wished to be accounted superior to other mortals, and would not put themselves on a level with the rest of mankind, by exposing themselves to the eyes of the multitude. Thus they gratified their pride at the expense of their happiness and usefulness. They could not enjoy the comforts of society, nor procure the information which they needed, of the state of their subjects and kingdom, whilst they secluded themselves from their people.

But there were seven princes of Persia and Media who had a right by law to see the face of their sovereign. It was highly necessary that these men should exceed their fellow-subjects in wisdom, from whom the king was to receive the greatest part of his information, and by whose counsels he was to regulate his measures. But it cannot be reasonably supposed, that the happiest selection should always be made of men intrusted with such privileges. Those who wish to raise themselves above the rank of mortals, are likeliest of all others to fall below it. Few men in Persia were likely to know less of the real state of the kingdom, than a king whose grandeur rendered him inaccessible to the greater part of his subjects.

Verse 15.—*What shall we do unto the queen Vashti according to law, because she hath not performed the commandment of the king Ahasuerus, by the chamberlains?*

Inflamed as the king was with rage, he wishes not to inflict any punishment upon the queen, but such as the laws warranted. Absolute princes, in their anger, commonly make their will their law; but this humane prince makes the law his will. The laws of kingdoms may be unjust; but it is far better to be governed by fixed laws, than by the capricious wills of men.

This pagan prince sets us in some degree an example for the government of our passions. In the heat of his rage, he seeks advice, according to the laws. Are you angry at your wife, or at any body else? Before you give vent to your displeasure, inquire what you may do to the offender, not according to the dictates of your anger, but according to the laws. The laws of Persia might mislead Ahasuerus, although they were less likely to do so than his own passion. You have for your direction the law of Christ, which cannot mislead you. Do you ask, what ought to be done, according to this law, to a disobedient wife? Endeavour to reclaim her in the spirit of meekness. It does not permit you to banish her from your bed and house. It requires you still to love her as your own body; to temper all your admonitions with love; and to overcome evil with good.

Verse 16.—*And Memucan answered before the king and the princes, Vashti the queen hath not done wrong to the king only, but also to all the princes, and to all the people that are in all the provinces of the king Ahasuerus.*

There is one malignant circumstance in open sins, which is not generally considered to the extent it deserves; what is the influence which our conduct is likely to have upon other persons? Are there many who are likely to follow our example? then we must share in their guilt. We are their tempters to sin. You know under what infamy the name of Jeroboam, the son of Nebat, lies, because he made Israel to sin. 'Woe to the world,' says our Lord, 'because of offenses! Offenses must needs come; but woe to that man by whom the offense cometh!'

Vashti's offense was likely to be hurtful to all the princes and people of all the great and large dominions of King Ahasuerus. So extensive might the influence of the queen's example be expected to prove. The great are under strong obligations to be circumspect. The greater they are, the greater will the influence of their good or bad behaviour be, and therefore, if they behave ill, their grandeur will be the occasion of their greater condemnation. Yet, let not persons of a low rank in life conclude, that they may take liberties to themselves which their superiors ought not to take. We have all our sphere of influence. If we are possessed of Christian charity, we will endeavour to do good to all, and hurt to none; Rom. xiii. 10.

Verse 17.—*For this deed of the queen shall come abroad unto all women, so that they shall despise their husbands in their eyes, when it shall be reported, The king Ahasuerus commanded Vashti the queen to be brought in before him, but she came not.*

It has been observed by heathen authors, that all the world regulates itself by the example of the king. It is to be lamented that the maxim holds too much even among Christians, who have an infinitely better model for their behaviour than the example of princes. If any man saith that he is a Christian, he saith that he abideth in Christ; and 'if any man saith that he abideth in him, he ought himself to walk even as He walked.' And yet, how common is it for those who call themselves Christians, to be conformed to this world, and to think that they can never degrade themselves, if they follow the example of the great! Read carefully the history of the bad kings of Israel and Judah, whose example their people followed. Did God count it any extenuation of their abominable idolatries, that their kings led the way in their wickedness? 'Ephraim was oppressed and broken in judgment, because he willingly walked after the commandment,' and after the example, of his princes. The Jews, in a subsequent period, brought calamities upon themselves, greater than any nation had ever suffered, because they followed the example of their rulers in crucifying Jesus, and rejecting his gospel. We are ready to follow the bad examples of others, chiefly in those evil things to which we are most prompted by our own prevailing corruptions. Submission to those whom God hath placed over us, is a duty not pleasant to our corrupt natures. Our pride continually tempts us to raise ourselves to an equality with our superiors. For this reason we see so many undutiful sons, so many disobedient wives. And those who do not willingly subject themselves to their superiors, are glad to find examples to patronize them. If queen Vashti refused obedience to her husband, why might not the ladies of Persia and Media refuse subjection to their husbands also? And if both the queen and inferior ladies refused this subjection, why might not women of low rank follow an example so gratifying to their love of independence? Can any husband in the king's dominions expect greater submission from his wife than the king himself?

Verse 18.—*Likewise shall the ladies of Persia and Media say this day unto all the king's princes, which have heard of the deed of the queen. Then shall there arise too much contempt and wrath.*

'Likewise shall the ladies of Persia and Media say this day unto all the king's princes.'—The king's nobles and princes trembled for their own dignity and authority. They durst not trust the good sense of their wives, but expected that Vashti's disobedience would by all of them be made a pretext for disobedience to themselves. Their fears were probably too just. What could be expected from women held in the chains of ignorance and slavery, as the women of the East generally were, but that they would embrace every opportunity, and seize every pretext, for disentangling themselves from their fetters? Better things may be expected from women in our land, who are trained up in the knowledge of the true religion, and indulged with all reasonable liberty. They ought to know better things than to plead the example of the great, as if it were the rule of their duty. Our gracious queen has always set a good example of conjugal duty; but were it otherwise, what excuse would her example give to those who have been taught, that God requires them to be obedient to their husbands in all things, as the church is unto the Lord? If the great should take the road that leads to damnation, will the sight of their misery in the regions of punishment alleviate our torments? Or will it be any comfort to the damned, that they have for companions in misery those heads that were once encircled with crowns? If so, then it will lessen their torments that they are to be associated with the devil and his angels, for these malignant spirits were once greater than the kings of any land.

Thus shall there arise too much contempt and wrath.—This would be the natural and necessary consequence of wives despising their husbands, that there would be fierce wrath and endless disputes between them. When authority is not acknowledged in a kingdom, there must be wars and seditions without hope of any termination; and when in a family honour is not given to the husband and father, the house is divided against itself, and peace and comfort are banished.

Wives! be obedient to your own husbands, if you value your peace and happiness above the gratification of a foolish unhallowed pride. Think not that you can ever find satisfaction in the indulgence of a perverse, rebellious, and imperious disposition. Your husbands know that you have no title to domineer over them, and must be provoked at that insolence which prompts you to usurp their place. Perhaps they may rather yield to your authority than live in perpetual war, but their tempers towards you will be soured. Their love will be turned into terror and aversion. You will no longer be considered by them as their dear and amiable companions, but as their tyrants. Is it not far better to engage their love, than to be feared by them? You cannot blame them for requiring obedience from you, because you have promised it. But when you require subjection to your government, it is impossible that they should not be aggrieved, when your conduct is so directly the reverse of your promises, and of the known will of God?

Contempt and wrath in families is an evil of such magnitude, that the princes of Persia thought it necessary to use the most vigorous and severe measures to prevent it.

Verse 19.—*If it please the king, let there go a royal commandment from him, and let it be written among the laws of the Persians and the Medes, that it be not altered, That Vashti come no more before king Ahasuerus; and let the king give her royal estate unto another that is better than she.*

What a happy difference is there between the Christian law and the laws of the Persians, if Memucan's advice was conformable to them! It is true, divorce for disobedience might serve the purpose which he had in view. It would greatly strengthen the authority of husbands. But that authority in husbands which is founded in terror, cannot contribute to the happiness of the conjugal life. What pleasure can it give to a man to find that his wife is careful to obey him, because she dares not behave otherwise? Or, why should laws be made to secure the authority of men, by the depression and misery of their wives and daughters? The Christian law, which does not allow of divorce, 'saving for the cause of fornication,' is acknowledged by the best writers, even of those who little regard the authority of Christ, to be exceedingly conducive to the peace of families. Wives, if they be not very inconsiderate, will see it necessary to submit to that authority from which they cannot be set free but by death: On the other hand, husbands, if they are not fools, will use their authority with mildness, when they know, that if they provoke their wives to give them disgust, by opposition to their will, they must bear all the miseries of a warfare which can be terminated only by the death of one of the parties.

The Persians, and most other nations, were careful to support the authority of men over women. But they paid little regard to the rights of women, who have as good a claim to kind usage, as men have to authority. And it will always be found, that where selfishness leads us to maintain our own claims, without any regard to the just claims of others with whom we are connected, the oppressed will find the means, one way or other, of retaliating upon their oppressors. Tyrants may find submission in those who are compelled to be their slaves; but the submission prompted by fear is attended with aversion or discontent. And what man can be happy in seeing misery around him, the fruit of his own lawless pride? Or, what pleasure can he take in the submission of a human creature, whom oppression may provoke to return his injuries by some methods which he cannot foresee nor prevent?

Let Vashti be deposed from her royal dignity, and her royal state be given to one that is better than she.—In the eyes of Ahasuerus, Vashti was more beautiful than any woman that could have been put in her place; and her beauty was probably the cause of her elevation. But let men who have wives to choose know, whatever they think at present, that they will soon be convinced from experience, that there are qualities in women of far greater importance than a fine set of features, or a blooming complexion. In the married state, that woman who is best disposed to perform her duty will be found the most agreeable companion; and the beauty of her mind will soon render her more lovely to the eye than any outward form would do.

Verse 20.—And when the king's decree, which he shall make, shall be published throughout all his empire, (for it is great,) all the wives shall give to their husbands honour, both to great and small.

This decree was, indeed, likely to inspire all the wives with fear of their husbands. But was it not as likely to make all the husbands tyrants? If the king tyrannizes over the queen in this wide-extended empire, and announces his own example as their model, will not all husbands, great and small, learn to rule their wives with a rod of iron? The wives will, of consequence, be obedient slaves whilst the eyes of their husbands are upon them, but will not cordially promote their interests and comfort. Let your wives be sharers in your happiness, if you wish that they should contribute to it. Let them be treated with tenderness, if you expect sympathy from them in your distresses. Let not their faults be punished with rigour, until you can say, that your behaviour has never tempted them to commit such faults.

Verse 21.—And the saying pleased the king and the princes; and the king did according to the word of Memucan.

We do not wonder that the king was pleased with a proposal which gratified his pride and his anger. The princes too, were pleased with a law which flattered their vanity, and sanctioned their domestic tyranny. Had they been taught to love their neighbour as themselves, no law would have appeared equitable to them which favoured the tyranny of the one-half of the human race over the other. It was, indeed, highly proper that the laws should secure the authority of men in their own houses; but this might have been as effectually done by a milder punishment. 'And the king did according to the word of Memucan;'

Verse 22.—*For he sent letters into all the king's provinces, into every province according to the writing thereof, and to every people after their language, that every man should bear rule in his own house, and that it should be published according to the language of every people.*

Great care is taken by this prince to prevent the bad effects which might result from the disobedience of Vashti. He not only divorces her, but publishes a decree through all his dominions, that every man should bear rule in his own house. He was afraid that a spirit of independence among the female sex would soon spread disorder through the kingdom, if he did not take strong measures to counteract the bad example set by the queen. It is certainly the duty of all princes to do what they can to promote good order in their dominions, and to prevent or suppress every immorality. The safety and honour of a prince is in the virtue, as well as in the multitude, of his people.

Let every man bear rule in his own house.—This is the law of God, as well as of Ahasuerus. Let every wife willingly submit to the authority of her husband in all lawful things. Consider what miseries you may bring upon yourselves by refusing compliance with that order which God hath settled for the peace of families. What did Vashti think of her own conduct, when she lost a royal diadem by one act of disobedience? Did she not curse that pride, which a little before she had considered as an instance of female delicacy?

You cannot lose a diadem by disobedience. Your husbands

cannot divorce you; but they can embitter your lives, by their resentment of your conduct. For this reason you ought to behave well in the married state, because nothing but death can dissolve it, and therefore the whole or the best part of your days are likely to be poisoned by discord, if you do not contribute your part to maintain that mutual love which alone can render it happy.

You will not lose a crown of gold by your disobedience; but you may lose a crown more precious than gold. 'The hoary head,' either in man or woman, 'is a crown of glory, if it be found in the way of righteousness.' 'A virtuous woman is herself a crown to her husband.' Whether would you choose to be a diadem of beauty to him, or to be 'rottenness in his bones'? God grant us grace to behave in such a way, in every situation of life, that some of the wise heathens may not rise up against us to condemn us in the day of Christ!

DISCOURSE III.

EXTRAORDINARY METHOD USED TO SUPPLY THE PLACE OF VASHTI.

CHAPTER II. 1–11.

Verse 1.—*After these things, when the wrath of king Ahasuerus was appeased, he remembered Vashti, and what she had done, and what was decreed against her.*

Absolute kings are envied by their inferiors, because they can do whatever they please, without contradiction. For this very reason they ought to be pitied. A man who may do what he pleases, will often do what will be very displeasing to himself in the recollection. Was Alexander the Great to be envied because his dominions were great, and his power absolute? He did not think so himself, when in his pride and drunkenness he had killed his faithful friend Clitus, and would next have killed himself, if he had not been forcibly restrained. When the fury of Ahasuerus against Vashti was cooled, did he rejoice in that absolute power by which he was enabled so easily to take severe vengeance on her disobedience? Did he not envy persons of a private condition, whose actions are placed under such restraints that they cannot expose themselves to such terrible remorses, as those which have often embittered the days of kings?

'When the wrath of king Ahasuerus was appeased, he remembered Vashti.'—He thought upon the happy days he had enjoyed in her society; upon the proofs she had formerly given him of her affection and obedience; upon the folly of his own conduct, which had tempted her, for once, to dispute his orders; upon the cruel punishment inflicted on her; upon the impracticability of reversing the sentence passed against her, upon a thousand circumstances which added to the disgust of his mind. Remorse now punished him almost as severely as his imperious device had punished the unhappy queen.

Verses 2–4.—*Then said the king's servants, that ministered unto him, Let there be fair young virgins sought for the king: And let the king appoint officers in all the provinces of his kingdom, that they may gather together all the fair young virgins unto Shushan the palace, to the house of the women, unto the custody of Hege the king's chamberlain, keeper of the women; and let their things for purification be given them: and let the maiden which pleaseth the king be queen instead of Vashti. And the thing pleased the king; and he did so.*

'He that reproveth a man shall afterwards find more favour than he that flattereth with his lips.' If the king's seven counsellors had advised him to moderate his anger against Vashti, to require and accept from her such acknowledgments of her fault as might have prevented the bad effects of her example, and to suffer her to retain her royal station, he would have thanked them, when his anger was appeased. They seem to have been apprehensive, that when he was restored to himself his anger would be turned upon them. What method must be taken for their security? It would be inconsistent with the fundamental laws of Persia and Media, to restore the degraded queen to her rank. Besides, her vengeance, in case of her restoration, might prove fatal to the authors of her disgrace. On the other hand, the queen's beauty was so highly admired by the king, that he is not likely to forgive the advisers of the divorce, unless he can find a wife equal in beauty. For this reason, his servants (among whom his great counsellors were the chief) advised him, by means of proper officers, to collect all the fairest virgins in the various provinces of his dominions, and to put them under the care of Hege, the chamberlain, to prepare them by proper purifications for converse with the king, that he might choose out of them, as his queen, the fairest woman in all his dominions, or (which was the same thing perhaps) in all the world.

This advice appears to us very strange and very barbarous.

Must the king engross all the beauty of his dominions, by taking to himself, as his queen or concubines, all the beautiful young women that could be found in all his provinces? Are women born for nothing else, but to be the property of any man that can purchase them by his money, or tyrannize over them by his power? Are a thousand of the most beautiful women to become the property and the prisoners of one man? If the king is so fond of female beauty, he should remember that other men feel the same desires, and claim the same right to gratification with himself.

The king's behaviour, however, was such as might have been expected in a country where men thought they had a right to multiply wives to themselves, if they had the means of procuring and supporting them. Where no regard is paid to equity and purity of conduct amongst a people, their prince will naturally think that his power and affluence entitle him to superiority in the inordinate gratification of his sensual appetites. Where reason and the law of God do not set limits to the desires of men, they will be carried beyond all bounds.

How much are we indebted to the Bible for present as well as expected happiness! We learn from it, that God has created one man for one woman. We could not value its discoveries too highly, were it only for the accounts that it gives us of creation, and of the great law of marriage resulting from it. The knowledge of the divine authority of this law, that a man ought to have only one wife, is equally essential to the happiness of both sexes of the human race. Why then do not both men and women resent every attempt made by the enemies of religion to weaken the authority of a book, which so effectually secures the natural rights of the male as well as of the female part of human kind?

The thing pleased the king, and he did so.—He did so, because it pleased him; but he ought to have considered, not only his own wishes, but the laws of justice and equity. He was not blessed with the knowledge of divine revelation; but did not his own heart tell him, that we ought to do nothing to please ourselves that is oppressive to those who are made of the same materials, and have the same feelings with ourselves? If Ahasuerus had not been a king, but a subject, would he have thought it reasonable that kings should inclose all the beautiful women of the country in their seraglios? Would he have thought it reasonable, in that case, that his own sisters, or daughters, should have been immured for life within the walls of a palace, to minister occasionally to the pleasures of a prince, if he should think of sending for them; or to live and die forgotten by their capricious lord?

We enjoy the inestimable advantage of knowing our Lord's will by divine revelation. We are very unworthy of that benefit, if we do what comes into our own minds, or what is suggested to us, merely because it pleaseth us. The first question with us ought to be, How we are to walk so as to please God? Nothing is a surer sign of reigning depravity, than to prefer the pleasing of our flesh to the pleasing of Him who made us; of him by whom we must be judged at the great day. If we make it our great business to 'fulfil the desires of the flesh and of the mind,' we 'walk according to the course of this world, according to the prince of the power of the air.'

Verses 5, 6.—*Now in Shushan the palace, there was a certain Jew, whose name was Mordecai, the son of Jair, the son of Shimei, the son of Kish, a Benjamite; who had been carried away from Jerusalem, with the captivity which had been carried away with Jeconiah, king of Judah, whom Nebuchadnezzar the king of Babylon had carried away.*

The greatest objection against the opinion that Ahasuerus was the same prince who is called Artaxerxes in the books of Ezra and Nehemiah, is taken from this passage, in which Mordecai is said to have been carried captive with Jeconiah king of Judah. If he was then carried captive, he must now have been more than a hundred and fifty years old, although he was afterwards capable of exercising the office of Prime minister to the king of Persia.

It is, indeed, improbable, though not impossible, that Mordecai might live, and be fit for business at this great age. We have often heard of a Countess of Desmond, who lived and enjoyed health for one hundred and fifty years. She lived during the reigns of Edward V. and his successors, to the reign of James I. In the reign of Charles I. John Par lived to the age of one hundred and fifty-two; and, in the following reign, Charles Jenkin to the age of one hundred and sixty-nine. Scripture itself informs us of a man who was a prime minister in the end of his life, although he died at the age of one hundred and thirty years; 2 Kings, xii.

But, perhaps, it is more to the purpose to observe, that in the time of Artaxerxes Longimanus, Ezra often speaks of the people of the Jews as if they had been captives in Babylon, although it is certain that very few of them had ever seen that land of captivity. 'Thus were assembled unto me,' says that inspired historian, 'every one that trembled at the words of the God of Israel, because of the transgression of them that had been carried away captive.' These words refer to an event that happened in the very year when Esther became queen of Persia, if Ahasuerus was the same with Artaxerxes; and yet the people are said to have been carried away captive. They certainly were not carried away captive in their own persons, but in the persons of their ancestors. Why may we not suppose, that the writer of the book of Esther uses the same mode of expression in speaking of Mordecai?

A still easier solution has been given of this difficulty, by referring what is said in the beginning of the 6th verse, not to Mordecai, but to Kish, his progenitor.

But why was Mordecai in Shushan the palace, when the Lord had turned again the captivity of his people? Why did he not rather reside in the Holy Land, that he might be near the house of the Lord? Was he not of a very different spirit from David, whose great desire was to dwell in the house of the Lord all the days of his life? We cannot, without rashness, condemn the good man for this part of his conduct. Even Daniel continued in Babylon after the proclamation of liberty to the Lord's captives. Both these men, doubtless, loved the habitation of the Lord's house; but they might have reasons which entirely justified their continuance in a foreign land. It was love to the habitation of the Lord that fixed Daniel at a distance from it, where he could perform services to Jerusalem, which he could not have performed at Jerusalem itself.

This, too, was Nehemiah's motive for residing at the king's court; and the same, in all probability, was the motive which induced Mordecai to dwell in Shushan.

Verse 7.—*And he brought up Hadassah (that is Esther) his uncle's daughter; for she had neither father nor mother, and the maid was fair and beautiful; whom Mordecai (when her father and mother were dead) took for his own daughter.*

Hadassah, otherwise called Esther, was daughter to an uncle of Mordecai. It is uncertain whether she was the immediate daughter, or more remote descendant of Mordecai's uncle, for it is well known that the word *daughter* may, with equal propriety, be taken in either of these senses. She must, at least, have been much younger than Mordecai, who took her not as a companion, or a wife, but as a daughter, her father and mother being dead. He performed a kind and laudable action to this poor orphan; and was well rewarded for it by the gratitude of Esther, and by the liberality of divine providence.

It is lamentable for poor infants, especially of the weaker sex, to be bereaved of both their parents. But, blessed be the Father of the fatherless! they often find friends no less kind, and no less useful, than fathers or mothers. Let young persons deprived of their parents learn to say, 'Though my father and mother both should leave me, the Lord will take me up.' Esther, through the favour of Providence, was well educated by a cousin; and was advanced to the highest dignity which could be conferred on her sex, although she neither expected, nor perhaps desired it.

Verse 8.—*So it came to pass, when the king's commandment and his decree was heard, and when many maidens were gathered together unto Shushan the palace, to the custody of Hegai, that Esther was brought also unto the king's house, to the custody of Hegai, keeper of the women.*

Poor Esther, who had been so kindly cherished by Mordecai, was now led away from his house to be the slave, or the beloved wife, of the great king, as his caprice should determine. Her consent was not asked; the consent of Mordecai, her adoptive father, was not asked. They were both slaves to a despotic master. Blame not Esther, therefore, but pity her, when you hear that, like so many other maidens, she was led away to the house of the king's women. Think not that she sets you an example of entering into marriage-connections with a partner of a false religion. She was not an actor, but a sufferer. Had she been left to her choice, it is probable she would have chosen the poorest Jew that was faithful to his religion for her husband, in preference to the great king.

Some young women may think it hard to be under the authority of parents, and under the necessity of paying great deference to their counsels in the choice of a husband. Be thankful that you are under the direction of such affectionate friends, rather than under the command of an unfeeling lord. How glad would Esther have been to be left under the direction of her second father! The time has been when, even in England, many young women were under the controul of haughty lords, who disposed of them in marriage at their pleasure.

Verse 9.—*And the maiden pleased him, and she obtained kindness of him; and he speedily gave her her things for purification, with such things as belonged to her, and seven maidens, which were meet to be given her, out of the king's house: and he preferred her and her maids unto the best place of the house of the women.*

Esther's singular beauty, her modesty, her unaffected simplicity of dress and behaviour, appear to have engaged the affection of all that conversed with her. It was God that gave her these lovely endowments which captivated all hearts. It was God that gave her favour in the eyes of beholders. She was, no doubt, deeply affected with the thought of separation from her beloved father, to be put under the government of strangers, and to enter into involuntary competition with so many beauties for the possession of the king's heart. She was certainly of the temper of the Shunamite who said to Elisha, 'I dwell amongst mine own people;' but God, for gracious ends, permitted her not to enjoy her wishes. He consoles her, however, by the favour that he gave her in the eyes of the man to whose care she is committed. His respect and attention made the change of her condition less painful to her. Every thing was done for her that she could wish, to make her confinement easy. She had her things for purification given her. She had seven maids given her to wait upon her. She had the best apartments in the house of the virgins. All the presents allowed by the king to his women were readily given her by Hegai with a good grace, and without any means used on her part to obtain them. This favour of the chamberlain might be considered by her as a pledge of the care that divine Providence took of her comfort, and a presage of the favour that she might expect from the king himself, when the year was expired.

Verse 10.—*Esther had not showed her people, nor her kindred; for Mordecai had charged her, that she should not show it.*

We must never be ashamed of our people, or our kindred, especially when we have the honour to be related to the godly. Yet it may be, on many occasions, a part of prudence to say little or nothing of our connections. We must never be ashamed of our religion, if we desire that Christ may not be ashamed of us at the day of his appearance. Yet there is a time to be silent, as well as to speak, of that blessed name by which we are called. Mordecai knew that many hated the Jews and their religion, and that Esther, by publishing her connection with them, might procure malevolence to herself, without serving the cause of her people. 'A wise man's heart discerneth both time and judgment.'

Esther's obedience to Mordecai is no less worthy of attention and imitation, than Mordecai's prudence. Let young women learn from her to pay a due deference to the instruction of their parents, not only when under their eyes, but when they are removed from them. What miseries to young people might be prevented, what happiness might they enjoy, would they but cease from their own wisdom and humour, and obey those whom God commands them to obey!

Verse 11.—*And Mordecai walked every day before the court of the women's house, to know how Esther did, and what should become of her.*

Mordecai, though the adoptive father of Esther, was not permitted to visit her. How much better are our laws calculated than those of the eastern nations, for the comfort of human life! Let us be thankful for our advantages of free intercourse with our friends, and 'not use our liberty for a cloak of licentiousness.'

Mordecai did not forget his favourite cousin when she was taken from him. He took care to be informed daily of her health and welfare. Our friends ought not to be out of our mind, when they are removed from our sight. We may be useful to them by our prayers, and by other means, when we cannot see them. When Paul was distant from the Christians whom he loved, he was always desirous to know their circumstances, and to inform them of his own; Eph. vi. 22.

DISCOURSE IV.

ESTHER MADE QUEEN OF PERSIA—BY HER MEANS MORDECAI DISCOVERS TO THE KING A CONSPIRACY FORMED AGAINST HIS LIFE.

CHAPTER II. 12-23.

Verse 12.—*Now, when every maid's turn was come to go in to king Ahasuerus, after that she had been twelve months, according to the manner of the women, (for so were the days of their purifications accomplished, to wit, six months with oil of myrrh, and six months with sweet odours, and with other things for the purifying of the women;)*

THE pleasures of sensuality were carried to the highest excess by those men who ruled over the Persian empire. The women designed for their embraces were obliged to undergo a wearisome purification, to render them the more agreeable to their pampered lords. Their eyes and their nostrils must be at once regaled by the presence of their beauteous companions. Voluptuousness must be turned into an art, and a toil, to gratify their senses. Had they never learned, that they who devote themselves to pleasure destroy it? Moderation in the pleasures of sense is necessary for the enjoyment of them; and those who can relish pleasure only in excess, prepare for themselves satiety, disappointment, or chagrin. If we will not regulate our enjoyments by the laws of God, made known to us by reason, religion, and experience, our pleasures will end in the worst of pains.

Verses 13, 14.—*Then thus came every maiden unto the king; whatsoever she desired was given her, to go with her out of the house of the women unto the king's house. In the evening she went, and on the morrow she returned into the second house of the women, to the custody of Shaashgaz, the king's chamberlain, which kept the concubines: she came in unto the king no more, except the king delighted in her, and that she were called by name.*

Such was the fate of those wretched beauties that were collected for the king's pleasure. They were gratified with rich presents. They might have what jewels or what ornaments they desired, when they were first admitted to the king's presence. But when they became his concubines, or secondary wives, and were committed to the custody of Shaashgaz, to be held in captivity for life, they were not so much as admitted into the king's presence, unless he was pleased to call them by name. How much better was it to be the wife of a peasant, than to be a concubine to the great king? And the peasant who loves his wife, and is beloved by her, enjoys pleasures which princes who love none but themselves cannot taste.

Verse 15.—*Now when the turn of Esther, the daughter of Abihail the uncle of Mordecai, (who had taken her for his daughter,) was come to go in unto the king, she required nothing but what Hegai, the king's chamberlain, the keeper of the women, appointed. And Esther obtained favour in the sight of all them that looked upon her.*

Esther had no wish to set off her beauty by such ornaments. She asked nothing from Hegai, although she had the complaisance to put on the ornaments which he gave her. Vanity very often disappoints itself: and no women are so beautiful in the eyes of beholders, as those that discover the least desire of admiration. Esther obtained favour with her unaffected ornaments in the eyes of Hegai, in the eyes of all beholders, in the eyes of the king himself.

Verse 16.—*So Esther was taken unto king Ahasuerus, into his house royal, in the tenth month, (which is the month Tebeth), in the seventh year of his reign.*

For the space of four years Vashti's place was unoccupied. It is not surprising that the king, who divided his love (if it may be called love) amongst so many women, should so long want a partner to his crown. He knew not the true pleasure of the conjugal life. He discerned, however, other qualities besides beauty, in Esther. He found her mind still more charming than her face.

Verse 17.—*And the king loved Esther above all the women, and she obtained grace and favour in his sight, more than all the virgins; so that he set the royal crown upon her head, and made her queen instead of Vashti.*

What a surprising revolution took place in the fortune of this orphan daughter of Abihail! Among so many hundreds of competitors, she could have but a poor prospect of rising above the rank of a concubine. But the king was charmed with her beauteous countenance, the indication of a virtuous mind; and set the crown-royal upon her head.

We are not, however, to ascribe this change in her circumstances so much to the king's admiration either of her person or mind, as to the over-ruling providence of God; in whose hand are the hearts of kings, to be more easily turned by him whithersoever he wills, than the rills of water in a field can be turned by the husbandman to water his ground. The same gracious providence which exalted Joseph to be lord over Egypt, that he might be 'the shepherd and stone of Israel,' raised Esther to the dignity of a great queen, that she might be the protector of the race of Jacob in a time of extreme danger.

Whilst we regret the unmerited fate of Vashti, who was degraded for a pardonable offense; whilst we deplore the effeminacy of a great king, who was a slave to the love of pleasure, and the unhappy fate of those ladies who were sacrificed to his vanity or lust; let us adore that all over-ruling providence, which managed the vices and weaknesses of the king of Persia in a subserviency to the interests of his despised people, and to the glory of that wisdom by which he brings safety and felicity to his chosen, out of those events which appeared to have no relation to them. 'Our help is in the name of the Lord of hosts, who is wonderful in counsel, and excellent in working.'

Verse 18.—*Then the king made a great feast unto all his princes and his servants, even Esther's feast; and he made a release to the provinces, and gave gifts, according to the state of the king.*

The king appears to have taken much delight in feasts. It was well that he did not take delight in something worse. A feast on occasion of his marriage with the accomplished queen whom he espoused, cannot expose him to blame. We find marriage-feasts common among patriarchs and judges in Israel. Jesus himself, and his disciples, attended a marriage-feast, where he performed the beginning of his public miracles. 'A feast is made for laughter;' and we may partake of it without sin, if we are careful to glorify God in eating and drinking, and in whatever we do.

The king, at the same time, gave a release to the provinces from their usual imposts, and bestowed gifts, according to the state of the king. His heart overflowed with joy at the acquisition of a queen so beautiful, and possessed of so many virtues. He wished his subjects to rejoice with him; and endeavoured, by his liberality on Esther's account, to procure for her the good-will and the blessing of his people. That man must be selfish to an uncommon degree, who can confine his joys to himself. The man of a truly generous spirit would have all around him, if possible, as happy as himself.

Verse 19.—*And when the virgins were gathered together the second time, then Mordecai sat in the king's gate.*

The virgins that had been collected for the king, were first put under the care of Hegai. They were now collected together, as secondary wives, under the care of Shaashgaz, to be left in perpetual solitude, or to be sent for by the king to share his bed, as his humour should direct him. Such was their unhappy condition; and such the condition of Esther would have been, if God had not given her favour in the sight of her lord. Esther was, doubtless, penetrated with gratitude to God, when she considered the condition of her rivals, who were buried alive by a perpetual seclusion from the pleasures of society. And have not the poorest of European women reason to thank the great Disposer of human affairs, when they consider the slavery imposed upon women in the East? How precious are those laws of Christ, 'Let every woman have her own husband—Husbands, love your wives, even as Christ loved the church'! What happiness has been diffused by them over all those places of the earth, where they have been received as the commandments of the Lord!

Mordecai sat in the king's gate at the time when Esther was made queen, and the other ladies of the king were collected into the house of the concubines. What was Mordecai's office at the king's gate, we cannot precisely say. It was probably not so mean as that of a common porter, nor so high as Mordecai might have expected, if it had been known that he was the queen's adoptive father. But his eyes were not lofty, nor his heart haughty, nor did he seek a great place for himself in the palace. He had even taken measures to prevent the knowledge of his relation to the queen.

Verse 20.—*Esther had not yet showed her kindred, nor her people, as Mordecai had charged her; for Esther did the commandment of Mordecai, like as when she was brought up with him.*

Esther was far from being ashamed of her people or of her kindred. She rejoiced more that she was the daughter of Abihail, than in her royal dignity. She was far from being unwilling, when occasion should require it, to solicit needful favours for her people and her kindred, whose welfare, we will afterwards find, was preferred by her to her life. But she did not choose to be needlessly troublesome to the king with her petitions; and, at the same time, she was under restraints by the commandment of Mordecai, who had charged her to say nothing about her kindred or her people.

But did not Esther forget her rank, when she would obey Mordecai as she had done when she was a child? Shall the wife of the great king be held under pupilage upon her throne? Esther is more truly great in the obedience she still yielded to Mordecai, than in the honours conferred on her by Ahasuerus. Her gratitude, her humility, her filial obedience, ennoble her more than a hundred diadems of the brightest gold could have done.

The woman, as well as the man, that enters into the state of marriage, must leave father and mother. But think not that your change of life sets you free from the obligations of honouring your parents, or even of obeying them, as far as obedience to them is compatible with your new duties. You must honour your father as long as he lives; and you must not despise your mother when she is old, and stands in more need than ever of the comforts which she will receive from your attentions.

You that have been left orphans, and have found parents in other friends, are bound, whether in the single or married state, to testify your respect and gratitude to them as if you were their children. In some respects you are more indebted to them than children to their parents. They took you under their protection when you were in a destitute condition, and when they were not constrained by such powerful obligations as natural parents.

Let no change in your condition be a pretext for forgetting the duties you owe either to parents, or to friends who have treated you with the tenderness of parents. Esther, when she was a queen, paid the same deference to Mordecai, as when she was a dependant upon his bounty. Our Lord Jesus Christ was more highly raised above his mother from the very beginning of his mortal life, for he was the Son of God; and yet he was subject to his parents whilst he lived with them; and when he was upon the cross, provided another son for his mother to comfort her, when he should leave the world.

Verse 21.—*In those days, (while Mordecai sat in the king's gate,) two of the king's chamberlains, Bigthan and Teresh, of those which kept the door, were wroth, and sought to lay hand on the king Ahasuerus.*

It was not the design of the writer of this book to give us the history of king Ahasuerus, or of his wicked servants, but to give us the history of a wonderful salvation wrought for God's scattered people. But events of many different kinds are combined, and co-operate under divine direction for accomplishing his gracious purposes to his people. Who would have thought that the conspiracy of Bigthan and Teresh, fatal only to themselves, had any relation to the salvation of Israel? But if their conspiracy had not been formed, it would not have been detected; and by detecting it, Mordecai gained that favour with the king which afterwards proved fatal to the great enemy of Mordecai and of Israel.

Bigthan and Teresh were wroth, and sought to lay hand on the king Ahasuerus.—You may envy kings, and think they are more fortunate than other people, because they were born to be great. But greatness ensures neither safety nor happiness. If kings were immortal, when other men must descend to the dust, or if their loyalty would protract their lives to the age of Methuselah, there would be some plausible pretense for looking up to them with an envious eye. But they die like men, although they are honoured with the title of gods. They are even exposed to dangers from which men of lower ranks are exempted. The father of Artaxerxes was treacherously destroyed by one of his own servants. One of his descendants and successors was killed by a favourite eunuch, and had his flesh given to the rats. This prince himself, one of the best that swayed the Persian sceptre, had his life sought by the treachery of those who did eat of his bread, and who had doubtless given him many assurances of their attachment to his person and government. The life of European princes, in our time, seems to be less precarious than that of many ancient princes, because their governments are so constituted as to obviate the hopes of ambition in their subjects. Yet, in our own days, we have seen two sovereigns cut off by the hand of violence, and the life of our own sovereign (whom may God long preserve!) exposed to danger from the hands of madmen.*

Bigthan and Teresh were wroth with king Ahasuerus; and therefore they sought to lay hands on him. Kings are often

---

*The recent foul assassination of his Excellency Abraham Lincoln, President of the United States of America, who was so universally respected and beloved for his integrity and amiable qualities as a man, and for his eminently patriotic administration as the Chief Magistrate of the great American Republic during the late deplorable rebellion, adds fresh point and emphasis to our author's observations, in regard to the peculiar dangers that beset supreme rulers and princes. Christians should, from these considerations, be impressed with the duty and obligation which specially rest on them as Christian citizens, to offer up prayers to God for the preservation of the life of their chief Magistrate. The Scripture prayer —'God save the King!' or, God save the President! should as earnestly and constantly go up to heaven from millions of Christian hearts, as the prayer—'Give us this day our daily bread!—ED.

ill informed of the real disposition of their subjects towards them. Flatterers assure them, that whatever they do pleases all the people; and there are few, or none, that choose to wound their ears with painful truth. But none are more exposed to ill-nature and dislike. It was the saying of Louis XIV. of France, that when he bestowed any office, he made ninty-nine men discontented, and one unthankful (meaning the person to whom he gave the office). What were the grounds of the wrath of Bigthan and Teresh, we cannot tell. But in the management of the affairs of a large empire, there must be many things daily done which will awaken the wrath of selfish and ambitious men. What man was ever so fortunate as to dispense a thousand favours, without giving disgust to some of those who did not share in them? and perhaps not less to those who have shared in them; for it is difficult to make a proud man believe, that he is respected according to his merits.

Mortify all your corrupt passions, and never let them be suffered to regulate your conduct. How often has the passion of anger involved men in blood and treason! Most justly does our Lord explain the sixth commandment to include the prohibition of anger.

Beware of speaking a word, or entertaining a thought, inconsistent with that high respect which is due to princes; 'for a bird of the air shall carry the voice, and that which hath wings will tell the matter.' Bigthan and Teresh afford but one of many thousands of instances in which the secret thoughts and speeches of traitors have been unexpectedly brought to light, by the providence of him who 'giveth salvation unto kings.'

Verse 22.—*And the thing was known to Mordecai, who told it unto Esther the queen, and Esther certified the king thereof, in Mordecai's name.*

We are not told how the thing came to the knowledge of Mordecai. But we know that, whatever was the means, God was the author of the discovery. It was by his good providence that the life of the king was preserved, that he might be useful to the Israel of God. It was by his good providence that Mordecai the Jew was the discoverer of the treason, that the king's favour might be conciliated to Mordecai, and to Esther, and to their people. May we not add, that the wicked designs of these traitors, Bigthan and Teresh, were permitted by the providence of God, that the detection of them might contribute to the advancement of his gracious purposes? He permits no more wickedness to take place, than he knows how to over-rule for good. 'The wrath of man shall praise him, and the remainder of his wrath shall he restrain.'

As soon as Mordecai came to the knowledge of the plot formed against the king, he took the best measures to prevent its execution, by revealing it to the queen, and by her to the king. It we forbear to deliver those that are drawn unto death, and those who are ready to be slain, we are partners in the guilt of their blood. We are bound especially to contribute our best endeavours, as we have opportunity, to preserve the lives of princes, those ministers of God for good, under whose protection we enjoy life and its comforts. Mordecai was under special obligations, as a servant of his king, who sat at his gate, to be careful of his life. But all the subjects of a king are under powerful obligations to seek and to promote, by all proper means, his life and welfare. Abishai procured to himself great honour, and yet did no more than his duty, when he put his life into his hand, and encountered a mighty giant, to save the life of David.

Esther certified the matter to the king in Mordecai's name. Here she appears to have acted without commandment from him. It was sufficient for Mordecai to do his duty, and to save the king's life, without seeking either praise or reward for a service which he could not neglect without baseness and treachery. But Esther, on the other side, wished not for those rewards and honours from the king which more justly pertained to another. She had now an opportunity of recommending to the king's favour her affectionate friend and father, and she did not suffer it to pass neglected. Never let us assume to ourselves the praises that belong more justly to another; but let us be ever ready to procure for our friends and brethren those honours and rewards to which they are entitled.

Verse 23.—*And when inquisition was made of the matter, it*

was found out; therefore they were both hanged on a tree: and it was written in the book of the chronicles before the king.

The king Ahasuerus would not by his absolute authority deliver up to punishment even men who had conspired against his life, till he had good proofs of their guilt. Happy would it have been for him and for his subjects, if he had never departed from this principle, that proof should go before punishment. Grievous and dangerous as the crime of idolatry among God's people was, he would not have it punished till proper inquisition was made about the fact; Deut. xiii. What safety can any man enjoy, if accusation is to hold the place of evidence?

Both traitors were hanged. Their punishment was just and necessary, and more moderate than punishments often were among the Persians. Ahasuerus would not suffer his enemies to escape vengeance, although he was a humane prince. And think not, you who are enemies and traitors to the Prince of the kings of the earth, that you shall escape the vengeance merited by your wickedness? 'Those mine enemies,' he will say, 'who would not have me to reign over them, bring forth and slay before my face.' Earthly princes are terrible in their wrath against the enemies of their crown or life; but all that they can do is only to kill the body. The King of heaven has power to kill both soul and body, and to cast both into hellfire.

And it was written in the book of the chronicles before the king.—It was a wise institution in Persia, that secretaries should commit to registers every remarkable action of the king, and every event of his reign. It was a great encouragement to well doing, and a powerful discouragement from evil doing, to know that what was done would not be forgotten. Suppose you knew that a register was kept by some invisible scribe of all that you think, or speak, or act, what manner of persons would you endeavour to be in the exercise of every virtue? Know, then, that none of your actions ever can be forgotten; that even your most secret thoughts are written in durable registers. The Lord hearkens and hears all that is spoken by us. He observes all that we think or do, and a book of remembrance is written before him, which will one day be opened, to the praise of them that do well, and to the confusion of the wicked.

Mordecai was not presently rewarded by the king for the eminent service which he had done him. No matter. It was marked down in the king's register. He may one day find, that it was a good thing patiently to wait the king's time. At present he wanted nothing. The time may come when the king's favour may be more valued by him than life itself. If he had never been rewarded by the king, the testimony of his conscience, and the assurance of divine approbation, were more to him than all that the king could bestow.

It was possible that the king of Persia might forget the services done to him, though they were recorded in his books. But let none of those who perform any services, in the fear of God, to God or to man, to kings or to beggars, be afraid of losing their reward. 'God will not be unrighteous to forget any works or labours of love' done for the name of his dear Son. 'A cup of cold water given to a disciple shall in no wise lose its reward; and whatever good thing any man does, the same shall he receive of the Lord, whether he be bond or free.'

DISCOURSE V.

THE ELEVATION OF HAMAN—HIS PRIDE, AND RESOLUTION TO REVENGE FANCIED INDIGNITIES, RECEIVED FROM MORDECAI, UPON THE WHOLE NATION OF THE JEWS.

CHAPTER III. 1–6.

Verse 1.—*After these things did king Ahasuerus promote Haman, the son of Hammedatha, the Agagite, and advanced him, and set his seat above all the princes that were with him.*

A THOUSAND years before this time, the family of Agag was renowned in the world. 'His king,' said Balaam concerning Israel, 'shall be higher than Agag.' The generous spirit of Ahasuerus might probably feel sentiments of compassion for the poor representative of a family once so glorious, and endeavour by his favour to make him some compensation for the fallen grandeur of his house and people; but why did God suffer a man to be raised high above the princes of Persia, who was to make such a bad use of his grandeur, as we will soon find Haman did? 'Promotion cometh not from the east, nor from the west, nor from the south. But God is the judge. He putteth down one, and setteth up another.' Why, then, is the basest and proudest of men set up so high, that all the princes of Persia must bow to him? It is needless to answer the question at present. We will find it sufficiently answered in the course of this history; which will teach us, that 'when the wicked spring up as the grass, and when all the workers of iniquity do flourish, it is that they shall be destroyed for ever; because thou, Lord, art most high for evermore;' Psalm xcii. 7, 8.

Verse 2.—*And all the king's servants, that were in the king's gate, bowed, and reverenced Haman; for the king had so commanded concerning him: but Mordecai bowed not, nor did him reverence.*

Many of the king's ministers had their stations in the king's gate, where, it is probable, convenient apartments were provided for them; and all of them honoured him whom the king delighted to honour. 'Where the word of a king is, there is power.' All will bow to the man on whom the king is pleased to smile. If the favourites of earthly kings are so highly respected, ought we not to honour those who are the favourites of Heaven? The mind of Christ is not in us, if we do not 'honour them that fear the Lord.'

Why did the king command his servants to pay such distinguished honours to Haman? Did he not believe that his own known affection to Haman, and the high honours conferred upon him, were abundantly sufficient to ensure to him all that honour to which the highest subject could be entitled? From this command it appears probable that the king desired greater honour to be given to Haman, than was usually given even to kings' favourites; and this was probably the reason why Mordecai refused to perform that homage to Haman, which he expected from the royal command in his favour. Many authors attest, that honours of a religious kind used to be given to the kings of Persia, by those who came into their presence; and some share of the like honour was, it is likely, required by the king for his favourite and friend.

This, at least, we may safely say, that Mordecai did not decline the required homage to Haman, either from motives of envy, or from narrow scruples of conscience in a matter where conscience was not concerned. He well knew that Abraham made no scruple of bowing himself to the ground before strangers who came to his tent; that Joseph accepted of the homage of the Egyptians, which (if our translation of Gen. xli. 43, is just) amounted to no less than bowing the knee before him; and that when the people of Israel worshipped the Lord and king David, they did nothing inconsistent with their religion. It was only civil homage that they performed to their fellow men. But, in all appearance, something more was understood to be signified by that homage which was required for Haman; and Mordecai would not in the least instance violate his duty, to please the greatest of men.

Verse 3.—Then the king's servants which were in the king's gate said unto Mordecai, Why transgressest thou the king's commandment?

The king's servants thought his commands entitled to implicit obedience. Whatever he said was a law to them. He was an image of God upon earth; and obedience of an unreserved kind seemed to them a part of their duty. Christians have not so learned to regulate their practice. There is one King whose commands must ever be a law to us: For 'why call we Christ, Lord, Lord, if we do not the things which he says?' Luke vi. 46. The commands of earthly princes are to be done likewise, out of conscience towards God, when they do not oppose his commandments. But when any thing is enjoined us contrary to the honour of God, and to the duty which we owe to Him, we must obey God, and not man; 'for whether it be right in the sight of God to obey God or man,' it is not difficult to decide.

Why transgressest thou the king's commandment?—Mordecai professed, and practised on former occasions, strict loyalty. He had recently saved the king's life, and might hope for a good reward, if he continued to satisfy the king by his obedience. Why, then, does he now act in express opposition to his declared will? Did he not know that kings must be obeyed, and will not suffer disobedience to their orders to pass unpunished?

Confessors of the truth, who exposed themselves to reproach and punishment for their fidelity to God, have been the wonder of the world in every age; especially when their opposition to the public laws seemed to turn upon small matters. The heathens who saw the Christians expose themselves to a cruel death, because they would not throw a few grains of incense into the fire, nor worship the genius of Cæsar, believed that they had lost their reason. The like notions were formed concerning Protestant and Presbyterian martyrs by their enemies. But surely true wisdom will direct us to choose the greatest sufferings, rather than the least sin. God can easily recompense our worst sufferings in his cause; but who can compensate the damage of the least sin? Remember the words of Jesus,—'Whosoever shall break one of the least of these commandments, or shall teach men so, he shall be called the least in the kingdom of heaven'; Matt. v. 19.

Verse 4.—*Now it came to pass, when they spake daily unto him, and he hearkened not unto them, that they told Haman, to see whether Mordecai's matters would stand: for he had told them taht he was a Jew.*

They spake daily unto him.—This they understood to be the office of friends; for Mordecai, they thought, was risking his life for a trifling scruple about his religion. They did not think it the part of a man of sense to throw away his life for the punctilios of religion; and used all their eloquence to persuade him to change his conduct. But their friendship to him was of the same kind with Eve's friendship to Adam, when she persuaded him to eat the forbidden fruit; or with Delilah's friendship to Samson, when she insisted upon a proof of his love that was to be fatal to his own life. Those are our true friends who warn us against declining the cross of Christ by sinful compliances. Those are our worst enemies, who persuade us to prefer our life and comfort to our duty. Our Lord Jesus Christ taught us this lesson when he said to Peter, 'Get thee behind me, Satan!' Peter's offense was, that he would not have his Lord to suffer. This he accounted an expression of his friendship; but Christ esteemed it an expression of enmity worthy of Satan, the great enemy of God and men.

When they spake to him day by day, Mordecai was still the same man. He laid it down as a principle, that he would do his duty, be the consequence what it would; and that no intreaties, no persuasions, no dangers, should induce him to violate the commands, or to sacrifice the honour, of his God. To what purpose do we enter into the way of righteousness, if we do not persevere in it? The importunities of those who would turn us aside from the path of duty, are to be considered as temptations of Satan by his emissaries; and shall they be set in opposition to the commands of God, or to the dictates of our own consciences? Would we listen to any man, if he persuaded us to inflict deadly wounds upon our bodies? But our bodies are less precious than our souls, to which every wilful sin gives a deadly stab. At length

They told Haman, to see whether Mordecai's matters would stand, and whether he would not at last be constrained to yield to their advices. They appeared to be his friends when they exhorted him to obey the king's commandment; but now they discover themselves to be his enemies, when they expose him to the vengeance of the haughty favourite. There are too many whose friendship is but little removed from enmity. They will show you great kindness, if you suffer them to be your masters: but if you think it necessary to judge for yourselves what you are to do, they reckon themselves affronted. If you follow their example, they will praise your understanding; if you act in opposition to it, they consider your conduct as a libel on their own, and care not what mischiefs may be the consequence.

For he had told them that he was a Jew.—And it seems they desired to see whether the Jews would be allowed to observe, with impunity, their singular customs.

It was high time for the Jews to be strict in observing the laws of their God; those laws, especially, which prohibited the alienation of religious worship from their own God. They had already smarted severely for idolatry, and now it was necessary for them, unless they wished for utter extermination, to stand at the utmost distance from this fatal crime. We find in the Grecian history, that the Jews were not the only people who refused to give that homage which was required by the kings of Persia. The Athenians put Timagoras, one of their citizens, to death, for saluting the king of Persia in the Persian mode; and some of the soldiers of Alexander the Great rebelled against him, when he demanded from them the honours usually given to the kings of Persia. But these blind heathens acted rather upon the principle of honour, than of religion. They might have performed religious homage to the Persian monarchs as reasonably and innocently as to the ordinary objects of their worship. But the Jews were taught of God to worship himself alone. Shadrach, Meshach, and

Abednego, chose to give their bodies to the burning fire, rather than worship any other god than their own God: and Mordecai chose to run every hazard, rather than prostitute to a creature those honours which belonged exclusively to God his Maker.

Mordecai would not comply with the solicitations of the king's ministers: but he gave them a good reason why he would not do it, when 'he told them that he was a Jew;' and that the laws of his fathers prohibited his compliance with their wishes. He forbade Esther to tell her people or her kindred: but, when occasion required, he was not ashamed to tell his own people, and kindred, and religion. Here he followed the example of David, 'who would speak of God's testimonies before kings, and would not be ashamed.' Why should any fearer of God, any follower of Jesus, be ashamed openly to avow his profession before the greatest of men? Nothing can be more shameful, than to be ashamed of our Creator and Redeemer. The followers of the Lamb 'have their Father's name written on their forehead.'

Verse 5.—*And when Haman saw that Mordecai bowed not, nor did him reverence, then was Haman full of wrath.*

Mordecai bowed not, nor did him reverence.—Was not Mordecai too full of scruples? Might he not have bent his body in civil homage, to which Haman was entitled by his station? He might then have been overlooked; the difference between his mode of paying homage, and that of the other servants of the king, might have been unobserved, and thus he might have escaped the danger that threatened him.

Mordecai would not, surely, have withheld civil homage from the king's favourite, although he was of the race of Agag, if he could have performed it without being supposed to give to him that religious respect which was paid to him by others. But he would have preferred peace to truth, and his own life to a good conscience, if he had rendered to him any kind of homage that would have been generally understood to contain the lowest acts of religious worship. It is a necessary duty to 'abstain from all appearance of evil.' We must give no offence to any man, even by doing those things that are in themselves lawful. But when, without practising any acts of idolatry, we do those things which may lead weak brethren into idolatry, we sin against our brethren, and against Christ who died for them. It is an excellent story that is told of old Eleazar, 2 Mac. vi, who refusing to eat swine's flesh at the commandment of the king, his pitying, but weak friends, proposed to bring some other kind of flesh to him, that he might eat it as swine's flesh, and thus escape the torments prepared him. But the good man would by no means sully his old age with the reproach of simulation to save his life; nor lay a stumbling-block before the younger Jews, by giving them any appearance of reason to think that he had done a thing so contrary to the laws of his fathers. He chose rather to bear the cruel effects of the royal indignation, than to flinch, even in appearance, from that good profession which he had maintained for ninety years; and Mordecai would rather encounter all the rage of a haughty favourite, than do any action which might prove a stumbling-block to any of his brethren of the children of Israel.

Haman was full of wrath, when he heard and saw that Mordecai refused him that homage which was given him by every other man, without excepting even the highest of the king's princes. How dreadfully this wrath flamed in his bosom, we learn from the method which he took to express it. We may observe, at present, what misery pride, by its own nature, and its inseparable consequences, brings upon men! No proud man ever received all that respect, or was treated with all that delicacy of regard, which he thought his due. Now pride, mortified by neglect or contempt, kindles a fire in the soul, which burns, and torments, and destroys. What man can be more miserable than he who burns for vengeance upon the objects of his displeasure, but torments himself in the first place by a fire which he is constantly feeding within his own bowels?

A wise man would have overlooked the supposed injury, and respected, or at the worst pitied, scruples that appeared to him unreasonable. Haman's master would have probably smiled at the singularity of Mordecai's behaviour. It is said that Darius, grandfather to this prince, was once, on a journey, solicited by one of his attendants to give him his embroidered robe, which happened to be torn. The king, knowing that it was a capital crime, by the laws of Persia, for any subject to wear the king's robe, gave it to the man, with a strict prohibition from wearing it. He no sooner received it, than he dressed himself in the gorgeous robe. When the king's other attendants were filled with indignation, the king said, 'I give him leave, as a woman, to wear the embroidery; and as a madman, to wear the robe.' If Haman had passed over the supposed indignity with such a jest, he might have saved himself from much misery, and would have lost none of his honours. But none are so proud as men raised from a dunghill to a seat near the throne. Cyrus, Darius, and Artaxerxes, whom we suppose to be the king Ahasuerus of this book, had Jews in their courts, who certainly did not give them honours unfit for men to receive; and yet those princes showed them great favour. But the upstart minion thought no punishment too severe for a man that would not honour him as a god. May God preserve us all from unexpected heights of prosperity; or give us grace to bear such dangerous changes in our condition as becometh saints!

Verse 6.—*And he thought scorn to lay hands on Mordecai alone; for they had showed him the people of Mordecai: wherefore Haman sought to destroy all the Jews that were throughout the whole kingdom of Ahasuerus, even the people of Mordecai.*

Pride thirsts for the blood of those by whom it is wounded. And this is certainly enough, and too much, for its gratification. When the Pharisees and priests were hurt by the fame and by the testimony of Jesus, they sought to destroy him; and his own blood would have been sufficient, whilst he lived among them, to satiate their fury. When they sent a band of men with Judas to apprehend him, they gave them no commission to apprehend his disciples along with him. But the wound given to the pride of Haman was too sore and deep to be healed by the blood of Mordecai alone. The blood of a thousand, the blood of ten thousand men, was not sufficient. The whole nation of the Jews must be sacrificed to his revenge. In some barbarous nations, atrocious crimes are punished, not with the death of the malefactor only, but with the death of every member of his family, or of all his kindred. The fury of Haman is not satisfied with the destruction of Mordecai, and of all his father's house; all the Jews throughout the wide-extended empire of Ahasuerus were no more than a sufficient sacrifice to his revenge. They were

The people of Mordecai.—This was his quarrel with them. Was this a reason for their destruction? Let Mordecai be the worst of men, it does not follow that all his countrymen must be wicked. If a whole nation were to be extirpated when a single atrocious criminal is to be found amongst them, all the nations of the world must have been long ago rooted out of the land of the living, and the earth left one large desert for lions, and tigers, and bears, and wolves, to prey upon the weaker animals. But the wrath of man cannot hear the voice of reason and justice. It wants ears; but it has a loud voice, crying, Blood! blood! If you desire to hold your innocence, give no ear to its clamours. Make it to appear that you have learned the truth as it is in Jesus, 'by putting off the old man with his deeds, which is corrupt, according to the deceitful lusts.' Among other lusts, 'put away all malice and envies'—'Be ye angry and sin not—Let not the sun go down upon your wrath; neither give place to the devil.' Your wrath may prove very troublesome to the persons against whom it is directed; but it will be beyond comparison more troublesome to yourselves. The wrath of Haman drew many tears and sighs from Mordecai: but it drew down fearful vengeance upon Haman himself, and upon all his family. God give us all that 'wisdom which is from above, which is first pure, then peaceable, gentle, and easy to be entreated, full of mercy and good fruits, without partiality, and without hypocrisy;' James iii. 17.

DISCOURSE VI.

HAMAN OBTAINS FROM THE KING A DECREE FOR THE DESTRUCTION OF THE JEWS.

CHAPTER III. 7–15.

Verse 7.—*In the first month (that is the month Nisan), in the twelfth year of king Ahasuerus, they cast Pur, that is, the lot, before Haman, from day to day, and from month to month, to the twelfth month, that is, the month Adar.*

THE meaning plainly is, that on the twelfth day of the month Nisan, they cast lots with reference to all the days and months of the year, to know what would be the lucky month for the business in agitation. The Vulgate translation runs thus:— 'On what day, and in what month, the Jews ought to be slain.' And the twelfth month, which is called Adar, came forth.

It was the reproach of some of the Jewish Kings, that they observed times. But it was common amongst the heathens to make a distinction between lucky and unlucky days. By this superstitious distinction, they sometimes suffered opportunities to be lost which could never be recalled, and thereby exposed themselves to great losses, or to extreme dangers.

The business which Haman had now in contemplation was important, and might prove dangerous. He therefore endeavours to discover the will of the gods by the use of the lot, concerning the most proper time for executing his purpose. But there was surely another point which ought previously to have been determined, whether he should attempt to execute his purpose, or forbear. It might have occurred to him, that possibly there was no time at all in which it would be safe to undertake an enterprise so full of horror. But his passions blinded him. The enterprise must be undertaken. He cannot enjoy life unless his enemies are destroyed. The time only is referred to the lot; and, through the good providence of God, it directs him to a very distant day, at the end of not less than eleven months.

Little did Haman know that the whole disposing of lots belonged unto the God of that people whom he proposed to exterminate from the earth, and that of consequence the season pointed out by the lot was likely not to be the best season for executing his purpose, but the most proper season for preventing the execution of it, and for turning the meditated vengeance upon his own head. 'The wicked is snared in the work of his own hands.' Whilst he crouches and humbles himself, and uses every artifice that the poor may fall by his strong ones, he is, in effect, spreading snares for himself.

Verse 8.—*And Haman said unto king Ahasuerus, There is a certain people scattered abroad, and dispersed among the people in all the provinces of thy kingdom; and their laws are diverse from all people; neither keep they the king's laws: therefore it is not for the king's profit to suffer them.*

It is surprising that it could ever come into the mind of any man, to seek the destruction of a whole nation for an offense given him by one man. But it is far more surprising that Haman could ever have the audacity to propose it to his sovereign, and to a sovereign known to be of a humane disposition. He stood high in the favour of his prince; but did he not risk the total loss of that favour by a proposal so evidently unjust and inhumane? Why did he not dread the wrath of the king, which is 'as messengers of death'? Might he not have heard such words as these, in answer to his proposal: 'Audacious wretch! what hast thou seen in me that thou shouldst hope to make me the murderer of my people? Man of blood! thou scruplest not to seek the destruction, at one blow, of thousands of my subjects, upon a vague unsupported charge which thou bringest against them! Wilt thou not another day follow the example of Bigthan and Teresh? Wilt thou be more afraid to lay thy hand upon one man, though a king, than upon many thousands of my subjects, who have done thee no wrong?'

But Haman had his reasons to justify his strange proposal to the king. The people whose destruction he sought were a contemptible people, scattered through every province of the king's dominions. They had laws peculiar to themselves, and they were not observers of the king's laws.

They were scattered through every province of the king's dominions. He speaks as if they had no country which deserved to be called their own. This, however, was not a fact, for the nation of Israel was now brought back to its own land; and although many of them still continued to dwell in foreign lands, were they therefore to be marked out for slaughter? Was Ahasuerus to make his name infamous among all nations, and to all posterity, by imitating the example of the tyrant Busiris, whose custom it was to sacrifice all strangers that he found in the land of Egypt, where he reigned? If the Jews must die because they dwell not in the land of their fathers, let Haman himself, and all the remnant of Amalek, perish. They have been brought, by the revolutions of time, or by the providence of God, into a condition still more contemptible than that of the Jews.

And their laws are diverse from all people.—True. But is this a reason why they should be destroyed, before it be considered whether these laws are better or worse than the laws of other people? Let this be considered before this people be condemned for having such laws. Have they laws to authorize murder, treason, hatred of mankind, robbery, or adultery? Then let them be compelled to abjure such laws, or be rooted out of the land of the living: But if their laws be found to be the best in the world, let it be acknowledged that this nation is a wise and understanding people; unless they are found careless about their own laws, and disposed rather to observe other rules of conduct.

But this was another charge against them, that they were too observant of their own laws, and did not regard the laws of the king. It is, indeed, a great crime, in most cases, to disobey the laws of the country where we dwell, and of the king under whose protection we live. Unless the king's authority be respected, good order cannot be maintained; nor can men be secured in their life, property, and honours, where kings do not enforce obedience to their good laws. Yet there are cases in which it is a virtue to transgress the laws of the greatest king. What if the laws of God are contrary to them? Kings themselves are but subjects to the everlasting King; and as subjects are bound to disobey their superior fellow-subjects when they require them to do things inconsistent with the laws of the king, so all subjects are bound to respect the will of God, in opposition to the will of an earthly sovereign. Nothing, indeed, can be more wicked then to violate good laws under pretense of conscience towards God. But wise princes themselves will respect those men most amongst their subjects who are least disposed to sacrifice their highest duties to complaisance for princes. The Emperor Constantius, father to Constantine the Great, once commanded all his Christian servants to offer sacrifices to the gods of Rome. If they refused to obey his command, they were to be dismissed from his service. Many of them obeyed; others did not, and accordingly were dismissed. But in a day or two he turned out all who had complied with his orders, and recalled those whom he had expelled; saying, that those would be most faithful to their prince, who were most faithful to their God; and that he would not trust men who were false to their religion.

Verse 9.—*If it please the king, let it be written that they may be destroyed; and I will pay ten thousand talents of silver to the hands of those that have the charge of the business, to bring it into the king's treasuries.*

If it please the king, let it be written that they may be destroyed.—Why? They are a worthless people, 'for they are scattered over all the king's dominions, and live according to their own singular laws, without observing the king's laws; and therefore it is not for the king's profit to suffer them to live.' And must the lives of hundreds of thousands be sacrificed to a vague, unproved accusation? If the Jews are a scattered people, that is their misfortune, rather than their sin. If they have singular institutions derived from their fathers, are they to be blamed for observing them, before it is proved that they are wicked, or inconsistent with the safety of other men's lives and property? It was commonly held among the heathens to be a virtue, rather than a vice, for men to respect the laws of their fathers. If they did not observe the king's laws, let them be punished for it, unless they can prove that their consciences required them to act as they did; but let them be punished according to the nature of their offense. The king's laws were not the laws of Draco the Athenian; which were said to be written in blood, because he made every fault capital. He thought that the smallest faults deserved death, and for the greatest crime he could find no greater punishment.

It is not for the king's profit to suffer such men to live; and therefore let them be put to death. But will it be profit to the king to put them to death? Will he derive much pleasure or advantage from the guilt of an hundred thousand murders; from the execrations of all his surviving subjects, and of all generations of mankind; from the horrors of a self-accusing conscience; and from the prospect of the vengeance which the Creator of mankind may be expected to inflict on the destroyers of the work of his hands?

But the profit of which Haman chiefly thought, was the flourishing state of the royal revenue. This nation was so poor, that the revenue would not be lessened by its destruction. If, however, the king was under any apprehensions that his revenue would suffer damage, Haman proposes to make a full equivalent by paying into the king's treasuries ten thousand talents of silver; which make several millions of our money. This sum he probably intended to raise in part out of the effects of the condemned nation, and to make up what was wanting from his own private estate. His revenge was so dear to him, that he would not only hazard the king's favour by the horrid proposal of murdering a whole nation, but expose himself to a severe loss in his fortune, rather than suffer the hated race to live. What liberal sacrifices will men make to their passions! They will give a great part of the substance of their house for the gratification of their hatred or their lust. Why then should we think it an hard matter to give a part of our substance to God? If our desires are as eager for the advancement of virtue and purity; if we are as earnest in our wishes to have the wants of the poor supplied, and the afflictions of the unfortunate relieved, as revengeful men, like Haman, are to gratify their ill-nature; it will give us pleasure to honour the Lord with our substance, and to minister to the necessities of our fellow-men.

Verses 10, 11.—*And the king took his ring from his hand, and gave it unto Haman the son of Hammedatha, the Agagite, the Jews' enemy. And the king said unto Haman, The silver is given to thee, the people also, to do with them as it seemeth good to thee.*

Here we see the danger of despotism, and the value of liberty. Ahasuerus was none of the worst of princes. Humanity appeared to characterize his government; yet we find him, in an unguarded hour, and in the effusions of his friendship to an unworthy favourite, giving his consent to a massacre, which, if it had been perpetrated, must have ranked him with the most odious tyrants that ever lived. What tyrant ever consigned a whole nation of subjects to destruction by a single decree? Caligula, it is said, wished that the whole Roman people had but one neck, that he might cut it off at a single blow. Yet we do not read that he ever attempted to destroy at one blow any of the numerous nations that were subject to the Roman empire. But Ahasuerus compliments Haman with the lives of a whole nation scattered through all his dominions, without putting himself to the trouble of asking what proof Haman had of the crimes, if they could be called crimes, that were laid to their charge. The mischief of arbitrary power and of slavery in nations, lies not chiefly in the insecurity of life, and of property, but in the tendency which they both have to corrupt the hearts and the morals of men. Could any man, not invested with unlimited power, have ever thought of making such a horrid present to one of his favourites? When men are taught that they may do what they please, they must be exempted from the weaknesses and vices incident to human nature, if they always confine their pleasure within the limits which men must prescribe to themselves who are limited by laws. Bondage under masters of unlimited power, has, on the other side, a strong tendency to debase and vitiate the soul. No wise man will wish to possess the power of doing evil. Every subject of a free government is no less bound to be thankful to God for that precious blessing, than for food and raiment.

Ahasuerus appears to have been a man of an easy temper, and ready to confer the greatest obligations, without deliberation, on those whom he loved. But there is no true virtue without judgment and steadiness. A thoughtless man, of an easy temper, is more likely to turn out a vicious than an virtuous character; because, in a world where so many more bad than good men are to be met with, he is likely to give himself up to the guidance of those who will lead him out of the way of understanding; or if he should be led in the right path by some of his friends, there are others that will lead him out of it. Ahasuerus would have heaped favours upon the Jews, if Mordecai had been to him at this time what Haman was. If he was the prince whom we take him to have been, he had already conferred very high favours upon the Jews in the seventh year of his reign; Ezra vii. And now, at the distance of five years, he signs a death-warrant for the whole nation, without knowing or thinking what he was doing. He does not appear to have so much as asked what that nation was which Haman solicited him to destroy. For aught he knew, he was giving consent to a decree for the destruction of his beloved queen, and of Mordecai, to whom he was indebted for his life. He now takes his ring, and gives it to Haman, to sign what decrees he pleased to make. How did he know that Haman would not sign a decree for his own deposition or death? Some say that Semiramis obtained her husband's permission to reign for five days, and in that time ordered her husband to be slain, that she might get perpetual possession of his throne.

Many have not duly distinguished between an easy and a good temper. An easy temper is a very dangerous one, when it is not under the powerful restraints of wisdom. It is vain to boast of a ready compliance with every good motion suggested to us, if we are equally ready to comply with bad motions. If we surrender ourselves to the direction of our friends, we may soon find that we have given up ourselves to our enemies. He is not our friend who desires to be our lord. A true friend will wish us to behave like men, and like Christians; and if we are Christians, we must not be slaves of the best of men on earth. 'Ye are bought with a price—Be not ye the servants of men, but of the Lord Christ—Please men for their good to edification.' Be always ready to grant reasonable requests, and to follow good counsels. But you must judge for yourselves by the light which God hath given you, what requests are lawful to be granted, and what counsels are worthy to be followed.

The silver is given to thee, and the people also, to do with them as it seemeth good to thee.—Observe in what light this prince viewed his people. He considered them as a part of his goods and chattels, of which he was at liberty to dispose at his pleasure. Unhappy the people whose kings are trained up in such notions! Still more unhappy the princes whose minds are swelled, and their hearts vitiated, by such conceits of their own powers! And yet, if the people had been as entirely the king's property, as cattle are the property of the husbandman who rears them, would he have been justified in transferring his right to an avowed butcher? The husbandman incurs no blame by giving up to the slaughter those animals that may be used as food; but if he should give up to the slaughter those beasts that are used in work only, would he not greatly abuse his power, and incur the just charge of wanton cruelty? A good man regardeth the life of his beast. A proud man little regards the life of his fellow-men in the lower ranks of life.

Verse 12.—*Then were the king's scribes called on the thirteenth day of the first month, and there was written, according to all that Haman had commanded, unto the king's lieutenants, and to the governors that were over every province, and to the rulers of every people of every province according to the writing thereof, and to every people after their language: In the name of Ahasuerus was it written, and sealed with the king's ring.*

The wickedness of the intended massacre does not rest with Ahasuerus and Haman. Great multitudes of the king's subjects must participate in the guilt. The governors and rulers of every province, and the people under their command, have letters written to them, sealed with the king's seal, to contribute their part to the massacre. Let the great consider what they do. If they are wicked, they are not wicked alone. They make others sharers with them in their guilt: and whilst they make their inferiors sin, they may expect to bear their execrations in hell for bringing them along with themselves to that place of torment.

These men were greatly to be pitied who lived under an absolute government, because, in many instances, they would find it necessary either to sin against their own souls, or to offend a prince whose frown was death. We ought to bless God that no man hath power to require us to do any thing but, according to the known laws of the land: And yet men of true virtue will not comply with the will of the most absolute monarchs, when it is not consistent with the laws of justice and of mercy. At the famous Bartholomew massacre, when the King of France sent his orders to the commanders in the different provinces to massacre the Huguenots, one of them returned him this answer: 'In my district your Majesty has many brave soldiers, but no butchers.' That virtuous governor never felt any effects of the royal resentment. It is to be feared that few of the Persian governors would have given such proofs of virtuous courage, if the king's edict had not been reversed. We find none of all the governors of the provinces of the Babylonian empire, that refused to bow their knees to the graven image which Nebuchadnezzar the king set up. The subjects of princes who rule with unlimited dominion, are for the most part slaves both in body and in soul. They are taught from their earliest days, by the examples which they see around them, to consider their princes as gods on earth, whose will must not be disputed.

Verse 13.—*And the letters were sent by posts unto all the king's provinces, to destroy, to kill, and to cause to perish, all Jews, both young and old, little children and women, in one day, even upon the thirteenth day of the twelfth month, (which is the month Adar,) and to take the spoil of them for a prey.*

Malice must have blinded the eyes of that wicked man to a strange degree. He gives as the reason why he would have the hated nation destroyed, 'That they did not keep the king's laws;' but in the edict against them are comprehended many thousands who could not possibly break them. The little children, who could neither do good nor evil, may reasonably be supposed to make a fourth or fifth part of the whole nation. There might be supposed, at least, as many in the whole nation of the Jews as at Nineveh in the days of Jonah, 'who could not discern between their right hand and their left.' The king's humanity must have revolted at the thought of shedding the blood of so many innocents, as soon as he reflected calmly on this horrible decree. It is said, that one of the hardened bigots who killed many of the Protestants in the Irish massacre, found his conscience tormented as long as he lived with the thought of some babes whom he had stabbed in the heat of his zeal. Their images often presented themselves to his fancy, and inflicted severer pangs than the gibbet could have done. What, then, must a prince, naturally of a clement disposition, have thought in his moments of reflection, concerning a favourite who had, in an unguarded moment, persuaded him to give a death-warrant against the poor babes of a whole nation, who could not in any manner offend him; as well as against their fathers and mothers, who had done nothing to offend him, but by observing the laws of their fathers? Although Providence had not so wonderfully interposed to turn Haman's mischief upon his own head, it is very probable he would not long have escaped the vengeance of his misguided prince; who could not have forgiven himself nor his favourite the guilt of so many causeless murders.

The Jews are the people expressly mentioned as the unhappy objects of this bloody edict. Haman did not know that Esther herself, no less than Mordecai, was included in this intended proscription. Had any one drawn his sword against the queen's life, what punishment could justly have been inflicted upon him by the king, when he could produce a warrant sealed with the king's seal?

But there was another point of still more importance unknown to this enemy of the Jews; that they were a nation which could not be extirpated, because they were under the special protection of the God of heaven. The malice of Haman could no more frustrate the ancient oracles relating to the Jews, than it could pull the sun out of the firmament, and deprive the world of the light of day. 'The sceptre was not to depart from Judah, nor a lawgiver from between his feet, till Shiloh should come.' The Shiloh was not yet come. Judah must therefore continue a distinct nation, under governors that proceeded from himself. Haman's malice will be so far from finding the means of extirpating Judah, that the glory of that people, though eclipsed, must again shine forth as the morning.

Verse 14.—*The copy of the writing for a commandment to be given in every province, was published unto all people, that they should be ready against that day.*

Nebuchadnezzar gathered the governors of all his provinces to Babylon, that they might witness the honours done to the graven image that he had set up. But the event was very different from his expectation. They all saw the disgrace of the worshippers of graven images, and the glory of the God of Israel, who preserved his faithful servants in the midst of that fire which consumed the king's servants that cast them into the furnace. Thus Haman caused the edict against the Jews to be published in the language of every people, that they might all be prepared to bear their part in the destruction of the Jews. But the enemies of Israel had one thing in view, and the God of Israel quite another. Haman intended to make the destruction of Judah as sure as possible, but God intended to make all nations attentive witnesses of his power and wisdom displayed in counteracting the designs of their enemies, and accomplishing their salvation. The effect of such an edict would be the fixing of all men's attention on the event; and the event was to make it evident, that there was no god like the God of Israel; nor any people on the earth so much the care of Heaven, as that nation which was held in abhorrence by Haman.

Verse 15.—*The posts went out, being hastened by the king's commandment, and the decree was given in Shushan the palace. And the king and Haman sat down to drink; but the city Shushan was perplexed.*

Haman was in great haste to publish the decree through all

parts of the king's dominions, though it was not to be executed till eleven months were elapsed from the time when it was enacted. His intention was, that every thing should be in readiness for the execution on the proper day. But did he not outwit himself? Would it not have been much better to have kept it a profound secret till it could be a secret no longer? Had he no reason to think that there might be some one or other in the king's large extended dominions that might befriend the oppressed nation, and make the king sensible how much he had been imposed upon? What if some one of the king's noble princes, envying Haman's credit, might take the advantage which the atrocious cruelty and injustice of the decree gave him, of opening the king's eyes to the wickedness of his conduct? The Jews themselves, at least, might be expected to adopt some measure, either to preserve themselves, or to sell their lives dear. What if despair should inspire them with courage to aim a deadly blow at the head of this oppressor? They could make the attempt without risking their lives, when they were already under sentence of death. Their losing their lives a few months sooner than the time fixed, would be a relief to them from so many months of anguish.

In the folly of Haman's conduct, we see the wisdom of God over-ruling the counsels of the wicked, to serve his own purposes; and infatuating them, that he might destroy them. The Jews have time to pray, and confess their sins. The terror into which they were thrown, would put them in mind of Him who was 'the Hope of Israel, and the Saviour thereof in the time of trouble.' God himself was in the mean time 'whetting his sword, and making it ready. He was preparing for him the instruments of death, that the violent dealing' of the wicked Haman 'might come down upon his own head.'

Haman, in the mean time, gives up himself to pleasure and jollity, in which he had the honour to be companion to the king. He will soon find that 'the end of this mirth is heaviness.' The city Shushan was perplexed, when the king and Haman were enjoying this merriment. What heart could be free from perplexity on such an occasion? The Jews were known to be as innocent as their neighbours. Many of them resided in the city of Shushan. The prospect of their miserable and unmerited fate was terrible. Who could tell where such mischiefs were to end? Haman might next day petition his deluded master to compliment him with a like sacrifice of other lives. The people of Shushan at this time would be in much the same state of mind with a Persian minister of state in later times, who said, that he never left the king's presence without putting his hand to his head, that he might feel whether it was still standing on his shoulders.

We have reason to bless God that most men in civilized nations feel an abhorrence at bloody crimes. Many who scruple not to lie, or to cheat, would be struck with horror at the guilt of murder in themselves or others. Many and gracious are the methods used by God for the security of the life of that favourite creature which he made after his own image. May we spend those lives to his glory, which are protracted by his goodness!

DISCOURSE VII.

THE GRIEF OF MORDECAI AND THE OTHER JEWS AT HEARING OF THE BLOODY EDICT—MORDECAI SOLICITS ESTHER TO INTERCEDE WITH THE KING ON THEIR BEHALF.

CHAPTER IV. 1–11.

Verse 1.—*When Mordecai perceived all that was done, Mordecai rent his clothes, and put on sackcloth with ashes, and went out into the midst of the city, and cried with a loud and bitter cry.*

MORDECAI was watchful over the interests of his people, and deeply affected with all their concerns; Chap. x. 3. Judge, then, what must have been his feelings, when he was informed that an edict had passed for their destruction! But what was still more distressing to him, was the consideration that himself was the occasion of it. He could not reflect upon his own conduct, indeed, as the proper cause of the mischief. He had done nothing but what his conscience approved, and what he still resolved to do in similar circumstances; Chap. v. 9. And who could ever have imagined that the revenge of Haman would have extended farther than his own life? But still he must have been penetrated with bitter anguish at the thought that the sanguinary decree originated in Haman's revenge against his own conduct. And, as David told Abiathar that he had been the occasion of the death of all the persons of his father's house, so he might be reflected on by the Jews as the death of every person of their nation. With cutting reflections he would think on the day when he first entered into the king's service. If he had not been one of the men that sat in the king's gate, he might never have seen Haman's face; and the decree would never have been thought of. Why did he still reside in a foreign land, when he might have been a dweller in the Holy

Land, with his brethren who had returned from their captivity? Why had he not rather chosen the meanest condition, which would have kept him at a distance from kings and courts, than a situation which had so unhappily involved himself and all his people in the danger of utter extermination? Had a sentence of death been pronounced upon himself; and his beloved Esther and all the persons of his father's house been comprehended in the sentence; his grief would have been very great, but in no wise comparable to what he felt from the present danger of all his people.

Poor Mordecai had it not in his power to confine his anguish to his own bosom, or to his own house. He published it through all the city of Shushan. You need not ask for what reasons persons overwhelmed with grief do not inquire what purpose the publication of their grief may serve. The strong impulse of sorrow often makes them publish their complaints to the winds or to the trees. Yet who knows what good end it might serve to announce the unmerited calamity of the Jews through the whole city of Shushan? There might be some compassionate hearts amongst the people that would be interested by such a dire calamity: and though the people had no direct access to the king, yet they could present their supplications to the counsellors who saw his face; or if nothing could be gained, nothing could be lost by men already doomed to death.

We are not, after all, to suppose that Mordecai's sorrow was altogether hopeless. His faith in God might be shaken, but it was not destroyed. He could not be ignorant of the many precious promises concerning the Lord's redeemed captives, which were to be found in the prophecies of Isaiah, of Jeremiah, of Ezekiel, and of many other prophets. The Jews, restored to their land, or scattered among the nations, might be sore vexed, but they could not be utterly destroyed. God's promise could not fail for evermore. 'Deliverance,' said Mordecai, 'shall rise up to the Jews.' Yet he did not know how or when it would arise. He did not know but many might lose their lives before deliverance came. He mourned sore, although he did not mourn like one that had no hope.

Verse 2.—*And came even before the king's gate: for none might enter into the king's gate clothed with sackcloth.*

Mordecai might go where he pleased with his sackcloth and ashes, excepting only to that place where his duty required his attendance. Not those who are clothed in garments of heaviness, but those who wear gay clothing, are in king's palaces. Within the gates of the palace of Shushan, badges of sorrow were criminal. The king could not banish trouble of heart; he could not banish sickness, or vexation, or death from his palace; but he banished all those ordinary signs by which grief is expressed. The maker of this law was certainly of a different judgment from a much wiser king, who advises men to go to the house of mourning rather than the house of feasting; Eccles. vii. 2. We have heard of princes that forbade death to be mentioned in their presence. How terrible must the harbingers of death have been to those great personages! Since the last enemy must be encountered by the greatest as well as the least of our race, is it not far better to be prepared for meeting him, than to banish him from our thoughts?

Verse 3.—*And in every province whithersoever the king's commandment, and his decree came, there was great mourning among the Jews, and fasting, and weeping and wailing, and many lay in sackcloth and ashes.*

'In this day did the Lord God of hosts call to weeping and to mourning, and to baldness, and to girding with sackcloth:' and the call was so loud and awful that it commanded compliance. All that loved their lives, all that loved their friends and brethren, mourned bitterly, and refused to be comforted. All that had any impression of religion among the Jews, joined religious fasting to their expressions of grief, that they might pour out tears unto God. And there is reason to believe, that religious impressions would be now felt even by those who had forgotten God in their days of prosperity.

If a sentence of death pronounced by an earthly sovereign produced such grief, such anxiety, such cries for deliverance, what impression ought to be made on the minds of sinners by that sentence which is passed against them in the court of heaven—'Judgment is come upon all men to condemnation!'

We are still under that sentence of condemnation, if we are not in Christ Jesus. Surely we believe neither law nor gospel, if we can enjoy peace in our own minds, without the humble hope of mercy through our Lord Jesus Christ unto eternal life.

Verse 4.—*So Esther's maids and her chamberlains came, and told it her. Then was the queen exceedingly grieved; and she sent raiment to clothe Mordecai, and to take away his sackcloth from him: but he received it not.*

Esther was advanced to the highest station which a woman could fill. She dwelt in a magnificent palace, where she might fare sumptuously, if she pleased, every day. Her wardrobe was filled with a rich profusion of raiment embroidered with gold. She was attended by maids and chamberlains devoted to her will. But did she find happiness in that magnificence which surrounded her, or in the riches which she might use, or abuse, at her pleasure? She might, indeed, be thankful that her condition was such as it was, when she considered the humiliating condition of the other ladies of the king. But her palace was a prison. She could not enjoy the society of her former friends, or even of her beloved Mordecai. She was, at this time, ignorant of the pitiable condition of her nation. She was cut off from her wonted sources of pleasure, and the man to whom she must now devote her life seemed almost to have forgotten her. The happiness of men and women is by no means proportioned to their station, their riches, their power, or their manner of living. There are vexations annexed to greatness, of which the poor have little apprehension; and there are comforts within the reach of the poor as little known to the great. Those who know the world will see little reason to envy their superiors; and the great have no reason to look down with disdain upon the lowest ranks.

Esther, in her elevation, and in her separation from her friends, was far from forgetting them. She was deeply afflicted when she heard of the mourning habit and sore affliction of Mordecai. She was vexed that he should appear at the king's gate in a dress in which he could not enter it, and therefore sent to him change of raiment. But she knew not the sources of his distress. Grief so firmly rooted, and so well founded, could not be removed without a removal of its cause. To send him change of raiment was like singing songs to a heavy heart. Mordecai was doubtless pleased with her kind attention: but she must do something of a very different nature to banish his sorrows.

Verse 5.—*Then called Esther for Hatach, one of the king's chamberlains, whom he had appointed to attend upon her, and gave him a commandment to Mordecai, to know what it was, and why it was.*

If we weep in sincerity with those that weep, it will be our desire, if possible, to remove their sorrows. But to this end it is necessary to know their cause. Physicians cannot administer proper medicines to their patients, unless they know the causes of their diseases. They may palliate the symptoms, the root of the distemper remains if the cause is not removed. So, we may soothe the minds of persons labouring under grief, and cause them for a time to forget their sorrows; but if they are rooted in the mind, they will soon recover their force, and hold the soul in misery, unless the causes are removed: And these cannot be removed but by a change in those outward circumstances which occasioned them, or by a change in the state of the mind, when it is convinced that the supposed causes do not exist, or that they are not sufficient grounds for the sorrows they occasioned, or that relief or consolation may be found, or virtue sufficient to counteract their force.

Esther could not now visit Mordecai, or call him to her palace, and therefore, conversing with him by means of a third person, inquires into the causes of his distress, with a sincere intention to do every thing in her power to set his heart at ease.

Verses 6, 7, 8.—*So Hatach went forth to Mordecai unto the street of the city, which was before the king's gate; and Mordecai told him of all that had happened unto him, and of the sum of the money that Haman had promised to pay to the king's treasuries for the Jews, to destroy them: Also he gave him the copy of the writing of the decree that was given at Shushan to destroy them,* to show it unto Esther, and to declare it unto her; and to charge her that she should go in unto the king, to make supplication unto him, and to make request before him for her people.

It is unpleasant to be the messenger of bad tidings. It is, however, often useful. If a physician saw you labouring under a mortal distemper, and insensible to your danger, he is the preserver of your life, when, by warning you of the peril of your condition, he rouses your fear, and excites to apply the proper remedy. Esther must have been shocked beyond measure at hearing of the sentence of death pronounced against her dearest friends, against her whole people, against herself, by the man who had raised her to a share in his bed, and in his throne, without a crime proved against any one of them. But it was better to hear of it at present, than ten or eleven months afterwards, when it would be too late to provide a remedy.

There are some who cannot bear to hear of any bad tidings, however true; and think those men their enemies who tell them the truth. They consider those friends or preachers as their enemies who speak to them of their sins, and of the judgments of God denounced against them. But was not Esther under deep obligations to Mordecai for informing her of the danger of her people, and urging her to exert her influence for preserving them? Whether was Ahab most indebted to those prophets who told him that the Lord was with him, and would give him victory at Ramoth-Gilead; or to him who told him that he would fall in the battle? By following the counsel of the former, he lost his life; he might have preserved it, if he had believed the latter.

It is indeed cruel to distress men by false or doubtful intelligence of calamities that have not happened, or, if they have happened, cannot be remedied. Mordecai was far from wishing to disquiet the mind of his royal friend by uncertain rumours. But he had too good intelligence to be mistaken; and he puts into her hands decisive proofs of the danger of her people, and of Haman's activity in procuring their ruin. Nor did he give her this intelligence to torment her before the time. If nothing could have been done to avert the danger, he might have permitted her to enjoy tranquillity till it could be concealed no longer. But who could tell what might be the result of supplication to the king, especially from a queen who was understood to be the object of his warmest love? He therefore desires, or rather requires, her to go in and make intercession to the king for her people, and for her own life.

Mordecai uses authority in his language to the queen, and does her great honour by using such language. He durst not have charged her to do her duty, if he had not known her humbleness of mind in her greatness. She was as much disposed as in her youngest days to give him the authority of a father; and this he knew so well, that he uses it without scruple or apology. Happy are those on whom prosperity makes no change but for the better!

He charges her to make intercession to the king. The knowledge of that dreadful situation in which the Jews were placed, was to be improved by all the Jews as a call to fasting and intercession with the God of heaven, on whom their hope was to rest. But it was to be improved by the queen in particular, as a motive to the exertion of all her influence with the king. All, according to their places and stations, are bound to do what they can to avert threatened miseries from their nation. But some are bound to do much more than others, because they have peculiar opportunities, which, if they are not improved, must render them in some degree accountable for the mischiefs consequent on their neglect. Those who can do nothing by their own power, may do much by their influence with others. In the reign of the bloody Jehoiakim, the princes of Judah saved Jeremiah from his hands. If these princes had not used their influence for this purpose, they must have shared in the guilt of his blood.

Verse 9.—*And Hatach came and told Esther the words of Mordecai.*

'A faithful messenger refresheth the soul of him that sent him.' Hatach was a faithful messenger, and yet he stunned his employer. But refreshment to her soul was the consequence in due time of his fidelity, and of Mordecai's firmness.

Verses 10, 11.—*Again Esther spake unto Hatach, and gave him commandment unto Mordecai; All the king's servants, and the people of the king's provinces, do know, that whosoever, whether man or woman, shall come unto the king into the inner court, who is not called, there is one law of his to put him to death, except such to whom the king shall hold out the golden sceptre that he may live; but I have not been called to come in unto the king these thirty days.*

Esther was not unwilling, but she was afraid, to go in unto the king. She does not absolutely refuse; but she objects against compliance with Mordecai's charge. If Mordecai can find out no other probable means of safety, she will undertake the business: but she earnestly desires to be excused, if some other can be found to undertake the cause, whose interest with the king may be greater than her's.

Some are too ready to undertake services for which they are unqualified. But dangerous services are too often declined by those who are both called to undertake them, and best qualified to execute them. Moses was eminently qualified by God to be the deliverer of Israel from Egypt, and clearly called; and yet he earnestly desired God to excuse him; and this he did again and again on various pretenses, till he saw God's anger kindled against him. Let us never trust to ourselves, as if we were able of ourselves to think so much as a good thought. But let us never distrust God, as if he would 'send us a warfare on our own charges.' If we can believe, 'all things are possible to him that believeth'—'when he is weak, then he is strong.'

Danger of death is one of Esther's objections against undertaking this business. This, too, was one secret reason that made Moses so unwilling to undertake the work of delivering Israel. There is a strong love of life implanted in us by God, and it is not easy to give up life even to Him that gave it. There are few so courageous as Paul, who was moved by nothing that is grievous to other men; and who 'counted not life itself dear to him, that he might finish his course with joy.' But when we compare Paul's courage with the fears of Moses or Esther, or other Old Testament believers, let us remember the advantages that Paul enjoyed above them, by living in that happy period when Jesus 'had abolished death, and brought life and immortality to light by the gospel.'

But why was Esther so afraid of her life, if she should make intercession to the king for the life of her people? Was it so criminal in the court of Persia to present a supplication to the king? Or, if it was a crime in others, was it a crime even in the queen? Yes; it was universally known, says Esther, and Mordecai could not well be ignorant of it, that if any person should venture, uncalled, to approach the king in the inner court of his palace, he must be put to death, unless the king was pleased graciously to pardon him; nor was the queen herself excepted from the penalties of this law. The laws of the Persians were strange indeed! No man was allowed in a mourning-habit to enter into the king's gate; and no man in any apparel was allowed to come near the king in the inner court. Did these kings ever consider for what end they were elevated above their fellow-men? Was it not to defend the poor and the afflicted, and to do judgment and justice to all their people? How could they do the duties of princes, if they were inaccessible to their people? But if it was a crime to intrude into the private apartments of the palace, and to disturb the privacy of the prince, was it one of those atrocious crimes that can be justly punished with death? Could no milder punishment assuage the wrath of a proud mortal, who wished to make himself invisible like his Maker? Surely it may be said of a law that punished an offense like this with death, that it was written in blood; and of a government which would establish such laws, that Daniel had too good reason to represent it by the emblem of a bear; Dan. vii. 5.

Blessed be God, the laws of heaven are not like those of the Persians! Our King 'who dwells on high,' is at all times accessible to the afflicted mourner. The poor and the afflicted had ready access to Jesus while he was upon the earth; nor is He less accessible in his state of glory. At all times we may come near to God, even to his throne of grace, that we may obtain mercy, and find grace to help in time of need.

Esther was believed by Mordecai to be a great favourite

with the king; and, doubtless, there was a time when she was very dear to him. But Esther was afraid that this time was past, and questioned whether Mordecai would insist upon the charge he had given her, when he was informed, that for thirty days past she had not been called to go in unto the king. This she considered as a sign that his affection was alienated, and that it was questionable whether the golden sceptre would be held out to her, if she should presume to enter the king's apartment. What reason the king had for this coldness to his virtuous queen, we know not. This is plain, that it was a providential trial appointed for Esther, by which it would be known whether she had the courage to serve her people and her God at the risk of her life. It was a severe trial of her faith and charity. She felt the force of the discouragement; and expressed her sense of it to Mordecai, that she might receive further directions from him.

To whatever difficult duty we are called, we may lay our account with trials. If thou desirest to serve the Lord, look for temptation. But remember, that 'the man is blessed who endureth temptation; for when he is tried, he shall receive of the Lord the crown of life which he hath promised to them that love him.' Those who have held on in the path of duty, under sore temptation, shall at last 'stand before the throne of God with white robes, and palms in their hands'—'But the fearful and unbelieving shall have their portion in the lake of fire burning with brimstone, which is the second death.'

DISCOURSE VIII.

MORDECAI INSISTS ON THE CHARGE TO ESTHER TO GO IN UNTO THE KING—SHE COMPLIES WITH HIS DESIRE; BUT REQUIRES HIM TO PROCURE FOR HER THE HELP OF THE SOLEMN PRAYERS OF ALL THE JEWS IN SHUSHAN.

CHAPTER IV. 12–17.

Verses 12, 13.—*And they told to Mordecai Esther's words. Then Mordecai commanded to answer Esther, Think not with thyself that thou shalt escape in the king's house, more than all the Jews.*

It is necessary for those who desire to be useful to the souls of their neighbours, not only to tell them, as occasion requires, what it is their duty to do; but to repeat their admonitions, to enforce them by reasons, and to obviate those objections which rise up in their minds against the performance of it. Those who desire a good increase from the seed sown in their fields, must plow the ground over and over, if it is stiff; must root up the weeds; must cover the seed with the harrow. In like manner, instructors must often repeat their good advices, and enforce them by arguments, and make it to appear how weak those reasons are which our slothful dispositions set in opposition to our duty. Eli admonished his sons to repent; but he did not follow up his admonitions with new reproofs, and warnings, and corrections. For this reason the Lord reproved Eli himself as an accessary to the sin of his children. Mordecai charged Esther to go in unto the king; but when Esther wished to be excused, he did not satisfy himself with what he had already done, as if he had already discharged his part of the duty. He renews his charge, he enforces it by powerful arguments, and he prevails. He was but a poor subject of that king who had made Esther his queen. But the grandeur of her station did not hinder him from using all freedom in dealing with her. He was her father. She was still his daughter in her heart as much as ever. He knew her modesty, her veneration for himself, her contempt of earthly grandeur; and makes use of his influence with her to excite her to her duty. Happy are those friends who freely make use of their mutual influence for such purposes!

Esther was afraid of her life if she should go in unto the king. Mordecai shows her, that if she valued her own life, she ought to go in unto him, and to make supplication to him for her people. Her safety lay not in shunning, but in doing, a duty so needful. She might risk her life in venturing to do a thing which was prohibited by the unreasonable laws of Persia; but she must lose it by refusing to obey the commandment of God, which requires us to use all lawful endeavours to preserve our own life, and the life of others.

It was natural for Esther to think that her own life was in no danger from the bloody decree. Her husband had unknowingly signed a warrant for her death: But who would venture to lift up his hand against the queen? Or what would it avail her murderers to allege the king's law, when the king himself, who was above the law, would consider the cause as his own? We must not, however, entertain such a mean opinion of Esther as to think, that she would be less zealous in the cause, because she might apprehend herself to be safe. Yet Mordecai hopes to quicken her zeal, by letting her know that she was not more safe than other Jews. God would find some means to free them from their danger; but Esther, though in the king's house, must not expect to escape if she deserted the cause of God, and of his people in their extreme danger.

Human probabilities were on her side. The king, though perhaps alienated from her, would not suffer himself to be insulted by a murder perpetrated upon his queen, and in his own palace. Even Haman himself would not dare to arm an assassin against the queen. But we are not to trust to human probabilities. God is the author and the preserver of our lives.

When He withdraws his protection, we are undone; and how could Esther expect his protection, if she refused, at the loud call of his providence, and at the pressing admonition of Mordecai, to seek the life of her people? 'If thou forbear to deliver them that are drawn unto death, and them that are ready to be slain; if thou sayest, Behold, we knew it not, doth not He that pondereth the heart consider it? and He that keepeth,' or He that observeth, 'thy soul, doth not He know it? and shall not He render to every man according to his works?' Are we worthy to have our lives preserved, if we show no concern for the lives of our fellow-men? Are we not in some measure chargeable with those deaths which we do not endeavour, if it is in our power, to prevent? Let it be remembered, that the life of the soul is infinitely more precious than that of the body, and that we have more frequent opportunities of contributing to the salvation of souls, than to the preservation of natural life; though we have more opportunities of the latter sort than we carefully improve, or perhaps think about. When we see men wasting their bodies, and shortening their days, by idleness, by intemperance, by the indulgence of those bitter passions which are as rottenness to the bones, we may contribute to the life of both soul and body, by good advice, by earnest expostulation, by our prayers to God. By our prayers, by our holy example, by well-timed and well-advised reproofs and exhortations, we may save souls from death. If we do not what God enables us to do for the salvation of perishing souls, are we not accessary to their perdition?

Think not that because thou art in the king's house, thou shalt be safe.—It is vain to trust in kings, or in the sons of men, in whom there is no confidence. Kings die. 'In that day their breath goes forth, and their thoughts perish.' Kings are changeable creatures, like other men. The kings were not like the laws of the Medes and Persians, which could not be altered. He that was in the morning their favourite, might, before the evening, be hanged by their orders. Herod, king of Judea, dearly loved his wife Mariamne, and yet he ordered her to be put to death without any crime, but what was committed in his own dark imagination. Monima was a beloved wife of Mithridates, the great king of Pontus, and yet, when he lost a battle against the Romans, that she might not fall into other hands than his own, he commanded her to die; and the only favour he showed her, was to give her the choice of her own death. Her choice was, to strangle herself by her royal tiara, which had long been hateful to her. But even in this she was disappointed, and her last, or nearly her last words, were, 'Poor bauble! canst thou not do me even this mournful office?'

Jesus forbids us to fear them that have power only to kill the body. Still less, if possible, are we to trust them; for they have no power even to save the body. God is to be trusted and feared. He is the Lawgiver, who is able to save and to destroy; Psalm cxlvi. 3–6.

Verse 14.—*For if thou altogether holdest thy peace at this time, then shall there enlargement and deliverance arise to the Jews from another place; but thou and thy father's house shall be destroyed: and who knoweth whether thou art come to the kingdom for such a time as this?*

What evidence had Mordecai to go upon, in alleging that deliverance and enlargement should arise from some one place or another to the Jews at this time? He had as good evidence as the word, and even the oath of God, could give him. The Lord had made a covenant with Abraham, to be a God unto himself, and to his seed after him. 'This covenant he ratified by his oath unto Isaac, and confirmed the same unto Jacob for a law, and to Israel for an everlasting covenant.' Haman's malice, and, what was more formidable than Haman's malice, the sins of God's people, could not make void the promise of God, nor make his oath and his covenant of none effect. We are sure, even in this age of the world, that no Haman will ever be able to extirpate the natural seed of Abraham: For 'the gifts and calling of God are without repentance.'

There were many prophecies published by Isaiah, by Jeremiah, by Ezekiel, by Daniel, and the other prophets, concerning the restoration of the captive Jews; concerning God's care of them in their own land, or in their dispersion; and concerning that Saviour who was to 'come to Zion, to turn away ungodliness from Jacob.' These prophecies were, doubtless, well known to

Mordecai. They were the life of his soul, and the joy of his heart.

The Lord had, in every age, been 'the hope of Israel, and the Saviour thereof in the time of trouble.' He had given enlargement to his people when they were shut up between rocks and seas, and the sword of an enraged enemy, who was much too strong for them; and he who had delivered his people from so great deaths, had assured them that he would still deliver them: 'The Lord said, I will bring again my people from the depths of the sea, and from Bashan hill.'

The hearts of the unbelieving Jews would sink within them in their present perilous condition; but believers in the word of God would not be confounded. They knew that the honour of God was as deeply interested in the event, as were their life and welfare; and that he who had so often wrought for his name's sake, would still work for his people. There were many and strong enemies; but they had the Almighty God for their friend.

Mordecai was one of those believers who, in the days of Israel's distress, 'remembered the years (or the changes) of the right hand of the Most High;' and in the words before us, he expressed his full assurance that God would frustrate Haman's plot. Blessed are they that trust in the Lord! God 'will keep them in perfect peace,' and enable them in the darkest days to express their joyful hope, that 'at evening-time it shall be light.'

But why did Mordecai mourn so bitterly, if he was assured that deliverance would arise from some place to the Jews? Because 'in that day did the Lord God of hosts call to mourning and to weeping.' In such a dark day the people of God were called to pour out their hearts like water before the face of the Lord, for their life, and for the life of their children. The faith of God's people does not interfere with the exercise of affections suited to mournful dispensations of providence. Faith encourages us to come before God with tears and cryings, because it assures us that he knows all our distresses, and puts our tears into his bottle.

Enlargement and deliverance will arise to the Jews; to the Israel of God, under the gospel, as well as under the law.

Amidst all the distresses of the church, we may rest assured that she cannot perish. Particular churches may be destroyed, but the church universal is 'built by Christ upon a rock, and the gates of hell shall not prevail against it.'

If Jews according to the flesh were blessed with the assured hopes of deliverance to their nation in every danger, however dreadful; those who are Jews in the noblest sense, may at all times expect help from God. 'He is not a Jew who is one outwardly, but who is one inwardly: neither is that circumcision which is outward in the flesh; but circumcision is that of the heart, in the spirit, whose praise is not of men, but of God.' If its praise be of God, he will be its almighty protector. He may 'sift Israel as corn is sifted in a sieve,' but one grain shall not be suffered to fall upon the ground.

If thou altogether forbear at this time, enlargement and deliverance shall rise up to the Jews from some other place.—Esther, though warmly solicited to interpose in the behalf of the Jews, must not imagine that their safety depends on her. If she succeeds, she will have reason to bless God for making her the honoured instrument of their deliverance; and the Jews will have great reason to bless her, and to bless God for her. But she will have no reason to be proud. She is assured, that whether she had any hand in their deliverance or not, their deliverance was sure. It by no means depended upon her exertions; for if she had never been born, if she had never been a queen, or if she had been a base apostate to the religion of the court, Israel was safe under the protection of the God of Israel. The safety of the church depends not on her best friends on earth; nor can her deliverance be prevented, either by the coldness of her friends, or by the power of her enemies. All, therefore, who perform eminent services to the church, ought humbly to thank the Lord for chusing to employ them rather than others; for He is never at a loss for servants to do his work. The life of Moses might have been thought by the Israelites so necessary for them when they were delivered from Egypt, that they could have little hope, without him, of obtaining possession of the promised land; and yet he died when they were come to the borders of it. But God could put a sufficient portion of Moses' spirit in Joshua to bring his people into the land of which he had sworn unto them; and when they were both in heaven, he could raise up other saviours to his people, to deliver them from their enemies.

But thou and thy father's house shall be destroyed.—Why? Because Esther neglected to do what she ought to have done for the salvation of Israel. It is a common, and not a false maxim, That sins of omission are less heinous than sins of commission. But let us not mistake the maxim; the meaning of it is, that sins of omission, as such, are not so atrocious as sins of commission. On other accounts, they may be criminal above most sins that you can name. It is worse to do what God plainly forbids, than to neglect the doing of what he requires; because (when other things are equal) it is a token of a more rebellious disposition, to be active in doing what is sinful, than, through negligence and inattention, to omit a duty required from us. Yet, if you saw a man drowning in the water, and did not attempt to save him from the danger, would not your sin be no less than murder, and consequently worse than an officious lie, or even than an instance of fraud? But if Esther had neglected to interpose in the present case, she would have suffered the whole nation to perish. If she did not so interpose, she had at least the guilt of not doing what she could to prevent it, and thus she exposed herself and her father's house to destruction from the anger of God.

But what had her father's house to do with her sin? Is it not said, that 'the son shall not die for the iniquity of the father, nor the father for the iniquity of the son?' This is a law which the universal Lord has prescribed for men, and not for himself. We know that God destroyed even whole families for the sins of their heads. Only we must remember, that the whole world is guilty before God. He can, without injustice, destroy a whole family when one member has sinned, and when the rest had no participation in the guilt, because guilt of another kind can be justly charged upon them. The punishment is therefore, properly speaking, the punishment of the single offender made ten-fold more heavy, by involving with him so many dear objects of his regard. His relations were chargeable with sins which exposed them to death when God pleased to require their souls; and they have no more reason to blame the righteousness of the divine procedure, than the debtor has to find fault with the creditor for demanding the money due to him, when he finds occasion to use it.

If thou art silent at this time, thou and thy father's house shall be destroyed.—But was it the exclusive duty of Esther to take this business upon herself? Where was that law to be found which imposed a burden upon this good woman, from which all the rest of the Jews were exempted? Was there a special commandment given to her, which she could not disobey without exposing herself and all her father's house to destruction? Esther was certainly under the same laws which bound all the rest of the Jews, and under none else. There was no special precept given to her, like that which was addressed by Jesus to the young man, who was commanded to sell all that he had, and give to the poor. Yet Esther, by that common law, had a special duty enjoined on her. All were bound to use the means competent to them to preserve their nation from destruction. Petitioning the king was a means of safety necessary to be used, and the providence of God plainly pointed out Esther as the petitioner most likely to succeed. The law of God is the only rule of our duty: but the providence of God often points out to individual persons, duties which the law requires especially from themselves. Those things may be necessary duties at one time which are not duties at another; or to one person, or to one class of persons, which are not required from others: and the neglect of those duties which are required from us, and not from others, or of those duties which are rendered so only by a particular train of providences, may involve us in deep guilt, and in great danger. A man who knows a particular remedy for a certain disease, of which others are ignorant, would be chargeable with the fatal consequences that may arise from the general ignorance, if he locks up his knowledge in his own breast. If Providence furnish us with talents which are not granted to others, we must account for our use of them. If we have opportunities of doing much good which others have not, and make no use of them, we make ourselves guilty of a crime which can be charged upon none but ourselves. The law is the same to all; but particular circumstances place us under the obligation of particular precepts, which take no hold of persons in different situations.

And who knoweth whether thou art come to the kingdom for such a time as this?—The circumstances which led Esther to a throne were wonderful, either in themselves, or in their combination. The daughter of Abihail the Jew, was astonished to find herself the wife of the great king Ahasuerus; and doubtless must have thought, that the providence of God, which shone so wonderfully in her exaltation, had some design in view, of which she was hitherto ignorant. When Joseph was raised to be lord over all the land of Egypt, God was making provision for the support of Jacob's family. When Esther was elevated to the dignity of a great queen, and when a sentence of death had gone forth against her whole nation, it appeared highly probable to Mordecai that God designed her to be the preserver of her people. It was, therefore, in his judgment, her necessary duty to make the attempt, that she might not be backward to second the designs of Providence. To hide our talent in a napkin is criminal and dangerous.

If God has done remarkable things for us, we have reason to believe that he expects some services from us suited to the situation in which he has placed us, and to the means of service with which he has furnished us. We ought, therefore, when we consider what God hath done for us, to consider at the same time what he requires from us. If our circumstances are peculiar, it is likely that some peculiar services are required; or if we cannot find out any particular service to be done at present, let us wait a little, and we may find calls to services suited to our condition. 'The Lord hath made all things,' and he still does all things, 'for himself.'

'What if thou art come to the kingdom for such a time as this?'—It is at least highly probable. But the duty itself is certain: and if we do not improve particular dispensations of providence for the purposes for which they are intended, we walk contrary to God, and provoke him to walk contrary to us. 'Whoso is wise to observe the doings of the Lord, even he shall understand his loving-kindness.' But when men do not know their times and opportunities, their misery is great upon them.

Verses 15, 16.—*Then Esther bade them return Mordecai this answer: Go, gather together all the Jews that are present in Shushan, and fast ye for me, and neither eat nor drink for three days, night or day: I also and my maidens will fast likewise: and so will I go in unto the king, which is not according to the law: and if I perish, I perish.*

Esther highly respected Mordecai; and she respected him not the less, but the more, because he continued to use the freedom of a father with her. She doubtless thought herself blessed in a friend who took the liberty to remonstrate with her concerning duties which she felt an aversion to perform. He that rebukes and admonishes, will be far more valued by us, if we are wise, than he that flatters with his lips.

Esther never intended to decline the perilous service recommended by Mordecai, when she should find it to be a necessary duty. Being now convinced that it was, she promises to go in to the king, let the consequence be what it would. But, as her hope of success was in God, she requires all the Jews in Shushan to fast for her three days. The Jews in other places would have been required to give her the same help, if it had been practicable to give them seasonable information of her wishes and intentions. Paul frequently seeks the help of the prayers of the church. Esther seeks the help, not only of the prayers of the Jews, but of all the devotional exercises of a solemn fast of three days continuance. The situation of the Jews was critical and dangerous in the extreme. Esther's hopes from her influence with the king were faint. If God did not pity his people, they were undone. Never did God more loudly call for fasting than at this time; and a single day observed in fasting, was thought by her too little to be employed in the exercise. Perhaps she called in mind the example of the Ninevites, and the happy success of their devotion. They observed a strict fast of three days, and cried mightily to God, and turned from their wickedness; and 'the Lord repented of the evil which he thought to do unto them, and did it not.' Esther would justly think that the Lord, who showed such favour to an Assyrian city, infamous for its former wickedness, would not turn a deaf ear to his own people in the day of their distress.

It would be folly to think that Esther placed the least dependence upon mere abstinence from food, when she required the Jews to fast. All her expectations of advantage from this fast were founded upon God, who had instituted this duty, and promised happy consequences to it, when it was observed according to his will. We have, therefore, no reason to say that the name of God is not to be found in this book, which speaks of his worship (a part of his name). The name *God*, or *Lord*, is not in it. But who does not know, that the exercise of fasting here enjoined by Esther, is a part of His service, and that no advantage can be expected from it but through divine mercy accepting this service, and hearing the supplications of his people? Esther, indeed, does not speak of the prayers, of the self-examination, of the confessions, of the reformation, that were to accompany this abstinence from food. The exercises proper to a day of fasting were already known to the Jews; or they would learn them from the history of Jonah, to which the similarity of the present danger of the Jews with that of the Ninevites would lead their minds; or if they needed any further information on the subject, Esther believed that Mordecai was better qualified than herself to give them proper directions. She insists, however, upon one thing, that they should neither eat nor drink three days, day or night; but observe the fast with strictness, like persons so deeply concerned in the business, that they would deny the strongest cravings of nature, and bear the extremes of hunger and thirst, that they might express the deepest humiliation of spirit before God, and pour forth their hearts before him. There are too many amongst us who would think it an intolerable hardship to be deprived of their food for a single day, or for half of a day, when they have the loudest calls to solemn fasting. How would such persons have acted in the time of Esther's fast? Would not the remedy have appeared to them almost as bad as the disease? Was it not as good to die by the sword of their enemies, as to starve themselves to death? Yet we do not find that any of the Jews in Shushan refused to comply with Esther's desire. The fear of death before their eyes, made their ordinary food a matter of indifference to them. What though they should deny themselves the ordinary comforts of life for three days, when their object was to obtain a reversal of a sentence of death given forth against them?

We are not, however, to understand the words so strictly as to make them a prohibition of all sorts of food for three days, even to those men, women, or children, whose bodies could not sustain such a long fast. Doubtless there were some among them who, through sickness or weakness, could as little bear a complete privation of food for three whole days and nights, as that Egyptian slave whom David relieved from mortal weakness, contracted by a fast of three days, when he was marching against the Amalekites that had burnt Ziklag. Esther did not think that it was any man's duty to destroy his body by a voluntary fast. She knew that God would have mercy and not sacrifice. Her desire was not to destroy, but to save the lives of her people. Her words may be reasonably understood to mean, that the Jews were not to take any regular meal, nor any other supplies of food, but such as might be necessary for the preservation of health and vigour. Perfect abstinence for three days and three nights would have been inimical, rather than favourable, to the great purpose of the fast. Paul said to the mariners that sailed with him to Rome, 'This day is the fourteenth day that ye have tarried, and continued fasting, having taken nothing.' Surely they did not want food during two complete weeks; yet they are said to have continued fasting, and taken nothing, because, amidst the agitation of fear and hope, they were incapable of taking any regular meal.

Fast ye for me, and neither eat nor drink for three days.—They were not called with Esther to go in unto the king. A service attended with no danger was required from them. But what they can do, and are called to do, they must do as conscientiously as Esther. There are many great works which are beyond our strength, or out of the line of our calling; and yet we may and ought to take a part in them, by strengthening the hands of those who are called to undertake them. Paul had many helpers in his work of the gospel, even among those who could not, or to whom it would not have been allowed to, speak in the church. We all ought to be fellow-helpers to the truth. While many go abroad to spread the gospel amongst heathens, we find it our duty to continue in the land of our nativity; but, without removing from it, we may promote the work in which they are employed, by our contributions, or at least by our prayers.

There are some who beg the prayers of others, and yet pray little for themselves. Esther, who requested the Jews to fast for her, told them that she also would fast, and would abstain as strictly from food as she desired them to do. She had been accustomed to a well-furnished table; but she was not thereby disqualified from afflicting her soul by fasting when she saw it to be her duty. She, no doubt, observed the annual fasts prescribed to the Jews; and she determined to observe this extraordinary fast which she herself prescribed. She hoped to obtain mercy from the Lord, that she might escape death by the laws of Persia, and might be the instrument of the salvation of her people. But if she miscarried, her fasting and prayer would be proper acts of preparation for her latter end.

I and my maids will fast.—Some, it is probable, of Esther's maids, were heathens when they came into her service; Chap. ii. 9. Yet we find her promising that they would fast. She can answer for them, as Joshua for his household, that they would serve the Lord. If mistresses were as zealous as queen Esther for the honour of God, and the conversion of sinners, they would bestow pains upon the instruction and religious improvement of their female servants. If women may gain to Christ their own husbands by their good conversation, may they not also gain the souls of their servants? and if they are gained to Christ, they are gained to themselves also. Esther expected much benefit from the devotional exercises of her maidens. Paul expected much from the prayers of his converts. Those whom we convert from the error of their ways, will probably be our joy and helpers upon earth; they will certainly be our joy and crown of rejoicing in the day of Christ.

'I and my maids will fast.'—Esther could not join in the public prayers of the Jews, when they met together out of many families to strive together in their prayers to God. But she will fast at home, not only by herself, but with her maidens. There are public fasts in which all are expected to join. There ought likewise to be secret and family fasts observed by us, according to the calls of providence, and the situation of our affairs, or the condition of our souls; Matt. vi. 16-18.

And then will I go in unto the king, which is not according to the law.—She would not go in unto the king, till she made her supplication to the Lord, and till the Jews had given her the assistance of their prayers. She was sensible, that though 'all men will intreat the ruler's favour, every man's judgment comes from the Lord;' and that the hearts of kings are turned by him according to his pleasure. What, therefore, she desires in the first place is, that she may obtain comfortable assurance of the divine favour. If the Lord be on her side, she is safe. If the Lord favour her suit, she need not fear the coldness of Ahasuerus, or the mortal enmity of Haman. 'The floods may rage. They may lift up their voices and make a mighty noise: but the Lord on high is mightier than the waves of the sea, or the voice of their roaring.

But when the fast is over, she will go in unto the king. She will not think that her duty is done, when she has prayed and fasted. She will seek, by the use of proper means, to obtain that blessing which she has been asking. The insincerity of our prayers is too often discovered by our sloth and cowardice. We ask blessings from God, and, as if he were bound to confer them, not according to his own will, but according to ours, we take no care to use those means which he hath appointed for obtaining them, or we do not use them with requisite diligence. Esther will go in unto the king, although she could not go in without violating the laws, and risking her life.

'I will go in unto the king, which is not according to the law.'—Who will keep the king's laws, if the queen herself does not observe them? Did not Esther know that Vashti

16

lost her crown, and her husband, for disobeying the king in a matter of less consequence than a standing law deliberately enacted by the king's authority? True; but necessity has no law. She will keep the king's laws as far as she can keep them and the laws of God at the same time. But in the present case, she must be a betrayer of her country, of her own life, of the laws of Heaven, if she hesitate any longer to go in unto the king, although it be not according to the law. We must obey princes, 'not only for wrath, but also for conscience sake.' But, for conscience sake, we must stop short where the law of God interposes; Acts iv. 19.

Esther may lose her royal dignity. She may be expelled from the king's bed. She may lose her life for disobeying the laws. But 'if I perish,' she says, 'I perish.' It is not necessary for me to live, but it is necessary for me to do my duty. If I perish in obeying the will of God, it is better than to live in disobedience.

If I perish, I perish.—Our lives are not our own; they cannot be long preserved by us. They will be of little value to us without a good conscience. That life which is purchased by neglect of duty, is shameful, bitter, worse than death. Whoever shall save his life in this manner, shall lose it in this world, as well as in the next. His life will be but a lingering death: for the dissatisfaction and painful reflections which fill it up are far less tolerable than the bodily pain which usually precedes death. But to lose life for the sake of Christ and a good conscience, is truly to live. A day of life employed in the most hazardous duties, by which we show that our love to God is stronger than death, excels a thousand days of a life spent in the service and enjoyment of the world.

Verse 17.—*So Mordecai went his way and did according to all that Esther had commanded him.*

Mordecai commanded Esther, and she obeyed him. Esther commanded Mordecai, and he obeyed her. They served one another in love. It would be happy for us if we knew how to command and how to obey in our turns, being 'subject one to another,' in the fear of God.

Mordecai required the Jews to fast three days according to

Esther's orders; and we have no reason to doubt of their ready and grateful compliance. They would not think it hard, but necessary and useful, to be called to afflict their souls to an extraordinary degree, when their lives and the lives of all their people were in question. And yet the present life of all the many thousands of Judah was not of equal importance to the eternal life of one precious soul. What, then, are we to think of ourselves, if the sentence of eternal death denounced against every sinner, has never induced us to devote as many hours to fervent prayer, as these Jews employed days in prayers and fasting to obtain deliverance from temporal death? Is it not to be feared, that we do not really believe what the Scripture tells us about that judgment which is come upon all men to condemnation, if we thing it too much trouble to spend some hours or days in considering our condition, and pouring out supplications for that mercy which we so greatly need? The Jews fasted. Esther went in to the king, uncertain about the event, but pressed by hard necessity. Necessity is laid upon sinners, yea, woe unto them if they do not obtain mercy! But great encouragement is given them to come to the throne of grace to obtain mercy. God himself puts words in their mouths, and will He not hear those prayers which are dictated by his own Spirit? Hos. xiv. 2–4: Jer. xxxi. 18–20.

DISCOURSE IX.

ESTHER GOES IN UNTO THE KING, AND FINDS FAVOUR IN HIS EYES
—HAMAN, INFLAMED BY REVENGE, PREPARES A GALLOWS FOR
MORDECAI OF FIFTY CUBITS HIGH.

CHAPTER V. 1–14.

Verse 1.—*Now it came to pass on the third day, that Esther put on her royal apparel, and stood in the inner court of the king's house, over against the king's house; and the king sat upon his royal throne in the royal house, over against the gate of the house.*

ESTHER was not one of those who resolve and promise well, but do not perform. How ready are we, like the disobedient son in the parable, to say, We will go and work in the vineyard, and after all go not! But what excuse will we have for breaking our promises through the mere power of laziness, when Esther kept her word at the risk of her life? She deserves to be ranked with the noble army of confessors, if not of martyrs. She went in unto the king when a law faced her which declared it to be death for any subject, not excepting the queen, to go in unto the king's private apartments without his leave.

Nor did she linger in doubt whether she should go in unto the king or not. If she had, new temptations, dangerous to her virtue, might have assaulted her. Her resolution had been already formed; and she makes haste, and delays not to do the commandment of Mordecai, which she considers as a commandment from God. On the third day, she went in unto the king. Her fast did not, it seems, consist of three complete days and nights. In the language of the Jews, 'three days and three nights' might mean one whole day and a part of two others.

Jesus is said to have been 'three days and three nights in the heart of the earth,' and yet he is said to have risen 'on the third day.'

She observed her fast, and it was no sooner over than she went in unto the king. It was wise in her, when she had finished her supplications, to present her petition to the king. When Hannah prayed in the bitterness of her grief, her heart was eased; she was no more sorrowful. We have reason to think that Esther's anxieties, too, were banished by her devotion. She had been lifting up her soul to the Lord. She had been, doubtless, 'remembering her song in the night,' and 'the wonderful works of former times' would inspire her with the hope of a happy event to her present enterprise. Thus she was able to approach unto the king with all that composure of mind, and cheerfulness of countenance, which were necessary for the occasion.

She put on her royal apparel when she went in to the king. She cared not for the distinction of her rank, and placed not her delight in the outward adorning of gold and pearls and costly array. But it was necessary to lay aside her mourning apparel, and to put on her beautiful garments, when she went in to the king. Good wives will endeavour to please their husbands by a decency in dress, as well as other things that may appear little when they are not considered as means to gain an important end. 'The married woman careth,' and ought to care, 'how she may please her husband'; and those women do not act as becometh saints, whose dress, or any part of their behaviour, naturally tends to produce disgust. Esther had a peculiar reason for dressing herself with her beautiful garments, when she went into the king's presence. But all women are bound to please their husbands in things lawful and innocent, because the law of Christ binds them to reverence their husbands: and their husbands, if they are not fools, will not desire them to transgress the laws concerning dress, which two apostles have thought it necessary to record for their direction; 1 Tim. ii. 9; 1 Peter iii. 3–6.

She stood in the inner court of the king's house, over against the king's house; that is, over against the king's private apartment in the palace. The word rendered *house*, may signify either a large pile of building, or particular apartments in it. In the first of these senses it is to be understood, when it is said 'she stood in the inner court of the king's house' or palace. In the second, when it is said that she stood 'over against the king's house.' She stood within his view as he sat upon his royal throne, waiting for the intimation of his will, either to leave her to the penalty of the laws, or to save her alive. We have already seen that Esther was a courageous woman. She would venture her life for the salvation of her people. It is probable, however, that she felt great agitation of spirit in this critical moment, when the sentence of life or death was in effect to be pronounced upon her. Her busy imagination would call up her fears, by setting in her view the cruel law, the coldness of the king, the severity exercised upon Vashti. But, in the multitude of her thoughts within her, it is to be presumed, that God's comforts delighted her soul.

Verse 2.—*And it was so, when the king saw Esther the queen standing in the court, that she obtained favour in his sight; and the king held out to Esther the golden sceptre that was in his hand. So Esther drew near, and touched the top of the sceptre.*

The countenance of Esther at this critical moment was highly interesting to the king her husband. Grief, anxiety, and pity, painted in her beauteous face, awakened his pity, and attracted his love. She found favour in his eyes, and he held out to her the golden sceptre, the sign of grace and pardon; which Esther touched, in thankful acceptance of the offered mercy.

'As a prince,' said God to Jacob, 'hast thou power with God; and with men also shalt thou prevail.' Esther had been weeping and making supplication, like her father Jacob, and had prevailed, and saw the face of the king as if it had been the face of God, and her life was preserved; and, what was still better, she had the happy presage of the preservation of the life of all her people, in that favour which was extended to herself. What wonderful favours from men may fervent supplication to God obtain! 'If He be for us, who can be against us?'

Verse 3.—*Then said the king unto her, What wilt thou, queen*

Esther? and what is thy request? it shall be even given thee, to the half of the kingdom.

The heart of the king, if it was formerly alienated from Esther, was now most effectually turned to favour her. He not only held out to her the golden sceptre, but addressed her with expressions of the tenderest love, and of the richest bounty. She may now confidently seek from him the life of all her people; for she was assured that she should receive the richest boon which discretion could suffer her to ask.

Our Lord teaches us to draw a comfortable instruction from the bounty of parents to their children: 'If even ye, being evil, know how to give good gifts unto your children, how much more shall your heavenly Father give good things to them that ask him?' May we not with equal assurance draw the same instruction from the kindness of Ahasuerus to his queen? A man who could wantonly devote a whole nation to destruction, and a nation to which his queen belonged, for aught he knew, will nevertheless give her what she pleases to ask, when she comes to him as a humble petitioner, although her coming to him was not according to the law. When we come to the throne of the eternal King, we have the law of grace on our side. 'Come boldly unto the throne of grace— Ask, and ye shall receive.' The King whom we approach is 'rich in mercy to all that call upon Him.' He will not withhold from us the desire of our lips. He will 'do for us above what we can ask or think.' We have perhaps come into his presence under discouraging apprehensions of his displeasure, but 'He will not contend for ever, neither will he be always wroth—He hath heard the desire of the humble—Thou wilt prepare their heart, thou wilt cause thine ear to hear.'

Verse 4.—*And Esther answered, If it seem good unto the king, let the king and Haman come this day unto the banquet that I have prepared for him.*

Esther had surely a good opportunity to present her request to the king, when he was so well disposed to grant it. But the importance of it was far more than life. Her timidity was not entirely removed by all the kind words which the king had spoken. He might take it kindly to find a rich banquet prepared for him by Esther. She hoped that his heart would be warmed with friendship, and inspired with generous and pleasing sentiments, by a banquet to his taste; and she wished for some more time of recollection, preparation, and prayer, before she made known her great request to the king. All, therefore, that she requests at present is, that the king and Haman might come to the feast which she had prepared for their entertainment.

A feast is, especially in the eastern countries, a seal of friendship; and, therefore, it may appear strange that Haman was invited along with the king, although Esther had it in view to present a petition to the king against him. But necessity was laid upon her, if she invited the king, to invite Haman also, who was as inseparable from him at this time as his right hand. The fault was in the king, and not in Esther, if any wrong was done him by cherishing those proud imaginations that were soon to be humbled to the dust. She was not in a situation to act with the delicacy of Saladin, sultan of Egypt, who gave a draught of refreshing liquor to his thirsty captive, Guy, king of Jerusalem; but when the king handed the cup to his companion in bonds, Arnold, lord of Brescia, the sultan desired him to observe, that it was not he, but the king of Jerusalem, that gave him the cup. The reason of this behaviour was, that Saladin had justly doomed Arnold to death for barbarities treacherously perpetrated by him against his people. No man, however, can say that Esther dealt unfairly with Haman. His presence was expedient at the presenting of the petition, that there might be no pretense to complain of injury. He was to be charged with the worst of crimes, and there was nothing unfair in giving him an opportunity, by being present, to exculpate himself, if that had been possible.

Verse 5.—*Then the king said, Cause Haman to make haste that he may do as Esther hath said. So the king and Haman came to the banquet that Esther had prepared.*

The king was not displeased at the timidity of Esther, but considered it as a mark of the profound reverence which she entertained for him. He was pleased with the respect showed to him in inviting him, with his friend Haman, to a banquet.

He knew that Haman would reckon himself highly honoured by the invitation, and sent for him to come in all haste to share in the entertainment. Thus far things went well with Esther. She was assured of the king's kindness, and furnished with an opportunity of ingratiating herself still more with the man to whom, under God, she must look for the life of her people.

Verse 6.—*And the king said unto Esther at the banquet of wine, What is thy petition? and it shall be granted thee: and what is thy request? even to the half of the kingdom it shall be performed.*

We find, in the second chapter, that the beauty and modesty of Esther gained the hearts of all who saw her. Doubtless, when the king, at the banquet of wine, had an opportunity of conversing with Esther, and of observing those lovely graces that appeared in every part of her behaviour, his love was inflamed, and he thought he could not give her too great proofs of his kindness. The pleasure he enjoyed in the entertainment, and in the society of those whom he most loved, opened his heart to liberality; and he again desires Esther to present her request before him, with the repeated assurance that it should be granted her to the half of the kingdom. The fears of Esther, however, seem not yet to have been altogether extinguished, although hope predominated.

Verses 7, 8.—*Then answered Esther, and said, My petition and my request is; if I have found favour in the sight of the king, and if it please the king to grant my petition, and to perform my request, let the king and Haman come to the banquet that I shall prepare for them, and I will do to-morrow as the king hath said.*

It was a great favour that she had already received, that the king honoured her banquet with his presence, and all that she will venture to ask more at this time is, that this favour may be repeated. But the great object of her desire for which she entered into the king's presence, she dares not yet to produce. She lays herself, however, under an obligation to vanquish her fears, and to acquaint the king with her wishes, if he will favour her with his presence to-morrow. The king would not take it amiss that Esther discovered such timidity in his presence. He loved her, and wished to be loved by her;

but he wished likewise to be feared with are verence greater, perhaps, than is due to mortals.

But, could Esther have a better opportunity than the present to present her chief request to the king? She could not, perhaps, prudently publish it in the king's apartments, where some of the princes might be present, who would be ready to declaim against the request, as a petition for the overthrow of the fundamental laws of the empire. Here none but the king and Haman were to be present, and Haman must be her enemy whenever the petition is presented. The king was now in the best humour imaginable, and nothing but courage in Esther seemed to be wanting to complete the business.

It is to be considered, however, that there was no occasion for great haste in the business, because more than ten months still remained of the time set for the destruction of the Jews; and if the queen had gained much this day upon the king's affection, she might gain still more by the entertainment and converse of the next. It is to be remembered, that there were difficulties almost insurmountable in the way of granting her request. It might seem to demand the overthrow of a fundamental law of the kingdom, that laws ratified by the king's authority, and sealed with his seal, should not be altered. It might even have been supposed, that the king's right to the throne was exposed to question, if he should attempt unconstitutional innovations in the government, by granting such a petition. We all know that a race of our own kings forfeited the throne by such attempts.*

The king's kindness to Esther was a great encouragement to her to present her request. But his attachment to Haman might well render it doubtful whether that favourite or the queen would prevail. It is not, therefore, strange that Esther desired another day before she presented her request. She trusted in God, but she must likewise use the utmost prudence. Paul believed God that he should be saved from the hands of the Jews, to testify concerning Christ at Rome; Acts xxiii, 11; and yet he made application to the chief captain to protect him

---

* Referring to the House of Stewart.—ED.

from their snares. The use of the best means for obtaining what we desire ought to accompany our hope in God.

It is good always to avoid undue delays in doing what is right; yet precipitancy is likewise to be avoided. We know not what a day may bring forth, when we wait for a proper season. Esther seems plainly to have been directed by the Divine Providence in deferring her petition to the following day. Very unexpected events fell out in the interval, which greatly favoured her request.

Verse 9.—*Then went Haman forth that day joyful, and with a glad heart: but when Haman saw Mordecai in the king's gate, that he stood not up, nor moved for him, he was full of indignation against Mordecai.*

Unhappy are they whose chief happiness lies in the favour of princes, or in any earthly object. Haman thought himself happy in the king's favour, which he enjoyed. He though himself happy in the queen's favour, which he did not enjoy. He was soon to know that he was equally deceived in both. The queen was already plotting his destruction, and the king's favour was soon to be converted into deadly hatred.

Vain are the joys of them that have their portion in this life. Double vanity is in the joys of the proud. They are exposed to misery no less by their own capricious fancies, than by the changeable nature of external objects. Although Haman had been able to secure the king's favour to the end of his life; although he had been no less the favourite of Esther than of Ahasuerus; what good would all have done him, when such a trifle as the stiffness of Mordecai's knees could make him unhappy? He must every day have met with something to deprive him of the possession of his own soul. A man who cannot be happy unless every person give him all the respect which he may think his due, will never be happy till the Almighty resign to him the government of the world.

Mordecai was as far as ever from bowing the knee to Haman. He acted on a principle of conscience, and no circumstances could alter the settled purpose of his soul. Haman can procure a sentence of death against him, and against his people; but he cannot turn sin into duty: and let death or life come, it was Mordecai's resolution to be found in that good path which leads to life and peace.—'Haman was full of indignation against Mordecai;'

Verse 10.—*Nevertheless Haman refrained himself: and when he came home, he sent and called for his friends, and Zeresh his wife.*

When proud men are seeking glory from others, they are often secretly ashamed of themselves. Haman was ashamed to disclose that secret rage which boiled in his bosom, when Mordecai bowed not his knees to him. He had indeed good reason to be ashamed, that a man so great, and blessed with such affluence of worldly comforts, should be a slave to his own vanity, and dependent on every man he saw for his happiness. What man is more to be pitied than he who cannot enjoy any comfort without the consent of all his neighbours, without excepting those whom most of all others he hates and despises? Such is the proud man. He despises all around him, and yet cannot taste of happiness if any of them think fit to deny him that homage which he wishes to enjoy. Let him hear the praises or the flatteries of nine hundred of his neighbours, his heart may be swelled with joy; but that joy is dependent for its continuance upon the next man he meets. The meanness of such a man's spirit must cover him with shame, when it is disclosed. Haman would not disclose his chagrin in the presence of Mordecai, but he could not conceal it from his friends. 'When he came home, he sent and called for his friends, and Zeresh his wife.'

Verses 11, 12.—*And Haman told them of the glory of his riches, and the multitude of his children, and all the things wherein the king had promoted him, and how he had advanced him above the princes and servants of the king. Haman said, moreover; Yea, Esther the queen did let no man come in with the king unto the banquet that she had prepared, but myself; and to-morrow am I invited unto her also with the king.*

Haman gives his friends an inventory of his happiness. He was immensely rich. He had many children to preserve his fame in the world. He was the unrivalled favourite of the king; and he was no less so of the queen, who honoured him almost as much as the king did. Amongst all the king's noble princes, none was admitted to the queen's royal banquet with the king but himself. Not one of the brothers or cousins of the king, not a relation of the queen, was called to the feast. Haman must, therefore, be considered as the second man of the kingdom.

Riches are good. The favour of kings and of queens may be very useful, and give great pleasure. But, unhappy is the man whose chief happiness lies in any of these things, or in all of them together. Riches soon make to themselves wings, and fly away; and during the time of their continuance, they cannot ease the body afflicted with the slightest disorder; far less can they produce that tranquillity of soul, without which men must be miserable were they in paradise itself. Children are no less mortal than their parents, and their life is often more grievous than their death would be. Princes may shower down favours upon us, and their smiles may gratify our vanity. But they may smile to-day, and frown to-morrow. To-day they may invite us to their banquets, and, if they are absolute princes, may to-morrow pronounce the sentence of our death. Besides, we know not the hearts of princes, and we may deceive ourselves with fond opinions of their friendship, which a short time will discover to have been illusions of our own imagination. Haman's fate ought to be a lesson to those who boast themselves because they are become exceeding rich, and because they are blessed with every thing that the heart of a man of the world can wish. We know not what a day may bring forth. On the morrow after Haman boasted to his wife and friends of his unequalled prosperity, his honour was laid lower than the dust. His great friends appeared to be his deadly enemies. His wealth became the property of one of the nation which he had devoted to destruction. His ten children were left unprotected, to feel the dismal effects of their father's crimes. How well-founded is the precept of the apostle!—
'Let them that have wives (or any relation) be as though they had them not; and they that rejoice, as though they rejoiced not; and they that buy, as though they possessed not: for the fashion of this world passeth away.'

Verse 13.—*Yet all this availeth me nothing, so long as I see Mordecai the Jew sitting at the king's gate.*

Haman himself confesses the vanity of his high-swelling words. Why does he talk of his riches, of his children, of the favour of the king and queen, of the grandeur of his condition? That his friends might congratulate him as the happiest man in the king's dominions. Yet with the same breath he declares himself unhappy. He confesses that all that confluence of blessings which swelled him with pride, were not blessings to him, because a certain man whom he despised did not bow the knee to him.

There are few who will confess so plainly as Haman the weakness of their own spirit. Men are ashamed to say that trifles disturb their minds and deprive them of self-enjoyment. But it is certain, that numbers, like Haman, are miserable amidst the means of happiness, because they want a disposition for enjoying happiness. They are so unreasonable, that a thousand enjoyments lose all their relish, for the want of something else which they cannot obtain. 'A good man is satisfied from himself;' and he that is not satisfied from himself, will not be satisfied from any thing without him. He is like a sick man surrounded with the richest dainties. He cannot relish them. He starves in the midst of plenty.

Give a whole world of pleasure to a man who loves the world, and the things of it, he will soon find that something is wanted, though perhaps he does not know so well as Haman thought he did, what it is. He finds some gall and wormwood that spread poison over his pleasures. All his abundance cannot compensate for the loss of some one thing or other that he deems essential to his happiness. The fact is, that the world cannot give a right constitution to his disordered soul, or be a substitute for that divine favour in which lies the life of our souls. Habakkuk, Paul, and other good men, could be happy in the want of every earthly enjoyment; nor could all the miseries which are the objects of aversion to the generality of mankind greatly disturb their tranquillity; Hab. iii. 17, 18: 2 Cor. ii. 14; for God was the portion of their inheritance, and in him they had what a thousand worlds could not give. But those who know not God, and his Son Jesus Christ, in whom are the light and the life of men, know not the way of peace. Whatever they have, they want the one thing needful, without which all things else are vanity and vexation of spirit.

'I have all things, and abound,' said an apostle, who was often in hunger, and thirst, and nakedness; and who, at the time when he wrote these words, was a poor prisoner, that had newly received a temporary supply from his friends. This man had nothing, and yet possessed all things. Ten thousand talents were but a small part of Haman's wealth; and yet he is miserably poor, for all that he had could avail him nothing. The believer in Christ must be rich in the midst of poverty; for he is possessed of 'gold tried in the fire.' The man who knows not Christ, is poor though he be rich, because he is utterly destitute of 'the true riches.'

Verse 14.—*Then said Zeresh his wife and all his friends unto him, Let a gallows be made of fifty cubits high, and to-morrow speak thou unto the king that Mordecai may be hanged thereon; then go thou in merrily with the king unto the banquet. And the thing pleased Haman; and he caused the gallows to be made.*

Miserable comforters were all those friends of Haman. They were all physicians of no value. What though Mordecai had been hanged, and, to make his ignominious end the more conspicuous, upon a gallows of fifty cubits high? Haman's disease lay deep in his heart. A day would not have passed till some other vexation would have disquieted him. He would have rejoiced for a moment at Mordecai's downfall; but the joys of murder cannot be pure. The bitterness of hatred, and the reflections of conscience, must have polluted and embittered his pleasure. His pride would have raised up other Mordecais. Some, through inadvertency, others through envy, would soon have disquieted his soul with new instances of disrespect, which to him would have been insufferable insults. Or, if fear had constrained every man in the Persian dominions to give him all the honour he desired, yet it was not to be hoped that it would be rain and sunshine at his pleasure; that dogs, and horses, and bulls, would always regulate their motions by his humour. He was not less proud than Xerxes, the father of his lord Ahasuerus, who exercised his impotent vengeance upon the winds and the seas, when they took the liberty to break down his bridge over the Hellespont!

If a proud man make his complaint to you of his unhappiness, you but make him more unhappy if you advise him to gratify his pride by unreasonable and sinful means. You might as well advise a man dying of a dropsy to pour into his throat large quantities of water. Advise him to mortify his pride, and to learn of Him who was meek and lowly in heart to deny himself; to prepare himself for bearing the cross; to take upon himself the yoke of Christ, which is easy. The humble man is always happy. The proud man never can be happy till he is effectually humbled. It is not consistent with the nature of things, nor with the will of the high and lofty One, who abhors the proud, that the gratifications which pride requires should ever give pure or lasting pleasure to the soul.

Haman was pleased with the advice of his friends, and began to put it in execution. But he found too soon, that 'he who flattereth a man spreadeth a net for his feet.' Haman prepared for Mordecai in intention, but for himself in reality, a gallows of fifty cubits high. Remember and believe the instruction of the wise man,—'He that diggeth a pit shall fall into it; and whoso breaketh an hedge, a serpent shall bite him.'

DISCOURSE X.

HAMAN IS COMPELLED TO CONFER A SINGULAR HONOUR UPON MORDECAI, WHICH HE HOPED TO PROCURE FOR HIMSELF.

CHAPTER VI. 1–13.

Verse 1.—*On that night could not the king sleep, and he commanded to bring the book of records of the chronicles; and they were read before the king.*

THE king could not sleep, any more than we, when he pleased. Of what use, some will say, is royal dignity, if it cannot procure sleep to the wearied eyelids? A king, by the wise administration of government, may procure sleep to his people; on the contrary, by his oppression, he may cause many wearisome nights to his subjects, in which their sorrows will not suffer them to sleep. But the regal dignity will not insure sleep to him who enjoys it. It is more likely to debar his eyes from rest by those anxious cares which attend it; or by those uneasy reflections which attend the abuse of power. Labour, and a good conscience, will procure sweeter sleep than all the riches in the world.

On that night could not the king sleep.—On what night? The night preceding the decisive day on which Esther was to present her petition, and the morning on which Haman had a petition of an opposite kind to be presented to the king. Observe how divine Providence kept sleep from the eyes of Ahasuerus, to serve his own gracious purposes. It is said that 'God giveth his beloved sleep.' But he sometimes, too, withholds sleep from them for good purposes; and he sometimes hath with-held sleep from other persons, or disturbed it with strange dreams, for their benefit. A dream was sent to Pharaoh, that Joseph might be delivered from his prison and exalted to power. Another dream was sent to Nebuchadnezzar, to procure the exaltation of Daniel and his friends. Ahasuerus was kept from sleep, that he might not suffer Mordecai to be hanged.

It is of great use to know how to improve those moments of the night in which we are debarred from sleep. Ahasuerus, it seems, thought he could not employ his waking moments better than by hearing the chronicles of his reign. Here, too, we may observe the superintending care of providence. Why did not a prince, who delighted in pleasure, rather call for the melody of the harp and viol, than for the chronicles of his reign? It was the will of God that he should be put in mind of what Mordecai had done for him, because now the fit time was come that he should receive the reward of his fidelity.

Verse 2.—*And it was found written, that Mordecai had told of Bigthana and Teresh, two of the king's chamberlains, the keepers of the door, who sought to lay hand on the king Ahasuerus.*

How came this part of the records to be read at this time, rather than the celebrated exploits of Cyrus, or some other passage which might be expected best to entertain the wearied king? Such was the appointment of Providence, which regulates the minutest events. 'The footsteps of a good man are ordered by the Lord' in wisdom and love; and the footsteps of other men are ordered by Him in wisdom and love to them that love God, 'to them that are the called according to his purpose.'

Mordecai might think that he had good reason to complain of the disregard showed to his eminent services. The king was a liberal rewarder of others who had done little, but seemed to have forgotten the man who had done so much in his service; the man to whom, under God, he owed his life. Yet Mordecai had this to comfort him, that his name and his services were recorded in the book of the chronicles, and therefore were not likely to be always forgotten. May not all God's faithful servants, when they think He hath forgotten them, comfort themselves with the assurance, that a book of remembrance is written before God, in which not a cup of cold water given to a disciple, in the name of a disciple, is omitted; and that infinite wisdom will choose out the time of their reward?

Verse 3.—*And the king said, What honour and dignity hath been done to Mordecai for this? Then said the king's servants that ministered unto him, There is nothing done for him.*

The king did not doubt but some honour and dignity had been conferred upon Mordecai for saving his life. He could not believe that he had been so thoughtlessly ungrateful, as never to requite for such a length of time a service so eminent as that which Mordecai had performed; and was astonished to hear his servants say that nothing had been done for him.

Let us take a review of our lives, and consider what we have done, or not done. If our memories are good, we shall be surprised at many instances of our conduct, or of our forgetfulness. Have we showed all that sense of gratitude to our benefactors, to which we must acknowledge them to be entitled? Have we not often intended to do what we have never done, although we must blush at the thought that we have not done it? And can we forget, that amongst our benefactors are to be reckoned our parents, and, most of all, God our Maker?

We are taught, likewise, by this question of Ahasuerus, not to impute to intention what may be the effect merely of inadvertence. We are apt to make louder complaints than we have any reason to make, of the ingratitude of those to whom we have performed good offices. Perhaps they have forgotten that they did not requite them. Perhaps their neglects have not originated in depravity of heart, or insensibility to benefits; but in thoughtlessness; or, it was occasioned by the many avocations of other affairs. We cannot, indeed, justify those who do not with the first opportunity requite benefits received; but we must not aggravate real evils. Who will say that David did not retain a grateful rememembrance of what Jonathan had done for him? And yet several years seem to have elapsed, after he was advanced to the regal dignity, before he inquired who were left of the house of Saul, that he might show them the kindness of God for Jonathan's sake; and several more years passed away, before he brought the bones of that beloved friend from Jabesh-Gilead to be interred in the sepulchre of his fathers; 2 Samuel xxi. 12–14.

There is nothing done for him, said the servants of Ahasuerus. This was a disagreeable truth which they could not conceal from the king. But the evil was not irreparable. Mordecai was still alive, and the king could yet testify his sense of the benefit received.

Verse 4.—*And the king said, Who is in the court? Now Haman was come into the outward court of the king's house, to speak unto the king to hang Mordecai on the gallows that he had prepared for him.*

'Woe to them that devise evil upon their bed,' or before they go to bed, 'and when the morning is light practise it.' Haman rose up early in the morning to obtain the accomplishment of his malicious designs against Mordecai. It is much to be lamented, that the children of the wicked one are often more active in the prosecution of their corrupt intentions, than the children of light in the accomplishment of their pious and charitable designs.

Who is in the court? said the king. He slept not for the whole night; and he heard, at the fittest time for God's purpose in keeping him awake, that Haman was in the court of the palace. When he was newly informed that Mordecai had never been rewarded for saving his life, he asked the question, 'Who is in the court?'

Verse 5.—*And the king's servants said unto him; Behold, Haman standeth in the court. And the king said, Let him come in.*

When the king had formed the resolution that Mordecai should be immediately rewarded with the highest honours, he was glad that Haman had come so opportunely to give him his advice what honours were fittest to be conferred on him.

Verse 6.—*So Haman came in. And the king said unto him, What shall be done unto the man whom the king delighteth to honour? Now Haman thought in his heart, To whom would the king delight to do honour more than to myself?*

Long as Mordecai had been overlooked, the king discovers a warm gratitude for his good service when it is called to remembrance. This teaches us one happy means of exciting gratitude in our heart to our benefactors. Let us call to remembrance their benefits, and we must be more brutish than oxen or asses if we feel not grateful impressions on our hearts. It was by this method that David awakened his soul to the praises of God for all his benefits.

You may likewise be of great use to your neighbours, by reminding them, when it appears necessary, of the benefits which they have received, either from their fellow-men, or from their Maker. You see in this part of the history of Ahasuerus, what happy effects a word read or spoken may have.

The king delighted to honour the man who had saved his life. What honour is due to our parents who have given us life? To those who have been instrumental in saving us from eternal wrath? Above all, to Him who gave himself for us, that we might be preserved from everlasting destruction? 1 Cor. vi. 20; 2 Cor. v. 14, 15.

Now Haman thought in his heart, To whom should the king delight to do honour more than to myself?—This proud conceit of Haman did not seem to be without ground. If the king had not wanted his sleep the foregoing night, it would have been well founded. How uncertain is the favour of men! and how much are those to be pitied, who mistake the rolling wave for a solid rock, on which they may build the foundation of their happiness!

Verses 7, 8, 9.—*And Haman answered the king, For the man whom the king delighteth to honour, let the royal apparel be brought which the king useth to wear, and the horse that the king rideth upon, and the crown-royal which is set upon his head; and let this apparel and horse be delivered to the hand of one of the king's most noble princes, that they may array the man withal whom the king delighteth to honour, and bring him on horseback through the street of the city, and proclaim before him, Thus shall it be done to the man whom the king delighteth to honour.*

Haman thought with himself that he was certainly the man whom the king delighted to honour; but he did not say so. The vainest of the sons of men affect modesty, to obtain gratification to their vanity. If the king had asked Haman what honour he wished for himself, he would not have asked what he now supposed he was asking for himself, without incurring the danger into which Adonijah brought himself by asking the concubine of David to wife. The kings of the East were jealous of all that affected, or seemed to affect, any badge of royalty. Alexander the Great, when he was sailing upon the river Euphrates, and suffered the diadem to drop from his head into the waters, punished with death a seaman who brought it out of the river upon his head.

But it was not professedly for himself. It was for the man, unknown to him, whom the king desired to honour, that Haman asked the glory, not hitherto allowed to any subject, of wearing for once the royal apparel, and of riding through the city on the favourite horse of the king, adorned with a royal coronet, under the care of one of the king's most noble princes, who was on that day to be the servant of the man whom the king delighted to honour. We see in what Haman placed the chief happiness of man. He could not hope to obtain the admired dignity of sitting upon the royal throne: but the happiness next to that, in his estimation, was to be adorned for once with some of the ensigns of royalty; to be served by the greatest of the king's princes during the exhibition of his royal pomp; and to be declared the favourite of the king. What an empty, what a transient shadow of felicity was this! Surely the man who sought it from the king was a child in understanding; and yet such children are the greatest part of mankind. What is there more solid or satisfactory in any of the objects of human pursuit, whilst men are unilluminated from above? 'Vanity of vanities, vanity of vanities, all is vanity?' But we can see and despise the folly of other men walking in a vain show, when we ourselves walk in a show equally vain. 'Surely every man is vanity!

Verse 10.—*Then the king said to Haman, Make haste, and take the apparel, and the horse, as thou hast said, and do even so to Mordecai the Jew, that sitteth at the king's gate: let nothing fail of all that thou hast spoken.*

This is a great infelicity which attends worldly pursuits, that there is no proportion between the pleasure of success and the pain of disappointment. How unsatisfactory to Haman would the wearing of royal ornaments for a small part of a day have been, and all the other honours which he expected to enjoy only for a few moments! We can scarcely suppose that the pleasure of this feast to his vanity would have lasted longer than a night, or a week. But how dreadful a stroke was given to him, by hearing that the man whom he mortally hated was the man whom the king delighted to honour; that *he* was to be invested with that royal pomp to which Haman himself looked as the perfection of felicity; and that he must become the servant of that man for whom he had erected a gallows fifty cubits high! What exquisite misery, if he had lived to endure it, must have been his portion, at the galling remembrance of his own disgrace, when the erection of the lofty gibbet published to the whole city the height of his hopes and the bitterness of his disappointment!

Let nothing fail, said the king, *of all that thou hast spoken.*—
He counted no honours too great for his benefactor. He would compensate by his liberality the time which Mordecai had lived unrewarded and unhonoured. If we have neglected to do good when we should have done it, let us use double diligence in doing it, if time is still left us to repair our omissions.

Verse 11.—*Then took Haman the apparel, and the horse, and arrayed Mordecai, and brought him on horseback through the street of the city, and proclaimed before him, Thus shall it be done unto the man whom the king delighteth to honour.*

Do you complain that you must deny yourselves, and take up your cross in following Christ? But who is the man that is exempted from trouble, or the man that does not find it necessary to deny himself on many occasions? And is it not better to deny ourselves for Christ, than to deny ourselves for the sake of any earthly object? You see that Haman, great as he was in the court of Ahasuerus, must serve Mordecai as his lacquey, and perform to him those services which to Haman himself appeared the most glorious of all others, when he would have given thousands of gold and silver for a warrant to slay him. The greatest earthly princes must often do things displeasing or omit things pleasing to themselves, for temporary advantage, or even without the prospect of advantage. What could Haman gain from Mordecai, or from Ahasuerus, for doing what he could not do without the most extreme reluctance? But the least instance of self-denial for the sake of Christ shall be attended with a great reward, worthy of the bounty of the Giver.

Mordecai was too wise to value those childish honours which appeared so glorious to Haman. He was, undoubtedly, struck with amazement when Haman brought to him the royal robes, and the royal horse. But it was necessary for him to yield obedience to the king's pleasure; and, doubtless, he saw the gracious hand of God in what was done to him. Mordecai had more sagacity than the friends of Haman, who saw his fall before Mordecai the Jew presaged by this instance of his humiliation. Jacob saw the love of God in the face of his reconciled enemy. Mordecai saw the favour of God in the reluctant services performed by an enemy as full of malice as ever, and was cheered by the dawnings of that deliverance to his nation for which he had been praying and looking.

Verse 12.—*And Mordecai came again to the king's gate: but Haman hasted to his house, mourning and having his head covered.*

If you desire to be happy, be clothed with humility, and mortify pride. Haman in prosperity was miserable, and in adversity was doubly miserable, because he was the slave of pride. Mordecai preserved the even tenor of his soul in prosperity and in adversity. When he was led in royal state through the city, and publicly proclaimed the king's favourite, he was the same man as before; and returned without noise to the duties of his humble station. Haman's disappointment crushed his spirits. He hastened to his house, to pour out his sorrows to his friends, who could give him no comfort. He came back with his face covered, in token of that anguish which preyed upon his heart, and that shame which would not suffer him to show his face. Yesterday he went out from the king's presence merry and joyful of heart. To-day he goes to his house pierced with incurable grief. For, since Adam was upon the earth, 'the triumphing of the wicked is short, and the joy of the hypocrite but for a moment; Job xx. 5.

Verse 13.—*And Haman told Zeresh his wife, and all his friends, every thing that had befallen him:—*

He would have acted as wisely, if he had left his sorrows concealed in his own bosom; but this was impracticable. They were too violent to be concealed. He probably expected some mitigation to his griefs from the kindness of his friends. But miserable comforters were they all! Their words were the piercings of a sword.

Then said his wise men and Zeresh his wife unto him, If Mordecai be of the seed of the Jews, before whom thou hast begun to fall, thou shalt not prevail against him, but shalt surely fall before him.

Who were these wise men? Either sages whom Haman patronised, and from whom he expected wise counsel when he required it; or diviners, who were believed to know more than men could know, without some communication with superior beings. Many of the heathens put much confidence in diviners, but we have learned better things from the word of God. By making it our counsellor at all times of perplexity, we shall find peace to our souls; Isaiah viii. 19, 20: Psalm cxix. 24.

'If Mordecai be of the seed of the Jews, before whom thou hast begun to fall, thou shalt not prevail against him, but shalt surely fall.'—If Mordecai be of the seed of the Jews. Why do they lay so much stress upon the stock from which Mordecai sprung? If Mordecai had been a native Persian, or a Babylonian, or an Egyptian, would they not have prognosticated equal success to him against Haman? No; it plainly appears that the dispensations of divine providence in favour of the Jews were so far known to them, as to assure them that Providence watched over their interests in a manner peculiar to their nation. Although most men are disposed to think that their own country is happy above others in the divine favour, and although the Persians at this time seemed to have good reason to flatter themselves with a special interest in the favour of Heaven, yet these wise Persians plainly confessed, that the Jews scattered through the nations were the special objects of the divine care. The wonders done in Babylon were known to all the world, and could not fail to impress all considerate persons with high sentiments concerning the God of Israel. Haman's wise men might have read the sacred books of the Jews, in which they would find that their God had wrought as great wonders for them in times past, as in the period of the Babylonian captivity. They learned instruction from the works of God. They saw that the same God who had preserved Daniel and his companions, watched over the safety and fortune of Mordecai; and they concluded that Haman, his irreconcilable enemy, would fall under the weight of his vengeance.

But it is strange that these wise men, and even the wife of Haman, whatever they thought, expressed to him their mind so fully. If they did not choose to flatter him, might they not at least have concealed their dismal conjectures, especially as he was led by their counsels to that public disgrace in which he had involved himself, by building a gallows for the man who was appointed to be the king's favorite? for although it was built in the court of his own house, yet the news of its erection was soon to spread. It appears from the freedom they used with Haman, that they already considered him as a lost man, whom it was useless to flatter. They were his friends as long as his friendship could profit them; and now they seem to have cared little whether he accounted them his friends or his enemies. Their prophecy must have been as unpleasant as the howling of a dog, or even a sentence of death, to his ears. The rich hath many friends; but when poverty is seen coming like an armed man, they vanish away like snow in the days of sunshine.

We may, however, learn useful instruction from a prophecy, dictated by reflection on the works of the Lord. Blind heathens have been forced to see, that God takes care of his people; that he often interposes wonderfully for their deliverance; and that he leaves not his gracious works in their behalf unfinished. Why do not God's own people, in the day of their distress, call to remembrance his judgments for their consolation, and for the support of their faith? When he begins to deliver them, why do they indulge distrusting fears about the accomplishment of that work which he hath taken into his own hand? Why are they not thankful for the day of small things, as the beginning of months of joy? After Jesus undertook to heal the daughter of Jairus, strong temptations met the mourning parent, when Jesus was on the road to complete his work, and fears began to overwhelm his soul. But what said Jesus? 'Fear not, only believe.' He believed, and received his daughter back from death.

DISCOURSE XI.

HAMAN'S FALL AND DEATH.

CHAPTER VI. 14—CHAPTER VII. 10.

Verse 14.—*And while they were yet talking with him, came the king's chamberlains, and hasted to bring Haman unto the banquet that Esther had prepared.*

WHEN Haman, on the former day, left the queen's banquet, he went forth joyful and glad of heart. One reason of his joy was, that he was invited to a like banquet next day. 'Boast not thyself of to-morrow, for thou knowest not what a day may bring forth.' Art thou invited to a banquet? Thou knowest not whether thou shalt partake of it, or whether it will give thee any pleasure to partake of it. Haman was in no haste to this day's banquet. He waited till he was sent for; and would have gladly gone to a house of mourning, rather than the house of feasting, for his mind was ill fitted for the joys of a banquet. But he is not his own master. He must comply, as far as he can, with the will of the king. With a heart full of grief he goes to a feast where he must eat the bread of sorrow, and drink his own tears.

CHAP. vii. 1, 2.—*So the king and Haman came to banquet with Esther the queen. And the king said again unto Esther on the second day at the banquet of wine, What is thy petition, queen Esther? and it shall be granted thee: and what is thy request? and it shall be performed, even to the half of the kingdom.*

Haman, honoured with the king's society at the banquet of wine, might expect to be consoled for his late disappointment, by new expressions of the royal favour. But soon did his hope, if any remained, prove like the giving up of the ghost. He was brought to the banquet, not that he might enjoy the queen's smiles, but that he might hear an accusation against himself, which touched his life, and to which he could not answer.

The king persisted in his kind sentiments towards Esther. For the third time he promises, whatever her petition was, to grant it, even to the half of the kingdom. Who would not have been emboldened by a promise so often given? To have deferred the petition any longer would have but argued an ungrateful distrust of the king's sincerity. Let us remember how much greater encouragement we have to present our requests to God; and what distrust we discover of his faithfulness, if we do not come before his throne of grace with boldness. No less than six times, in the compass of one sentence, does our Lord Jesus assure us that our prayers shall be heard; Matt. vii. 7, 8.

Verse 3.—*Then Esther the queen answered, and said; If I have found favour in thy sight, O king! and if it please the king, let my life be given at my petition, and my people at my request:*

Esther, at last, ventured to bring forth her request. The nature of the case pressed her. The king's solicitations urged her. His kindness and his promises encouraged her. Unnecessary delays are dangerous, especially in matters of great importance.

The request was for her life, and the life of her people. The king was no less surprised at this petition, than Festus was at hearing the accusation of the Jews against Paul. It was, certainly, not for any such thing as the king supposed. It never came into his mind, that his beloved queen could have any occasion to present a petition to him for her life. Although by his own authority, (but without his knowledge,) a sentence of death had been pronounced against her, it must have astonished him to hear, that she and her people were doomed to destruction; and it must astonish the reader of this history, that the king, five years after his marriage with the queen, should have passed a sentence of death upon her whole nation, without knowing it. Into such absurdities are princes led, who are too indolent to look into their own affairs, and leave them to be managed without control by favourites, who have their own interests to serve, and their own passions to gratify.

Verse 4.—*For we are sold, I and my people, to be destroyed, to be slain, and to perish. But if we had been sold for bond-men and bond-women, I had held my tongue, although the enemy could not countervail the king's damage.*

The good queen enforces her petition with resistless eloquence. 'I and my people are sold to be destroyed, to be slain, and to perish.' These words are borrowed from the king's edict against the Jews. The king must have been greatly moved to hear that the queen was sold like a sheep to be slaughtered; and not the queen herself only, but all her friends, and, what was more, her whole nation. His heart must have been a thousand times harder than flint, if he had not been moved at this representation of the danger to which she and her people were exposed. If a humane prince will exert his power for the protection of the meanest of his subjects exposed to unmerited danger, what might not the great king of Persia be expected to do for the preservation of a beloved queen, and of all that were dear to her!

It is plain that she was not putting her husband to unnecessary trouble by her petition, which was extorted from her by the most pressing danger; and she informs him, that if the danger had been less dreadful, she would have been silent. If she and her people had been sold like bond-men and bond-women, then she would have left it to time to convince the king that his own interest required his interposition, or she would have left their deliverance to be effected by the gradual operation of divine providence in their behalf. But the case was very different as matters stood. The year was not to end before their utter destruction, unless something was presently done for their preservation; and it was not to be expected that God would show wonders to the dead, and make them to arise and praise him. The king could not bring them again from the dust of death, however he might regret the loss of so many faithful subjects.

But would it not have been the duty of Esther to supplicate

for their relief, although they had been doomed only to slavery? Perhaps she might have seen it her duty to do it, if this had really been the case. But at present, her mind was so deeply possessed with the awfulness of their danger, that she thought, if their misery had been any thing else than what it was, she could have borne it without troubling the king with her complaint. Thus, a man racked with the pains of a gravel, thinks, that if it had been only the gout, he could have borne it with patience; or, if he finds his life endangered by a sore disease, he will tell the physician that his anxiety is raised only by the dangerous symptoms, and that if these could be removed, he could easily endure the pains of his distemper.

It is to be remembered, that what the queen desired from the king, however necessary and reasonable, was difficult to be granted, because the laws of the Medes and Persians could not be altered. It was therefore necessary to assure the king, that nothing but bitter necessity could have induced her to give him so much trouble. Modest petitioners are heard with favour, when impudent beggars are repulsed with scorn.

The king's interest was deeply concerned in this request on other accounts. The safety of a prince consists in the multitude and happiness of his people. If the Jews had been sold for slaves, the enemy could not have compensated the king's damage, although he had given twice ten thousand talents into the royal treasury. Far less could he have compensated the loss to be sustained by the king in the destruction of so many thousands of useful and laborious subjects, scattered throughout every part of his empire. Divine Providence has so closely connected the interests of princes and people, that the throne is established by righteousness and mercy, and subverted by unrighteousness.

Verse 5.—*Then the king Ahasuerus answered and said unto Esther the queen; Who is he, and where is he, that durst presume in his heart to do so?*

What! to compass the death of the queen; and, as if that were too small a wickedness, the destruction of all her people also! Was a man so wicked to be found in any of the hundred and twenty-seven provinces of the king's dominions? If there were such a daring criminal to be found, no death was too terrible for him.

What, then, will our Lord do when he riseth up to revenge the wrongs done to himself in the persons of his brethren; of those who 'are espoused to him in righteousness, and in judgment, and in loving-kindness, and in mercies?' Will he not account the wrongs done to them to have been done to himself? When he maketh inquisition for blood, woe to them that are stained with bloody crimes against his people! The wrath of Ahasuerus against the enemies of the Jews was a fruit of God's wrath against them. He forgot not his promise to Abraham, 'I will bless him that blesseth thee, and I will curse him that curseth thee.'

Who and where is he that durst do this thing?—What if Ahasuerus himself is the man? although it would have been unwise in the queen to tell him that he was. He was, certainly, though unconscious of it, a partner in this wickedness; and yet he was filled with horror at hearing that any person could dare to load himself with such guilt. Thus David was filled with anger against a man who was only the emblem of himself; 2 Sam. xii. Consider what abhorrence you have of the sins of other men, and consider how like your own sins are to theirs, and let your souls be humbled within you. Take care how you speak of the sins of other men, lest your tongues condemn yourselves. Your sins are probably much liker to theirs than you could imagine till you have well considered the matter. Perhaps they are a great deal worse, when every circumstance is considered.

Verse 6.—*And Esther said, The adversary and enemy is this wicked Haman. Then Haman was afraid before the king and the queen.*

Haman now finds for what reason he was invited by the queen to her banquet. It was, to be accused to his face of the blackest of crimes. He had an opportunity of saying what could be said (if any thing could be said) in his own vindication, or in mitigation of his offense. But if he had nothing to say, it was to be expected that the confusion of his face would be a witness against him.

This was actually the case: 'Then Haman was afraid before the king and the queen.' He had too good reason to tremble for his life. The queen had brought a dreadful accusation against him, and his guilt was too apparent to be denied, or to be extenuated. And it was of a nature fitted to excite the king's fiercest indignation, and bitterest rage.

In what light did Haman's pride and greatness now appear to him? If he had possessed worlds, he would cheerfully have parted with them to have his former conduct buried in oblivion. In all our conduct let us have an eye to that future day which will assuredly come, when our behaviour will appear to ourselves in its true light; and to that day which may come before we quit the world, when it will be followed with its just consequences. How many things that are done would be left undone, if, at the doing, men would realise in their own minds what will be realised one day by the divine providence!

There was a time when Haman thought that life was not life, unless all men bowed the knee to him. But how happy would he now have been if he could have obtained life upon any terms! What did all his honours formerly avail him, whilst he saw the hated Mordecai at the king's gate? But in his fear he would gladly have bowed the knee to Mordecai as the price of life.

Verse 7.—*And the king, arising from the banquet of wine in his wrath, went into the palace-garden: and Haman stood up to make request for his life to Esther the queen; for he saw that there was evil determined against him by the king.*

The king was agitated by his indignation to a degree beyond what we can well conceive. The angry passions rage in the breasts of men, in proportion to the sense they have of their own dignity, of the insults they apprehend to be offered to them, and of the obligations violated by the offender. Ahasuerus was so great a king, that he would think the smallest offense against himself almost unpardonable; but an attempt to destroy his beloved queen was the greatest of all crimes, next to an attempt upon his own life. How unpardonable did this crime appear in one whom he had loved, and trusted, and honoured above all his subjects! No punishment which his power could inflict, appeared to him equal to a crime so atrocious. And yet this was not the worst of the matter. Haman, by his artifice, had drawn his master into partnership of his own crimes. It is propable that Ahasuerus now saw, that Haman's guilt was the decree obtained against the Jews, passed by the consent and authority of Ahasuerus himself. For how could Haman, without such authority, destroy a whole nation of the king's subjects? His wrath must have burnt like a furnace, when he considered how he had been betrayed into a decree so absurd, so wicked, so infamous, that might have proved so fatal to the wife of his bosom, and to all her kindred.

Ahasuerus could not keep his seat. He could not bear the sight of Haman. He ran to the garden, not to give his wrath time to cool, but to give it time to devise proper means for executing all the furiousness of its rage upon a man whom he had devoted to destruction. While Haman was already suffering for his wickedness by the terrors that tormented his heart, Ahasuerus himself suffered some part of what his rashness deserved, by the fiery indignation that raged in his bowels. How miserable is it to feel the torments which either of these passions inflict, when they obtain dominion over the soul!

Haman wished still to live, though in disgrace; and made supplication for his life to a woman whom he had offended beyond hopes of forgiveness. Although it was her duty to forgive him so as to wish well to his soul, it was not her duty to desire his pardon from the king, after he had involved himself so deeply in the guilt of blood. Or, if she had interceded for his life, it was not to be hoped that the king would spare the serpent that had almost stung the wife of his bosom to death. The case was hopeless; but drowning men will grasp at straws or shadows, when they can find no better supports.

The wicked now 'bows before the righteous;' and Haman was not the first, nor will he be the last, of the enemies of God's people, that shall be made to 'bow before them, and to lick the dust of their feet;' Isa. xlix. 23: Rev. iii. 9.

Verse 8.—*Then the king returned out of the palace-garden,*

into the place of the banquet of wine; and Haman was fallen upon the bed whereon Esther was. Then said the king, Will he force the queen also before me in the house? As the word went out of the king's mouth, they covered Haman's face.

When men are enraged, neither their thoughts agree with facts, nor do their words agree with their thoughts. Haman could not well be thought a worse man than he was, and yet the king was disposed to put a worse construction upon his conduct than it deserved. It is not, however, to be supposed, that the king really thought he meant to force Esther before him in the house. Anger is a short madness; and the words of an angry man are like 'the speeches of one that is desperate, which are as wind.' If we desire, therefore, to behave uniformly like wise men and like Christians, we must keep our mouths as with a bridle when our hearts are hot within us; and we must keep our hearts with all diligence, that our passions may not overpower our reason.

It is likewise necessary for us to beware of all irritating behaviour, that we may not kindle up fierce passions in the breasts of other men. If they should think, or speak, or act unreasonably, when we have strongly tempted them to be angry, a share of the blame belongs to us; and if we condemn their fury, we should condemn ourselves as sharers of the guilt. Surely the king could not imagine in good earnest that Haman meant to force the queen in his presence; yet Haman, by snares laid for her life, gave the king too good reason to suspect him of every thing wicked.

The king's fury drove him from the palace to the garden, and from the garden to the palace. It had the entire government of his thoughts, of his temper, and of his actions. A petition from any of the king's servants, or from Esther herself, at this time, in favour of Haman, would rather have increased than abated his fury. But, indeed, Haman had no friends in the king's house to take his part. Some of the king's servants covered his face, and others of them brought in new reports to his disadvantage. A proud man may be flattered, but he cannot be loved. When he falls from prosperity into adversity, he begins to know what sentiments are entertained concerning him.

Whilst he spoke these words, they covered Haman's face; which the king could not now behold without detestation. The faces of the condemned used to be covered; and sentence of death had already been passed against this wicked man. What a miserable change did a single hour produce! How justly may the words of Bildad concerning the wicked be applied to this wretched man!—'Yea, the light of the wicked shall be put out, and the spark of his fire shall not shine. The light shall be dark in his tabernacle, and his candle shall be put out with him. The steps of his strength shall be straitened, and his own counsel shall cast him down. For he is cast into a net by his own feet, and he walketh upon a snare; Job xviii. 5–8.

Verse 9.—*And Harbonah, one of the chamberlains, said before the king; Behold also the gallows, fifty cubits high, which Haman had made for Mordecai, who had spoken good for the king, standeth in the house of Haman. Then the king said, Hang him thereon.*

New charges are produced against Haman, when it was seen that the king was no longer his friend. Had Haman taken care to gain the love of his inferiors during the time of his greatness, he might have found some few, perhaps, that would have expressed their gratitude when he fell; and not many would have assisted in pushing him lower. But his misery was, that he trusted in the multitude of his riches, and in the favour of the king. When the king was his enemy, all men were his enemies; and he had given abundant occasion to complete his destruction. His own hands had made the cords with which he was now girded and strangled.

Harbonah told the king of the gallows that Haman had erected for Mordecai, fifty cubits high. Here was an instance of his intolerable presumption, that he had built this gallows without the king's previous knowledge. But what was sure to inflame the king's revenge beyond measure was, that the servant of the king, for whom the gallows was prepared, was the very man to whom the king owed his life when it was endangered by two wicked conspirators. It looked as if Haman had been in a confederacy with these men, and wished to revenge their death.

Then the king said, Hang him thereon.—The king was impatient to have such a viper crushed, and removed out of his sight. He had been considering with himself, perhaps, by what means he might chase him out of the world, so as best to express his own detestation of his conduct, and load him with ignominy. The words of Harbonah decided the business. What can be more ignominious for him than to be hanged on a gallows higher than most of the houses of the city; on a gallows constructed by himself for one of the king's friends; and on the very day on which Haman hoped to have enjoyed the pleasure of seeing Mordecai hanging on it till he died!—'Hang him thereon.'

Verse 10.—*So they hanged Haman on the gallows that he had prepared for Mordecai. Then was the king's wrath pacified.*

There is no law more just, says an ancient author, than that the contrivers of destruction should perish by their own contrivances. Who pities Haman hanged on his own gallows? Who does not rather rejoice in the divine righteousness, displayed in that destruction which his own art brought upon him? In his dismal end, how fully verified are the words of David! 'He (the Lord) ordaineth his arrows against the persecutors. He hath made a pit, and digged it; and he is fallen into the ditch which he hath made: his mischief shall return upon his own head, and his violent dealing shall come down upon his own pate. I will praise the Lord according to his righteousness; Psalm vii. 13–17.

Let the workers of iniquity tremble, and turn to the Lord, and seek pardon through the blood of Jesus. Saul of Tarsus was a persecutor, who sought the utter destruction of the Israel of God; and yet he obtained mercy, and the grace of our Lord was abundant to him. 'But the Lord shall wound the head of the wicked, the hairy scalp of him that goeth on still in his trespasses.'

Let not the children of Zion despair, when their enemies are successful, and no hope seems to be left them. God knows how to find expedients in desperate circumstances, and to turn the blackest darkness into light. He knows how to bring upon the head of his enemies that destruction which they prepare for his own people, and to save them that love him from the greatest deaths.

The king's wrath was never pacified till Haman received the punishment which he so justly deserved. Then his mind enjoyed some ease when he heard that Haman was hanged on his own gallows. But he soon found that much yet remained for him to do, to put away the mischief of Haman the Agagite. 'When the wicked perish, there is shouting;' but their wickedness may outlive them, and cause much distress and toil when they are gone to receive their reward.

DISCOURSE XII.

MORDECAI IS ADVANCED TO GREAT HONOURS—LIBERTY IS PROCURED FOR THE JEWS TO DEFEND THEMSELVES AGAINST THE INTENDED MASSACRE.

CHAPTER VIII. 1-14.

Verses 1, 2.—*On that day did the king Ahasuerus give the house of Haman, the Jews' enemy, unto Esther the queen. And Mordecai came before the king: for Esther had told what he was unto her. And the king took off his ring, which he had taken from Haman, and gave it unto Mordecai. And Esther set Mordecai over the house of Haman.*

BE not solicitous about treasuring up the riches of this world. What you can gain is to-day yours, to-morrow you know not whose it shall be. Should it fall into the hands of your children after you, you know not whether they will be wise men or fools; whether they will be losers or gainers by the possession of it. Nay, you know not whether it may not fall into the hands of your most abhorred enemies. This is often the fate of ill-gotten riches. 'The wealth of the sinner is laid up for the just.' With what vexation would Haman have thought of that wealth in which he gloried, if he had foreseen that it was to be possessed by a Jewess! Would he not rather have chosen to live a beggar all his days, than leave his wealth to persons whom he so mortally hated?

The queen was enriched beyond her expectations and wishes. Yet the wealth bestowed upon her would enable her to perform important services to her beloved nation. The donation of it by the king, to whom it was forfeited, was a testimony of his affection, to which she still must have recourse, with new petitions for her people. Above all, this donation was a remarkable testimony of the kindness and justice of the divine providence, which put into her hands that immense wealth of the enemy of her nation, by which he would have bribed the king, if a bribe had been necessary to procure their destruction. The Lord had already not only wrought deliverance for her, but had given her an accession of riches out of the snares that had been laid for her kinsman; and she was thereby encouraged to hope, that he would bring to a happy conclusion that great work that occupied her mind.

Her kinsman, too, was highly advanced, both on her account and his own. The king had formerly caused his favour for Mordecai to be proclaimed through the city of Shushan; but now he loaded him with real and substantial honours, which would put him into a proper condition for protecting his nation, exposed to danger for his sake.

It was now the fifth year since the adopted daughter of Mordecai was seated upon an imperial throne, and hitherto it was not known that he stood in any relation to the queen, or had showed to her the kindness of a father.

The king must, surely, at least have condemned his own thoughtlessness in inquiring so little after Esther's friends. He now discerned, that besides his unrequited obligations to Mordecai for saving his life, he owed to him likewise the graces and accomplishments of his queen, and almost her life; for he had been to her a second father, without whose kind care none knows what might have befallen her in her tender years.

It would be, likewise, a powerful recommendation of Mordecai, that he had hitherto lived quietly in a low station, without so much as mentioning his claims to preferment. It appeared plainly that he was more careful to deserve the king's favour than to enjoy it, and that greatness had no charms but the opportunities it might give him of doing good, or preventing evil. Those are fittest for high stations that are best satisfied with any station in which Providence is pleased to put them.

The king put Mordecai into Haman's place; and the queen, who now thought it highly expedient to inform the king or

Mordecai's kindness and relation to her, did likewise make him her steward. To her dying day she forgot not the kindness showed to her in the days of her youth, and behaved as the best of daughters to the best of fathers.

Gratitude to benefactors is essential to a virtuous character. If you call a man ungrateful, you need say nothing more of him, you have already said every thing that is bad; nor will the highest elevation excuse forgetfulness of benefits received in a lower condition. The blessed Jesus, exalted above men and angels, forgets none of the kindnesses shown to him in the persons of his brethren in a low condition upon earth; but what is done to the least of them is rewarded as if it had been done to Himself. We need not envy those women who ministered to him of their substance in the days of his humiliation the glorious rewards bestowed upon them in his state of exaltation. We still have it in our power to feed Him when he is hungry, to give Him drink when he is thirsty, to clothe Him when he is naked; and He will not be unrighteous to forget our works and labours of love to His name. Did Esther in her royal condition retain such a kind remembrance of the friends of her low estate, and shall we doubt of the infinitely superior virtues of him who is the fairest among the children of men; to the operation of whose Spirit we owe every thing that is lovely in our temper and conduct?

Esther, on the throne, retained the kindness of her youth, not only to Mordecai, but to all her friends and all her people.

Verse 3.—*And Esther spake yet again before the king, and fell down at his feet, and besought him with tears to put away the mischief of Haman the Agagite, and his device that he had devised against the Jews.*

Esther now appeared to be in a very safe condition, and her friend Mordecai had little reason to be apprehensive for his life, when he was honoured to be the king's favourite; but neither of them thought themselves safe or happy till their brethren and people were placed in a like condition. They would have rather chosen, if it had been the will of God, to perish, if their people could obtain deliverance and enlargement, than to live and see the misery threatened fall upon them. Esther, therefore, again ventures to trouble the king with her requests. She falls down before him. She weeps and makes supplication with floods of tears for her people. Happy were they in such an intercessor. Her beauty, her tears, the strong emotions of her heart apparent in her gestures, the amiable virtues which shone forth in her generous concern for her poor friends, were sufficient to have melted the most marble-hearted prince in the world. The humane Ahasuerus could not stand out against such forcible and pleasing importunities. He was requested to do what might expose him to difficulties and dangers; for the fundamental laws of Persia deprived him of the power of abrogating his own laws. But what he could do he would doubtless perform, at such importunities of such a suppliant.

Although Esther had wept and made supplication to God for her people, she did not reckon that she had done what was incumbent on her, without weeping and supplicating the king likewise, at the risk not only of displeasing him, but of her head. When she had by her supplications made some progress in the important business, she wept and supplicated the king a second time, till she obtained all that could be obtained for her people. It is not enough to begin a good work, but we ought to hold on till it be completed, although great difficulties meet us in the face, which it may appear almost impossible to surmount. When we stop short before we have finished what we were called to perform, may we not be confounded by that question, 'Ye did run well, who did hinder you? Are ye so foolish, having begun in the Spirit, to end in the flesh?'

The queen solicits the king to undo the mischief of Haman. The king himself might, with too good reason, have been implicated with Haman. He was under obligations, from strict justice, to put away the mischief which could not be done without his own consent. But the queen wisely overlooked this important consideration, and chose rather to address herself to the king's mercy than to his justice. 'Grievous words stir up anger; soft words turn away (or prevent) wrath.' It was, indeed, highly proper that the king should be sensible of his own part in the wrong done to the Jews; but his own conscience would not fail to perform that office, and probably it operated the more powerfully in him, that the Jews themselves kept silence. We feel most powerfully the injuries that we have done, when those to whom they are done show little disposition to complain.

Verse 4.—*Then the king held out the golden sceptre toward Esther:—*

She would now venture with greater boldness than before to go in before the king, for she was assured of his favour. When we know that we are beloved by superiors, we can go to them with boldness to ask any reasonable favour; yet so variable are the tempers of men, that we may be sometimes deceived in our hopes.

Esther was not, at this time, ashamed of her hope of the favour of Ahasuerus. God himself was her hope, and he inclined the king's heart to favour her.

Verses 4, 5.—*So Esther arose, and stood before the king, and said, If it please the king, and if I have found favour in his sight, and the thing seem right before the king, and I be pleasing in his eyes, let it be written to reverse the letters devised by Haman the son of Hammedatha the Agagite, which he wrote to destroy the Jews, which are in all the king's provinces:*

Observe with what humility and modesty, yet earnest importunity, she presents her request to the king. Esther was well furnished with those amiable qualities which must endear a wife to her husband, and obtain from him every reasonable request. Pride and petulance can obtain nothing without reluctance on the part of him that grants. Humility and submission are the weapons by which a wise woman will encounter opposition in her husband, and the means by which she will obtain what can be obtained by any methods fit to be used by a wife.

If Esther had any interest in the king's favour, the great use she desires to make of it is for the preservation of her people from the mischief devised by Haman. Patriotism and piety were shining ornaments of this princess. She desired not great things for herself. She was well satisfied with her own condition, if she could but see peace on Israel; for Jerusalem was near to her heart, and the welfare of the people of God was dearer to her than either grandeur or life.

Verse 6.—*For how can I endure to see the evil that shall come unto my people? or how can I endure to see the destruction of my kindred?*

Esther was now the queen of Persia, but still the people of Israel were her people and her kindred. Let a true fearer of God be placed ever so comfortably among the sons of men, still it will be his leading desire to 'see the good of God's chosen, to rejoice in their joy, and to glory with God's inheritance.'

. The king had secured Esther's life, but she lets him know, that the destruction of the great enemy of her people, and her security under the king's protection, would be of small avail to her, if her kindred must perish. Her life was bound up in their life. If her heart was broken and crushed by their ruin, what good could her life do her, or what pleasure could the king have any more in beholding her when she was drowned in perpetual sorrows?

There was a consideration that endeared the people of Israel to the queen still more than their relation to herself. They were the people of the Lord of hosts, the God of Israel. Esther did not think fit to mention this motive of her tender regard to her people when she was presenting her supplications to the king, because he could not have felt the force of it. Thus Nehemiah, in his supplication to the king for Jerusalem, does not speak of it as the centre of the Jewish religion, as the city of the God of Israel, but as the place of his fathers' sepulchres. The king could easily understand the interest that his cup-bearer must take in the place of his fathers' sepulchres; but he knew nothing of that delight which good men take in 'the habitation of God's house, in the place where his honour dwelleth.'

Verse 7.—*Then the king Ahasuerus said unto Esther the queen, and to Mordecai the Jew, Behold, I have given Esther the house of Haman, and him they have hanged upon the gallows, because he laid his hand upon the Jews.*

The king could not grant to Esther every thing that she requested. But he assures her, that it was not for want of good will, either to herself or to her people, that he did not in direct terms reverse the decree procured by Haman. His love to Esther appeared in the rich present of the confiscated estate of Haman. His good wishes to her people appeared in the ignominious death of their capital enemy. But kings cannot do every thing. The most noble and potent prince in the world had not the power of rescinding his own decrees, however desirous he might be of undoing foolish things done by himself.

Verse 8.—*Write ye also for the Jews, as it liketh you, in the king's name, and seal it with the king's ring: for the writing which is written in the king's name, and sealed with the king's ring, may no man reverse.*

The king himself could not reverse it; and therefore we find that Darius the Mede laboured in vain till the going down of the sun, to save Daniel from the lion's den, and passed a miserable sleepless night in the anguish of a fruitless repentance, for passing a mischievous law, which he could not abolish. The Persians thought their kings highly honoured in that law by which their decrees were made inviolable. But this honour, like some others enjoyed by absolute princes, was a burden too heavy to be borne by mortals. It precluded them from the comforts of repentance, too often necessary for vain men, who, though they would be wise, are born like the wild ass's colt.

The king, therefore, could not give Esther and Mordecai a warrant to pass an act rescissory of his own decrees against the Jews. But he allows them to frame a decree in his name, and to seal it with his ring, for counteracting its effects. As the first decree retained its force, the king could not legally punish those wicked enemies of the Jews who might take the advantage of it to gratify their malice. Their murders were already legalized by a decree that could not be altered. But a law for the protection of the Jews, which did not rescind the former, might possibly be devised by the wisdom of Mordecai; and to establish such a law, the king gave him his ring. He had been too ready on the former occasion to lend his authority; but now he commits it to a safe hand, and under necessary restrictions. He gave his ring to Haman, to seal a bloody decree; he now gives it to Mordecai, to seal a just and necessary decree for the preservation of many precious lives. The inviolability of the king's decrees, which gave him so much trouble by guarding the wicked laws procured by Haman, would guard the intended decree from violation.

Verses 9, 10, 11.—*Then were the king's scribes called at that time, in the third month, (that is, the month Sivan,) on the three and twentieth day thereof; and it was written, according to all that Mordecai commanded, unto the Jews, and to the lieutenants, and to the deputies and rulers of the provinces, which are from India unto Ethiopia, an hundred twenty and seven provinces, unto every province according to the writing thereof, and unto every people after their language, and to the Jews according to their writing, and according to their language. And he wrote in the king Ahasuerus's name, and sealed it with the king's ring, and sent letters by posts on horseback, and riders on mules, camels, and young dromedaries: Wherein the king granted the Jews which were in every city, to gather themselves together, and to stand for their life, to destroy, to slay, and to cause to perish, all the power of the people and province that would assault them, both little ones and women, and to take the spoil of them for a prey:*

Glad would Mordecai and Esther have been, could they have written to all the provinces letters in the king's name, recalling the permission given to the enemies of the Jews to destroy them. But this the laws of Persia would not permit. What, therefore, must be done to save the devoted nation? They are permitted by a new decree to defend themselves, and to destroy their enemies. This, it might be hoped, would have much the same effect as a decree repealing the bloody decree passed against the Jews. When it was known that the queen and the prime minister were Jews, and that the king favoured their cause, it might have been presumed that few would be bold enough to attack them; which would be, by the new edict, to rush upon their own destruction, and to expose the lives of their wives and children, as well as their own. Some, indeed, might entertain such deep-rooted malice against the Jews, as to take advantage of the former edict; but the fault was their own, the risk was chiefly their own; nor could any thing be done by Mordecai or Esther to prevent the mischief. It was to be attributed, not to them, but, in the first place, to the king's former rashness in gratifying the bloody enemy of the Jews; and, in the second place, to that fundamental, but absurd law of the empire, that the king's edicts, whether good or bad, could not be repealed. If men will presume to claim the prerogative of immutability in their counsels, let them take the consequences. Men are never more foolish than when they affect the perfection of wisdom.

We regret that permission was given in this edict to the Jews to destroy the wives and children of their enemies that might rise up against them. But the manners of ancient times are to have some allowance made for them. Jesus, the light of the world, had not yet humanized the nations by the light of his gospel. Besides, it was natural to think, that this permission to the Jews would be a means of preventing the effusion of blood; because many who will risk their own lives, will neither risk the lives of their wives, nor of their children, to gratify their passions. Retaliations in war sometimes involve the destruction of innocent persons, and yet are thought necessary to prevent greater mischief. But we are not bound to justify all that may be done by good men, or every circumstance of good actions. Mordecai and Esther might err, but their errors were not voluntary. It was their desire to prevent, and not to promote, the shedding of innocent blood.

The decree which they framed was sent to every nation of the empire in its own language. All wise lawgivers will address their subjects in a language they understand. God himself wrote the great things of his ancient law in the language of his chosen people; and the laws and doctrines of Christianity were communicated to the world in the language then most generally understood. It is better to speak five words in a known tongue, than ten thousand in an unknown language. Mordecai would have shown little regard to the life and comfort of his brethren, if he had not caused the decree to be translated into the languages of the different provinces. Those preachers of the gospel discover as little regard to the eternal life of their hearers, who do not use great plainness of speech, in showing unto them the way of salvation. Obscurity in our own language is not much less prejudicial than the use of an unknown tongue.

The decree was no sooner passed, and translated into the different languages, than copies of it were sent through every part of the empire, and the swiftest methods of conveyance were used. Mordecai and Esther had sufficient time to give seasonable intimation of the new decree to the Jews and to their enemies. Yet, considering the distance of some provinces, the possibility of untoward accidents, and the advantage of early information, they had no time to lose. Why should that be deferred till another day, which may be better and more safely done at present? How many have lost the season of good works, or the benefits expected from them, by deferring them! How many by delays have lost their precious souls! Eccles. ix. 10. But in the present case, the greatest possible expedition was likewise requisite, for the comfort of the trembling Jews. Let us not leave those persons under the power of despondency a single hour, whom we may cheer by happy tidings, or by other effectual methods of consolation. If happiness is preferred by ourselves to misery, we do not to others what we wish them to do to us, if we suffer them to languish under heaviness of heart, when we may, by a good word, make them glad.

Verse 12.—*Upon one day, in all the provinces of king Ahasuerus, namely, upon the thirteenth day of the twelfth month, which is the month Adar.*

The day was fixed by Haman, but the disposing of the lot by which he fixed that day was evidently of the Lord. The lateness of the time gave sufficient opportunities for spreading the new edict, by which the day intended for the destruction of the Jews became a day of destruction to their enemies.

Verse 13.—*The copy of the writing, for a commandment to be given in every province, was published unto all people, and that the Jews should be ready against that day to avenge themselves on their enemies.*

It was published to all people, that all the king's subjects might know the real wishes of the king, and might take their side accordingly, as they valued his favour. The knowledge of the decree might make many friends to that nation, and, doubtless, affrighted many of their enemies. 'Where the word of a king is, there is power; for all men seek the favour of the ruler.'

It was published unto all people, chiefly as an alarm to the Jews, that they might prepare themselves to resist their enemies, if any enemies made their appearance. They were not so entirely to depend on the favour of their sovereign, as to be unprepared for the contest. He had bound up his own hands from assisting them, or revenging their wrongs. All that he could do for them was, to give them the liberty of self-defence, and to afford them his countenance. They must stand up for their own lives, and for the lives of their little ones, if they were attacked. It is to be expected, that those who are not only forewarned of danger, but instructed in the proper means for guarding against it, and encouraged with the prospect of success in the use of them, will be ready for the day of decision. Do not they well deserve to perish, who are careless about their own safety? Who will bemoan those who may be safe in the day of evil, and despise the things that belong to their peace till they be hid from their eyes?

Verse 14.—*So the posts that rode upon mules and camels went out, being hastened and pressed on by the king's commandment. And the decree was given at Shushan the palace.*

The posts were hastened by the king's commandment.—He was now made sensible of the great wrong he had done to the Jews, and made all possible haste to undo, as far as he could undo, what he had done. Are you sensible you have done wrong? Make haste, and delay not to repair the wrong, if it is in your power. How can you say that you repent of the evil that you have done, if you hold it fast? The light of nature teaches men that they ought, with the first opportunity, to put away the evil of their doings, and to redress the injuries done by their hands, or their tongues, or their pens. As soon as Jesus brought salvation to the house of Zaccheus, he said, 'Lord! if I have wronged any man by false accusation, I restore him four-fold.' Is it your intention, in some future part of your life, to compensate the wrongs you have done in the former part of it? But are you sure that you shall see another week, or even another day? Boast not thyself of to-morrow, unless a prophet of as much credit as Isaiah has brought a message from God that some more years of life are allotted you.

And the decree was given in Shushan the palace.—Little good was now expected by the people of God to come from Shushan the palace. From Shushan came the edict for their destruction. But God can make good to spring up to his people where it was least expected. In the very place where it was said, 'Ye are not my people,' has it been said, 'Ye are the children of the living God.' The valley of Achor is made by divine wisdom and grace a door of hope. The best of all things in the world came out of Galilee and Nazareth.

DISCOURSE XIII.

MORDECAI'S GREATNESS, WITH THE HAPPY CHANGE IN THE CONDITION OF THE JEWS.

CHAPTER VIII. 15—CHAPTER IX. 5.

Verse 15.—*And Mordecai went out from the presence of the king in royal apparel of blue and white, and with a great crown of gold, and with a garment of fine linen and purple: and the city of Shushan rejoiced and was glad.*

MORDECAI, not long before this time, was clothed with sackcloth; and refused, at the request of the queen, to put it off. But now he is clothed with royal apparel, and his head is encircled with a crown of gold. What happy changes has God often made in the outward condition of his people! Let us never say in our prosperity, that 'we shall never be moved.' Let us never say in the day of adversity, that 'our eyes shall never more see good;' or, whatever our outward condition may be, let us not despair of obtaining those changes in our inward condition which the Redeemer, whom we are called to trust, hath accomplished in innumerable instances. The Lord anointed him 'to comfort all that mourn, to give unto them the oil of joy for mourning, the garments of praise for the spirit of heaviness.'

Mordecai was now adorned with the ensigns of that high station to which the king advanced him. Perhaps some may ask, whether Mordecai's happiness was increased by his elevation, or not? It certainly was. The greater part of men are fitted to enjoy more happiness in a middling, than in a high condition. But, when men are furnished with talents and opportunities for public usefulness, and when their pleasure lies more in doing good to others than in the enjoyment of ease and social delights, a station that enables them to gratify their wishes, and to exert their power for the public welfare, must afford them more exquisite and sublime pleasure than they would have enjoyed in domestic felicity, or in the endearments of friendship. Joseph was happier in the government of Egypt, which fitted him to be 'the shepherd and stone of Israel,' than in the tents of his father Jacob; although he was his father's delight. David found much more trouble on a throne than ever befel him when he was following the ewes with young; but he was happier on the throne, because his elevation enabled him to do greater services for God and for Israel. Mordecai was raised on high by Divine Providence to be a saviour to Israel, and enjoyed the sublime pleasure of knowing that millions blessed God on his account.

Let us not, however, envy the great. Multitudes of them might have been far happier, if they had moved in a lower sphere. We are not all Davids or Mordecais. Agur was a very good man, and yet he prayed that God might give him neither poverty nor riches. Think not that you are better fitted than Agur to resist the temptations attendant on riches. Christ tells us, that 'it is as easy for a camel to pass through the eye of a needle, as for a rich man to enter into the kingdom of heaven.' But nothing is impossible with God; and Mordecai, amidst all his wealth and power, hastened towards the possession of that kingdom which cannot be moved.

The city of Shushan rejoiced and was glad for the fall of Haman, and the exaltation of Mordecai. 'When the righteous are in authority, the people rejoice; and when the wicked perish, there is shouting.' Mordecai was an exile, and a worshipper of the God of Israel; yet the people of Shushan, who now knew his virtues, rejoiced that he was put into the place of Haman, who undoubtedly was an oppressor to other subjects of the king besides the Jews. The perplexity into which the city was thrown by the cruel decree against the Jews, prepared it for rejoicing in the exaltation of a man who employed his power for their protection. Bloody men are abhorred by their fellow-creatures, and virtue recommends itself to the admiration of those whose practice is not in all things conformable to its rules. A Herod venerated John Baptist!

Verses 16, 17.—*The Jews had light, and gladness, and joy, and honour. And in every province, and in every city, whithersoever the king's commandment and his decree came, the Jews had joy and gladness, a feast and a good day. And many of the people of the land became Jews; for the fear of the Jews fell upon them.*

Many expressions are used to signify the joy and exultation of the Jews on this occasion; and no expressions are sufficient to describe those transports of gladness which they must have felt when the king's commandment and decree came abroad. According to the days wherein they had sorrow, and wherein they had seen evil, they were made glad. Let us never sink under the weight of affliction, if the Lord is our God. Who had ever more reason than the Jews, in the interval between the two edicts, to say, 'The Lord hath led us, and brought us into darkness, and not into light?' The Babylonian captivity was a less hopeless calamity than the situation to which they were reduced by a general sentence of death. But the Lord 'brought them again out of darkness and the shadow of death, and broke their bands asunder.' Now might they sing with pleasure these delightful words of David, 'Thou wilt save the afflicted people, but wilt bring down high looks; for thou wilt light my candle. The Lord my God will enlighten my darkness.'

'No affliction for the present is joyous, but grievous;' yet afflictions have often terminated in joys never felt by those who never had changes. Men never feel the joys of health that were never sick; and those whose souls have been failing within them, through trouble, oppression, and fear, know best the pleasure of ease and safety. It will be a great enhancement of the blessedness of heaven to redeemed saints, that they were once in a state of sin and sorrow. When we are in trouble, let us consider by what means joy may be brought out of it, that we may learn to rejoice in hope. Through the grace of God, thorns may be made to bear grapes, and thistles figs, for he is 'wonderful in counsel, and excellent in working.'

There is one thing that deserves observation in this joy of

the Jews, that it was occasioned, not by a full security given
them for their safety, but by that liberty which was given
them to defend themselves from their enemies. They had still
reason to dread an attack, but they had reason, too, to hope
for victory. We would never taste joy in the things of this
world, if we could not take pleasure but in prospects altogether
unclouded. Who can say that he shall never more meet with
dangers, or taste sorrows? We may be assured, on solid
grounds, that all things shall work together for our good, and
that heaven shall be our final portion; but what unpleasant
things, in the present life, may appear to divine wisdom a proper preparation for our final happiness, we cannot tell. This
we know, that when our prospects are in some degree pleasant,
we ought to be thankful, and especially when the dark prospects are brightened, although the events in question cannot
be certain. Some of the Jews might lose their lives, yet God
had wonderfully interposed for their safety; and they had
good reason to praise God for what was done, and to trust him
for what was yet to be done.

They had 'a feast and a good day,' wherever the king's decree came. 'A feast is made for laughter.' Feasts, on proper
occasions, are not unbecoming the people of God. Jesus himself did not refuse his presence to feasts. Doubtless, on this
feast and good day the hearts of the Jews were enlarged, not
only with joy, but with kind affections towards their brethren,
'partakers with them of the benefit,' and with gratitude to the
God of their salvation. Whilst they congratulated one another,
and praised the exertions of Mordecai and Esther, they did
not forget to praise the Lord, who had turned the heart of the
king of Persia to favour them; Ezra vii. 27, 28; and who had
turned a gracious ear to the voice of their prayers and their
supplications. These are pure and lasting joys which terminate in God, the Father of lights, from whom every good
and perfect gift comes.

The Jews had honour, as well as light and joy. The Babylonian captivity, and their dispersion among the nations,
brought them into contempt: 'They were made a reproach
unto their neighbours, and a by-word among the people.' But

God's signal interposition in their behalf filled beholders with wonder and respect. They appeared to be the favourites of the God of heaven. 'They said among the heathen, The Lord hath done great things for them.' God hath promised to wipe away the reproach of his people, and get them fame and glory, when he rises up to plead their cause. Let us 'never fear the reproach of men, nor be afraid of their revilings.' Our honour, as well as our life and property, is in the hand of God; and those who are precious in his sight will sooner or later be honourable in the eyes of men.

And many of the people of the land became Jews; for the fear of the Jews fell on them.—It is not impossible for those who are not sprung from Abraham to become Jews. 'They are not all Israel that are of Israel;' and those may be 'Israelites indeed' who are sprung from Japhet or from Canaan.

'Hath a nation changed their gods, which are yet no gods?' says Jeremiah. Under the Old Testament dispensation, the nations were steady to their false religions. No nation changed their gods, which yet were no gods (if you except the Edomites, who were subdued by Hyrcanus, and adopted the Jewish religion; but these Edomites were only a part of the nation that had taken up their residence in the land of Judea). It was reserved for the glory of the New Testament dispensation, that nations under it should be born in one day to God; yet, in the days of old, many individuals became Jews after their return from the Babylonian captivity, especially at those seasons when God showed forth his glory in doing marvellous works for his people.

'The Lord is known by his judgments.' He was made known to many of the heathen throughout the Persian empire at this happy time, when the king Ahasuerus's heart was so unexpectedly turned to favour God's people. They saw that the God of heaven was the God of Israel, and that works were done by Him which no other god could do. The fear of the Jews fell upon them, for they saw that the greatest man, next to the king, in the whole empire, was broken and crushed in his contest with them.

If the observation of single acts of the divine procedure had such happy effects in the conversion of the Gentiles, what effect ought the consideration of all God's works of wonder to have upon our hearts? The salvation of the Jews, in the days of Ahasuerus, is one of the manifold salvations which God wrought for his people in ancient days. But what are all the temporal salvations wrought for ancient Israel, to the great salvation wrought for Jews and Gentiles by our Lord Jesus Christ! and how wonderful are the salvations that have been wrought in different ages for the church! 'Among the gods there is none like unto thee, O Lord! neither are there any works like thy works. All nations whom thou hast made shall come and worship before thee, O Lord! and shall glorify thy name. For thou art great, and dost wonderful things; thou art God alone!'

Who could have believed that the contrivances of Haman for the destruction of the Jews would have terminated in the increase of their nation? The lovers of the name of the God of Israel would tremble at Haman's devices, lest the name of Israel should be put out, and the worship of the God of Israel should be extirpated from the earth. But the revolution of a few weeks convinced them that their God was the same God that he had ever been; and that wherein his enemies dealt proudly, he was still above them. Death and destruction are in the hand of the Lord, and he can make them instrumental for the life, and for bringing about the safety, of his people. 'Before him darkness becomes light, and sorrow is turned into joy. He taketh the wise in their own craftiness, and carrieth the devices of the froward headlong. So the poor have hope, and iniquity stoppeth her mouth.'

CHAP. ix. Verse 1.—*Now in the twelfth month (that is, the month Adar), on the thirteenth day of the same, when the king's commandment and his decree drew near to be put in execution, in the day that the enemies of the Jews hoped to have power over them, (though it was turned to the contrary, that the Jews had rule over them that hated them:)—*

'The hope of the righteous is gladness, but the expectation of the wicked shall perish.' Of the truth of this maxim of wisdom, we have a remarkable instance in the events of the month Adar, when the decree of king Ahasuerus was put in execution. The enemies of the Jews had looked forward to that day with great pleasure. It was to be the day on which the name of Israel was to be abolished, and the worship of their God utterly extinguished. But, by the good providence of God, it was a day in which the bitter enemies of the Jews were destroyed, and their nation blessed with a testimony of the favour and power of their God, which made his name known through all the hundred twenty and seven provinces of the Persian empire. 'The God of their mercy prevented them;' and at the time when their enemies had hoped to gain a complete victory, they were subdued and destroyed. Little do the enemies of Zion know the intention of the God of Zion, when he covers her with a cloud, and gives scope to their malice. Their conjectures appear to be built on solid grounds when they predict the downfall of Zion; but the wisest conjectures of men must give place to the most improbable predictions of the word of God, which assure us that the enemies of Zion shall be covered with confusion, and that God himself will establish her. The times have been, when many nations were gathered against her, that said, 'Let her be defiled, and let our eyes look upon Zion:—But they knew not the thoughts of the Lord, neither understood they his counsel; for He gathered them as sheaves into the floor, and made the horns of the daughter of Zion iron, and her hoofs brass, that she might arise and thresh, and beat in pieces many people, and consecrate their gain unto the Lord, and their substance unto the Lord of the whole earth.' Wait patiently for God in the day of clouds and thick darkness. He often makes the day dark with night, when at the evening-time it shall be light.

Verse 2.—*The Jews gathered themselves together in their cities throughout all the provinces of the king Ahasuerus, to lay hand on such as sought their hurt: and no man could withstand them; for the fear of them fell upon all people.*

'Thou shalt not kill.' This commandment, in some cases, binds us to kill. It requires us to use all lawful endeavours to preserve our own life; and in preserving our own lives, we may be reduced to the unpleasant necessity of taking away the lives of other men. The Jews were compelled, on the thirteenth day of the month Adar, to take arms into their hands, to destroy all that might rise up against them; and they acted wisely in uniting themselves in large bodies to resist the power of their enemies. Had they stood single in arms, they might all have been destroyed with ease. But their combination in the various cities of the king's dominions made them terrible and irresistible. Let us learn from their example to stand fast in one spirit, and with one mind striving together against the enemies of our souls, who endeavour to rob us of our faith, more precious than our lives.* The church is terrible, like an army with banners, when her rulers and members are closely united under the Captain of salvation, to oppose her enemies.

No man could now withstand the Jews, for the fear of them fell upon all people. They had the king, the queen, the prime minister upon their side; and, what was still more, they had the providence of God upon their side. 'He caused judgment to be heard from heaven,' as audibly as if an angel had proclaimed his favour to the Jews, and his indignation against their enemies. The wonderful works of Providence have oft struck terror into the hardiest enemies of Zion; Psalm xlviii. 5, 6.

Verse 3.—*And all the rulers of the provinces, and the lieutenants, and the deputies, and officers of the king helped the Jews; because the fear of Mordecai fell upon them.*

---

* These weighty sentences fully vindicate the defensive leagues and covenants entered into by the Reformed Christians of the churches of the Reformation—such as the Huguenots of France, the Lutherans of Germany, and the Covenanters of Scotland, not to mention the primitive evangelical churches of the valleys of the Alps—by which they solemnly bound themselves to defend, even by resort to arms if necessary, their civil and religious rights and liberties, more precious to them than their lives, against the intolerable oppressions of Popery and the tyranny of their rulers. They equally condemn the principle of the 'Society of Friends' and our modern 'Peace Society' and others, who maintain that even defensive warfare for a just cause is unchristian and wrong; and who would even forbid to the individual the resort to self-defence for the security of his life and property. Away with such weak and contemptible principles as these! They are equally opposed to the dictates of nature, of reason, and of the Word of God.—ED.

There were two decrees in equal force, which might have given them a fair pretense for taking the part of the Jews, or of their enemies, as they pleased; but it was plain that the king's favour was towards the Jews, and that if they expected any favour from him, it was necessary to secure the good-will of Mordecai. They chose that side in the contest which their own interest prescribed. What a pity is it that all princes do not favour the cause of religion! If they did, iniquity would be compelled to stop her mouth, and those men who do not value religion would treat it, at least, with respect.

Verse 4.—*For Mordecai was great in the king's house, and his fame went out throughout all the provinces: for this man Mordecai waxed greater and greater.*

He was famous for his virtue and wisdom, as well as for the honours to which the king had advanced him. He gained more and more respect the better he was known, and all the respect entertained for him by the king, or by his subjects, contributed to the success of the Jews in the day when their fate was to be decided. It was this that made Mordecai's fame and greatness a pleasure to himself, and the cause of thanksgiving from him unto God. He had been formerly as an humble shrub in the valley, and then his obscurity was so little disagreeable to him, that he never called to the king's mind the great services he had done for him in saving his life, nor would suffer the queen to make any mention of his relation and kindness to her, although, by the bare mention of these, the king would have been induced to place him in a much higher station. He was now like a tall cedar, with spreading branches, and a shadowing shroud; and he was highly pleased with this change in his condition, because it enabled him to afford shelter to all his people.

Verse 5.—*Thus the Jews smote all their enemies with the stroke of the sword, and slaughter, and destruction, and did what they would unto those that hated them.*

It may appear strange that the Jews now found any enemies bold enough to contend with them in battle. The king was their friend, God was their friend, what could those expect who sought their lives, but destruction to themselves? It is indeed wonderful, but not uncommon, for men to value the gratification of their malignant passions above their best interests, and above their safety. At the destruction of Jerusalem by the Romans, it is well known that the Jews themselves did more mischief to one another, than all the harm they suffered from the fury of their conquerors. The different parties, when they found respite from the Romans, destroyed one another within the walls, and destroyed their provisions, and thus brought upon themselves a famine, which destroyed them by thousands. But we need not look seventeen hundred years back to see the tyrannizing power of malice and hatred over the minds of men. Are there not many who subject themselves to bitter remorse, to ruinous fines, or to an ignominious death; are there not many more who subject themselves to the curse of God, merely to gratify their accursed spite against their fellow-men?

Many of the enemies of the Jews, doubtless, were overawed by the power of Mordecai, and either sat quiet in their dwellings, or joined with the Jews. Many chose rather to be quiet than to venture their lives in battle with enemies that were sure to be victorious. But there were others, not in small numbers, who chose to venture or rather to sell their lives, and the lives of all that were dear to them, rather than lose the opportunity given them by law, of attempting to destroy a race of men whom, though innocent, they hated with a deadly hatred. These men combined in the different cities to fight against the Jews. But their confederacy was against the God of heaven, who spoiled them of their courage, and gave them into the hands of the Jews, to do to them as they would. They were so far from gaining their malicious purposes at the expense of their lives, that victory, and glory, and triumph to their hated enemies, were the fruit of their cruel attempt. Vain it is to fight against God, or against those whom he loves and protects. If God be against us, who can be for us? If we harden ourselves against the Almighty, we cannot prosper. It were better for us to dash our heads against the craggy rock, than to rush upon the thick bosses of the buckler of the Almighty.

Why should men fight against God? And yet there are too many who fear not to carry the weapons of an unrighteous warfare against their Maker and their Judge. 'Whatever ye have done, or not done, to one of the least of my brethren,' says Christ, 'ye have done, or not done, to me.' Enmity against the people of God is enmity against God himself; and surely 'all that are incensed against Him shall be ashamed.'

DISCOURSE XIV.

NUMBERS OF THE SLAIN—A SECOND BATTLE AT SHUSHAN.

CHAPTER IX. 6-19.

Verses 6-10.—*And in Shushan the palace, the Jews slew and destroyed five hundred men. And Parshandatha, and Dalphon, and Aspatha, and Poratha, and Adalia, and Aridatha, and Parmashta, and Arisai, and Aridai, and Vajezatha, the ten sons of Haman the son of Hammedatha, the enemy of the Jews, slew they; but on the spoil laid they not their hand.*

Even in Shushan the royal city, under the eye of the king, there were more than five hundred men that combined, in defiance of the king's known sentiments, to attack the Jews. But they meddled to their own hurt. When we consider the audacity of that behaviour to which their malice prompted them, we see that Mordecai had too much reason to tell Esther that she would not be safe in the king's palace if she did not intercede with the king. The men that could take the pretense of a law to attack the Jews to their certain destruction, might have been prompted by the same outrageous malice to attack Esther in the palace, when they could plead the king's authority for their enterprise.

These five hundred men in Shushan, who sold their lives in this desperate cause, were, doubtless, some of Haman's creatures, who had learned from him to hate the Jews with a bloody hatred. Haman's ten sons were at the head of them, and shared in their fate. They were, doubtless, trained up by their father in the hatred of that nation; and his miserable end, instead of opening their eyes, irritated their resentment, to their own destruction.

It was natural, some will say, for Haman's sons to account that people their enemies, by the means of whom their father suffered an ignominious death. It was natural, it must be confessed; but it does not follow that it was right. Children are to honour their parents while they live, and venerate their memory when they are dead, but not to follow their example in any thing that is evil. The children of wicked parents ought to remember, that their duty to their Maker must have the precedency of all other duties; and that to rebel against God because their parents rebelled against him, is not more excusable, than for a man to be a thief, or a traitor, or an adulterer, because his father was so before him. God commanded his people, when they were carried away captives for their transgressions, to confess their own iniquity, and the iniquity of their fathers. The holy son of the wicked Ahaz made a full confession of the sins committed by his father, and by the people under his influence, and deserved high praise for reversing all his wicked institutions; 2 Chron. xxix. Jeroboam had only one son in his house who discovered a dislike of his father's conduct, and was the only member of the family who died in peace. 'Fill ye up the measure of your fathers, said Jesus to the Jews; warning them that their fathers' example would be so far from justifying their wicked conduct, that the vengeance of Heaven was brought the nearer to them that their sins were but a continuation of the sins of their progenitors.

Parents! pity your children, if you will not pity yourselves. You know what force the example and influence of parents has. If you profess bad principles, you of course train up your children in the profession of the same. If you openly practise wickedness, you teach your children to practise it likewise. Thus you pull down vengeance, not only upon yourselves, but upon your houses. You see that Haman was the enemy of the Jews, and of the God of the Jews; and the punishment of his wickedness fell heavy, not only on himself, but upon all his family, which was probably rooted out of the earth. His sons might have been suffered to live in obscurity, if they had been willing to live peaceably. But they had drunk deep of their father's spirit, and followed his example; and ten (probably all) of them perished on that fatal day on which their father, a few months before, had hoped to feast his eyes with the blood of those whom he chose to account his enemies.

But on the spoil laid they not their hands.—It is not always good to seize all the money to which one has a legal right. There are many cases in which a regard to our own credit, and there are others in which a sense of duty, resulting from singular circumstances, should bind up our hands from receiving what we might otherwise take without injustice. The king's edict gave the Jews a right to take the spoil of their enemies; Chap. viii. 11. But for their own honour, and for the credit of their religion, they chose to leave the spoil of their enemies to be enjoyed by others. The tongue that slandereth might have alleged that they had slain innocent persons with the guilty, to enrich themselves.

They had been accused as a wicked people, whom it was good for mankind to destroy from the face of the earth. Their noble disinterestedness was a refutation of this calumny. It was evident from their conduct that they were not lovers of money; and 'the love of money is the root of all evil.' The apostle Paul showed disinterestedness of spirit in a higher degree, when he laboured for years in places where, for the honour of that gospel which he preached, he would receive no recompense from his hearers, that it might not be accounted a fable cunningly devised for the profit of them who preach it; Acts, xviii. 3.

Verses 11, 12.—*On that day the number of those that were slain in Shushan the palace was brought before the king. And the king said unto Esther the queen, The Jews have slain and destroyed five hundred men in Shushan the palace, and the ten sons of Haman; what have they done in the rest of the king's provinces? now what is thy petition? and it shall be granted thee: or what is thy request further? and it shall be done.*

The king had an account brought to him of the number of the slain in the imperial city. It was highly proper that he should cause this account to be brought before him. If husbandmen be diligent to know the state of their flocks, and look well to their herds, how much more ought kings to inform themselves of the affairs of their kingdom! Ahasuerus might learn wisdom from the account brought him of the slaughter of the enemies of the Jews. By his rashness he had occasioned the slaughter. If five hundred men were slain in Susa, what numbers might be supposed to be slain throughout all the provinces? What bloodshed had been the fruit of one thoughtless act of government! It may be hoped that Ahasuerus learned wisdom for the time to come. Never in the succeeding years of his reign was he chargeable with such folly. At a great expense he learned a very needful lesson, To do nothing without consideration of the consequences.

The king brings to the queen his information concerning the slaughtered enemies of the Jews. 'The Jews have slain and destroyed five hundred men,' says he, 'in Shushan the palace,' besides the ten sons of Haman, the most formidable and the most enraged of them. The king could not yet tell how many were slain through the large extent of his dominions, but he justly infers from the number of the slain in one city, that it must be very great in all the cities and provinces together. This piece of information the king hoped would be very grateful to Esther, as it would ease her mind of those griefs which had long oppressed it. She, indeed, had good and well-grounded hopes before this time, that the enemies of her people would fall in the contest; and now she enjoyed the satisfaction of knowing that her hopes were realized.

We must not rejoice in the destruction of our enemies, nor must our hearts be glad when they stumble. This is the doctrine of the prophets, as well as of the apostles; Prov. xxiv. 17. Yet God's people have good reason to rejoice at the fall of their irreconcileable enemies, when they see the mercy of God to themselves, and when they see the safety of the church in the destruction of those who hated them: 'When God shoots at the wicked with an arrow, and wounds them suddenly, the righteous shall be glad in the Lord, and shall trust in him, and all the upright in heart shall glory; Psal. lxiv. 7–10.

Now, what is thy petition? and it shall be granted thee: or, what is thy request further? and it shall be done.—It is reported of Mary Queen of Scotland, that her household-servants were always glad when she was put into a passion; for, when she was restored to good humour, she made them more than a sufficient recompense for all past unkindnesses. Thus Ahasuerus, sensible of the wrongs he had done to his queen, endeavoured to banish all remembrance of them, by heaping upon her unexpected kindnesses. All of us are liable to starts of bad humour, and may behave unkindly to those who are dearest to us; or we may, through want of due consideration, give them much pain without intending it. When we are made sensible of such conduct, let us repair it with advantage. Whilst our friends live, if we have treated them with unkindness, there is opportunity to obliterate the wrong. They may die, and then it will be sealed up, and nothing will be left for us but unavailing regret.

Verse 13.—*Then said Esther, If it please the king, let it be granted to the Jews which are in Shushan to do to-morrow also according unto this day's decree, and let Haman's ten sons be hanged upon the gallows.*

'Dearly beloved,' says the apostle, 'avenge not yourselves.' 'Love your enemies,' says Christ, 'that ye may be the children of your Father who is in heaven.' Was Esther not a daughter of the Lord Almighty? or was the spirit of the Old Testament dispensation of religion different from that 'spirit of love, and of a sound mind,' which is given unto us?

Esther was undoubtedly a saint of God, and the spirit of love dwelt in her. We have already seen that the writers of the Old Testament, as well as those of the New, forbid revenge; Prov. xxiv. 17. But self-defence is licensed and required under the New, as well as the Old Testament. Esther knew that there were still many deadly enemies of the Jews in Shushan, who might, if they were suffered to live, harass or destroy them. She desires that they might receive the just reward of their malice.

Lukewarmness, and even cruelty, have often assumed the dress of charity. The children of Israel, after the death of Joshua, were cruel to the rising generation, when they spared the wicked Canaanites. Saul brought wrath upon himself, when he spared Agag. Samuel performed an act of humanity, when he hewed to pieces before the Lord a tyrant who had made many women childless, for a warning to other despots. 'Cursed be he,' says Jeremiah on a certain occasion, 'who doth the work of the Lord deceitfully. Cursed be he who keepeth back his sword from shedding blood.' A curse came upon Meroz, for sparing the blood of the Canaanitish enemies of Israel. A worse curse might have come upon Esther, if she had neglected the opportunity graciously afforded her by God, for securing the peace of Israel by the destruction of Haman's creatures. They were a race of vipers. Their venom was not diminished. If they had not been crushed, they might have found an opportunity to sting the man who had brought destruction on their companions in wickedness.

Beware of making a bad use of this piece of history. Such circumstances as those in which Esther was placed, will probably never occur to any of you. The care of the lives of all the people of God came upon her, and the enemies of the Jews, by their late behaviour, were seen to be hardened beyond all hopes of reformation. When the hand of the Lord was lifted up, they would not see it, but rushed upon him, even upon the thick bosses of his buckler. Your enemies may be reclaimed. Your duty, according to Solomon and Paul, is, if your enemies are hungry, to feed them; if they are thirsty, to give them drink. Thus you will heap coals of fire upon their heads, and the Lord will reward you. Remember how Jesus, when he was dying for your sins, prayed for his murderers. You know not what manner of spirit you are of, if you draw into an ordinary precedent extraordinary cases, from the histories of Elijah, or Moses, or Esther. Christ left you an example to follow his steps on every occasion.

Let Haman's ten sons be hanged upon the gallows; on that gallows which their father set up for Mordecai. Kings can take away our lives, that is all they can do against us; and yet, when we are dead, they may expose our bodies to infamy. Haman's ten sons could feel no more pain from the hand of men. But their ignominious exposure on the gallows erected by their father was an awful warning to other enemies of the

Jews. It was a standing proclamation of the favour of God to that nation; of his indignation against their enemies; and of the righteousness of his judgments. Those who saw them, saw good reason for saying, 'Truly there is a reward for the righteous; truly there is a God that judgeth in the earth.' The Lord causeth his wonderful works to be remembered. He would not have us forget his awful, any more than his pleasant works, that he may be glorified by us as a great God and a Saviour.

Verse 14.—*And the king commanded it so to be done: and the decree was given at Shushan; and they hanged Haman's ten sons.*

From the ready acquiescence of the king in Esther's request, we may reasonably conclude that he saw it to be just and proper. After what had newly happened, it was not likely that he would give a rash assent to a bloody decree. But 'a wise king will crush the wicked, and bring the wheel over them.'

By the king's commandment, 'the ten sons of Haman were hanged upon the gallows.' The king soon relented after he had passed a too severe decree against Vashti; but he did not repent, nor had he any reason to repent, of what he did against Haman. All the children of that insolent favourite were given up to infamy after death. We need not on this occasion reflect on the uncertainty of royal favour. Haman and his family might still have enjoyed the smiles of the king if they had deserved them. Their own wickedness destroyed and disgraced them; for 'they drew iniquity to themselves with cords of vanity, and sinned as it were with a cart-rope.'

Verse 15.—*For the Jews that were in Shushan gathered themselves together on the fourteenth day also of the month Adar, and slew three hundred men at Shushan; but on the prey they laid not their hands.*

They provided for things honest in the sight of all men. When they laid not their hands on the prey, it would easily be believed that they had killed no innocent persons. It was evidently not the desire of gain, but a just regard to their own safety, that induced them to kill so many of their enemies.

These enemies of the Jews that escaped on the thirteenth day of the month, would think that the bitterness of death was past. The law, as it then stood, exposed them to no further danger. But these enemies of God who escape shall not flee away. 'Mischief shall hunt the violent man till he be ruined.' If he is not ruined to-day, he will be ruined to-morrow; if not to-morrow, on some following day known to the Lord, and probably on a day when he is not expecting it. The bitterness of death cannot be past whilst the sentence of the Almighty is standing in force against the wicked.

Verse 16.—*But the other Jews that were in the king's provinces gathered themselves together, and stood for their lives, and had rest from their enemies, and slew of their foes seventy and five thousand; but they laid not their hands on the prey,—*

How many were the enemies of the Jews, even after they were known to be favoured by the king, when, in all appearance, avowed enmity against them was to end in speedy destruction! But many as they were, there were more with the people of God than against them, and their enemies were made to lick the dust. Let not those who have God on their side tremble at the multitude and strength of their enemies. 'Associate yourselves, O ye people! and ye shall be broken in pieces; and give ear, all ye of far countries: gird yourselves, and ye shall be broken in pieces; gird yourselves, and ye shall be broken in pieces. Take counsel together, and it shall come to nought; speak the word, and it shall not stand; for God is with us.' Immanuel is our security from every danger.

The Jews, in none of the provinces of the king's dominions, laid their hand upon the spoil. They had been in great fear of death, and they thought it a great matter to have their lives saved, without making gain of their enemies. 'The life,' says our Lord, 'is more than meat, and the body than raiment.' When men are in extreme danger of their lives, or have newly escaped from it, money goes for little. Were we possessed with a due concern about deliverance from that sentence of death which has passed upon all men, or with a fervent gratitude for deliverance from so great a death, our attachment to the things of the present world would be greatly weakened. What will money avail us, if we must perish? If we are redeemed from destruction, we will be happy and thankful, whether we possess much or little, or nothing at all, of the good things that perish in the using.

Christians have often censured the whole body of the Jews, as men of a selfish and rapacious spirit. The charge has, probably, exceeded truth. But, as far as occasion has been given for it, it has been owing, in a great measure, to the oppressions exercised upon that unhappy nation, which have irritated their spirits, and weakened or destroyed their sense of justice towards those whom they considered as their enemies. Certain it is, that they were far from discovering a rapacious spirit in the days of Esther. Many who name the name of Christ might learn from them to set their minds on things above, rather than on things of the earth. They chose to adorn their profession, by making it apparent that they sought not riches by means which they disapproved, although they would have appeared safe and honourable to any others but themselves.

Verse 17.—*On the thirteenth day of the month Adar; and on the fourteenth day of the same rested they, and made it a day of feasting and gladness.*

On the thirteenth day they fought for their lives, and on the fourteenth they rested and rejoiced in their preservation and victory. The battle was probably sore in some places where their enemies were strong and many; but every where they gained the victory, and the joys of God's salvation were an abundant recompence for their toils and dangers. Let all God's people patiently endure the tribulations assigned to them, and courageously fight those battles which they are called to sustain. There is hope in their latter end, and the greater their fight of affliction, the sweeter is that rest which the Lord will give from their sorrows and fears. Jesus fought and conquered, and entered into his rest; and 'it is a faithful saying, that if we suffer with him, we shall also reign with him;' and, before the time of reigning with him is come, we may hope that in this world days of rest and joy will often succeed nights of sore affliction; Isa. iv. 3: Psalm cxxv. 3: Isa. lvii. 15, 16: Chap. xl. 1, 2.

Verse 18.—*But the Jews that were at Shushan assembled together, on the thirteenth day thereof, and on the fourteenth thereof;*

and on the fifteenth day of the same they rested, and made it a day of feasting and gladness.

The Jews of Shushan did not so soon obtain rest, as the Jews of the provinces. They were fighting on the fourteenth day of the month, when their brethren were resting and delighting themselves in the abundance of God's goodness. Yet they rested at last, and had as good a day on the fifteenth as their brethren had on the fourteenth. We must wait God's time for days of rest and gladness, and His time is always the best. It was good for the Jews at Shushan to be employed two days in encountering and destroying their enemies. Their rest was the more pleasant when it came, that they had made an utter end of those who plotted against their life.

The day of feasting and rest was sweetened by the preceding days of labour and fear. Pleasant is health after sickness. Safety is delightful after extreme danger; and gladness is double joy to those whose souls were depressed with sorrow. In days of prosperity it is good to look back to days of adversity, that we may feel the value of our present enjoyments, and that our hearts may be filled with the praises of him who hath turned our darkness into light, and our mourning into dancing.

Verse 19.—*Therefore the Jews of the villages, that dwelt in the unwalled towns, made the fourteenth day of the month Adar a day of gladness and feasting, and a good day, and of sending portions one to another.*

Their hearts overflowed with joy and gladness. They wished never to forget what God had done for them, and therefore they resolved annually to observe that day on which they had obtained joy and gladness, as a day of joy, and of the exercise of mutual benevolence. We ought never to forget the happy changes which God has made in our condition. Often should we call back to our remembrance the mercies of former days. This will be our wisdom and our happiness. It will be a frequent renewal of former joys, and a means of preserving alive that gratitude which we owe to the God of our mercies.

DISCOURSE XV.

ORDINANCE OF MORDECAI AND ESTHER FOR OBSERVING THE DAYS OF PURIM.

CHAPTER IX. 20–32.

Verses 20, 21.—*And Mordecai wrote these things, and sent letters unto all the Jews that were in all the provinces of the king Ahasuerus, both nigh and far, to stablish this among them, that they should keep the fourteenth day of the month Adar, and the fifteenth day of the same, yearly,—*

SOME of those days of the year in which God appeared in the glory of his power to his people, by working signal deliverances for them, or by giving them signal testimonies of his favour, were appointed by him to be annually observed as days consecrated to his honour. Thus the Passover was a yearly commemoration of the redemption of Israel from Egypt, and the Pentecost of the giving of the law.

But it is not within the power of men to give holiness to a day. God alone, therefore, has authority to appoint stated days for religious services. He alone can bless such days as means of spiritual improvement. Without His presence and blessing, we meet together for the worse, and not for the better; and therefore we must be assured, when we expect his blessing, that we have his warrant for our meetings. That occasional fasts and thanksgivings, on proper calls of providence, may and ought to be appointed by public authority there is no reason to doubt; but stated fasts or thanksgivings can be warrantably appointed by no less authority than His, on whose shoulders the government of the churches is laid. We must observe all things whatsoever He has commanded us, and nothing else, as a religious ordinance, and, lo! he will be with us always.

But why, then, did Mordecai appoint the feast of Purim? Surely Mordecai could not take it upon him to appoint a religious festival without a divine warrant. He knew that neither Joshua nor David had appointed holy-days to be annually observed by the nation, as commemorations of their glorious victories, or of the happy settlement of the people in consequence of their victories. He knew that Moses himself, the lawgiver of the nation, had appointed no solemn feasts by his own authority. He would not even authorise those who could not observe the passover on the ordinary day to observe it on another day, till he had received commandment about it from heaven.

We must conclude, therefore, either that Mordecai was authorised by the Holy Ghost to appoint this festival, or, which appears rather to be the truth, that the feast of Purim was not one of the holy festivals, but a civil festival appointed for joy and feasting, in commemoration of an event that ought never to be forgotten. Mordecai gave no orders concerning sacrifices to be offered on this day, or even concerning any act of religious worship. He, doubtless, hoped that thanksgiving and praise would be offered to God on every return of this joyful festival, but did not reckon himself authorised to publish a law for this purpose. His intention was to perpetuate the remembrance of a glorious deliverance, and he left it to the consciences and grateful feelings of the people to determine what acknowledgements should be made to God, according to the general rules of his word.

Mordecai wrote to the people far and near, to keep both the fourteenth and the fifteenth day of the month Adar as days of rejoicing. They were both of them days of rest, the former day in the provinces, the latter in Shushan; and he would have the people, in every part of the world, to remember, not only their own particular deliverance, or those which their fathers obtained, but deliverances granted to others of their people. Jews were bound, and Christians are surely not less bound, to consider themselves as members one of another, and to consider the mercies bestowed upon their brethren as mercies to themselves.

Verse 22.—*As the days wherein the Jews rested from their enemies, and the month which was turned unto them from sorrow to joy, and from mourning into a good day: that they should make them days of feasting and joy, and of sending portions one to another, and gifts to the poor.*

All things work together for good to the people of God, by promoting their happiness, as well as their holiness. The remembrance of their toils sweetens the rest which succeeds them. The sleep of the labouring man is sweet, although he should sup sparingly before he goes to rest. The tears which the Christian must often shed are remembered with joy, when they are wiped away by returning prosperity. Mordecai wished the Jews to be ever mindful of their sorrows, that their joy might be full.

The days of Purim were intended to be days of feasting and gladness. In the season of their distress, they would scarcely be able to eat that bread which was necessary to the preservation of their life: when they thought of their deliverance, and of the mercy of God in their deliverance, they would eat their bread with gladness, and drink their wine with merry hearts.

These days were to be *days of sending portions one to another.* Their common danger, and their common deliverance, would endear them to one another, and open their hearts to mutual kindness. How much more ought our common salvation by Christ from our general misery, to bind the hearts of Christians to one another. We were all involved in guilt and ruin by sin, and the same sin was the source of misery to us all. We are all redeemed by the same precious blood; we are all saved by the same Almighty arm: Let our common joy in Christ's salvation overflow in mutual love. If we are penetrated with the love of Christ, will we not love all those who are the objects of the same exceeding riches of grace?

Sending of gifts to the poor, was to be another of the duties of this happy day. There might be many poor Jews, who were not able to afford an entertainment for this day of joy.

But Mordecai would have the poor to rejoice as well as the rich. Although we find our circumstances unprosperous, we must not on that account reckon that we have no right, or that we are not bound, to rejoice in public mercies. That the poor may not be tempted to repine when others rejoice, as if they were cut off from the public happiness, we should be ready to communicate to them a share of our blessings, especially when our hearts overflow with joy in God's goodness to ourselves. Why should the rich eat their morsel alone, whilst others are pining with hunger? If you desire the continuance of your own happiness from divine mercy, endeavour to diffuse it by wise liberality. Every expression of divine goodness to ourselves is a new obligation laid upon us to do good, to those especially who have most need of our bounty. Above all, the redemption by Christ binds us to be merciful; 2 Cor. viii. 9.

Verse 23.—*And the Jews undertook to do as they had begun, and as Mordecai had written unto them;—*

They cheerfully promised to comply with Mordecai's wishes, both from a regard to his authority, and from a lively sense of the mercy bestowed upon them. It is a happy thing when superiors require nothing from their inferiors but what themselves see to be just and reasonable.

Mordecai's letters could not but have a mighty influence upon a nation who were indebted to him for their lives. He could not be blamed for bringing them into the dangers which they had escaped, because it was his steadfast adherence to his duty which provoked Haman's wrath. But he deserved no less praise than Esther herself for their preservation. Gratitude will induce us to do many things for those who have been the instruments of preserving our lives. What shall we render to the Author of our lives, and to him who hath redeemed our lives from destruction?

Verse 24.—*Because Haman, the son of Hammedatha the Agagite, the enemy of all the Jews, had devised against the Jews to destroy them, and had cast Pur (that is, the lot) to consume them, and to destroy them;—*

The remembrance of Haman's fearful plot against all the

Jews, powerfully instigated them to observe those days of joy that were appointed by Mordecai. When they considered how formidable the enemy had been, and how bent upon their destruction, they could not think of their deliverance without surprise, and joy, and thankfulness.

It would be useful to us for increasing our joy in the Lord, to think upon those enemies of the church that have often brought her into extreme dangers, that we may see the glory of that grace and power to which she is indebted for existence. If we think upon the Pharaohs, the Hamans, the Sennacheribs, the Antiochuses, the Dioclesians, the beast with seven heads and ten horns, that have opened their mouths like dragons to swallow up the people of God, will we not see good reason still to sing that song of ancient times?—'Many a time have they afflicted me from my youth, may Israel now say; many a time have they afflicted me from my youth; yet they have not prevailed against me.'

Haman was the cause of much terror to the Jews, but this terror ended in triumphs and joyful feasts. Unhappy are the enemies of the people of God. They labour for the profit of those whom they hate. Amongst those things that are made subservient to the advantage of the people of God, are to be ranked all the devices of their most malicious enemies, Satan himself, their greatest enemy, not excepted. Sennacherib was a tremendous enemy of Judah, and struck terror into the minds of the most valiant of the inhabitants of Jerusalem. But what was the event of his formidable invasion? Disgrace and ruin to himself, gladness and joyful feasts to the Jews; as Isaiah foretold, when he was marching along in all the pride of his heart at the head of his innumerable army, collected from his extended dominions: 'They had a song, as in the night when a holy solemnity is kept; and gladness of heart, as when one goeth with a pipe to come into the mountain of the Lord, to the mighty One of Israel.'

Verse 25.—*But when Esther came before the king, he commanded by letters that his wicked device which he had devised against the Jews should return upon his own head, and that he and his sons should be hanged on the gallows.*

In Mordecai's letters, he puts the Jews in mind, not only of Haman's plot against them, but of the means also by which it was disconcerted. Let us observe and call to mind the procedure of the providence of God in the works which he accomplishes for his church, or for ourselves in particular. Every step of his goings of majesty deserves to be remarked and admired. They are all beautified with wisdom and grace.

Who could have expected that Esther, whom the king had not desired to see for thirty days, should obtain such favour in his eyes, as to turn his wrath against his favourite Haman, whose face he saw every day with smiles? Yet, when Esther came before the king, the mischief of Haman was turned upon himself, and he and his sons were hanged on the gallows. Let us do our duty, and leave the consequence to God. Without the protection of his providence, Esther would have fallen under the sentence of that cruel law which made the king inaccessible to his subjects. But her life was preserved by that God to whom she had poured out her soul in fasting. She did great things, and prevailed; and her name shall live to the latest posterity in the records of those heroes and heroines, who 'wrought righteousness, escaped the edge of the sword, out of weakness were made strong, and turned to flight the armies of the aliens.'

'Wherever this gospel is preached,' said Jesus, 'there shall also this that this woman (who poured precious ointment on his head) hath done be told for a memorial of her.' Mordecai hoped, that what Esther had done would be told in every succeeding generation to her honour; and for the encouragement of women, as well as men, to do every thing in their power to promote the interests of the church. Women are too ready to say, What can we do to serve the public interest? our mode of life confines us to our own families. But Esther is not the only woman that has gained just praises by her public spirit. Lemuel's mother taught her son to be a blessing to his people, and has left lessons behind her, by which women, to the end of the world, will be taught to excel in virtue. To Priscilla, as well as to Aquila, all the churches of the Gentiles gave thanks for what she did for Paul; and many of them had reason to thank her for what she did to Apollos likewise. Males and females are one in Christ Jesus. They are equally saved by his grace; they are equally obliged to promote his interest in the exercise of virtue, and the practice of duties suited to their respective situations; and women, as well as men, have sometimes found singular opportunites of service to their generation, which they could not safely neglect to improve.

Verse 26.—*Wherefore they called these days Purim, after the name of Pur.*

The very name of these days afforded a useful lesson to the people of God, and might have afforded a useful lesson to their enemies. It appeared from the event of the lots which gave name to this day, that although time and chance happen to all men, yet nothing is contingent to God. Chance is under his management, and those things which to us appear most accidental, are managed by his providence to accomplish his designs of mercy to them that love him, and of vengeance to his enemies. Why, then, should the friends of God give themselves any anxious trouble about the most uncertain events? The whole disposal of the lot is of Him. Haman's lots directed his measures to his own destruction, and the salvation of Judah.

Verses 26, 27.—*Therefore, for all the words of this letter, and of that which they had seen concerning this matter, and which had come unto them, the Jews ordained, and took upon them, and upon their seed, and upon all such as joined themselves unto them, so as it should not fail, that they would keep these two days, according to their writing, and according to their appointed time, every year.*

The Jews, partly induced by Mordecai's letter, and partly by what they had seen and what had happened to them, agreed that the observation of Purim should be considered as an ordinance and a statute in Israel throughout every generation. They not only engaged for themselves, but for their seed, and all strangers who should join themselves to their nation, to observe this festival.

They did not take more upon themselves than there was a probability of accomplishing, when they engaged that it should not fail. When a joyful festival is appointed by the rulers, with the cheerful consent of the people, to be observed annually, it is not likely to fail amongst posterity, if the occasion of it was some signal revolution in favour of the nation, especially if the very existence of the nation depended upon it.

It may be justly questioned, whether a nation can bind their posterity to any thing further than the laws of religion, justice, and good order in society, bind them. But posterity would not too narrowly inquire how far the authority of their fathers extended, in a matter no less agreeable to themselves than to their progenitors. This, however, is certain, that when men command their children and their seed after them to keep the way of the Lord, future generations cannot turn aside from the good old way of their ancestors, without greatly aggravated guilt; Jer. ii. 10-13.

The Jews expected that proselytes would observe the festival with no less joy than the posterity of Abraham. If we have joined ourselves to the church, we ought to consider ourselves as deeply interested in all the ancient as well as the later dealings of God with her. We partake of the root and fatness of the olive, and therefore ought to bless God for all the care he hath taken of this tree of righteousness, which by his goodness has been so long preserved from destruction, and made to flourish in beauty, and abound in branches and fruit.

Verse 28.—*And that these days should be remembered and kept throughout every generation, every family, every province, and every city; and that these days of Purim should not fail from among the Jews, nor the memorial of them perish from their seed.*

Not only did the Jews resolve and promise to observe these days, but they did every thing in their power to promote the observance of them in every province and city where any of their brethren dwelt, and to perpetuate the observance of them among their seed. Such was the pleasure they felt for their deliverance, and such their gratitude to God their deliverer, that they wished all their brethren, wherever they were scattered, to rejoice with them, and to magnify the Lord together. Their posterity, to the latest generation, could not fail, they thought, whilst these days were observed, to admire, to praise, to glorify the God of their fathers, their King of old, by whom manifold salvations had been wrought in the midst of the earth. They would, whilst this deliverance was recent, be disposed to think that none of the ancient salvations was more worthy of remembrance; and that as they had no authority to appoint any religious festival for the commemoration of it, they could not do less than concur in the appointment of a common festival, which would annually recal it to mind.

Verse 29.—*Then Esther the queen, the daughter of Abihail, and Mordecai the Jew, wrote with all authority, to confirm this second letter of Purim.*

Far be it from us to suppose, that either Esther or Mordecai had their own glory in view, when they were at such pains to promote and perpetuate the observance of the feast of Purim. It would be unjust, as well as uncharitable, to ascribe such selfish intentions to persons who had laid down their necks for the honour of their God, and for the deliverance of their people.

That their design was good in writing the second letter of Purim with all authority, cannot be reasonably doubted. It may, indeed, admit of question, whether they did not expect more than prudence could justify them in expecting, from the perpetual observance of this feast. They probably thought, that whilst the memory of the wonders of the month of Adar continued, all posterity would abound in thanksgivings to God. The reverse has been the case. The feast of Purim has long since been turned into a drunken revel. The blinded Jews, it is said, lay it down as a maxim, That they ought to be drunken with wine in remembrance of Esther's banquet. How strange is it for human creatures to think that they are delivered to work abomination!

Esther and Mordecai 'wrote with all authority.' They thought that they could not use their power for a better purpose, than to perpetuate the remembrance of that day when God delivered their souls from death, their eyes from tears, and their feet from falling. But in the exercise of their authority, they forgot not that kindness which was due to their brethren, the Israel of God.

Verse 30.—*And he sent the letters unto all the Jews, to the hundred twenty and seven provinces of the kingdom of Ahasuerus, with words of peace and truth,—*

When we are exalted above our brethren, we are too ready to forget both them and ourselves, as if the change of our condition had raised us to a higher rank of creatures. Mordecai and his adopted daughter were not negligent in the exercise of their authority for purposes that appeared to them good and salutary to the nation; but they still retained their humbleness of mind, and their kind affections to their kindred. They sent these letters to all the hundred and twenty-seven provinces, 'with words of truth and peace;' with expressions of the warmest benevolence. Nor were these expressions, like many of our mutual compliments, merely dictated by a politeness which too often conceals a perfect indifference to our neighbour's welfare under good words and fair speeches. Their words were words of truth, as well as of peace, when they expressed their desires and prayers, that the Lord might bless his people with peace.

Let men maintain that authority which God hath given them, that they may attain the ends for which it is given them; but let it be always tempered with charity and gentleness. Paul, in his epistles, asserts his authority as an apostle of Jesus Christ; but he writes with words of peace and truth, when he prays for grace and peace to the churches from God the Father, and from the Lord Jesus Christ.

Verse 31.—*To confirm these days of Purim in their times appointed, according as Mordecai the Jew and Esther the queen had enjoined them, and as they had decreed for themselves, and for their seed, the matters of the fastings and their cry.*

At the motion of Mordecai, the Jews were unanimously determined to observe the festival, and to enjoin the observance of it to their posterity. The Jews were confirmed in their resolution by the second letter of Mordecai, in conjunction with Esther. And one consideration which would dispose them to observe the commemoration of this deliverance with joy and exultation, was, that they had fasted and cried for it under the pressure of the danger. They could not eat their ordinary food. They cried out with exceeding loud and bitter cries.

They fasted and cried unto the Lord, and he heard the voice of their supplications.

Spring is the pleasantest season of the year, because it follows the dreary desolations, and the piercing cold of winter. Those days of health are especially delightful which follow days of extreme sickness, when we had the sentence of death in ourselves. Remember the dismal thoughts that engrossed your minds, the terrifying apprehensions that embittered your troubles, and the exquisite felicity which you promised to yourselves, if it should please God, beyond your expectations, to send you relief. Thus will the troubles you have endured spread happiness in the retrospect over the remaining part of your life. You still must meet with trials; but you will be thankful that they are so light and easy to be borne, when they are compared with those which you have formerly endured.

Have you fasted and cried unto the Lord, and has He graciously inclined his ear to your complaints? With what joy and peace ought you to recollect the mercy which has preserved you from going down to the chambers of the grave, perhaps to the regions of destruction! David will teach you what improvement to make of your fasting and cries, when the Lord has been pleased to grant you the deliverance which you supplicated: 'I love the Lord, because he hath heard my voice and supplications. Because he hath inclined his ear unto me, therefore will I call upon him so long as I live. The sorrows of death compassed me, and the pains of hell gat hold upon me; I found trouble and sorrow. Then called I upon the name of the Lord: O Lord, I beseech thee, deliver my soul! Gracious is the Lord, and righteous; yea, our God is merciful. The Lord preserveth the simple: I was brought low and he helped me: I will walk before the Lord in the land of the living'; Psalm cxvi. 1–6, and 9: Psal. xviii. xxx. Isa. xxxviii. 11–20.

Verse 32.—*And the decree of Esther confirmed these matters of Purim; and it was written in the book.*

The high and beloved name of Esther was sufficient to establish the decree of Purim. She had been the saviour of the Jews. At the risk of her life she had preserved theirs. What do we not owe to Him who, not merely by endangering his life, but by giving up himself to an accursed death, hath delivered us from the wrath to come?

And it was written in the book of the Jewish institutions, or in the register of the Jewish transactions. Books are necessary for recording those things that are intended for the use of posterity. Were it not for books, we would all be children in understanding. Let us carefully improve those things that were written aforetimes for our learning, especially those things which divine wisdom hath directed the holy men of God to record for our benefit.

The feast of Purim is still observed, though not in a manner agreeable to Esther's intention. The observance of this and other festivals of the Jews, from the most ancient times, is attended with this great advantage, that it affords a convincing argument of the truth of those facts which they were designed to commemorate, when we take this into the account, that these facts were recorded in books at the time when they were instituted which are still extant. The observance of the ancient Jewish feasts is a public declaration of the firm belief of the Jewish nation in the Old Testament Scriptures. This is one of the most powerful rational arguments of the truth of our holy religion. If the Old Testament Scriptures are true, the Messiah expected by the Jews is come long ago into the world; and none but Jesus of Nazareth can be that Messiah. Thus the most determined enemies of Jesus give a decided, though indirect testimony, that he is the Son of God, by attesting the truth and divine authority of those ancient Scriptures that testify of him.

DISCOURSE XVI.

GREATNESS OF AHASUERUS—CHARACTER AND GRANDEUR OF MORDECAI.

CHAPTER X.

Verse 1.—*And the king Ahasuerus laid a tribute upon the land, and upon the isles of the sea.*

Too many subjects are disgusted with the governments under which they live, when new taxes are imposed. Here we find, that the increase of taxes is no new thing, and that it may be necessary under the best and wisest governments. When the tribute here spoken of was laid upon the land, and upon the isles of the sea, Ahasuerus had his counsels directed, not by Haman, but by Mordecai. Ahasuerus might perhaps have saved his subjects their new burdens, if he had been more frugal in his expenses. The multitude of his concubines must have put him to a very great, and a worse than needless expense; Chap. ii. He was liberal in his donations. His wars could not be carried on without great sums; and when his wars with the Greeks came to an end, he expended much money in political intrigues, to preserve himself from more wars. He therefore found it necessary to lay new burdens upon his subjects. But the protection which government affords makes the payment of necessary taxes an act of justice. 'Rulers are the ministers of God to us for good; and for this cause we must pay them tribute, because they are the servants of God, waiting continually upon this very thing.' We are not excused from this duty by the supposition that government ought to be more economical than it is. Who of us does not sometimes spend money that might be spared? It is one of the laws of the Turkish empire, that no new tributes can be imposed on the people. The consequence is, that when their government must have money, it must be raised by oppression of individuals, who, in their turn, indemnify themselves by oppressing others. The Persians were much more wise, when they allowed a tribute to be laid upon them which came with equal weight upon all. 'He laid a tribute upon the land,' upon the vast regions on the continent under the Persian empire, and upon the many 'isles of the sea' which they possessed. A burden borne by all will be light, when it would be unsupportable to a few.

Subjects may, under unwise governors, have too much reason to complain of burdens laid upon them; Prov. xxviii. 16; yet complaints of this kind are often without ground. Rulers can best know what sums are requisite for the honourable support of government, and for the defence of the country. Although we think our burdens heavy, let us bear them conscientiously. We claim support to our just rights from government, and must not defraud it of its own rights; Rom. xiii. 6, 7.

Verse 2.—*And all the acts of his power, and of his might, and the declaration of the greatness of Mordecai, whereunto the king advanced him, are they not written in the book of the chronicles of the kings of Media and Persia?*

The Bible is incomparably the best of all books, and yet it is not the only book from which we may derive instruction. Luther wished all his books might be burnt, rather than men should be kept by them from reading the Scriptures. But we may daily read the Scriptures, and find some time likewise for consulting other books. We find the apostle Paul quoting the books of poets and philosophers; Acts, xvii. 28: Titus, 1. 12: 1 Cor. xv. 33. Here the inspired writer refers to the chronicles of Media and Persia for a further account of the power and greatness of Ahasuerus; and for a confirmation of what has been said of the greatness of Mordecai. We are often referred by the sacred writers to uninspired histories for larger accounts than they were directed to give us of the lives of persons eminent for their stations, and for their virtues and vices. Much useful instruction is to be drawn from credible histories. We learn from them many of the works that God has done on the earth, and the perfect conformity between his words and works. Many examples of goodness are set before us, which we ought to imitate; many instances of vicious conduct, which we ought to abhor.

The registers of the ancient kings of Persia do not now exist; but the reference made to them is a confirmation of the history of this book. The writer would not have sent his contemporaries to the public records for further information, if he had written any thing which did not agree with them. Learned men have made a happy use of ancient writings of heathens, as well as of Christians, to establish the authority and truth of Scripture, in opposition to infidels.

Although the records of the Persian kings are lost, we have books left us which inform us of the greatness, and power, and long reign of Artaxerxes, or Ahasuerus, the husband of Esther. Many worthy deeds were done by him to the church of God, as we are informed by Ezra and Nehemiah; and he was well rewarded by Divine Providence. The prayers of the people of God for his prosperity were heard.

Although we have no account of Mordecai in the Grecian histories of this long reign, we have no reason to doubt of what is said concerning him in this book. The Greeks had but a partial acquaintance with the affairs of the Persian court, and the most ancient Persian histories, written by Persians themselves, give some cause to suspect, that through ignorance or partiality the Greeks have frequently omitted or misrepresented the most important facts. Mordecai the Jew, and Ezra, and Nehemiah, had access to the knowledge of many facts concerning the government of Ahasuerus, that were unknown to strangers.

Verse 3.—*For Mordecai the Jew was next unto king Ahasuerus, and great among the Jews, and accepted of the multitude of his brethren, seeking the wealth of his people, and speaking peace to all his seed.*

Mordecai the Jew was next unto king Ahasuerus. This was wonderful; a poor man of the dispersion of Israel was raised high in dignity, by the favour of Ahasuerus, above all the princes of Persia. The elevation of men from the lowest to the highest rank is not unusual in the east, even at present. But Mordecai professed a religion which seemed an unsurmountable obstruction to grandeur in a land of heathens; and he held it so firm, that he would not conform to the fashions of the court in any thing that did not consist with a good conscience. Haman hoped that all the men whose laws and customs were so different from the king's laws would soon be extirpated. He little expected that one of the most inflexible adherents to those laws and customs would supplant and succeed him in the king's favour. 'There be many that seek the ruler's favour' with such eagerness, that they will bend their consciences into a ready compliance with his wishes, whatever they are; 'but every man's judgment cometh from the Lord.' He exalted Daniel and Mordecai in the courts of Babylon and Shushan; and these were men that would not have turned a hair-breadth out of the path of duty to please any prince on earth. Their unshaken firmness might, very probably, be one cause of their advancement. Inflexibility in what is right must be a respectable quality in the eyes, not only of the good, but of every man of sense.

Ahasuerus showered favours upon Esther, upon Mordecai, upon Ezra, and upon Nehemiah, and yet continued all his days to adhere to the religion of his fathers. Herod Antipas did many things gladly because of John Baptist, and yet he was not a good man. Love to the brethren is a scriptural mark of a saint; but men that are not saints may have a warm attachment to good men, on account of qualities that all the world hold in esteem. We love the brethren, when we love believers as the children of God, as our brethren in Christ, partakers of the same divine nature. But integrity, generosity, unshaken constancy in virtue, are qualities for which men that have not passed from death to life may esteem and love their neighbours, whether they are saints or not.

Mordecai was great among the Jews, and accepted of the multitude of his brethren.—They venerated and loved him as the saviour of their nation, as their father and protector. Envy too often attends the exaltation of one's equals. Joseph's brethren would rather murder him, or sell him to strangers, than see him advanced above themselves. Ingratitude too often follows the greatest benefactions. The children of Israel requited evil to the house of Gideon for the deliverance wrought for them from the hands of the Midianites, at the risk of his life. But Mordecai met with returns of the sincerest gratitude from the multitude of his brethren. He still behaved to them as a brother, and they considered him both as their brother and their prince.

It was a great happiness to the good man that he was accepted of the multitude of his brethren; for 'a good name is better than precious ointment, and loving favour is rather to be chosen than silver and gold.' This, however, is a happiness not always to be expected by good men; and therefore, as our Lord teaches us, we must learn to do good without the expectation of a return from those to whom we do it. Paul was still happier than Mordecai, when he found ungrateful returns for the noblest services, and yet could say in sincerity, 'I am ready to spend and be spent for you, although the more abundantly I love you, the less I be loved.' If we do not perform our good works to be seen of men, we will be content with the honour that comes from God only. The favour and gratitude of men are highly useful, by enabling us to be still more useful to them; but then we have the testimony of our own hearts that our works are wrought in God, when the course of our goodness is not interrupted by bad returns from its objects; Heb. vi. 9, 10: Gal. vi. 12–16.

Seeking the wealth of his people.—Many, when they have attained the utmost summit of their wishes, become unhappy, because they have obtained what they sought. Desire faileth, and their hearts become like a stone in them, because they have nothing more to desire. This is the effect of selfishness reigning in the heart. Give a good man ten times more wealth or honour than he ever desired to possess, he is not unhappy because his wishes are completely gratified, for he will still find new desires operating in his heart. Although he has nothing more to wish for on his own account, he finds opportunities to do much good to others, which he did not formerly enjoy. His desires are roused by the means of executing them.

Mordecai was, doubtless, richer than he ever expected to be, when he was made the queen's treasurer, and the king's favourite. But there was a nation in which he was deeply interested, and which he had new opportunities given him to serve. These opportunities he did not neglect. Whilst he faithfully served a prince to whom he was highly indebted, he sought, and by all wise and honest means promoted, the wealth and prosperity of his people. A rare talent was entrusted to him, and he did not hide it in a napkin. When we have nothing to do for ourselves, it will be our wisdom and happiness to do much for others. 'The liberal man deviseth liberal things, and by liberal things shall he stand.'

The Jews were Mordecai's people. This was one though not the chief reason why he sought their wealth. Patriotism is certainly a virtue recommended to us by the best of saints. The apostle Paul was, perhaps, worse treated by his countrymen than ever any other man, and yet he would willingly have died for them a thousand deaths. He 'magnified his office as the apostle of the Gentiles, that if possible by any means, he might stir up to emulation his brethren according to the flesh.'

Paul could not procure the love of his kinsmen, like Mordecai; although he certainly sought the welfare of his people with an affection no less ardent. The reason of the difference may be, that Mordecai sought their outward prosperity, and Paul their spiritual advantage. We are not to suppose that Mordecai was careless about their spiritual interests. That expression which we translate 'the wealth,' might have been rendered 'the good' of his people. He sought their happiness of every kind. But his station gave him opportunities chiefly to promote their external prosperity. Paul laboured for their spiritual advantage; and we know what difference men put between services done to their bodies and services done to their souls. If the preachers of the gospel, who call men to come and share in the unsearchable riches of Christ, should call them to come and receive thousands of gold and silver, not one of them would hear the invitation without a thankful compliance; and yet they will not come unto Christ, that they might have life. Alas! how little regard is paid to the words of the Wisdom of God: 'Receive my instruction, and not silver; and knowledge rather than choice gold. For wisdom is better than rubies; and all the things that may be desired are not to be compared to it; Prov. viii. 10, 11.

And speaking peace to all his seed.—The generous soul of this good man was filled with kindness to the rising race, and projected the happiness of succeeding generations. 'He spake peace to all his seed' (or rather, their seed). He was courteous in his deportment to the young, and behaved so as to discover a warm regard for the welfare and happiness of the race that should be born. Thus Peter, in the view of laying aside his earthly tabernacle, took care that Christians should have necessary truths in remembrance, when they could not enjoy the opportunity of hearing them from his mouth.

The expression seems to imply, that Mordecai procured the peace of the seed of Israel by the words of his mouth. 'Death and life are in the power of the tongue.' Mordecai, by his credit with the king, gave him a favourable opinion of the Jews, and extinguished all suspicion that might be entertained by that prince to the prejudice of a nation whose laws were different from the laws of other people; and, by his influence with the Jews, promoted that spirit of loyalty and good behaviour on which their welfare greatly depended.

Few have it in their power to be such benefactors as Mordecai: all have it in their power to do much hurt; and who has it not in his power to do some good? We are not required to do what we have it not in our power to do, or what is not competent to our station. But all of us are bound to live under the influence of those tempers which were eminently displayed in those great saints whose examples are recorded in the Bible. They obtained their good report through faith, which animated them in all their undertakings. If we live by the faith of Christ, we will be active according to the ability that God gives us, and the calls of his providence, in promoting his glory, and the best interests of men.

Fervent charity operated in Mordecai; and if our faith is genuine, it will work by love. Love is not a dead, but a vigorous affection. If the spirit of love and faith dwell in us, we will be trees of righteousness, whose leaves will not wither, and whose fruit will be produced in its proper season; for 'the fruit of the righteous is the fruit of a tree of life.'

If we cannot reasonably hope to do much for posterity, we certainly may do something to promote the welfare of our own generation. If our goodness extend not far, it may reach to parents, servants, wives, neighbours. Our dutiful behaviour towards them, our example, our prayers, may greatly promote their present comfort, and their eternal welfare.

And why may not the most inconsiderable Christian hope to be of some use to posterity? Train up your children in the fear of God, and they will be a blessing to the next age. They will probably follow your good example, and thus you will be useful, by their means, to generations yet unborn. If you have no children, you may be useful to young persons around you: 'A word spoken in season, how good is it!'

THREE

SERMONS

ON

PARENTAL DUTIES.

SERMON I.

THE DUTY OF PARENTS TO THEIR CHILDREN.

EPHESIANS VI. 4.

And, ye fathers, provoke not your children to wrath: but bring them up in the nurture and admonition of the Lord.

It is a common, and a too just complaint, that religion is in a less prosperous state amongst us than it was forty or fifty years ago.* What is the cause of this unhappy change? The Spirit of God is the only author of true holiness. Why hath God withdrawn his Spirit from us? It is certainly owing to ourselves that he testifies his displeasure by with-holding, in a great measure, those gracious influences which were communicated to our fathers. 'The Lord is with you,' said the prophet Azariah, the son of Oded, 'while ye be with Him; and if ye seek him, he will be found of you; but if ye forsake him, he will forsake you; 2 Chron. xv. 2.

It is owing, say some, to the difference between the ministers of former and present times, that the means of grace appear to produce so little effect upon men. And we do not deny that our hands are in the trespass. Our spirits are not animated with the same sacred fervour in the work of the Lord as those of many of our fathers; and the Spirit of God does not crown our labours with success like theirs. But it will not be equitable to lay the whole blame upon us. 'Are there not with you, even with you, sins against the Lord our God?' and such sins as provoke the Holy Spirit to testify his displeasure by with-holding that gracious influence, without which we must continue in our present melancholy condition? When

---
* These Sermons were first published in the year 1804.—Ed.

ministers do not make full proof of their ministry, can they hope to save themselves and those that hear them? When professors of religion do not use, or use as if they used not, the means of grace, can they wonder that the Holy Spirit does not bless these means to their souls? When parents do not follow the instructions of the Holy Spirit, requiring them to train up their children in the way wherein they should go, have they any reason to be surprised when their children are left by God to walk in the way of their own hearts, and after the sight of their own eyes? When means by which the Spirit uses to work—means prescribed by the Spirit himself—means for obtaining the most precious blessings—means which he has encouraged us, by great and precious promises, to use with diligence,—when such means are either not used at all, or when they are used with such carelessness as makes it apparent that we pay little regard to the authority of God, place little confidence in his promises, and give ourselves little trouble whether we enjoy his influence or not, the Spirit himself is despised and grieved, and justly provoked to leave us to ourselves, that we may know, by sad experience, how little we can do, either for ourselves, or for those that are dear to us.

It cannot be reasonably expected that great benefit can be derived from sermons by men who understand little of what is said to them. And much cannot be understood by persons uninstructed in the first principles of the doctrine of Christ, which ought to be taught by parents to their children in the years of childhood. It is only once or twice in the course of a year, that we who are ministers of the gospel can give private instructions to your children; and therefore it is impossible for us to prepare their minds for our public instructions. This is the work chiefly of parents, who are commanded to 'bring up their children in the nurture and admonition of the Lord.' If you neglect this part of your duty, we justly impute to you a great part of the blame of the unsuccessfulness of our ministry. When men hear the word, and understand it not, the devil commonly finds it easy to steal away from them that little of which they may form some apprehension. But how can they understand sermons, if they have not been taught their catechisms? Do you expect that the teachers of your schools can make your children to read words, and sentences, and discourses, before they have been taught the letters of the alphabet? As little can it be expected that sermons should be understood by those who have not learned the first lessons of religion.

That other sermons may be better understood, I shall endeavour in this discourse to persuade you, if possible, to train up your children in the way wherein they should go: and for this purpose I shall endeavour to explain and enforce,

I. The caution given to parents against provoking their children to wrath.

II. The direction given them to bring up their children in the nurture and admonition of the Lord. After which, I shall,

III. Consider why the caution against provoking your children to wrath is joined to the command to bring up children in the nurture and admonition of the Lord.

I.—*I shall endeavour to explain and enforce the caution against provoking your children to wrath.*

Perhaps you will say, that you love your children, and therefore scarcely need to have this caution explained to you. You would be sorry to see your children causelessly provoked to wrath by any person whatever, and therefore you think you are not likely to provoke them by any part of your own conduct.

I doubt not but you love your children; but you may, nevertheless, need a warning against harsh behaviour towards them. Is it not too well known, that wives and husbands will sometimes make one another very uneasy by harsh behaviour or by provoking language; and yet if a third person interpose to terminate the difference, they will both turn against him, in defence of either of the parties? This is a plain evidence that love does not always ensure good behaviour to the object of it. They love one another too well to endure any harsh word from a third person to either of them; and yet their love does not hinder them from plaguing one another with rude behaviour. Discretion is necessary, as well as love, to preserve you from making your wives or your children unhappy by your conduct.

Suffer me, then, to speak a few works to you concerning that behaviour which your children have a right to expect from you. We have heard of books about the rights of men, and the rights of women. The rights of children, too, deserve our consideration. They are human creatures, made after the image of God. 'Of such is the kingdom of God.' They are not able to plead their rights against tyrannical parents. Suffer me to plead on their behalf. I do not say that any of you are tyrants in your families. But all of you have much power over your children; and such is the present state of human nature, that there are few who do not, on some occasion or other, make a wrong use of their power. David himself, on some occasions, made a rash and unwarrantable use of that regal power which God gave him over Israel. Can you say that you are chargeable with fewer errors in the use of your parental power? If you are, you may, however, need to be warned against abuses of authority to which you may be prompted by temptations not yet experienced.

1. *Ye fathers, provoke not your children to wrath, by austerity or rudeness in your behaviour to your children.*

Some seem to think, that, in all places except their own houses, they are bound to behave with gentleness and good manners. I am fully persuaded not only that they err in making this exception, but that this mistake is the source of a great part of the misery of human life, and of a great part of those iniquities whereby men are offended, and whereby God is dishonoured.

'Whosoever is angry with his brother without cause, shall be in danger of the judgment; and whosoever shall say to his brother, Raca, shall be in danger of the council; but whosoever shall say, Thou fool, shall be in danger of hell-fire.' Will you say that you are not, in the sight of God, the brethren, but the fathers of your children? But, although you are their fathers, you are the children of the same God, who made both you and them. You are redeemed by the same precious blood.

And because you are their fathers, to transgress any of the laws of love, in your behaviour to them, is a greater iniquity than a like transgression in your behaviour to other persons. The more nearly we are related to any of the human race, the greater are our obligations to perform to them all the numerous duties comprehended in the royal law of love; and the greater is the guilt which we contract, by doing any of those things which are forbidden in this law.

Some parents will not scruple to call their children idiots, brutes, blockheads, asses. Is not this as bad as to say unto them, Raca, or, Thou rebel? (for so it is probable the word rendered, *Thou fool*, signifies.) Would you take it well if any other person should call them by such names? But why should you take those freedoms which you will not allow to other people? You are their fathers, you say, and have rights over them, which none else have. This is true. But what are these rights? Have you a right to treat them with indignity and outrage, because you are connected with them by a relation which binds you to love them with a tender affection? Because you are obliged to do them much good, have you a right to do them hurt? Parents have surely as little right, and less if possible, to be injurious to their own children, than any other persons living.

But they have provoked you by bad behaviour? Well; admonish and chastise them, and teach them to behave better. But if you treat them with rudeness, you teach them to behave worse. If you call them bad names, you teach them to give the same, or as bad names, to any persons that happen to displease them. Will you chastise them for calling their brothers or sisters, or any other persons, brutes or blockheads? You are blamable to a high degree if you do not. You are blamable to as high a degree, if you punish them for imitating your own conduct, unless you, at the same time, make them sensible that you abhor yourselves for having taught them such lessons.

What do you think of Saul's behaviour to his son Jonathan, when he said to him in his wrath, 'Thou son of the perverse rebellious woman' ('Thou son of harlots,' as the most ancient translators understand it), 'Do not I know that thou hast chosen the son of Jesse to thine own confusion, and to the confusion of thy mother's nakedness?' How different from such language was that of Abraham to his son Isaac; of Isaac to his sons Esau and Jacob; of David to his son Solomon! Gen. xxii. 7, 8; xxvii. xxviii. 1 Chron. xxii. But we scarcely need such examples to teach us that gentleness of behaviour which parents owe to their children. Nature itself taught the heathens, who knew not God, that a man who is surly in his behaviour to his children deserves not the honourable name of a father.*

Parents, even when they justly correct their children, ought by no means to treat them with proud disdain, or to load them with opprobrious epithets. What would be thought of a judge who should load a criminal with insult at the time he is pronouncing sentence upon him? Fierce passions are never worse timed than when a judge gives sentence on a pannel, or a father corrects his child. Correction of children, and the punishment of criminals, are divine institutions, which ought to be administered with all gravity, and with perfect calmness of temper.

Correction, as well as punishment, ought to be proportioned to the fault, or the crime. And whatever the fault or the crime is, it must be remembered, that the offender hath the honour to be a human creature, and must not be treated as a brute. Do you not remember the law of Moses concerning stripes? Whatever the offence was, the offender was not to receive more than forty; 'lest,' says the divine Lawgiver, 'thy brother should appear vile unto thee.' He is still thy brother, whatever he has done. Thou must still respect him as a brother, and beware of loading him with ignominy, when necessity requires that he should be punished. This humane law was so strictly observed by the Jews, even in their worst degeneracy, that though they accounted Paul the most execrable of men, and often punished him with stripes, they never inflicted upon him the full number of forty. Shall the spirit

---

* This is a part of the character which Homer gives to one of his most distinguished heroes:—'He was mild as a father.'

of this law be less regarded by Christian parents, than the letter of it by Jewish persecutors?

2. *Parents must not provoke their children to wrath by injustice, or unkindness, in with-holding from them what they have good reason to expect from the affection of a father.*

Those men who are the instruments of being to their fellow-creatures, are bound to protect and cherish their tender years, and to provide whatever is necessary for them, till they are in a condition to provide for themselves. If children find themselves left destitute of needful provision and support, by the idleness, the prodigality, or avarice of their parents, they must be tempted to complain and fret at such barbarous usage, when they come to those years at which they can form a judgment of the cause of their distress; and these years sooner arrive than some parents suppose. 'If a man provide not for those of his own house, he is worse than the infidels.' He has less understanding than the beasts of the field, or than the fowls of heaven—except the ostrich.

Children have a right to expect from their parents food and clothing suited to their circumstances, together with such other comforts and conveniences as are generally enjoyed by the children of parents of equal rank; and, therefore, parents tempt their children to be angry with them, when they are compelled, by excessive frugality on the part of their fathers, to blush and hide their heads at their own mean appearance in the presence of young persons whose parents are not richer than their own, nor disposed to throw away their money on superfluities.

I am speaking to parents only, and not to children; nor to other people, who have no right to judge of the behaviour of parents to their children, and who, if they judge at all, must judge without proper evidence. I said, that parents ought to make such allowances of necessaries or conveniences to their children as their income will permit; not such as their station, in common estimation, may seem to require. To proportion men's expenses to their station, rather than their income, is one of the greatest follies in the world. It is the cause of continual misery to many of mankind, and leads to much wickedness. Now, parents are the only good judges of their own circumstances; which are but very imperfectly known to their neighbours, and perhaps still more imperfectly to their own children. You are not, therefore, young persons! to give ear to those impertinent meddlers in other people's affairs, who tell you that your parents are not generous in their behaviour to you. I have given to your parents my advice to treat you with that justice and generosity, which may be expected from their affection to the fruit of their own bodies. But both you and I must leave the application of this instruction to their own prudence. We have no right, nor have we that knowledge of their situation, which might enable us to mention particulars. It is very possible that some of your parents may carry their frugality too far in the allowance they make you; but you have no right to think that they do so, or to believe those who tell you so, unless better proof could be given of it than can be commonly had.

Although parents may be in circumstances which render it difficult for them, they ought not to with-hold from their children, grown up to proper age, the necessary means of enabling them to provide for themselves, by acquiring skill in some profession suited to their genius and their inclination. If industry is required from all men, it must be incumbent on parents to do what lies in their power to qualify their children for some kind of industry that may be useful to themselves, and to the public. Amongst one of the wisest nations of antiquity, it was a law, that the man who did not cause his children to be taught some useful profession, should have no claim upon them for support, when himself became infirm through sickness or old age. I do not commend this law. It would not became Christians to act according to its spirit towards their parents. What I infer from it is, that parents, in the estimation of the wise, act unjustly to their children, and tempt them to give place to resentment against the instruments of their own being, when they grudge the expense and trouble necessary to prepare their children for making that figure in the world which might be expected from the station and circumstances of their parents.

3. *Partiality in behaviour to children is certainly unjustifiable in parents.*

But let me not be mistaken. I do not say that parents ought either to love all their children equally, or to affect the appearance of an equal love to them all. Who will say that Jacob sinned in loving Joseph more than his brethren, when Joseph so well deserved to be loved above them all? And yet it will not be easy to free him from the charge of indiscretion, in distinguishing him so remarkably by singular testimonies of his love, when he might have been so justly apprehensive of some bad effects from it, considering what he knew of the haughty and passionate temper of some of his other sons; Gen. xxxvii.

Parents are not to be blamed for distinguishing, by the tenderness of their love, such of their children as need, above others, parental pity to soothe them under infirmities or misfortunes. God is pleased to illustrate the tenderness of his mercy to his people, by the pity of a father or a mother to their distressed offspring; Psalm ciii. 13; Isaiah lxvi. 13.

Parents are not unjust in giving peculiar marks of their affection to those children who have merited it by their piety, their prudence, the sweetness of their tempers, their industry in acquiring useful accomplishments, their virtuous actions, their attachment to their parents, their kindness to their brothers and sisters, their discreet and kind behaviour to friends or strangers. 'A wise son maketh a glad father;' why may he not express his gladness? Can any child of the family, who has not merited such regard, take it amiss that he should? Such a child must not only be destitute of wisdom, but blind to its beauties; and there is no hope, without a miracle of grace, that a regard either to God or man will ever make him wiser than he is.

But parents provoke their children to wrath, when they hate some, and love others of them, though their children have given them no reason to make this invidious distinction; or, when they make a difference between them, far exceeding the causes that have been given. Distinctions founded in reason and religion may be attended with good effects. They are just encouragements to virtue, piety, and dutiful behaviour on the one side; on the other side, they are discouragements to sin and folly. But distinctions that are arbitrary and capricious can do no good, and will probably do much evil. Your favourite child, we hope, will not, like Joseph, be cast into a deep pit, or sold into Egypt by his brethren; but, what is worse for him, he may be swelled with vanity and arrogance; he may learn to despise his brethren, and even to treat with insolence the father that cannot prevail upon himself to find fault with any thing that he does. You may, besides, draw upon him the envy of his brethren, which will more than counterbalance all the fruits of your partial favour. Had not the Lord been on Joseph's side, and turned all his calamities into blessings, the envy of his brethren, although they had neither killed nor sold him, would have done him more hurt, and given him more pain, than his father's partiality could have given him pleasure.

There is the more need of warning parents against groundless partialities to their children, that we find the best men too much disposed to indulge them, and the wisest men too little sensible of the mischiefs that may be produced by them. Who would have thought that Isaac would love Esau better than Jacob, when a divine oracle had declared that the elder should serve the younger? especially after the plain proofs which Jacob, no doubt, gave of his piety, whilst he was yet in his father's house. And little did Isaac think, whilst he was indulging his ill-judged partiality, that he was tempting his beloved Rebekah to impose a cheat upon himself, in conjunction with the best of his sons; or that he was sowing the seeds of a bloody dissension amongst his children, and his children's children to many generations. That behaviour of Jacob, which gave rise to an 'anger that did tear perpetually, and to wrath which was kept for ever,' took its rise in part from Isaac's unjust design to give the blessing to his eldest son; who had already forfeited the birth-right by his profane conduct, and who was never entitled to the blessing.

Partiality in distributing the possessions or goods of the father amongst his children, is inconsistent with justice. We do not deny that parents may justly give much more to one child of the family than to another; nor are they bound to account to strangers for the preference. But a great inequality, without any other reason but the will of the father, cannot be justified. Why should all his children but one be left beggars, for the sake of a favourite? Are they not all equally related to him? Have they not all their virtues and their faults? If some have distinguished themselves by their virtues, or by their faults, it will not be unjust to make them sensible of their father's sense of their conduct. Jacob was not to be blamed, but commended, for leaving the double portion to Joseph. He was, indeed, guided by the Spirit of God, in giving this instance of regard to that son who was 'the shepherd and the stone of Israel'; and in the dissatisfaction he expressed with the conduct of his three oldest sons; in the farewell blessings given to his family. But many parents, by their last will, appear to be actuated by the spirit of the world, which prompts them to rob all their younger children, to enable the eldest to keep up the honour of the family.

Why should daughters have merely a trifle left them when perhaps all the sons have a rich provision, though daughters have not the same means in their power which the sons have, to improve their condition? Daughters are often found to love their father better than his sons, and are less likely to squander away the fruits of his goodness. When partiality in their father deprives them of what they had reason to expect, are they not tempted to indulge those sentiments which are the common effects of unrequited affection?

The offspring of first marriages have sometimes been deprived of their rights, to gratify a second wife. But why should the dead be injured for the sake of the living? Your deceased friends may be still wronged or favoured in the persons of their living representatives. If you loved your wife while she lived, she has done nothing since she was taken from you to merit what is no less unjustifiable than an alienation of your regard. But, if you did not love her so well as you do the present, her children are still entitled to justice from their father. The law of Moses absolutely prohibited the Jews from making the son of a beloved wife the heir of the double portion, instead of the son of a wife that was hated. I do not say that this law binds us in the letter of it; but it certainly teaches us, that it is injustice in parents to prefer some of their children to others equally deserving of regard, from a partial attachment to their mother.

4. *Children must not be provoked to wrath by violence done to their consciences.*

Conscience must be regulated by knowledge and judgment. Till knowledge is gained by enlightening the consciences of young persons, parents certainly have a right to direct their religious behaviour; and it is the duty of parents to afford them all the means in their power to enable them to form a judgment for themselves, and to endeavour to convince them of the truth and importance of those doctrines which appear to themselves to be founded in the Bible. But they must by no means claim any powers which can belong to none but the Lord of conscience, the Lawgiver, 'who is able to save and to destroy.'

Amongst the different forms of religious profession, (which are too numerous amongst us,) you no doubt believe your own to be the best. I believe so too. We would deserve damnation for our hypocrisy, if we solemnly professed a belief of any religious principles which did not appear to us to be agreeable to the mind of God. And therefore it must be very desirable to us, that our children should make the same profession, if they can view the truths of religion in the same light with ourselves. If they cannot be convinced by our arguments, or their own inquiries, that we are in the right, we must not be displeased with them because they dissent from us. The rights of conscience are sacred. We step into the throne of God, and claim honours equal to his, if we require even our own children to make a profession of religion which pleases ourselves, rather than a profession which appears to them to please God.

What advantage can we propose by urging them to associate in church-fellowship with that body of Christians with which we are connected, unless we can convince them that our particular form of profession is warranted by Scripture? We may make them hypocrites, but cannot make them believers; and it is of little importance what profession they make, or whether they make any at all, if they are, in their profession, dissemblers with God. I should rather have said, that it were better for them intirely to lay aside all profession of religion, than to profess before God what they do not believe with their hearts. Wretched and wicked are the men who make no pretensions to any religion; but not so wretched and wicked as those men who wilfully 'compass God about with lies and deceits,' as all those men do who profess, before God, any thing which they do not believe.

I am far from meaning, by any thing I have said, that it is not a matter of importance in religion, to be steadfast in that form of profession which we think it our duty, upon proper examination, to make. We must first 'prove all things, and then hold fast that which is good.' But that which is our duty, is the duty of our children also. They ought first to prove, and then to hold fast. To hold fast, without having proved, is behaving neither like Christians, nor like honest men. I greatly dislike the religion of Popery, and yet I think it far better to be a conscientious Papist, than to want honesty; and, amongst all our transactions, honesty is most requisite in our dealings with God. He is the Searcher of hearts, and will not be mocked.

There is, indeed, one piece of deference in religion due to parents, and they have good reason to be displeased with their children if it is not paid to them. Children certainly ought to associate in the public exercises of religion with their parents, till they can choose for themselves what appears to be good. They ought not to desert that profession in which they have been trained up because it is less fashionable than others; or because it may oblige them to a stricter course of religion; or from any other motives but a persuasion, upon due examination, that some other form of Christian profession is more agreeable to the mind of God. To alter a religious profession in which young persons have been educated, on any other ground, is not only extremely disrespectful to their parents, but exceedingly offensive to God, and cannot be reconciled with that godly sincerity which is essential to the Christian character.

Parents have undoubtedly a right to deal with their children on this subject, and to learn what are their reasons for joining in a religious communion different from their own. But they ought to make the same allowance for their children that they require for themselves. If their children appear to act from bad motives, or without motives, they should admonish them of the infinite importance of dealing sincerely, and in the exercise of their best judgment, with God, 'who will bring every work into judgment.' But if their children appear to act sincerely, according to the best judgment which they can form, their parents have no right to deprive them of the privileges of children, for differing in sentiment from themselves.

'He that doubteth is damned if he eat; and whatsoever is not of faith is sin.' This maxim is of very comprehensive import, and is no less applicable to our forms of religious profession, than to the disputes which took place in the church of the Romans, when Paul wrote his epistle to them. Most certainly, any part of our religious profession which is not of faith is sin; and it cannot be of faith, unless it is founded upon the word of God, which we all acknowledge to be the rule, and the only rule, of religion. We cannot believe, if the Scripture is the rule of faith, that any point of doctrine or practice is an article of religion to be professed and held fast by us, unless we can find it in Scripture. That persuasion which depends upon the authority of persons, cannot be any part of that religion which is regulated purely by the word of God. Our fathers may communicate to us what they please of their goods, and may give us good instructions; but they can give us no part of their faith. They may, indeed, persuade us to believe many things upon their authority, and these things may be true and good; but they are no points of faith to us, till we know and believe them upon a higher authority.

On the whole, it is the duty of parents to remember that they once were children themselves, and to govern their sons and daughters with that mildness, and attention to their happiness, with which they wished to be themselves treated in their early years. Childhood and youth, under the direction of good parents, are a happy period of life; perhaps the only happy period which is ever to be enjoyed. Why should young persons be deprived of a happy day, or even a happy hour, but for their greater happiness? All our connections with one another are intended, by a gracious Providence, to make us happy; and they are perverted and abused, when they are not improved for this purpose. It must not, however, be forgotten, that our happiness in youth or age depends not on unstrained liberty. If parents wish to see their children happy, let them 'beware of provoking them needlessly to wrath, lest they be discouraged.'

SERMON II.

THE DUTY OF PARENTS TO THEIR CHILDREN.

EPHESIANS VI. 4.

And, ye fathers, provoke not your children to wrath; but bring them up in the nurture and admonition of the Lord.

II.—Let parents be careful, especially, to 'bring up their children in the nurture and admonition of the Lord.' By 'the Lord' we are to understand the Lord Jesus Christ, our Saviour, and the Author of our religion. 'The nurture and admonition of the Lord' is that course of discipline and instruction, which becomes believers in Christ; which is appointed by Christ; which is well-pleasing to Him; which fits young persons to be followers of the Lord; which he is ordinarily pleased to bless, as the means of faith in Himself, and of obedience to his laws. More particularly:—

1. *Educate your children in the knowledge of Christ, and of their duty.*

It is a great benefit to us who live in Scotland, that we were required, in our younger days, to commit that most excellent of human compositions, the Shorter Catechism, so exactly to memory, that we can scarcely forget the words of it, as long as our memories are able to retain any thing. Be not less careful of the grandchildren of your fathers, than they were of you. See that they learn, and that they remember the instructions of that book, which contains almost every doctrine and duty of our religion within such a short compass, that it can be bought for one of the smallest of our coins, may be read in half an hour, and may be easily learned by heart in the space of one hundred and seven days, although a few minutes only of each day be employed for the purpose.

But the words which the Holy Ghost teacheth are the grounds of our belief of every religious truth; and there is an energy in them which exceeds all human compositions, as much as the sound of thunder exceeds a whisper. Let your children, therefore, by all means, learn the proofs annexed in some of your little catechisms to the various questions. I will not take it upon me to commend any parts of scripture, as if they excelled all other parts of it; but the proofs from scripture adduced in your small catechisms to establish the various articles of religion are not, certainly, inferior in value and usefulness to any other passages of the Bible, and deserve to be imprinted on our memories, for the sake of those doctrines which they establish.

There are other small catechisms well known to you, which may be of great use to parents, as well as children, because they will enable them, with advantage and ease, to explain the important truths of our Shorter Catechism. I wish that they were more used than they are, by persons of mature age; for there are questions in them which many young, or even middle-aged persons, cannot answer. I would not, however, rigorously insist on young persons learning them so exactly as the Shorter Catechism. If they learn them so well as to understand the Shorter Catechism by means of them, the chief design of them is gained.

Let parents encourage, or even request, public teachers to teach their children the Catechism. But this is not all that is necessary for them. Let parents themselves hear their children repeat the questions and answers, and endeavour to make them understand what they repeat, as far as they can be supposed capable of understanding it; for it cannot be expected that they should be able to understand even the Shorter Catechism in every part, and in its utmost extent of meaning. The time and labour, however, are not lost, which are bestowed on every part of it. Having the questions in their memories, they will find them of great use when they are able to understand them better.

Besides the incapacity of children to understand every part

of the Catechism, there is another thing which ought to be considered; that it is difficult, if possible, to engage them to attend to the meaning of the truths contained in it. For this reason, it appears to me highly expedient to try another method of drawing their attention to the capital truths of our religion. The method I mean is, to make them early acquainted with the history of the Bible, by repeating it in their ears, as soon as they are disposed to listen to it, which they will be before they are able to read it, and long before they can derive much profit from the reading. It happens, very disadvantageously to our young people in North Britain, that the language generally spoken is very different in multitudes of words, from the language which we read. Young persons, therefore, have learned to read long before they can form clear apprehensions of the meaning of what they read; nor can they be expected to pay the same attention to the meaning of what they read, as of what they hear. A minute's discourse from the mouth of one whom they respect, will give them, in their earliest years, more knowledge than an hour's reading, if he adapts his manner of speaking to their understanding, and to their taste. Nor will it be difficult for him to know when they understand and relish what he says. Tell them the story of Joseph in a manner suited to their years, and their eyes will be fixed upon you. They will drink in your words as the earth drinketh in the rain. They will almost weep when you speak of the pit, and of the tears of Joseph. They will beg to hear the story an hundred times. They will submit to any task you may choose to impose on them, if you will give them stories about Joseph, or Elijah, or Daniel, or the three children.

When you teach them the histories of the Bible, you teach them its most important doctrines and precepts; for these are contained in the facts which you relate, or arise out of them so naturally, that they will impress themselves upon the minds of your children, whether you mention them expressly or not. What though they cannot tell you what is meant by the almightiness of God, when you have given them the history of the creation? They do not yet understand what is meant by the words used in expressing that attribute of the Most High;

but they see that God does every thing he pleases by the word of his power. Or what though they cannot tell what is meant by original sin? When you have told them the story of Adam's fall, and of the introduction of death into the world by his sin, do they not see as plainly as they can be made to see it, that man was made in a holy and happy state, and that he is now in a state of sin and misery? When you give them the history of the birth, of the life, of the death, of the resurrection of the Son of God, have they not heard the great doctrines that relate to our redemption? Have you not taught them all that you can teach children of the grace and glory of our Redeemer? and if the Spirit of God give the blessing which you seek and expect to your instructions, are they not prepared to love and trust the only Saviour?

By such instructions as these, it may be hoped that they will, with ease, be enabled, in a few years, to form a far clearer judgment than they could do without them, of the truths taught in their catechisms. They will know what is meant by 'Christ's offering up of himself a sacrifice to satisfy divine justice'; what is meant by 'the righteousness of Christ imputed to us'; what is meant by 'the Spirit's application of the redemption purchased by Christ.' For they have already often heard how the Son of God came into the world; how he fulfilled all righteousness; how he became obedient unto death, even the death of the cross; and how he sent his Spirit to men, after he was taken up to heaven.

But, before they can form these apprehensions of the doctrines of religion, which persons of mature age learn, with advantage, from systems of divinity, they may probably derive another advantage of infinitely greater consequence. The things which they have been taught, may be the seed of true faith, and of holy obedience, through the effectual working of the blessed Spirit. When Peter told Cornelius the leading facts of the history of Jesus, intermingling his discourse with a few observations naturally connected with them, the Spirit of God came upon Cornelius and his friends. When the apostles preached the gospel every where, the great subject of their discourses was the things recorded by the evangelists; the life, the works, the sufferings, the death, the resurrection, and exaltation of our Lord. And wherever the gospel was preached, the story of the holy woman that poured oil on his head was told.*

Will it be asked still, What authority I have to recommend this mode of teaching? Do you not remember that Jesus still taught his disciples, and the multitudes, as they were able to to hear and understand? If you are followers of Jesus, teach your children as they are able to hear. What would you think of ministers who preach sermons to their audiences, that can be understood only by students of divinity? Would they not be worthy to be turned out of their pulpits? Do not parents owe the same care to their children, that preachers owe to their hearers?

'Because the preacher was wise, he still taught the people knowledge,' and, that he might do it effectually, 'he sought to find out acceptable words.' Indeed, if your words are not acceptable to your hearers, you may speak as much, and bring forth as much hidden knowledge as you please, but you will

---

* These admirable advices by our author, to parents, in regard to the religious instruction of their children, are as fully suited to our circumstances and times, as they were in his own day to the circumstances of Scottish Christians, to whom they were originally addressed. In some respects, indeed, they may justly be regarded as more specially applicable to Christian parents in these United States of America. In Dr. Lawson's days, and indeed, we may truly say, down to the present time, religious instruction,—particularly, the careful commission to memory of 'the Assembly's Shorter Catechism,' with the use of the Bible as a common school book,—was, and continues to be, an essential part of the common education received in the Parish schools of Scotland; which correspond to our Common schools in the United States: whereas it is well known (and we have taken special pains to ascertain the fact), that, with the exception, perhaps, of the daily reading of a chapter of the Bible by the teacher without note or comment (which last is forbidden by the Directors), religious instruction is systematically and purposely excluded from our American Common schools. That is, by common consent, left to parents and to Sabbath-schools. This is greatly to be regretted. We do not advocate the *forcing* of religious instruction upon children in our Common schools against the wishes of their parents, especially if those objecting parents profess another religion or a different doctrinal faith; but there is little practical difficulty in providing, by proper regulations, for due freedom of conscience in such exceptional cases—as is done in

neither receive thanks, nor can you have the reasonable prospect of doing good; and I do not think you will find out any method of teaching that will be more acceptable to young persons, than that which I have been recommending.

The 78th Psalm may safely be commended as one of the most useful in the whole sacred collection; and one to which we ought to pay a very particular attention, if the address with which it begins is divinely authorized. Now, in this psalm we have a specimen of the manner in which the ancient believers taught their children the truths of God, and nourished them up in the words of faith and of sound doctrine. 'Give ear, O my people, to my law,' says the holy psalm-writer; 'incline your ear to the words of my mouth. I will open my mouth in a parable; I will utter dark sayings of old, which we have heard and known, and our fathers have told

---

the National schools of Ireland, and indeed has always been practically done in the schools of Scotland.

We specially recommend these excellent instructions of our author to parents, to the diligent attention and practice, also, of Sabbath-school teachers. This class of religious instructors has greatly increased since Dr. Lawson's day. And yet we will say, that with all our boasted modern light and improvement in the art of imparting religious instruction to the young in Sabbath-schools, we have never read in any published addresses delivered in modern Sabbath-school Conventions, or listened to from the mouths of modern Sabbath-school orators, any thing at once so pointed and so suitable, as is contained in these few pages by our author, of advices to parents in regard to the religious instruction of their children. How far advanced was our author, even in his time, in regard to the breadth and comprehensiveness of his views, of many in our own day who consider themselves 'representative men,' and who loudly blow their own trumpets in our modern Sabbath-school Conventions!—in some of which, it is to be feared, novel and sensational plans and methods occupy too prominent a place; while too little attention is given to the great business of the Sabbath-school, namely,—the imparting sound and solid religious instruction in the Word of God to the souls of the young.

The subsequent remarks of our author in this passage may also suggest to Pastors the important duty of frequently preaching Sermons exclusively to the young—the lambs of their flock. We are happy to know that a number of Pastors have adopted the practice of preaching a Monthly Sermon to the children of their Sabbath-school—an example worthy of general imitation.—Ed.

us.' What were those things which their fathers had told them? The facts which Moses and Joshua, and other prophets, recorded in their histories. And as their fathers had told them these pieces of history, they were bound, in duty to their fathers, to God, to their own children, to speak of them to the rising race, and might promise themselves the happiest effects from such instructions. 'We will not hide them from their children, showing to the generation to come the praises of the Lord, and his strength, and his wonderful works that he hath done.' They did no more than God had commanded them to do, when they showed to their children the praises of the Lord, and his strength, and his wonderful works. 'For he established a testimony in Jacob, and appointed a law in Israel, which he commanded our fathers that they should make them known to their children; that the generation to come might know them, even the children which should be born, who should arise and declare them to their children, that they might set their hope in God, and not forget the works of God, but keep his commandments.'

We are all commanded to speak of the works of God to one another; and how can we pretend to be lovers of God, if we reckon this commandment grievous? Parents, in particular, are required to speak of the works of God to their children. 'These words,' says Moses, 'which I command thee this day, shall be in thine heart, and thou shalt teach them diligently to thy children, and shalt talk of them when thou sittest in thine house, and when thou walkest by the way; when thou liest down, and when thou risest up.' This precept, as its importance well deserves, is found, almost in the same words, in two different passages of the concluding exhortations of Moses to his beloved nation of Israel; Deut. vi. 6, 7; xi. 18, 19. 'These words which I command thee:'—What words? Not merely the laws which were to be observed by the people, but the histories recorded by Moses, in which alone the meaning of many of them is to be found, and by which they are all powerfully enforced. When the histories were forgotten, the laws were disregarded, or the observance of them was perverted into a mere form, or into something worse. How could it be otherwise, when the express intention of several of the laws was to preserve alive the remembrance of the works of the Lord; to excite the curiosity of those who had not yet heard of them; and to give to parents a favourable opportunity for communicating the knowledge of them to their children. The ordinance of the Sabbath was intended to keep up the remembrance of the work of creation. The ordinance of circumcision was intended to keep up the remembrance of God's gracious 'covenant made with Abraham, the word which he commanded to a thousand generations.' Various other ordinances were appointed to preserve the remembrance of what the Lord did in Egypt, and at the Red Sea, and in the wilderness. 'And it shall be,' said Moses concerning the law of dedicating the first-born to the Lord, 'when thy son asketh thee in time to come, What is this? then thou shalt say unto him, By strength of hand the Lord brought us out of Egypt, from the house of bondage. And it came to pass, when Pharaoh would hardly let us go, that the Lord slew all the first-born in the land of Egypt, both the first-born of man and the first-born of beasts; therefore I sacrifice unto the Lord all that openeth the matrix, being males; but all the first-born of my children I redeem'; Exod. xiii. 14-16. A like injunction is given to the people concerning the feast of the Passover; Exod. xii.

'When Israel was a child, God loved him, and called his son out of Egypt,' and 'led him about, and instructed him,' as a father does the son whom he desires to train up in the way wherein he should go. And one of the ways whereby he instructed him, was by directing Moses to write, for his use, a history of all the most wonderful things that the Lord had done, from the time that man was placed upon the earth. If God suited the means of knowledge and grace to the state of his church when she was yet in her childhood, ought not parents to suit their instructions to the capacity of their children also, and to place before their eyes those sensible displays of divine truth with which we are furnished in so rich abundance by God himself? And if those discoveries of divine things which suited the childhood of the church were effectual means of faith and salvation, who can doubt but means of instruction, suited to the tender age of our own children, may be attended with the same happy effects? Gal. iv. 1–7.

The duties of religion may be taught with great advantage in the same way. Tell them of the faith of Abraham; of the centurion; of the Syro-phenician woman; of Paul; that you may teach them to rely on the power, on the mercy, on the word of God. When you tell them the history of Joseph, you teach them to obey their parents; to love their brethren; to forgive injuries; to bear afflictions; to abhor sin, even when it promises the greatest advantages; and to resist temptations to sin, at the risk of liberty and life. Tell them how Jesus lived, and how he died, and you teach them every virtue.

Whilst the disciples of Jesus were yet but children in understanding, he put them in mind of the miracle of the loaves, when they were afraid of wanting bread; and censured them for not drawing that conclusion which naturally arose from the miracle.

Our Lord exemplifies another method of instruction, which may be very profitably used with children by parents qualified to use it with advantage. He drew the most precious instructions from such objects as were best known to them; and often, perhaps, when these objects were present to their view. At a feast, he spoke of that feast of fat things which is set before us in the gospel. It is probable, that some lilies were in the view of the disciples, and that they beheld some fowls flying about in the air, when Jesus said to them, 'Behold the fowls of the air—Consider the lilies of the field;' Matt. vi. 26–34. Luke xiv. John vi. 26, 27.

I might farther observe, that we are not bound to confine ourselves to the histories of Scripture, in teaching young persons what they are to believe concerning God, and what duty God requires of man. It will be of great use to them, when they are qualified to profit by it, to entertain them with some accounts of God's dealings with the Christian church, in various places of the world, and especially in our own land, and to set before them the brightest examples of virtue which the annals of our forefathers, or any other uninspired writings furnish. Scripture itself often refers us to human histories for useful information; Esther x. 2. Numb. xxi. 14, 15.

2. *Parents must bring up their children in the nurture and admonition of the Lord, by the due exercise of parental authority over them.*

'I know Abraham,' says the Lord, 'that he will command his children and his household after him, to keep the way of the Lord, to do judgment and justice.' If Abraham had only told his family what it was fit for them to do; if he had only advised and urged them to do their duty, without enjoining them to do what was agreeable to the mind of God; he would not have obtained this commendation from the Lord. Eli told his children that their conduct was very offensive to God, and would be followed with fatal consequences to themselves; but because he did not exert his authority to enforce his admonitions, the Lord justly complained of him as a partner in the wickedness of his sons, and threatened to inflict such vengeance on the house of Eli, as would cause the ears of all that heard of it to tingle.

Eli was, indeed, more than a father to his sons, for he was the judge of Israel, and ought to have inflicted on them the penalties of the law; but any father of such sons in Israel might, by a legal process, have procured the execution of these penalties: and although we are neither in Eli's station, nor under the political laws of the Jews, yet we are kings in our own families, and ought to have our children in subjection; for the Lord hath given the father honour over his children, and hath established the authority of the mother over her sons.

When you find it required in those who are to be invested with the office of bishops, that they must 'have their children in subjection with all gravity,' you are not to think that other parents are left at liberty to surrender the authority with which God hath entrusted them over their children. When God will admit none into the sacred ministry that knows not how to govern his own house, he sets a mark of his disapprobation upon all those parents, who, through sloth, or weakness, or foolish fondness, suffer their children to do what they please; 1 Tim. iii. 4, 5; 12.

What would you think of a king, who was so averse to severities in his administration, as to suffer every man in his dominions to do what he pleased? Could the worst tyrant in the world do more to make his subjects miserable and wicked? The mischief that would result to a single family from the want of due control, would bear the same proportion to the state of such a king's dominions, as a family bears to a nation. The exercise of authority in a family where the children are young, is more necessary, if possible, than the due exercise of royal power in a nation; because men of mature age may possibly be able and willing to govern themselves, but every child left to himself must bring his parents to shame. Indeed, the shame of his conduct must fall upon them, rather than upon himself; because it belongs to them, more than to himself, to govern his conduct.

Every father will find it necessary, in many instances, to exercise authority over his children. His house would soon become an unpleasant dwelling to him, if he suffered young children, without restraint, to do whatever they pleased. He will not suffer them to carry burning sticks through the house, or to dash the cups and platters upon the ground. But if parents find it absolutely necessary, for the security of their life and property, to exert authority, why should they not exert it likewise to enjoin on them those duties which God requires, and to restrain them from doing what he forbids? What are we to think of parents who will not allow their children to break a china-cup, and yet will suffer them to break the commandments of God? Can those men be called Christians, who will tolerate sin in their families, whilst they tolerate nothing that is, in the smallest degree, injurious to their secular interests?

Command your children to read the Bible; to learn the questions of their Catechism; to pray every morning and evening. Take them with you to the public assembly of worshippers, and see that they behave with decency and propriety. Forbid them to lie, to sport themselves on the Lord's day, or to behave disrespectfully to those whom they ought to reverence for their station or their age. See that no corrupt communication come out of their mouths. And let your injunctions be suited to their circumstances, their years, and their temptations.

There is nothing in which you will find it more necessary to exert your authority, than in guarding your children against bad company. In that golden book which Solomon wrote, 'to give subtilty to the simple, to the young man knowledge and discretion,' the first precept, after that of fearing the Lord, and giving due honour to parents, is contained in these words: 'My son, if sinners entice thee, consent thou not: My son, walk not thou in the way with them, refrain thy foot from their path.' Nor did the wise man think it sufficient to lay down this precept in the beginning of his book. He often resumes it: 'Enter not,' he says again, 'into the path of the wicked, and go not in the way of evil men: Avoid it, pass not by it, turn from it, and pass away. He that walketh with wise men shall be wise; but a companion of fools shall be destroyed. Hear thou, my son, and be wise, and guide thine heart in the way. Be not amongst wine-bibbers, amongst riotous eaters of flesh.' Admonitions to young persons are admonitions to parents likewise, because parents ought to watch over them as those that must give account. Young children cannot be expected to make a proper choice of their companions, without direction from their parents. And as many vicious young persons are possessed of insinuating manners, and an engaging behaviour, they may render themselves too agreeable to other young persons; in which case, authority, as well as advice, will be necessary to prevent a connection that may be attended with disagreeable consequences. What father would suffer the child whom he loves to go into a house where other children are dying by a putrid fever, or by the small-pox, if he had not already escaped from that disease? How much more pernicious is the infection of bad manners than the small-pox, or the most pestilential fever? Where is our regard to God, or to the souls of our children, if we do not guard them, with greater anxiety, from every thing that may ruin their souls, than from those distempers which may prove fatal to their bodies?

As virtue is a part of religion, and industry is essential to virtuous conduct, it is necessary for those who desire to bring up their children in the nurture and admonition of the Lord, that where circumstances will admit of it, they should make use of their authority to educate them in habits of industry. Men were not made by God to play on the dry land, like the leviathan in the waters. But if habits of industry are not acquired in early years, it will never become pleasant; and those who are not employed in doing something that is good, if they enjoy health, will be doing something that is not good; 1 Tim. v. 13. I do not, however, mean that you should restrain them from employing a reasonable portion of time in those sports which are useful to cheer their spirits, and to strengthen their bodies; especially in that period of childhood when they are yet unfit for useful labour. We behold one of the many instances of divine mercy which we enjoy, when we pass through our towns, and see them full of boys and girls playing in their streets; Zech. viii. 5.

When I exhort you to use your authority over your children, to train them up in the way that they should go, some of you will probably allege that you find it very difficult to maintain your authority; and that you would be glad of some directions on this subject. You have sufficient direction in the text, and in the Proverbs of Solomon. Here you are taught to treat your children with justice and mildness. If you do so, your children are very perverse if they do not obey you. They soon feel their dependence upon you; and if, at the same time, you make them to love you, which it is not difficult to do, your word will be a law to them. There is nothing which they will dread more than offending you, and forfeiting your smiles. A slight hint will do more with them, than a hundred lashes from a tyrant whom his unhappy children despair of pleasing.

Foolishness, however, is bound up in the hearts of children, and words of reproof, or the rod of correction, and, for the most part, both together, are necessary to drive it far from them.

You must reprove and rebuke your children, when they wilfully transgress your orders, or break the commandments of God. It is not mentioned to the honour of David, that he had never said to his son Adonijah, 'Why hast thou done so?' If David had been less sparing of his reproofs, it is probable that Adonijah would not have rebelled against him in his old age. His ambition prevailed over his love to his indulgent father, for his love was not coupled with fear. As a twofold cord is not easily broken, so the united principles of fear and love to parents will, for the most part, be a powerful restraint upon those corrupt dispositions of children, by which they may be tempted to embitter the days of their parents.

When I exhort you to reprove and admonish your offending children, do not imagine that I call you, on any occasion, to cast away the bowels of a father. What father on earth is to be compared, for kindness to his children, with our heavenly Father? and yet he often rebukes, and reproves, and chastens. 'He scourges every son whom he receives;—Be ye followers of God, as dear children,' and frequently recollect, for the direction of your parental behaviour, that you also have a Father in heaven.

Your heavenly Father spares you, 'as a man spares his son that serves him.' He does not enter into judgment with you, because you are not so perfect as the angels of heaven, but he restrains your corruptions by his gracious discipline; and when you do not vigorously oppose the workings of the law of sin in your members, he makes you sensible of his displeasure by the withdrawment of his heavenly consolations, by the upbraidings of your own consciences, or by his rod upon your persons, your estates, your characters. Are you not thankful that he does not leave you to yourselves, but rebukes and chastens you, that you may be partakers of his holiness? Were there any passage of the Bible which assured you of exemption from chastisement, would you consider it as a promise? Would you not consider it as one of the most tremendous threatenings that could be uttered by the mouth of God? Why, then, do you imagine that parental love should hinder you from speaking an unpleasant word to your children? You do not love them, you hate them with a deadly hatred, if you do not reprove and rebuke them with all authority, when you see them sinning against their own souls. If you saw them sporting with a sharp knife, you would run and pull it with all haste out of their hands. If you saw them amusing themselves with an adder, and pleased with the sight of its speckled skin, would you not venture your own lives, to remove it from their reach, before they received a fatal wound from its deadly sting? But no serpent is so deadly as sin. Flee from sin, and cause your children to flee from it, as from the face of a serpent. The teeth thereof are as the teeth of a lion, slaying the souls of men.

When God rebukes his people, he 'remembers mercy in the midst of wrath.' He will not lay upon them more than is meet and necessary for accomplishing the purposes of his love. He adjusts his corrections, not to their demerits, but to his gracious designs of promoting and perfecting the work of their sanctification. Thus, in reproving our children, we ought still to have their benefit in view. We may testify hot displeasure, but we must not discover any degree of hatred or revenge. They are but children, and we who are men have our faults. Their spirits may be crushed, they may despair of ever pleasing us; and such despair may harden their hearts against reproof, when they find us inflamed with fierce resentment for every fault.

The Lord will not contend with his children, nor even with his enemies, without good reason. He would not destroy the Sodomites, though wicked, and sinners before the Lord exceedingly, without 'knowing whether their iniquity was altogether as the cry that had come up unto him.' It is said of our Lord Jesus Christ, that 'he shall not judge after the sight of his eyes, nor reprove after the hearing of his ears, but shall judge with righteousness the poor, and reprove with equity for the meek of the earth.' Thus parents, in reproving their children, are not to proceed upon mere surmises, nor to prostitute their authority by reprimands that may very possibly be undeserved. If a matter is dubious, and yet deserving cognizance, let them rest satisfied with such admonitions as do not imply a presumption of guilt, or let them make proper inquiries before they fix blame. But it is not safe, for the most part, to interrogate children themselves, so as to require them to be their own accusers. This is strongly tempting them to lie; and it is better to let some faults pass uncensured, and to rest satisfied with general admonitions, even where there is a presumption of blameable conduct, than to refer their guilt or innocency to their own testimony. If you tempt them to lie once or twice, you may lead them into a habit of one of the meanest and most pernicious vices of which human nature is capable; for what can be worse than to become exact resemblances of the father of lies? Few men ever lied for the first or the second time, without an inward sense of shame or terror. But, let a child be strongly tempted to lie now and then in order to conceal his faults, and it is very probable that lying will become his habitual practice, and will ruin him both in this world and in the next.

The Lord will not be always contending with his children, he will not draw out his displeasure against them for ever; and fathers that deserve the name will not be constantly reproving their children. This would be to alienate their hearts from their parents, and tempt them to think that parental authority is a yoke too heavy to be borne. It might prompt them to some desperate attempts for shaking it off, and thus produce effects that would be sorely felt to the day of the death of both parents and children, and through eternity itself.

'The Lord is wonderful in counsel, and excellent in working,' both when he smiles upon his children, and when he contends with them. He mingles judgment with mercy, and he regulates and proportions his chastisements with a variety of procedure wonderfully calculated to accomplish the ends which he designs; Isa. xxviii. 23-29. We cannot pretend to a close imitation of the wisdom of His conduct in the management of our children, because we have but a very contracted view of those circumstances, events, and effects, which would determine our conduct if they could be known. We can only conjecture what effect particular acts of parental discipline may have. Yet there are general rules of procedure which it is safe to observe, and which afford no reason for bitter self-reflection, and give no occasion for censure from others, when we observe them, although the consequences may not be such as we wish and expect; for we are not bound to be prophets. We are accountable for the morality of our conduct, but not for its effects.

We ought, in reproving (and the same rule ought to be applied to correction), to consider persons, times, places, circumstances of several different kinds, that the end may, if possible, be gained. There is no partiality in correcting or reproving one child more severely than another for the same fault, if there be a good reason for the difference that is made between them. 'A reproof entereth into a wise man, more than an hundred stripes into a fool.' Some children are wise, and some are foolish. To some a word, or even a hint, is sufficient. To some ten, or a hundred blows, are insufficient to convince them of their errors. Why should parents run into an error, when they are correcting error? Too much, or too little, are both errors. Only, the last can more easily be repaired, because what is undone may be done, but what is done cannot be undone.

There is a time for every thing. There is a time for correcting, and a time for with-holding correction. With-hold not correction when it may be profitable; but, although a fault has been committed, it may be inexpedient to correct, till a more convenient season is come. If, for instance, you correct your child before he is duly informed concerning the nature of his fault, he will be only exasperated and hardened.

There is a sense of honour in the minds of young persons, as well as of their seniors. If you are too open with your reproof and corrections, their sensibility is awakened to violence of passion; and whilst you endeavour to amend a fault, you tempt them to the commission of worse faults. There are, however, cases in which publicity of reproof or correction may be necessary, either to make the impression sufficiently deep on the mind of the child corrected, or for a warning to others. Wisdom is profitable to direct in what cases this may be necessary. So many circumstances must come into account, that it is not easy, if possible, to lay down particular rules, without multiplying and modifying them without end.

One of the most necessary rules concerning admonition and correction is, never to begin without intending to make an end. I do not say, without making an end; because you may have been unwise in beginning, and ought to proceed no further; or circumstances may occur, which render it inexpedient to finish what is begun. But this I say, that when you enter into controversy with any of your children, it is of the utmost importance that you should prevail in the contest. If he gains his point, your authority is weakened, and he is encouraged and emboldened to repeat his offenses. Never, therefore, enter upon a business of this kind, without a reasonable prospect of success. Better to leave your child unchastised, than to chastise him into greater perverseness; which is likely to be the case when you leave him without making him to repent of what he has done, and to resolve that he will do so no more.

There are some parents who do not consider the difference between reproving and threatening. When they are displeased with their children, they do not endeavour to make them sensible of the evil of what they have done, that they may be convinced and reformed, but they terrify them by threatenings; the effect of which will be, that the repetition of the fault may be prevented for some little time, whilst the child is under the eye of the parent, but he will soon lose the impression; or even, whilst it continues, will not scruple to commit the same fault, when he hopes to escape detection. And we know that children easily form such hopes, when they feel themselves inclined to do what they are forbidden to do.

I do not, however, forbid you to make use of threatenings as well as reproofs; for the fear of your displeasure is necessary to check their corrupt propensities; and it is easier to make them sensible of the danger they may incur from your displeasure, than of the baseness of their conduct, or of the danger of punishment from God. But join both together, that they may be taught to hate sin as well as punishment; to fear God, as well as to fear their parents. And take care to threaten no punishment for their faults but what you seriously mean to inflict, and what you are warranted to inflict. Don't tell them that you will break their heads, or that you will cut out their ears, if they again offend you. If they believe such threatenings, they will dread you as they would do a wild beast; and when they find that you do not execute these threatenings, they learn from you to lie. With what face will you ever punish them for lying, if you have taught them, by your example, to speak things that are contrary to their designs, or their thoughts?

But, if you have threatened only such punishment as you are warranted to inflict, let them never have cause to think, that your reproofs and threatenings are but morning-clouds which pass away, and leave no trace behind. Chastise them with all that severity which you have given them reason to expect, that they may not secretly laugh at your great swelling words of vanity, and set at nought all your future reproofs. What would you think of a country that enjoyed the best of laws for checking vice, whilst they were seldom or never executed? If you were born in such a country, you would be compelled, by the abounding of wickedness and violence, to exchange your native country for a place of voluntary exile. And you will soon find your own house a habitation no less uncomfortable, however sharply you threaten, if you never proceed to punish. It may be said of most children (though not all), as Solomon says of servants, that they will not be corrected by words; for though they hear, they will not answer.

I know there are many parents who are sufficiently forward with their reproofs and threatenings; but if their children will not be reclaimed by words, they cannot proceed any farther. The rod of correction would give ten times more pain to themselves than to their children. They will use reproof as well as instruction, to give wisdom to their little ones; but if the rod, too, is necessary for the purpose, they will suffer them to die fools.

But, consider attentively what Solomon says to you on this subject: Bring forth your strong arguments, and he well soon put you to silence.

You will not use the rod to give your children wisdom; but if you do not, you are cruel both to your children and to yourselves. You are cruel to their mother that bare them. You are rebellious against God, who vouchsafes, by Solomon, to give you, not one, but many directions concerning the correction of your children; and who tells you, in plain terms, that 'the rod and reproof give wisdom, but a child left to himself bringeth his mother to shame;' Prov. xxix. 15.

You feel the blows of the rod so sensibly on your own bowels, that you cannot make use of it. But Solomon assures you from God, that your pleasure will greatly overbalance your pain. Your grief must be lasting and incurable, if, through the neglect of any needful part of discipline, that foolishness which is bound up in the hearts of your children is suffered to remain. But, 'correct thy son, and he shall give thee rest; yea, he shall give delight to thy soul;' Prov. xxix. 17.

You love your children, and therefore you cannot bear the thought of making them uneasy. But, if you really love your children with an affection that becomes either a saint or a man, you will not scruple to give them those pains which are requisite for their welfare. Will you not, if they break their legs by a fall, compel them to submit to all that uneasiness which is necessary to restore them the use of their legs? If they are sick, will you not oblige them to swallow those bitter drugs which are necessary for the restoration of their health? Confess that you are more solicitous about the health of their bodies, than the welfare of their souls, if you will not correct them when they do amiss; and that your love to them is of that wretched kind, which, in the language of the Holy Ghost, is rather to be called hatred than love; for 'he that spareth the rod hateth his child; but he that loveth him chasteneth him betimes.'—'He that spareth the rod hateth his child.' I do not deny that this language is figurative; but it is just, it is expressive, it is striking. It contains a just and much-needed admonition respecting that love which all parents ought to bear, and every wise parent will bear, to his children. And if any man should choose to understand the expression literally, his mistake will only be about the meaning of the expression. The sentiment will be just, which the expression, in this sense, conveys. A child left to himself will very probably become odious, even in the eyes of his parents, by behaving so ill as to compel them to hate him, although they were most powerfully prompted by the instincts of nature to love him.

Do you allege, that you may possibly procure to yourselves the hatred of your children, by reproving and correcting them? You are much more likely to procure it by a criminal indulgence of their follies: 'He that maketh too much of his son shall bind up his wounds, and his bowels will be troubled at every cry. A horse not broken becometh headstrong, and a child left to himself will be wilful. Cocker thy child, and he shall make thee afraid: play with him, and he will bring thee to heaviness. Laugh not with him, lest thou have sorrow with him, and lest thou gnash thy teeth in the end. Give him no liberty in his youth (that is, no licentious liberty), and wink not at his follies. Bow down his neck while he is young, and beat him on the sides while he is a child, lest he wax stubborn, and be disobedient unto thee, and so bring sorrow to thine heart. Chastise thy son, and hold him to labour, lest his lewd behaviour be an offense unto thee;' Ecclus. xxx. 7–13. These words are not Solomon's, but they are the words of a venerable Jewish sage, who had learned much from Solomon, and from his observation of human life. And they agree with Solomon's doctrine: 'He that reproveth a man, shall afterwards find more favour than he that flattereth him with his lips. Chastise thy son, and thou shalt have joy of him.'

But what if I should kill him, or crush his spirit?—Why are you afraid of such consequences as these? It is not the sword, but the rod, that is recommended to you, and you are commanded to use it with the wisdom of a man, with the affection of a father: 'With-hold not correction from thy child; for if thou beatest him with the rod, he shall not die.' He shall live. The rod is a preservative from death, and from what is a thousand times worse than death: 'Thou shalt beat him with the rod, and shalt deliver his soul from hell.' You have perhaps heard the story of a young man led to the gallows, who said, 'It is not the judge, it is my mother, that has brought me to this shameful end.' The same thing might have been said by many of those who have suffered for their crimes. And those who are hanged for their crimes are far from being the one-half of those that come to a miserable and untimely end by the fault of their parents, in the neglect of needful discipline.

3. *Parents must bring up their children in the nurture and admonition of the Lord, by setting them a good example.*

Example has a mighty influence upon full-grown men. Peter's example at Antioch had a kind of compulsory influence upon the minds of the Jewish disciples. They knew that Peter was a wiser man than themselves; and when they saw that he would not eat with the Gentiles, 'Surely,' said they within themselves, 'the mind of the Lord is with him;' it must be sinful to eat with the Gentiles; at least, it must be safest, if the case is doubtful, to do as this great apostle does. Thus, a disingenuous bigotry, to the great prejudice of the church, would soon have taken deep root at Antioch, and that city, which gave birth to the Christian name, might have become the beginning of one of the most Antichristian iniquities, if Paul, through divine mercy, had not been strengthened to plead the cause of Christian liberty, against the man to whom, perhaps, of all others, he paid the greatest deference.

What Peter was to Barnabas, and to others that 'were carried away by his dissimulation,' you are to your children, if they possess the modesty which belongs to their age, and feel that affection which becomes their relation to those who gave them birth. Although you are far from equalling Peter, yet your children probably pay you as much deference as Barnabas paid to Peter, and will be as ready to follow your example, and to think that they do well in following it. Have you not heard that the children of Mahometans, for the most part, follow the doctrines of Mahomet; that the children of Papists worship saints and angels; that the heathen nations worship the gods of their fathers, and would reckon it shameful to abandon that religion which has been transmitted to them from many generations of ancestors? Do you not observe, that, for the most part, the children of men who make no pretensions to religion are equally indifferent to it with their parents; and that those who have the happiness to be born of religious parents appear to tread in the footsteps of their fathers; or, if they do not, are despised by those who are no better than themselves, except that they are less inexcusable, because they did not enjoy the same advantage of religious education?

Solomon's words are all true. They are the faithful sayings of God, however little some regard them in their practice; and who is ignorant of the earnestness with which he warns young persons against the company of bad men and bad women? Parents who deserve the name, will endeavour to preserve their children from that pestilence of bad example, which has been the destruction of so many millions of our race. But what are we to think of those parents who are themselves the corrupters of their children, by the practice of those vices which cannot but bring the wrath of God upon all that practise them? Do they deserve the honourable name of parents? Is the life which they have given to their children sufficient to counterbalance that eternal death to which they expose them? Will not many children of Christian parents wish at the last, that their fathers had buried them alive, rather than trained them up in the service of the devil, whose wages are everlasting burnings? Are not godless parents bringing up their children to the great murderer of our race? Is not that death to which they are exposing them, by their pernicious example, a thousand times more dreadful than to be buried alive before they are capable of doing good or evil; before they are capable of adding any actual transgressions to that sin which they bring into the world?

No sentence of a heathen writer hath come more frequently into my mind than one of a Roman poet, who says, that 'the greatest reverence is due to a child.' We must cast no stumbling-blocks, or occasions to fall, in the way of any of our brethren of the human race, but least of all in the way of children; because they are most likely to be hurt, perhaps ruined by them. How do they learn most of the things which they learn, but by imitation? Nature, or rather the God of nature, has wisely appointed this to be the way of learning most of those things which are necessary for the support and comfort of the present life. Without this principle of imitation, we would grow up more rude and uncultivated than the Hottentots. But do not turn this principle into an instrument of destruction to their souls. If you will needs be wicked, be wicked by yourselves, and let no part of your bad conduct appear in the eyes of those who, in all probability, will think that they do right in following your example. You will find the guilt of your own blood heavy enough to bear; why should you go to the eternal world laden with the guilt of destroying more souls than one?

Remember that young persons are neither qualified nor disposed to make the distinctions that you may think easy and natural. You can distinguish between a lie and a jest, which, in the early part of childhood, they cannot do; and therefore, by jesting with them, or in their presence, you may teach them to lie. Although evil-speaking, in general, is sinful, yet you reckon it lawful, on some occasions, to speak of the bad things you have heard of some of your neighbours. But by doing this unguardedly, you may teach them to be backbiters. Abstain from every thing that has the appearance of evil, especially before those who have not yet learned to distinguish between realities and appearances. If one of your elder boys should climb upon the branches of a tree, you will not be displeased with him if he does it only in company with boys of the same size, because they may amuse themselves with the same sport without danger; but if he should do the same thing in the presence of your younger children, you will beat him with severity, because he has taught his younger brothers a lesson that may cost them a broken leg. If you expect that little boys should pay some regard to the consequences of their actions, what excuse remains for you, if you do those things which, though innocent in themselves, may, in their consequences, be productive of eternal misery to persons whose salvation ought to be the object of your constant care?

But it is not sufficient for you to set no bad example, and no example that may prove bad in the use that will be made of it before your children. You must not only cease to do evil, but learn to do well, and make your light so to shine before every beholder, and especially before your own families, that they may see your good works, and glorify your Father which is in heaven.

When you wish to have your children taught a profession to be the employment of their life, you do not send for a man of that profession to come to your house, and lay down and explain all the rules of it. You know, that if he should repeat these rules a hundred times, till they were all deeply fixed in your son's mind, very little is gained. He must see those things done that he is to do, and by careful imitation learn to do what has been done by his teacher; and, therefore, you bind him to an apprenticeship of several years. Does not this consideration convince you of the importance of teaching, by a good example, what is infinitely more important than all arts or sciences?

I do not say, that you are to make a show of your religion before your families, or before the world. That would be setting a bad, and not a good example before them. An ostentatious piety cannot hide that folly and self-conceit which is the principle of it. But there are many duties which are public in their nature; and if you neglect them, or perform them in a careless manner, you wrong, you greatly wrong, the souls of your children. They have eyes in their heads, and perhaps they see better than you imagine, and can apply the proverb, 'Physician, heal thyself,' with no less readiness than yourselves. When you see preachers negligent of those duties which they warmly recommend, you despise them, you look upon them as the most contemptible of all human beings, because they affect airs of seriousness in the pulpit, and show themselves destitute of it every where else. Will not your children think the same of yourselves, when they often hear you recommend prayer, and never hear you pray? when you tell them, that they must daily read the Scriptures, and never take that blessed Book into your hands?

The wise among the heathen nations were very sensible of the importance of being trained to virtue by domestic examples. When the Spartans, subdued by Antipater the Macedonian, were required to give him a certain number of their children as hostages for their good behaviour, their ambassadors answered, that they would rather give him double the number of old men. And when the people in their public assembly were threatened with Antipater's vengeance, if they did not comply with his requisition, they unanimously answered, that it was better to die, than to suffer what was worse than death. Of such importance did the whole city reckon it to be that their young persons should be educated in the observation of the customs of their fathers, which they preferred to all others in the world. Did they value so highly that mode of living which they learned from Lycurgus? What excuse can be made for us, if we discover no anxiety to train up our children in the observation of those holy practices which we have learned from Christ?

'In all things that I have commanded you,' says God, 'be circumspect.' All Christians ought to be careful that they transgress not the least of the commandments of Christ. But parents ought to be doubly circumspect, lest, by some undesigned omission of duty, or some inconsiderate action of life, they hurt the interest of religion in their families for generations to come. There were many good kings of David's family who were much inferior to David their father, because they neglected one thing which probably appeared to them to be of such inferior importance to other parts of duty, that they did not greatly attend to it; and when the more ancient of them, who deservedly obtained a good report, did not attend to it, his descendants would think themselves happy when they walked in his steps, without proceeding any farther in the reformation of the people. You will probably guess that I have in view that defect in the character of Asa, and many of his successors, that they did not remove the high places, where the true God was worshipped, though not agreeably to his own appointment. Asa was the first of Solomon's successors who walked in the ways of David and Solomon. His heart was perfect all his days, but he did not remove the high places. Jehoshaphat was an eminent saint, and yet he did not reckon it necessary to do what his good father Asa had not done.

The following kings, for several generations, were either wicked men, or were far inferior to these two princes in piety; and the high places kept their ground, till a man arose to bless Judah, who was not inferior to David himself, and who was too wise to pay any regard to what either Asa or Jehoshaphat did, unless he found it agreeable to the law of Moses. Hezekiah was a second David; and although his son and grandson were wicked, the third in descent from him, Josiah by name, trod in his steps, and like these two men there was no king in Judah, before or after them.

The wise and good should endeavour, for the sake of their children, as well as for their own sake, to be wise and good in every thing. Solomon was the wisest of men, but he was unwise in multiplying wives, and in multiplying horses: and we find, that his two next successors took many wives, and that all his successors made more use of horses than the law of Moses allowed, till that King of Zion appeared, who came 'riding into Jerusalem upon an ass, and upon a colt, the foal of an ass.'

Abraham was wise and good beyond most men that ever lived. There are, however, two things in his conduct that do not merit imitation: his marrying Hagar, and his dissimulation about Sarah. The first of these was not likely to mislead Isaac; he knew too well what it was to have an Ishmael for a brother, and a Hagar for a stepmother and a rival to his true mother, to bring a Hagar or an Ishmael into his own family. But in the other blameable, or suspicious instance of his father's behaviour, he made no scruple of following him. What Abraham did in Egypt, and in Gerar, Isaac made no scruple of doing at Gerar. What Abraham did, not once, but twice, Isaac might think could scarcely be wrong.

Perhaps you may think, that the instances I have produced, instead of being warnings against uncircumspection of conduct, are rather apologies for your defects. You cannot hope to be better men than Abraham, and therefore you deserve little blame if your conduct deserves as little reprehension as his. But have you Abraham's virtues to set against his defects? or, have you the same excuses for the defects of your conduct that

Abraham had, who enjoyed but a very small part of that revelation of the will of God which you enjoy, and whose temptations were a thousand times harder to be overcome than yours? But remember, besides, that if you live uncircumspectly because Abraham erred twice or thrice in his conduct, you can have no pretense to say that you walk in the steps of Abraham. He did not walk uncircumspectly. The strictest Christians amongst us are chargeable with more defects in conduct than Abraham. If you will not take good heed to your ways, your errors in conduct will be perhaps every day more numerous, or worse than the errors of his whole life after he attained to the knowledge of God. When you have done all that you can to guard against offensive conduct, you will not be more free from blemishes than the holy men of ancient days.

Remember also, that the good men of ancient days were far from approving of those evil things which, through the overpowering force of temptation, they sometimes did. No saint spoken of in the Bible gave more offense by some parts of his conduct, than Solomon; but none could be more sensible than Solomon, after he repented, of the mischief which may follow single instances of misconduct in the wise and good. There is a warning in the last of his books, which, if men would attend to it, might do more good than ever the example of his irregularities did hurt: 'Dead flies cause the ointment of the apothecary to send forth a stinking savour: so doth a little folly him that is in reputation for wisdom and honour'; Eccl. x. i.

I have spoken of what parents ought, in their own persons, to do for bringing up their children in the nurture and admonition of the Lord. But it is not to be expected that most fathers can do every thing needful to be done for this purpose. Children are commonly sent to school, where they ought to receive instruction in religion, as well as in reading and writing; and parents, if they have the opportunity of making a choice, ought to give a preference to those schools where their children are likely to be best educated, by instruction and example, in the knowledge of religion, and in the practice of virtue. If we have horses to be trained up for riding, we put them into the hands of those men who are most likely to break them to the saddle, and to cure them of every vicious habit. If we have ground to cultivate, we employ such servants as are best skilled in the use of the plough, and in every part of husbandry; and we do not grudge the best wages to those who are likeliest to give us satisfaction by their work. If we are less careful to find proper teachers for our children, we deserve the reproof which the philosopher Crates gave to the Athenians, 'O ye Athenians! why are ye so careful to provide estates for your children, and so careless about providing children for your estates?'

There is a complaint among some parents, that schoolmasters are not so careful as they have been in some former times, to teach their pupils the principles of religion. The complaint, I am afraid, is just: but parents ought to leave a part of it on themselves. Schoolmasters, I think, would be more careful of this part of their duty, if the parents of their pupils would roundly inform them that the neglect of it is very disagreeable to them. When we think we have reason to complain of our neighbours, let us complain first of all to themselves. Perhaps they will reform their conduct, and leave us no reason to complain to others. If they do not, we will complain to others with a better grace.*

Sabbath-schools are now set up in many parts of our land. These, it is to hoped, will be an excellent help to those parents who desire to educate their children in the fear of God; for emulation will prompt children to learn those things with

---

* See Note on p. 354 of this edition. These observations of the author should suggest to Christian parents the importance of their using their utmost exertions to have pious Common school teachers appointed in their School District; and to Ministers of the Gospel the duty of exerting their influence to that end: and to see to it that *religious instruction* form an essential part of the instruction received in the Common School. Especially should they exert themselves to have religious as well as well-informed and intelligent School Directors elected (among whom there should always be one or more godly Ministers); who will take a deep interest in securing that our youth be educated in the fear of the Lord.

When this cannot be obtained in the Common Schools, it should be a serious consideration with parents whether these important benefits might not be secured for their children in private schools.—ED.

alacrity, which they will not easily be induced to learn without companions. Fathers, therefore, it may be presumed, will encourage them, from a regard to the welfare of their own children, as well as to the welfare of the rising generation in general. And if any parents are too negligent to bestow all that care which is requisite for the instruction of their own families, it is to be hoped, that they will at least take the trouble of sending them to places where they may be taught without any expense to themselves. There are some parents whom poverty may excuse for not employing physicians to cure the diseases of their children; but no excuse could be made for them, if they refused to employ a physician who undertook to cure their children without reward. Instruction is as necessary to the mind of a child, as medicine to his body in a fever; and so much the more necessary, that there is not the same natural vigour in the mind, as there often is in the body, to expel disease without the application of means.

But nothing is more necessary for bringing up children in the nurture and admonition of the Lord, than fervent prayer to God, for his blessing upon all the means used for this purpose. The endeavours of parents must be as ineffectual as the endeavours of ministers, to communicate good impressions, without divine influence; and yet all will acknowledge, that those preachers are unworthy of the pulpit, who do not accompany their public ministrations with the fervent devotions of the closet. Melancthon, that great reformer, when he was yet a young man, and not acquainted by experience with the perverseness of mankind, flattered himself with the hope, that men would find it impossible to resist the force of those truths which he was able to represent to their minds; but he soon found, when he proceeded to the trial, that 'old Adam was too strong for young Melancthon.' And old Adam is strong in the youngest of his off-spring. The wise man speaks of young persons who, with bitter remorse, will be compelled to say at the last, 'How have I hated instruction, and my heart despised reproof, and have not obeyed the voice of my teachers, nor inclined mine ear to them that instructed me!'

There are, indeed, several proverbs of Solomon which give

us ground to hope, that good and seasonable instruction will have the desired effect. These passages are proverbs, not direct promises. They express what is generally found by experience to be the case; not what will always be the case. They are not, however, to be considered as words of human wisdom. They are proverbs dictated by the Spirit of God, and imply a promise in them, to be understood with the same limitations as many other promises in the Bible. God does not intend by them to limit his own sovereignty, by bringing himself under obligations to communicate saving grace as an hereditary right to the children of the faithful, any more than he binds himself by the promises of success to faithful ministers, to convert, by the power of his Spirit, all their hearers; 1 Tim. iv. 16. Parents, therefore, must not trust to the best means they can use for promoting the spiritual welfare of their children. Sensible of their own unfitness to perform any useful service to God without help from above, they must pray for that wisdom and fervency of spirit which is necessary for themselves, that they may perform the important duties of a parent, in a manner acceptable to God, and useful to their children. Sensible of the power of that corruption which dwells in the hearts of their children, and of the absolute sovereignty of divine grace, they must pray for a divine blessing on the instructions, admonitions, and corrections, which they dispense to them. The use which they ought to make of the promises of success to their endeavours, is to encourage them in praying to the Father of lights, the God of all grace, that he would verify his words, and fulfil the delightful hopes which they are fitted to inspire. If you ask a blessing on your children's food, as well as your own, because you know that God only can give a nutritive virtue to our bodily provisions; is it not equally necessary to solicit his blessing on their spiritual provision? If, when you call the physician to apply remedies to their distempers, you would reckon it presumptuous to 'seek to the physician, and not unto the Lord'; is it not equally blamable to expect any benefit from the means you use to heal the distempers of their souls, without fervent applications to the throne of grace for a blessing on these means?

SERMON III.

THE DUTY OF PARENTS TO THEIR CHILDREN.

EPHESIANS VI. 4.

And, ye fathers, provoke not your children to wrath; but bring them up in the nurture and admonition of the Lord.

III.—I now proceed to consider with what propriety the apostle conjoins, in our text, the caution against provoking your children to wrath, with the command to bring them up in the nurture and admonition of the Lord.

1. *Love to parents is an essential part of that religion in which they are to be educated; and, therefore, parents should do nothing that may be expected to alienate the affections of their children.*

You know very well that it is your duty to love your wives; and yet if your wives are every day teazing and disquieting you with clamour, contradiction, reflections, and sullen behaviour, you find it almost, if not altogether, impossible to love them. Although your consciences tell you that it is your duty, although common sense teaches you that it is your interest, although the gospel suggests motives of infinite strength to enforce the duty; yet you will find it very difficult to refrain from hating them, and wishing that their tongue were silenced for ever by an incurable palsy. How, then, do you imagine that your children will love yourselves if you hold them in constant uneasiness, by a severe and stern behaviour? Can you reasonably hope that, at their years, they will behave more wisely, or feel the power of conscience more forcibly, or make a better use of the motives of the gospel enforcing obedience, than yourselves might be expected to do in a similar case?

Many parents complain of the disregard shown them by their children. Children are exceedingly blamable, when they give just occasion for such complaints. But parents, in many cases, deserve a share and a double share, of the blame. They are Satan's agents in tempting their children to hate themselves, by a behaviour naturally calculated to inspire aversion.

Now, if you tempt your children to hate their own parents, how can you teach them that religion which is summed up in the love of God and man? 'If a man say, that he loves God, whom he hath not seen, and hates his brother, whom he hath seen, he is a liar'; and whom shall a man love if he love not his own parents, who are, under God, the instruments of his being?

2. *Parents ought to avoid all that behaviour which may excite disaffection in their children, that their instructions and admonitions may be received with pleasure.*

Young persons will learn nothing, unless they taste some pleasure in what they endeavour to learn; and they are very unlikely to take any pleasure in instruction when it begins to be communicated to them, if they feel an aversion to the persons of their instructors. They cannot be expected to know and relish the pleasures of what they learn, till they make some advances in knowledge, and feel, in some degree, the energy of truth; Prov. ii. 10, 11.

Before the trouble of learning is sweetened by this experience, they must be allured by the kindness of their instructors; and even after religious knowledge is become in some degree pleasant, the remaining toil of learning, and the pain that attends necessary admonitions and corrections, must be qualified by that love to their teachers which kind usage cherishes, and which unnecessary rigour tends to destroy. Scripture tells us, that we ought to esteem very highly in love, those who are over us, and admonish us. For what reason? That with pleasure we may drink in their intructions and admonitions. For this reason, public teachers ought to behave in such a manner as to gain, if possible, the love of those whom they are appointed to teach. Such was Paul's behaviour. No man valued human applause less than Paul, 'for if I should yet please men,' says he, 'I should not be the servant of Christ;' yet no man was more careful, by a meek and gentle behaviour, to gain the attachment of those whom he taught. 'We were gentle among you,' says he to the Thessalonians, 'even as a nurse cherisheth her children. So, being affectionately desirous of you, we were willing to have imparted unto you, not the gospel of God only, but our own souls also, because ye were dear unto us.' And again, 'You know how we exhorted, and comforted, and charged every one of you, as a father doth his children.' The blessed apostle could find no happier illustration of that gentleness and kindness which he showed to his beloved hearers, than the gentleness of a nurse in cherishing the tender babe committed to her care; or the tenderness with which a father exhorts, and comforts, and charges his son: as if that man were not a father, but an alien, or an enemy, who deals harshly with his children.

If even full-grown men must be treated with mildness by their teachers and rulers, that they may receive instruction, and submit with cheerfulness to lawful authority, how much more is this gentle treatment necessary for children, who are less able to understand the advantage of instruction and government? If those who are parents in a figurative sense only, ought to treat their children with kindness, may it not be expected still more from those who are parents in the literal sense; from those who are parents, both in the flesh, and in the Lord; from those to whom kind behaviour is so natural, and from whom it is so ordinarily to be expected, that other relations to whom authority belongs are called fathers, to express the kind regard which they ought to bear towards those who are under their authority?

3. *Parents are to teach their children by example, as well as by their words.*—Now, that mildness of behaviour which the apostle recommends, is one distinguishing part of that Christian conduct which they ought to recommend by their example; because it must be visible to the eye of every beholder.

There are many of the most essential parts of religion which are secret in their nature, and cannot be made public without the appearance of affectation. Many are the aspirations of the

Christian after God, which none can witness. Many are the charities dispensed by an affluent Christian, with such secrecy, that his left hand scarcely knows what his right hand doth. The Christian feels bitter pangs for his sins, which no eye but the eye that sees all things can discern. To proclaim such acts of religion would not exhibit a good example. It would discover a vain and ostentatious temper of mind, as remote from the spirit of religion as pride is from humility. But there are good works which cannot be hid where they exist, and, by care to excel in them, we must make our light to shine before men. 'Whatsoever things are lovely, whatsoever things are of good report; if there be any virtue, if there be any praise, we must think on these things,' and practise them before the world, and in particular before our families, that they may glorify God, by walking in our steps.

I know you think that you ought to read God's word, to pray, to sing God's praises before your family. You would be ashamed to teach your children such duties, witthout letting them see that you practise them. But he that said, 'Thou shalt worship the Lord thy God, and him only shalt thou serve,' said likewise, 'Ye parents, provoke not your children to wrath, lest they be discouraged. Let your moderation (or meekness) be known unto all men.' If it must be made known unto all men, it ought especially to be made known unto your own families, whom you are bound to love with the most tender regard. Give no indulgence to an imperious temper any where, but especially in that place where no redress can be obtained if you act the tyrant. Remember that the meekness and gentleness of Christ was one eminent part of that lovely example which he left us; and that he no where appeared more amiable than in his own family. Remember that meekness and gentleness are distinguishing characters of that wisdom which must appear in your own conduct, and which you must teach your children: 'Who is a wise man, and endued with knowledge among you? let him show, out of a good conversation, his works with meekness of wisdom.' That wisdom which is not joined with meekness is not the Christian wisdom. It is not 'the wisdom from above.' It is 'earthly, sensual, devilish! But the wisdom which is from above is first pure, then peaceable, gentle, and easy to be intreated, full of mercy and good fruits, without partiality, and without hypocrisy;' James iii. 13-17.

We are all most deeply affected and impressed by those things that come nearest to ourselves. You may, then, believe that your children will be most deeply impressed by that part of your conduct which most nearly affects their comfort and happiness. No part of your behaviour will more likely be imitated by them, than your behaviour to themselves. If you wish them, therefore, to make themselves amiable to all around them, behave towards them with every reasonable expression of kindness. If you desire to see them contentious and quarrelsome, and ready on every occasion to pour forth torrents of abusive language, you cannot train them up more effectually in such an odious manner of behaviour, than by frequently provoking them to anger without any justifiable cause.

4. *It is of vast importance to guard young persons against the common, but false and pernicious notion, that the ways of wisdom are not pleasantness and peace.*—But, instead of guarding them against this notion, you infuse it into their minds by harsh and rigorous behaviour.

All men desire to enjoy pleasure; but, above all, young persons and children, who have yet little relish for profit or honour, and therefore place the greatest part of the happiness of life in pleasure, and its chief misery in being denied those gratifications from which it results.

We have often heard of religious parents, whose days of old age have been imbittered by the bad behaviour of those children that have been, with the utmost care, educated in the knowledge and practice of religion. One cause of it has sometimes been, that the parents have over-done in this great duty of educating their children religiously. They have been too severe and harsh in their admonitions and reproofs. They have held the reins of discipline with too strait a hand, and have not duly considered the difference between youth and mature age; between babes, and young men, and fathers in Christ.

I am far from wishing any indulgence in sin to be granted to children, or connivance at the neglect of any necessary duty.

I do not say that they ought to be allowed too much time even for their lawful diversions. But this I say, that they ought to be governed as much as possible by love, and that the love of their parents should be made apparent to them in their general course of behaviour, unless their faults exceed the ordinary faults of young persons of their age. I plead not for sin, but for the honour of religion, when I contend, that compassion and kindness should be shown even to offending children, when they give signs of repentance; and often, too, before they give signs of repentance, that they may be the more easily induced to repent. 'When Israel was a child,' says God, 'then I loved him. I taught Ephraim also to go, taking them by the arms. I drew them with cords of a man, with bands of love, and I was to them as they that take off the yoke from their jaws, and I laid meat unto them.' If the Lord had not showed all that sparing mercy and tender kindness to his nation in their state of childhood, he would not have accounted their defections so inexcusable as they were. 'What iniquity,' says he, 'have your fathers found in me, that they are gone away far from me? Have I been unto Israel a barren wilderness, or a land of darkness? Wherefore say my people, We are lords, we will come no more unto thee?' Had God been a barren wilderness unto them, they might have pleaded something to excuse themselves, when they came no more unto Him. If he had not drawn them with the cords of love, and with the bands of a man, they could not, indeed, have alleged that there was any unrighteousness with Him; but their alienation from God would have been ten times less aggravated. Thus, likewise, if, through the austerity of parents, religion feels as a load to their children, which they will shake off as soon as it is in their power, they deserve pity as well as blame; and those, whosoever they be, that give occasion for unjust suspicions concerning the ways of God, must bear their own burden.

Our blessed Lord, by his example, taught us how to avoid both the dangerous extremes of suffering sin in his pupils, and of discouraging their hearts by needless austerities. When Peter spoke against the cross, he reproved him with severity as an agent of the devil; and yet, when the same man, with his companions, gave way to sleep in the time of our Lord's agony, he only said, 'What! could ye not watch with me one hour?' He never with-held needful admonitions, but administered them in such a way as to show that his love to his disciples was not abated by their infirmities. He taught and enjoined every needful duty, and yet he did not require from them such frequent fastings as those of which John's disciples and the disciples of the Pharisees boasted. The reason for this part of his behaviour was, that his disciples were yet but children in their attainments, and that the time was not yet come when such fastings were requisite; Mark ii. 18–22. 'He fed his flock like a shepherd; he gathered his sheep with his arm; he carried the lambs in his bosom; he gently led those that were with young. The bruised reed he did not break; the smoking flax he did not quench.' He behaved with all that meekness of wisdom which became the author of our salvation, the great pattern of all that is amiable and condescending. Thus he still acts towards his people; thus he acts towards us who have the inspection of the souls of our fellow-mortals; thus he acts towards those whom he has placed under our inspection; and if we have ever seen the glory and beauty of the meekness and gentleness of Christ, we will endeavour to recommend his laws to all around us, by making it to appear, that, according to our measure, we are changed into the same image.

HAVING thus shown, that the apostle, with his usual wisdom, requires parents to show forth the meekness and gentleness which becomes the followers of Christ to their children, whilst they endeavour to 'bring them up in the nurture and admonition of the Lord'; and having recommended the leading duties necessary to be practised by Christians, in the holy education of their children; I shall conclude this discourse with an address, first to children, and then to parents.

1. *To children.*—From what has been said, you who are children must not infer, that your parents are to blame when they do not gratify your humours, or when they administer the rod of correction at times, or in a degree, that you may think unneces-

sary. You are not so wise as your parents. They know far better than you do what methods of behaviour are best calculated for your advantage. It does not, at least, become you to think otherwise. You are apt to be partial to yourselves; and in nineteen instances out of twenty you will mistake in judging for yourselves against them, in your own favour. A modest child will be, for the most part, disposed to think that his parents treat him as well as he ought to be treated, although he cannot discern the reason of their conduct.

I confess there are too many instances in which parents violate the rule of the apostle, which I have been endeavouring to explain; and there are some instances in which they may violate it so palpably, that children themselves must see it, unless they should seal up their eyes. Jonathan could not but see that Saul did not act the part of a father to him, when he loaded him with bitter words, and threw the javelin against him. But remember that your duty to your parents does not lose its obligation by their bad behaviour. They are your parents still. The fifth commandment is still in force. It is harder to observe it, but it must be observed, if you mean not to transgress the laws of your heavenly Father, who surely never treated you harshly.

A certain Roman, in the days of Paganism, called Titus Manlius, was extremely ill treated by his father, for no other reason but a defect in his speech. A tribune of the people brought an accusation against the father before the people, who hated him for his imperious conduct, and were determined to punish him with severity. The young man came one morning very early from his father's country-farm, where he was forced to live in the style of a slave, and, finding out the house of the tribune who had impeached his father, compelled him to swear that he would immediately drop the prosecution. Oaths being at that time held inviolable in Rome, the tribune declared before the people, that he withdrew his charge against old Manlius, because his son Titus had obliged him to promise upon oath that he would carry it no farther. The people, charmed with the filial piety of Titus to an unnatural father, not only forgave the old man, but next year advanced his generous son to the supreme honours of the state. Here you see how men, guided only by the light of nature, approved and admired filial love to an imperious father. How inexcusable, then, will you be, if, under the light of divine revelation, you cannot, for the sake of Christ, who died for you when you were his enemies, behave dutifully to relations who do not behave dutifully to you?

Did Jonathan rebel against his father for affronting him in the most outrageous manner, and seeking the blood of a friend whom he loved as his own soul? No: Jonathan speaks in a becoming manner of his father to David, when he was forced to acknowledge his injustice, and fought and fell by his father's side in the fatal battle of Gilboa. If he had not continued to behave with propriety to a harsh father, David would not have found reason to say in his funeral elegy, 'Saul and Jonathan were lovely in their lives, and in their death they were not divided.'

You have an infinitely nobler example than Jonathan, to teach you to behave well to friends that give you too good reason to be dissatisfied with their conduct. You have the example of our suffering Redeemer. He called the apostles 'his friends and his brethren'; yet they all forsook him, and fled, when he was suffering for them. But did he desist from his redeeming work? did he abate in his love? 'Having loved his own which were in the world, he loved them unto the end,' and gave them the brightest displays of his love at the very time when they dealt deceitfully with him, like the stream of brooks that pass away.

Seek grace from God to behave dutifully to every friend that behaves undutifully to you, and you shall in no wise be unrewarded. Consider what Peter says of the duty of servants to bad masters. May it not be applied to the duties of children to parents, and to the duties of every other relation, where harsh severity on the one part takes place of that gentleness which the nature of the relation requires? 'Servants, be subject to your masters with all fear; not only to the good and gentle, but also to the froward. For this is thank-worthy, if a man for conscience towards God endure grief, suffering wrongfully. If, when ye do well, and suffer, ye take it patiently, this is acceptable with God. For even Christ suffered for us, leaving us an example that we should follow his steps'; 1 Peter ii. 18–25.

2. *To Parents.*—I might now dismiss the subject with a very short appeal to the consciences of those who are parents, whether there is any thing in the present life to which you are bound more carefully to attend, than to the duties which are here enjoined by the authority of Christ? But I will yet beg your patience a little longer, that I may say something more on your children's behalf. Their souls are exceedingly precious. If, by a few more arguments, I can prevail on any parents to do what they can for the salvation of their children, the patience of the whole assembly will be well bestowed, and well recompensed. If a single child in the assembly had fallen down dead, like Eutychus, from the loft, would you think your time ill bestowed, if you should all wait together a full hour, to see if any of you could do any thing that might be a means of restoring him to life?

I need not exhort you separately, To beware of provoking your children to wrath; and, To be careful about training them up for God. When you are exhorted to bring them up for God, you are exhorted at the same time to show them all that kindness which is so necessary to sweeten your instructions and reproofs. When the physician prevails on you to administer some bitter drug to your child, he will not need many words to persuade you to cover it over with some palatable ingredient.

(1.) *For God's sake, who has commanded you to 'bring up your children in the nurture and admonition of the Lord,' neglect not this comprehensive duty.*—Are you Christians? Then you are the servants of God; and what has the servant to do but what his master requires? Every good servant will cheerfully endeavour to execute the commandments of a good master.

The least intimation of the will of God will certainly be regarded by all that 'join themselves to the Lord to serve him, to love the name of the Lord, to be his servants.' But the commandment in our text is certainly to be considered as one of the greatest commandments. What doth your gracious Master require from you, but that you should promote his glory to the utmost of your power, by working out your own salvation, and by contributing your influence to promote the salvation of your fellow-sinners? those, especially, who are under your authority. Say not, 'If I work out my own salvation, what more can be required from me?' You cannot work out your own salvation, if you are not deeply concerned about the salvation of your children. If God 'work in you both to will and to do,' you will feel ardent desires to promote the salvation of your fellow-men; and these desires will not sleep in your bosoms. They will be expressed in earnest endeavours, where there is a probability that these endeavours will not be in vain in the Lord.

Attend, all ye who call yourselves the people of the Lord, unto one of his laws which I am going to recite in your ears. It is a law which he hath established in his church, that the glory of his name might be advanced in every age, and transmitted by every present generation to every succeeding generation: 'He established a testimony in Jacob, and appointed a law in Israel, which he commanded our fathers, *that they should make them known to their children.*' This, certainly, is not one of those temporary laws which were to be abolished at the time of reformation. If we 'surname ourselves by the name of Israel,' we will certainly acknowledge that this law of the God of Jacob demands our most attentive regard.

What is the most earnest desire of every Christian? Is it not that he may be enabled to walk worthy of the Lord unto all pleasing? If so, let it be remembered, that the way of pleasing God is, 'to stand perfect and complete in all the will of God.' And this is certainly an eminent part of his revealed will, that we should endeavour to train up our children for his service. How well he is pleased with obedience to his will in this point, is plain from the gracious words spoken concerning Abraham; Gen. xviii. 18, 19. Abraham was the friend of God, and God would hide none of all those secrets from him, which it might be of use to him to know. But, how did it appear that Abraham was the friend of God? 'Shall I hide from Abraham,' said the Lord, 'that which I do, seeing I know Abraham, that he will command his children and his household after him, and they shall keep the way of the Lord to do judgment and justice, that I may bring upon Abraham that which I have spoken of him.' Abraham's children that were chiefly to enjoy and improve his instructions were not yet born; but God knew that Abraham would command them, as soon as it was possible to command them, to keep the way of the Lord; and God will not suffer Abraham to go unrewarded at that time, for what he was afterwards to do. Many good works had Abraham already done for God, and yet God mentions none of them. The God who knows all things, knew that he would command his children, and his household after him, to keep the way of the Lord. This instance of his piety is singled out from all others by God, when he designed to do him honour, and to reward his piety with a distinguished token of his friendship. Think not within yourselves that Abraham is your father, if you do not the works of Abraham; or that Christ will acknowledge you as his friends, if you keep not this important commandment, of bringing up your children in the nurture and admonition of the Lord. By obeying it, you not only prove your fidelity in one part of your duty, but, as far as lies in you, you cause the commandments of the Lord to be observed by your children after you. By neglecting it, you are chargeable with innumerable acts of disobedience in one, because the iniquities of your children, the consequences of your neglect, will be justly placed to your account.

(2.) *I urge you to perform this duty from a regard to your children.*—You love them. But how do you show your love to them? Is it only by providing for them those things that are necessary for their bodies? But, wherein are you better than the most stupid or ferocious animals, if your views, either for yourselves or for your children, are confined within such narrow bounds? Do not even tigers and lionesses provide what is needful for the subsistence of their young? Perhaps you say, that you educate them to be useful and accomplished members of society, by giving them instruction in arts or sciences. This is certainly good in its place. But what do you more than heathens, if you do not likewise teach them to fear God? Or do you not rather come short of the heathens, who used to train up their children in the knowledge and worship of the gods of their fathers?

You know that your children were born in a state of sin and misery, and that it would have been good for them never to have been born, if they are never recovered from that state. None can recover them from it but God, who has appointed parental instruction and discipline as one of the principal means for this purpose. If you do not apply this mean, what obligation are they under to you for giving them a life, which, for any thing that you will do to prevent it, must be miserable beyond expression through endless ages? If you saw them ready to be cast into a burning fiery furnace, what would you not do to save them? Would you not part with every shilling of your property, with the clothes on your back, almost with your lives, to buy them a pardon, if they were condemned by human laws to the flames? But such flames soon exhaust their power to torment. The flames of hell are eternal, and all sinners must 'dwell with these everlasting burnings,' who are not 'washed, and sanctified, and justified in the name of the Lord Jesus, and by the Spirit of our God'; whose ordinary method of operation is not by immediate inspiration, but by that knowledge of the truth which is obtained through the means appointed by himself. No doubt, the Spirit of God can work by other means than parental instructions, or without means, if he pleases. But God can likewise provide food and raiment for children without the help of their parents, or he could feed us all with bread from heaven, as he fed the children of Israel in the desert; and yet no man will neglect the ordinary means of providing for himself, or for his family, unless he is deprived of the use of his understanding.

Would you not be very diligent in labouring for your families, if you saw a rational prospect of providing a rich estate for them by the blessing of God upon your industry? No man can have a more rational prospect of laying up a rich portion for his children by his utmost industry, than Christians have of being instrumental in the 'deliverance' of those children whom they train up for God, 'from the power of darkness,' that, being 'translated into the kingdom of God's dear Son,' they may possess 'the inheritance which is incorruptible, undefiled, and that fadeth not away.' Will you be more careful to provide for the fruit of your bodies the meat that perisheth, than the meat which endureth unto eternal life? Are you more anxious to see them in possession of enjoyments which cannot continue with them seventy or eighty years, and probably will not continue with them half that time, than to be blessed with the transporting hope of seeing them in possession of those eternal pleasures which are at the right-hand of God; of those pleasures which were purchased, not with corruptible things, such as silver and gold, but with the precious blood of Christ? What, then, must we think of your temper of mind? Are you to be ranked with those who mind earthly things; or with those who have their conversation in heaven, from whence we look for the Saviour? with those who look at the things which are seen, and are temporal; or with those who look at the things which are not seen, and are eternal? Judge for yourselves!

I know what some will think, although, perhaps, they will not say it. They love their children very well; but they see that the duties recommended to them would put them to a great deal of trouble, and the success of their endeavours is very uncertain. They would gladly submit to all the toil, if it were certain that their children would obtain all those advantages from it which have been mentioned. But good parents have sometimes bad children, after all the pains they can bestow upon them, and therefore they will leave it to God to deal as he pleases with their own children; only using such means to instruct them in their duty, as other people around them use.

Why do you grudge the trouble of doing your duty to your children? Did you ever hope to bring up a family without trouble? You certainly read the Bible before you married your wives, and heard Paul telling you, that those persons who wished to have wives, or husbands, must expect trouble in the flesh. Is trouble to be grudged only when it is intended to serve the best purposes in the world? You must have some trouble while you live in a troublesome world. But no troubles are so well recompensed with pleasure and advantage, as those which are cheerfully endured in the service of God. Indeed, if we are faithful servants to God, our troubles will be turned into pleasures. Love to Rachel made Jacob's service of Laban pleasant, although he was exposed to the scorching heats of the day, to the freezing colds of the night, yea, to what is more grievous than both, the ill usage of a hard uncle. Will not love to Christ, and love to your children, make those labours pleasant, which are designed to promote the glory of Christ in the salvation of your children?

But here, you will say, lies the hardship,—'What reason have I to hope that my children will receive any saving benefit?' I say, on the other side, what knowest thou, O man! whether thou shalt save thy children? If this is not a sufficient motive for trying it, Paul was a bad reasoner, although he was taught by a greater master than Gamaliel. I confess that your labours may be unsuccessful; but you must grant that it is very possible, if not highly probable, that they may be successful. If they are not successful with all your children, they may be with some. 'I know Abraham, that he will command his children, and his household after him, and they will keep the way of the Lord.' Well do we know that many of Abraham's children after him did not keep the way of the Lord. The number of his natural seed that kept the way of the Lord, has not hitherto been nearly equal to the number which has not kept it. And yet, in God's own estimation, his labours have been crowned with glorious success.

Perhaps those very children which, at present, cause to your minds the greatest uneasiness by their perverseness, may yet be your greatest comforts, if you persist, against discouragements, in doing your duty. The woman of Canaan saw her desire at last upon her daughter, although she met with greater discouragements in the means she used for obtaining her cure, than you have yet met with in your endeavours to do good to the souls of all your children together. The great Augustine, in his younger days, was a Manichee (one who ascribed the work of creation to the devil). He was a libertine in his conduct, and cost his mother many tears, and many prayers; but she was told by her pious friends, that the child of so many prayers and tears could not be lost; which was accordingly verified to her happy experience. Perhaps from the day that John the divine died, there has not been a greater man in the church than Augustine.

If you should lie down in the grave without seeing any happy effects of your instructions, you may hear of them in another world. Manasseh, the son of Hezekiah, was, no doubt, instructed with all possible care by his father, and by the prophet Isaiah. 'The father to the children,' says Hezekiah, 'shall declare thy truth.' His own son, however, did not know the Lord for a long time after his father's death. But the Lord sent upon him sore affliction, to put him in mind of what he learned from his father; and 'then Manasseh,' though formerly the worst of men, 'knew the Lord that he was God.' When he was among the thorns, he knew and called to mind the way of finding mercy; for he had learned it in the days of childhood, although he had long forgotten it.

Although your own immediate children should derive little benefit from your dealings with them, your grandchildren may. So much knowledge of religion may be transmitted to your descendants as may have little effect on one generation, but a saving effect on another; for religion, kept up in the knowledge of it, though useless to those that hold the truth without feeling its power, may be transmitted by them to those whom the grace of God may enable to make a better improvement of it. We do not read of the good effects of Abraham's instructions upon Ishmael; though, from the expression of his being 'gathered to his people,' and from the prayers of Abraham for him, which were graciously answered by God, we may with some probability infer that he died a saint; Gen. xvii. 18, 20, 23: xxv. 17. We do not read of any good effects of Isaac's instructions upon Esau. But we know, that the posterity of Ishmael and of Esau lived in Arabia, where the knowledge and practice of true religion seem to have been still preserved amongst the descendants of Abraham, and of his friends, when other nations were generally, if not universally, idolaters. 'Who knoweth not in all these,' says Job, 'that the hand of the Lord hath wrought this?' And elsewhere he speaks of the worship of the sun and moon, the earliest species of idolatry, as a crime to be punished by the judges; which may indeed mean, that it is a crime which will certainly be punished by God, the Judge of the universe (who is frequently spoken of in the plural number). But, at any rate, this, and many other passages in the speeches of Job and his friends, make it evident that the country where they dwelt was very far from being destitute of the knowledge or fear of the true God. And the names of Eliphaz, Teman, Buz, leave little room to doubt whence the friends of Job had learned religion.

What knowest thou, O man! whether thou shalt save thy children, or whether thou shalt be instrumental in the salvation of thy grandchildren, and of their children, to the tenth and twentieth generation? Was not Jeroboam the plague and the curse of his people from generation to generation? It is highly probable, that many of their descendants are, to this day, practising those idolatries which he taught their fathers, or other worse idolatries, to which they were led of course, when they were driven from following the Lord. It is to be confessed, that the instruction which causeth to err from the words of knowledge, has ordinarily a greater influence upon men, than those holy instructions which are drawn from the Scripture; because, through the corruption of human nature, sin pleases men more than holiness. Yet the grace of God can give that efficacy to good instructions, which will render them the seed of holiness to many succeeding generations. Abraham's endeavours to transmit religion to his posterity, seemed to have lost their effect during the course of many generations; and yet God, by the unseen workings of his providence, preserved the knowledge of his doctrines from being utterly extinguished amongst his posterity, and often revived his work in the midst of the years of apostasy. Divine grace can certainly give that permanency to the effect of instructions that are well-pleasing in his sight, which the corrupt bias of the human heart gives to the influence of error and wickedness; and therefore we ought, for the sake of generations yet unborn, for the sake of generations to be born hundreds of years hence, to take care what education we give to our children, and what example we set them. The effect of our conduct towards our children may operate upon their children to remote ages. If we train them up in ignorance and irreligion, it is probable that they will transmit ignorance and impiety to their children also, and to their children's children. If we train them up in the fear of God, we may be instruments, under divine influence, of preserving the knowledge of God in our land, till that happy period come, when 'the knowledge of God shall cover the earth, as the waters cover the sea.' Our instructions and example may contribute to that glorious revival of religion which is to take place in the latter days, although it should yet be removed from us to the distance of two hundred years. It is a question whether we shall live to see that happy period of the church, but we daily pray that it may come. Our works and our prayers are inconsistent with one another, if we do not endeavour to sow that seed which, in the last days, will spring up so abundantly. If we are in heaven when that period comes, it will double our joy to know, that any thing which we did whilst we were in the world has contributed to effect such a happy change. This, I think, we may freely infer from what our Lord says to his disciples; John iv. 36–38; concerning the advantages which his disciples derived from the labours of their predecessors, and the joy which will be felt by sowers and reapers together, when the harvest is gathered in.

(3.) *Let your own comfort and advantage in the effect of your labours, excite you to make full proof of all that can be done for the salvation of your children.*—Train up a child in the way that he should go, and when he is grown up, he will be wise; and what joy can exceed that of a father in the wisdom of his son, especially when his own instructions and example have greatly contributed to make him wise? Will not such children be the crown of their parents, both in this world, and at the appearance of Jesus Christ?

Allowing, what may be true, although we hope otherwise,

that your children should remain to the end blind and hardened, after all that you can do for their souls, your labour is not lost. You shall have your reward. The reward of Christ's servants is according to their work, not according to their success; 1 Cor. iii. 13, 14. This, surely, may satisfy you, when it satisfied Christ in a like case. 'I said, I have laboured in vain, I have spent my strength for nought, and in vain; yet surely my reward is with the Lord, and my work with my God.' Whilst you are in this world, your compassion for your perishing children will, indeed, greatly abate your comfort: but, in this world, whilst they live, you cannot certainly know that your labour will always remain uncrowned with success. If they should visibly die in their iniquities through their own folly, your bowels of compassion must be greatly troubled within you: but the pain you feel will not be, by a thousand times, so distressing as your self-tormenting reflections would be, in the consciousness that their perdition must be in part imputed to yourselves. David mourned bitterly the fate of his unhappy son Absalom; but, from some of his last compositions; Psalms xviii. lxxii. 2 Sam. xxiii. 1–5; we may justly infer, that he recovered his wonted cheerfulness of spirit and joy in the Lord. We have no reason to think that Eli, if he had lived many years after the death of Hophni and Phinehas, would ever have enjoyed a day's happiness. The assurance of heaven to himself could scarcely have made a man happy on earth, whose sons had perished through his neglect. There will be no sorrow in heaven. But, if it were possible that any grief could enter into the abodes of bliss, I believe it would seize upon those men, some of whom may have an humble place in those dwellings, whose children had perished through their negligence, or the influence of their bad example. Although parents obtain repentance for their own faults, they cannot give it to their children, to repair their former errors.

(4.) *Your duty to your parents, or to your remote ancestors, who transmitted unto you the truths of God, binds you to transmit their religion to their posterity.*—Many of them jeoparded their lives in defense of the truth, that it might come down unadulterated to you. Read the history of the contendings of your fathers in the various reformation-periods of our church, and especially in days of bloody persecutions. Will not their perils, their solemn covenants, their prisons, their scaffolds, bear witness against you at the day of judgment, if it is found that, by your negligence or misbehaviour, you have done what was in your power to make all their generous efforts useless to their posterity? Do you wish to resemble those wicked kings of Judah, who did not that which was right in the sight of God, like David their father?

(5.) *But, I have more powerful arguments still to enforce parental duty. They are taken from the redemption purchased for us by Christ.*—No considerations will be more effectual to impress us with a sense of the importance of our own salvation, or of the salvation of our children and friends, than those which are drawn from the works that Christ performed, and the sufferings that he endured, for our salvation. Think, careless sinners! of our Lord's deep abasement. Why did he come into our world, clothed with a mortal body? Why did he endure pain, and shame, and the wrath of God? Was it not to obtain salvation for us? And will you, hereafter, think it a matter of small concern, whether you share in his salvation or not? Will you account it a hardship, that you must put yourself to some trouble to promote the salvation of those whom you love? O that the mind which was in Christ were in us also! We would, like Paul, be willing to endure all things for the elect's sake, that they may obtain the salvation which is in Christ, with eternal glory. You know not, indeed, whether your children are elected or not, till the fruits of their election appear in their lives. But do you think that Paul could distinguish the elect, before their effectual calling, any more than yourselves? You do not defer their baptism till you are assured of their election. Instruct, admonish, correct them for them; and your work shall be rewarded.

www.ingramcontent.com/pod-product-compliance
Lightning Source LLC
Chambersburg PA
CBHW021232300426
44111CB00007B/523